P9-DMK-054

STOP!

You are going the *wrong way!*

Manga is a *completely* different type of reading experience.

To start at the *BEGINNING,* go to the *END!*

That's right! Authentic manga is read the traditional Japanese way--from right to left, exactly the opposite of how American books are read. It's easy to follow: just go to the other end of the book, and read each page--and each panel--from the right side to the left side, starting at the top right. Now you're experiencing manga as it was meant to be.

A Kodansha Comics Trade Paperback Original
Attack on Titan volume 7 copyright © 2012 Hajime Isayama
English translation copyright © 2013 Hajime Isayama

Published in the United States by Kodansha Comics, an imprint of Kodansha USA Publishing, LLC, New York.

Publication rights for this English edition arranged through Kodansha Ltd, Tokyo.

First published in Japan in 2012 by Kodansha Ltd., Tokyo as *Shingeki no Kyojin*, volume 7.

ISBN 978-1-61262-256-9

Original cover design by Takashi Shimoyama (Red Rooster)

Printed in the United States of America.

www.kodanshacomics.com

9 8 7 6 5 4 3
Translation: Sheldon Drzka
Lettering: Steve Wands
Editing: Ben Applegate

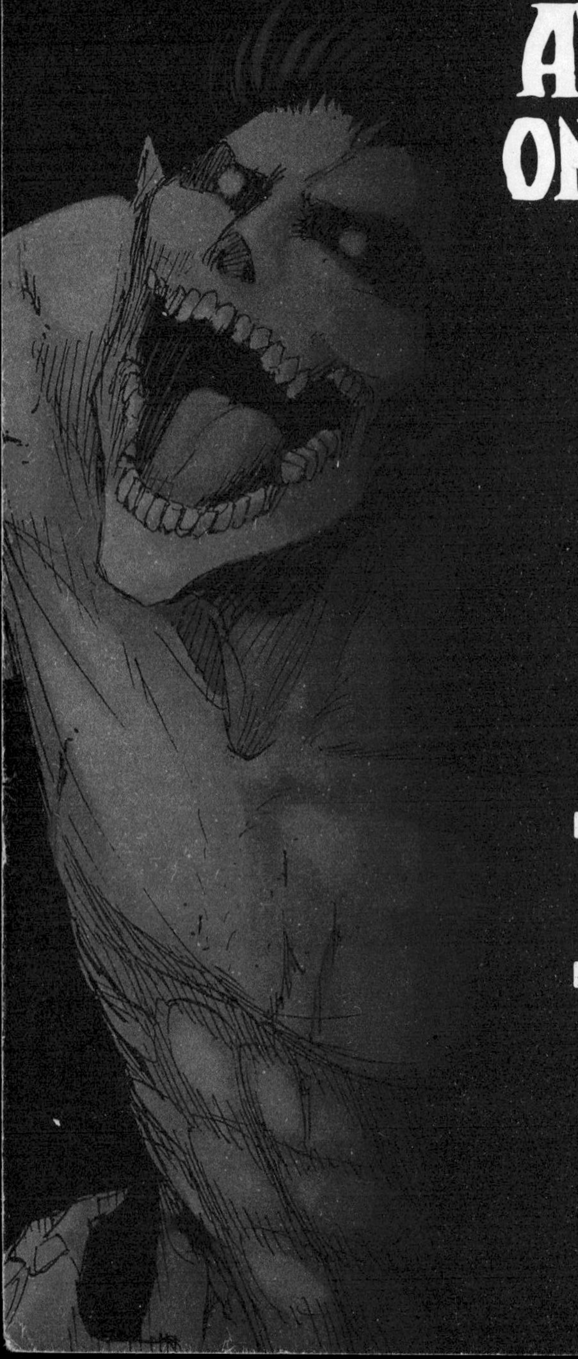

ATTACK ON TITAN

7

HAJIME ISAYAMA

Attack on Titan Character Introductions

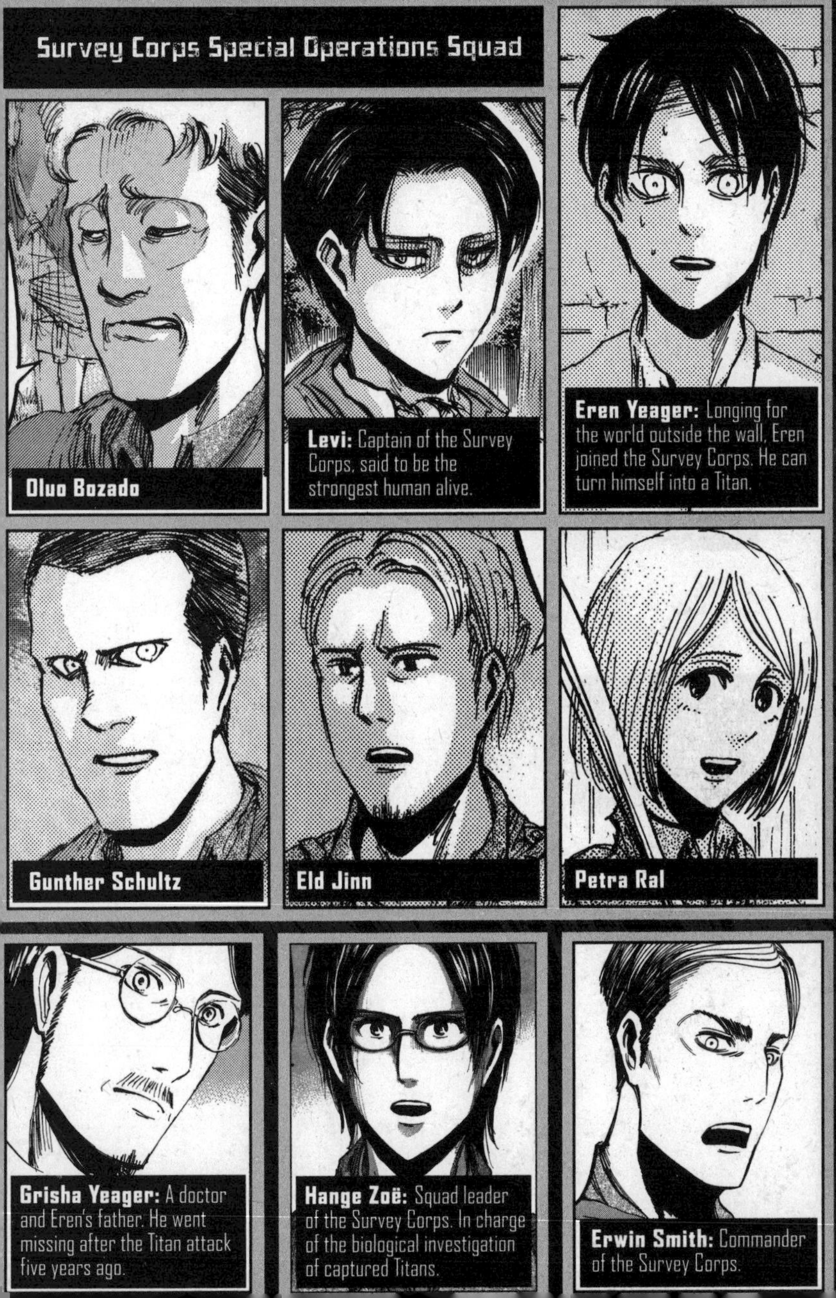
Survey Corps Special Operations Squad
Oluo Bozado
Levi: Captain of the Survey Corps, said to be the strongest human alive.
Eren Yeager: Longing for the world outside the wall, Eren joined the Survey Corps. He can turn himself into a Titan.
Gunther Schultz
Eld Jinn
Petra Ral
Grisha Yeager: A doctor and Eren's father. He went missing after the Titan attack five years ago.
Hange Zoë: Squad leader of the Survey Corps. In charge of the biological investigation of captured Titans.
Erwin Smith: Commander of the Survey Corps.

104th Corps

Armin Arlert:
Eren and Mikasa's childhood friend. Though Armin isn't athletic in the least, he is an excellent thinker and can produce unique ideas. A member of the Survey Corps.

Mikasa Ackerman:
Mikasa graduated at the top of her training corps. Her parents were murdered before her eyes when she was a child. After that, she was raised alongside Eren, whom she tenaciously tries to protect. A member of the Survey Corps.

Connie Springer:
Effective at vertical maneuvering, but is slow on the uptake, so his comprehension of tactics is less than stellar. A member of the Survey Corps.

Jean Kirstein: Superior at vertical maneuvering. Jean is honest to a fault, which often puts him at odds with other people. A member of the Survey Corps.

Bertolt Hoover:
Has a high degree of skill in everything he's been taught, but is indecisive and lacks initiative. A member of the Survey Corps.

Reiner Braun: Graduated second in his training corps. Reiner is as strong as an ox and has the will to match. His comrades place a great deal of trust in him. A member of the Survey Corps.

Marco Bott: Yearned to join the Military Police Brigade so he could serve the king. Marco died during the Titan mop-up operation.

Annie Leonhart: Annie's small stature belies her great skill in the art of hand-to-hand combat. She's a realist through and through, and tends to be a loner. A member of the Military Police Brigade.

Krista Lenz: Extremely short, with a friendly, warm-hearted personality. A member of the Survey Corps.

Sasha Blouse: Sasha is very agile and has remarkable instincts. Owing to her unconventionality, she isn't suited for organized activity. A member of the Survey Corps.

ATTACK on TITAN

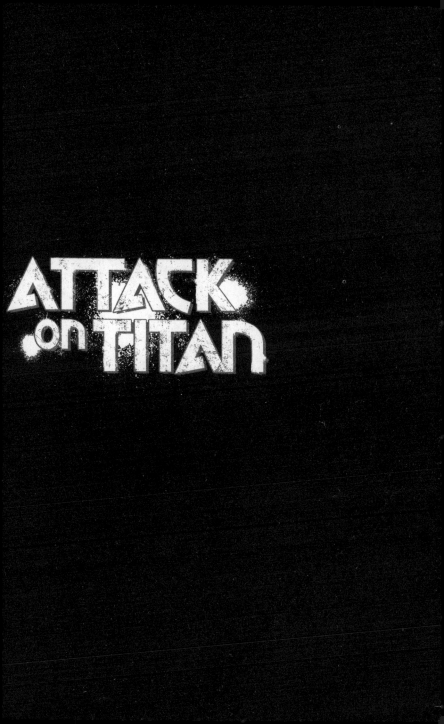

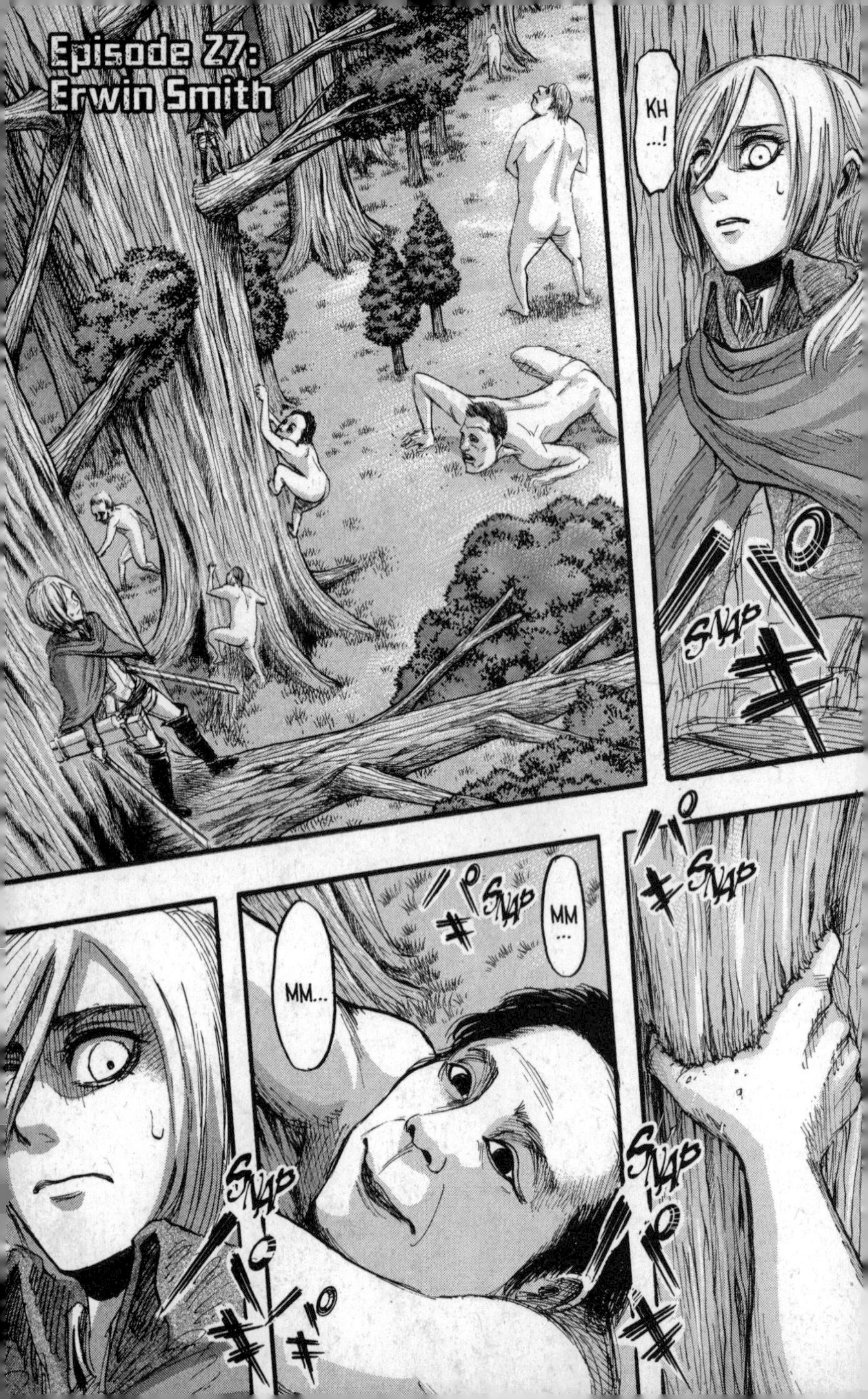
KH ...!
SNAP
Episode 27: Erwin Smith
SNAP
SNAP
MM...
SNAP
MM...
SNAP

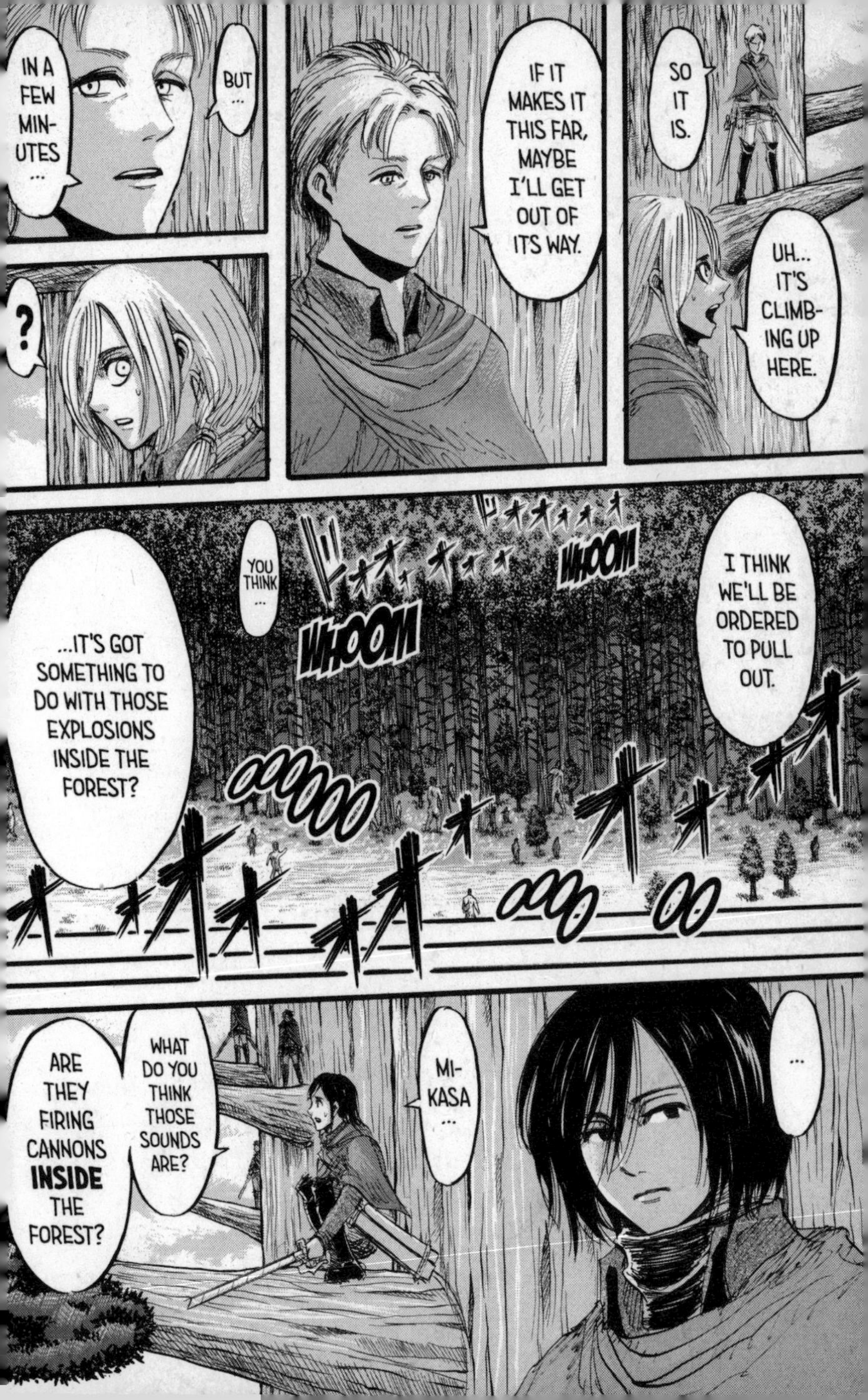
SO IT IS.
UH... IT'S CLIMBING UP HERE.
IF IT MAKES IT THIS FAR, MAYBE I'LL GET OUT OF ITS WAY.
BUT ...
IN A FEW MINUTES ...
?
I THINK WE'LL BE ORDERED TO PULL OUT.
WHOOM
WHOOM
YOU THINK ...
...IT'S GOT SOMETHING TO DO WITH THOSE EXPLOSIONS INSIDE THE FOREST?
...
MIKASA ...
WHAT DO YOU THINK THOSE SOUNDS ARE?
ARE THEY FIRING CANNONS **INSIDE** THE FOREST?

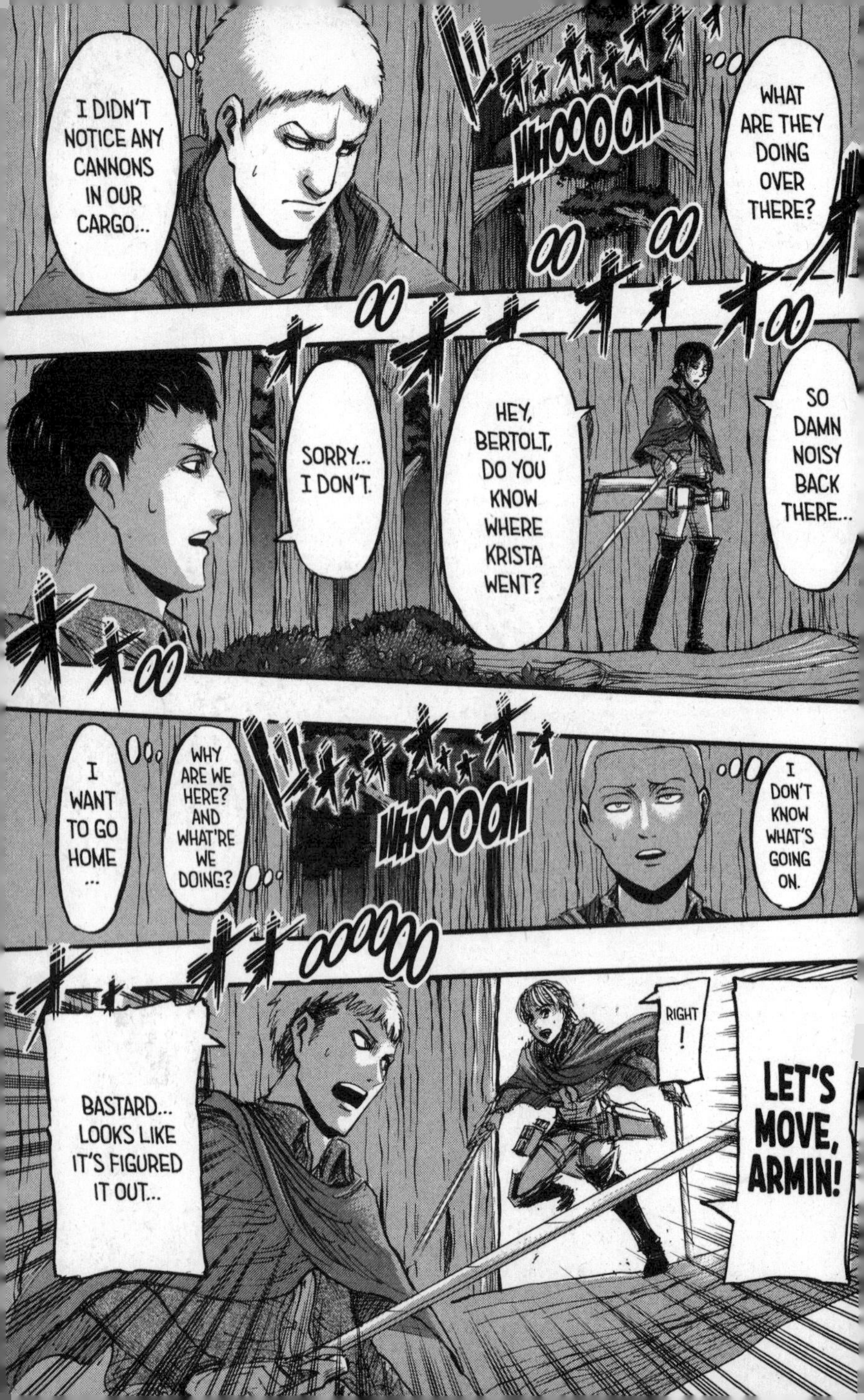
WHOOOOM
WHAT ARE THEY DOING OVER THERE?
I DIDN'T NOTICE ANY CANNONS IN OUR CARGO...
SO DAMN NOISY BACK THERE...
HEY, BERTOLT, DO YOU KNOW WHERE KRISTA WENT?
SORRY... I DON'T.
I DON'T KNOW WHAT'S GOING ON.
WHOOOOM
WHY ARE WE HERE? AND WHAT'RE WE DOING?
I WANT TO GO HOME ...
LET'S MOVE, ARMIN!
RIGHT!
BASTARD... LOOKS LIKE IT'S FIGURED IT OUT...

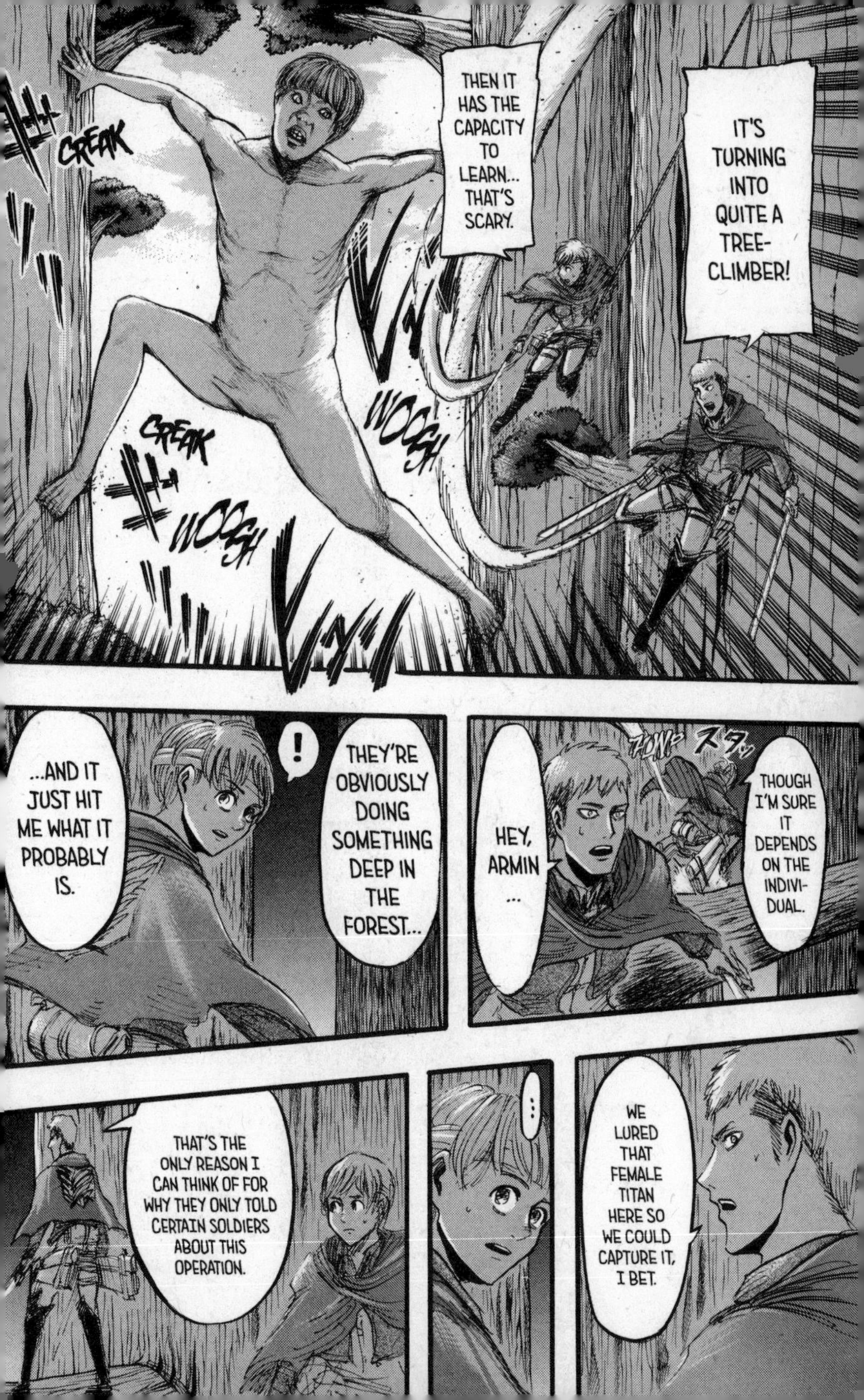
IT'S TURNING INTO QUITE A TREE-CLIMBER!
THEN IT HAS THE CAPACITY TO LEARN... THAT'S SCARY.
CREAK
WOOSH
CREAK
WOOSH
スタッ
THOUGH I'M SURE IT DEPENDS ON THE INDIVIDUAL.
HEY, ARMIN...
THEY'RE OBVIOUSLY DOING SOMETHING DEEP IN THE FOREST...
!
...AND IT JUST HIT ME WHAT IT PROBABLY IS.
WE LURED THAT FEMALE TITAN HERE SO WE COULD CAPTURE IT, I BET.
...
THAT'S THE ONLY REASON I CAN THINK OF FOR WHY THEY ONLY TOLD CERTAIN SOLDIERS ABOUT THIS OPERATION.

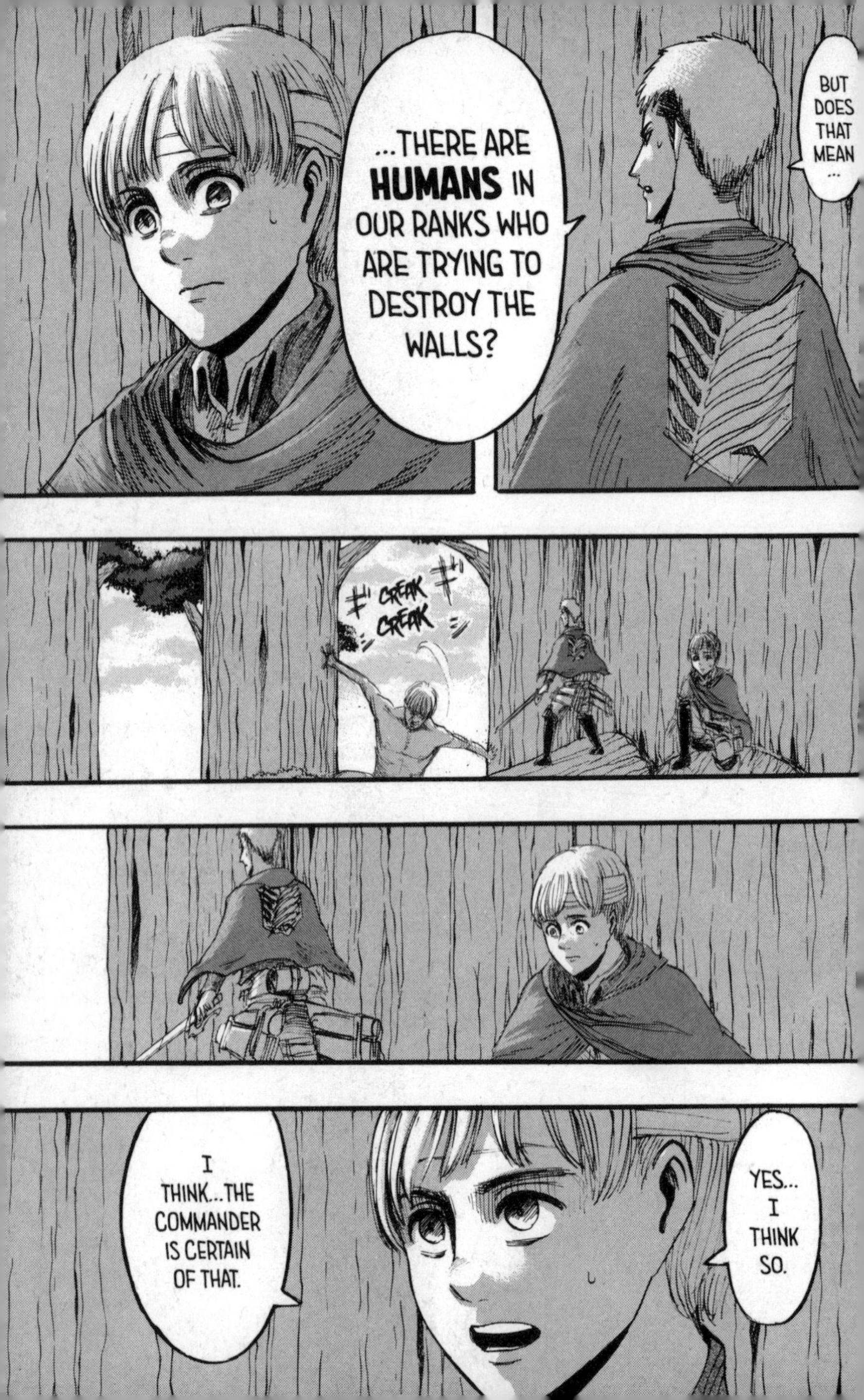
BUT DOES THAT MEAN ...
...THERE ARE **HUMANS** IN OUR RANKS WHO ARE TRYING TO DESTROY THE WALLS?
CREAK CREAK
YES... I THINK SO.
I THINK...THE COMMANDER IS CERTAIN OF THAT.

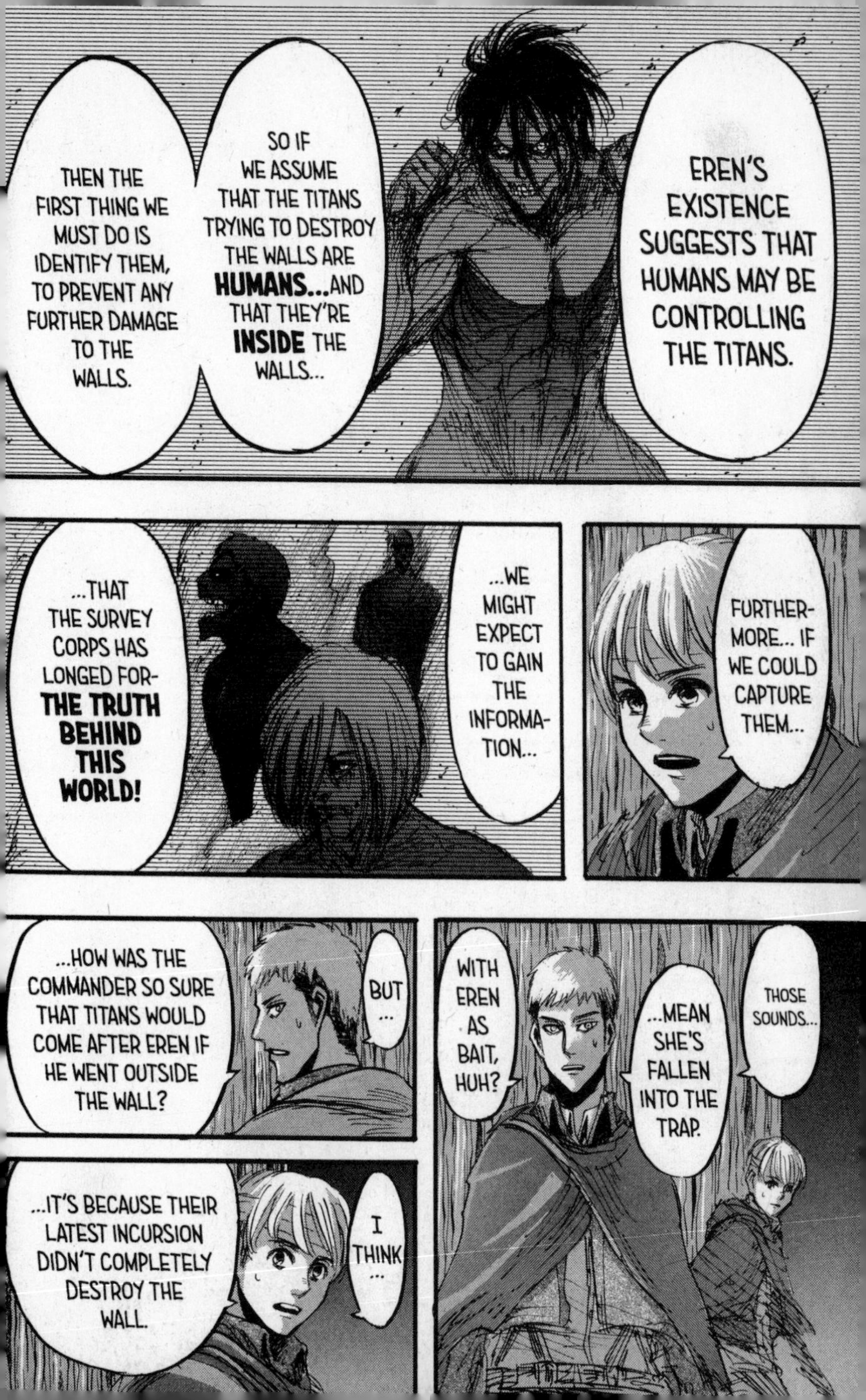
EREN'S EXISTENCE SUGGESTS THAT HUMANS MAY BE CONTROLLING THE TITANS.
SO IF WE ASSUME THAT THE TITANS TRYING TO DESTROY THE WALLS ARE **HUMANS...**AND THAT THEY'RE **INSIDE** THE WALLS...
THEN THE FIRST THING WE MUST DO IS IDENTIFY THEM, TO PREVENT ANY FURTHER DAMAGE TO THE WALLS.
FURTHER-MORE... IF WE COULD CAPTURE THEM...
...WE MIGHT EXPECT TO GAIN THE INFORMATION...
...THAT THE SURVEY CORPS HAS LONGED FOR-**THE TRUTH BEHIND THIS WORLD!**
THOSE SOUNDS...
...MEAN SHE'S FALLEN INTO THE TRAP.
WITH EREN AS BAIT, HUH?
BUT ...
...HOW WAS THE COMMANDER SO SURE THAT TITANS WOULD COME AFTER EREN IF HE WENT OUTSIDE THE WALL?
I THINK ...
...IT'S BECAUSE THEIR LATEST INCURSION DIDN'T COMPLETELY DESTROY THE WALL.

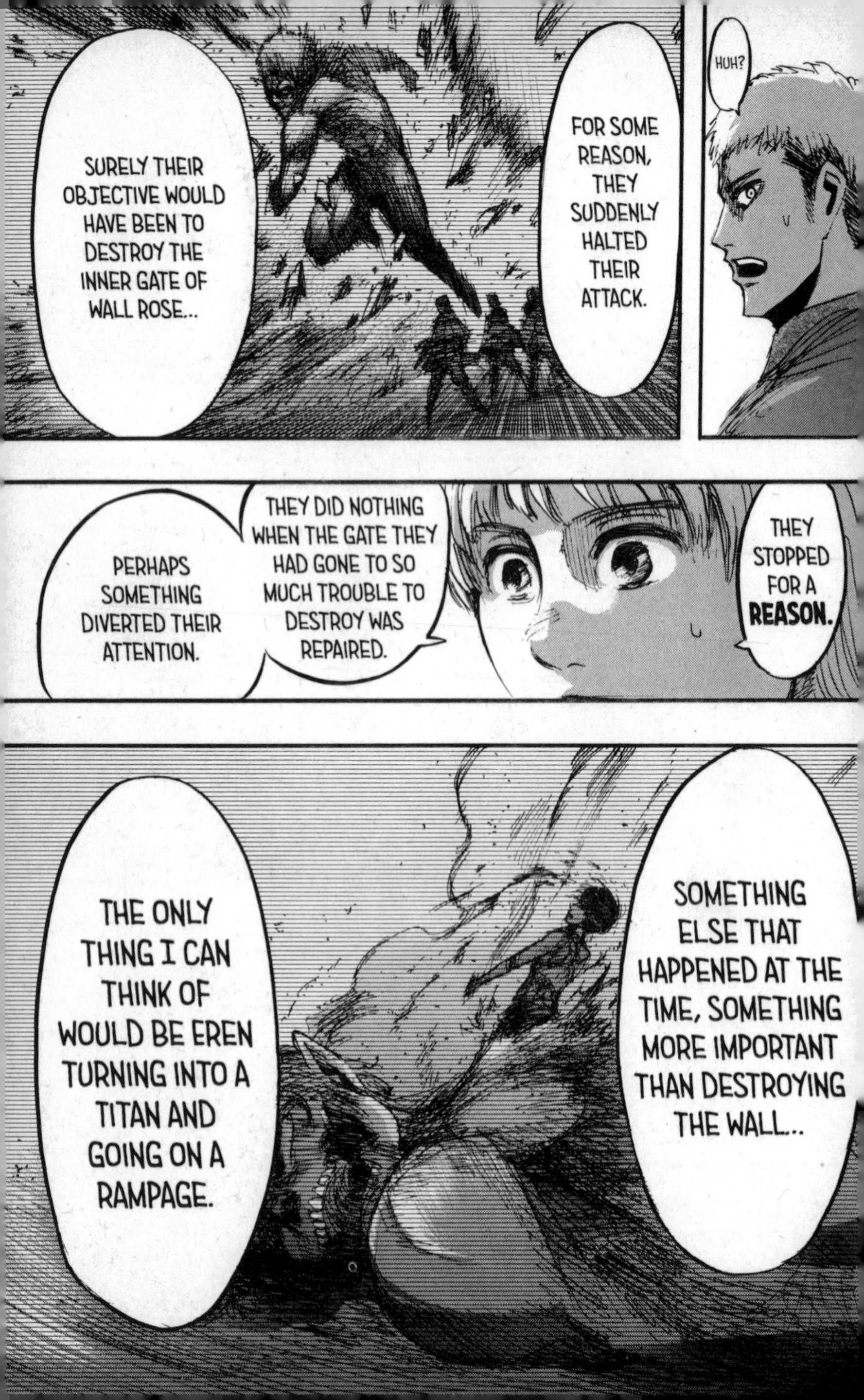
HUH?
FOR SOME REASON, THEY SUDDENLY HALTED THEIR ATTACK.
SURELY THEIR OBJECTIVE WOULD HAVE BEEN TO DESTROY THE INNER GATE OF WALL ROSE...
THEY STOPPED FOR A **REASON.**
THEY DID NOTHING WHEN THE GATE THEY HAD GONE TO SO MUCH TROUBLE TO DESTROY WAS REPAIRED.
PERHAPS SOMETHING DIVERTED THEIR ATTENTION.
SOMETHING ELSE THAT HAPPENED AT THE TIME, SOMETHING MORE IMPORTANT THAN DESTROYING THE WALL...
THE ONLY THING I CAN THINK OF WOULD BE EREN TURNING INTO A TITAN AND GOING ON A RAMPAGE.

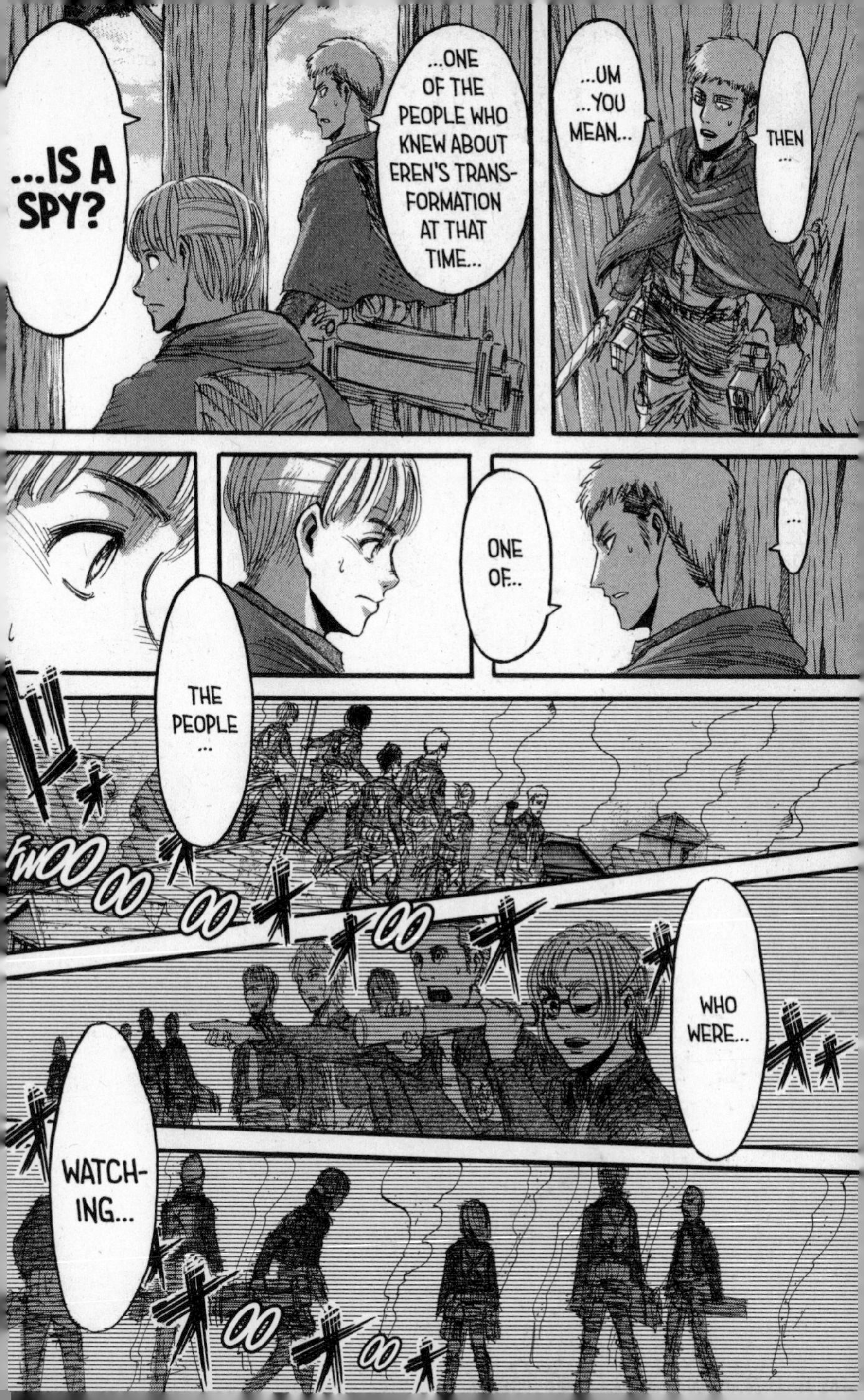
THEN...
...UM ...YOU MEAN...
...ONE OF THE PEOPLE WHO KNEW ABOUT EREN'S TRANS-FORMATION AT THAT TIME...
...IS A SPY?
...
ONE OF...
THE PEOPLE...
FWOO OO OO OO
WHO WERE...
WATCH-ING...
OO OO

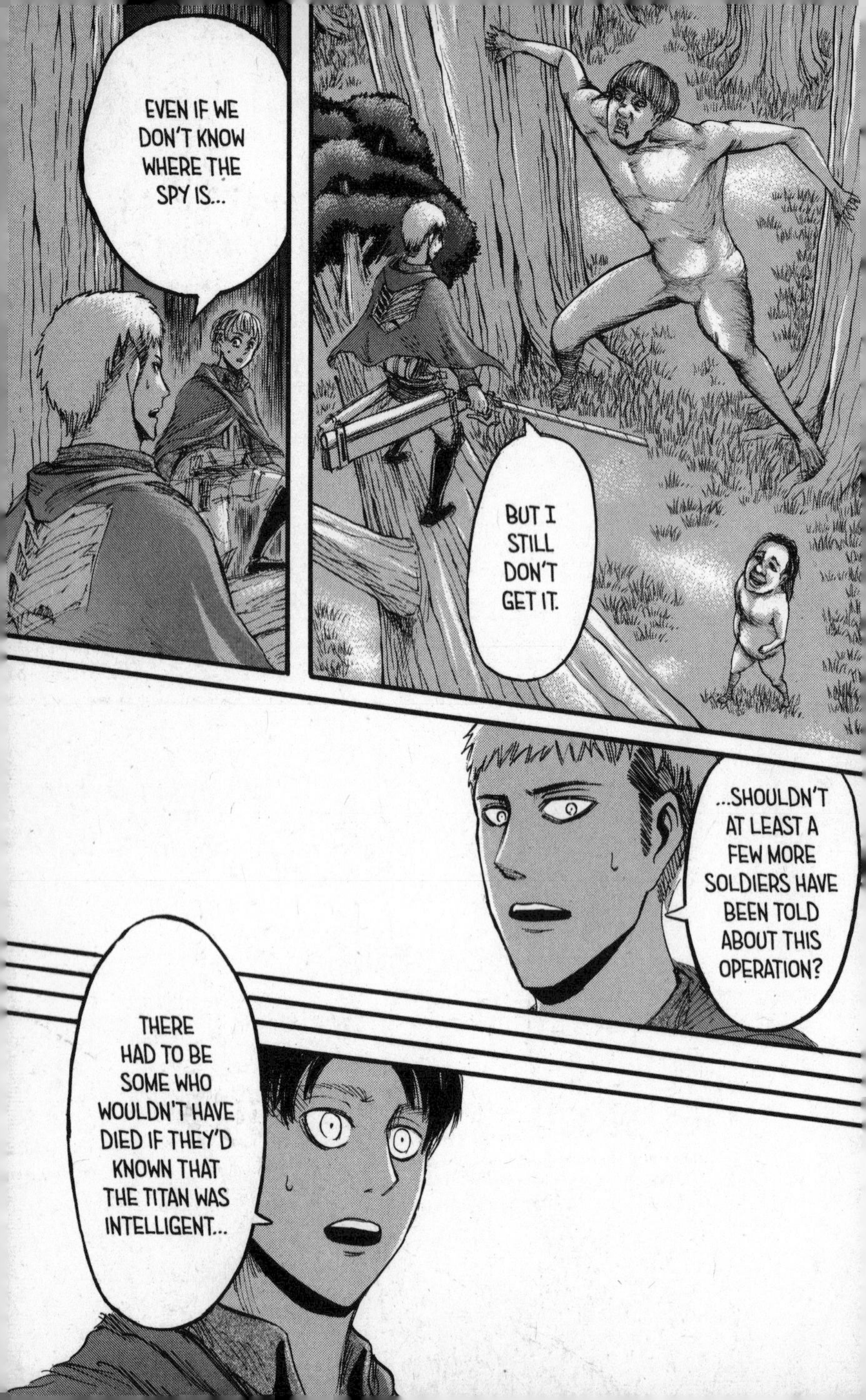
BUT I STILL DON'T GET IT.
EVEN IF WE DON'T KNOW WHERE THE SPY IS...
...SHOULDN'T AT LEAST A FEW MORE SOLDIERS HAVE BEEN TOLD ABOUT THIS OPERATION?
THERE HAD TO BE SOME WHO WOULDN'T HAVE DIED IF THEY'D KNOWN THAT THE TITAN WAS INTELLIGENT...

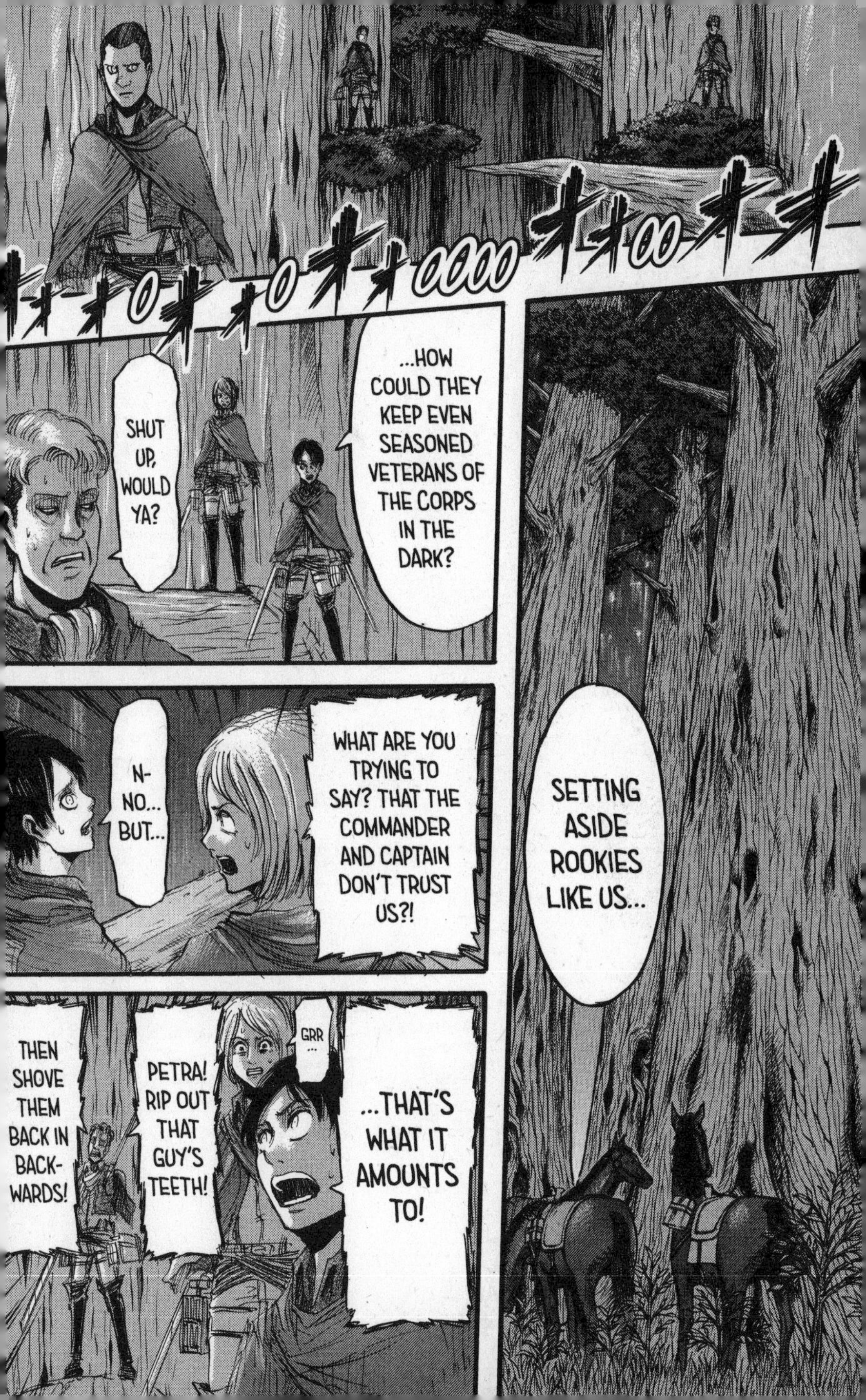
SETTING ASIDE ROOKIES LIKE US...
...HOW COULD THEY KEEP EVEN SEASONED VETERANS OF THE CORPS IN THE DARK?
SHUT UP, WOULD YA?
WHAT ARE YOU TRYING TO SAY? THAT THE COMMANDER AND CAPTAIN DON'T TRUST US?!
N-NO... BUT...
...THAT'S WHAT IT AMOUNTS TO!
GRR...
PETRA! RIP OUT THAT GUY'S TEETH!
THEN SHOVE THEM BACK IN BACKWARDS!

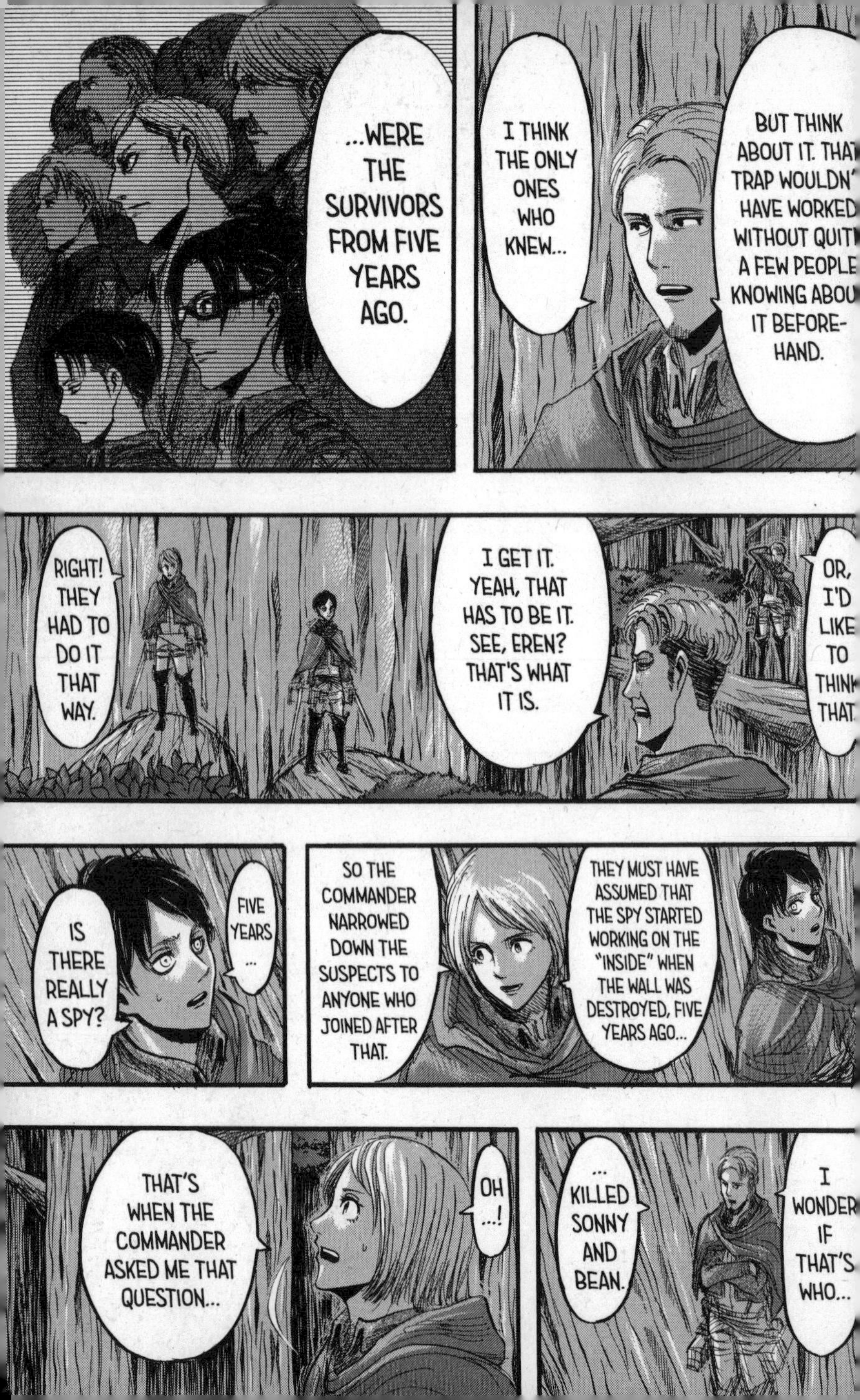
BUT THINK ABOUT IT. THAT TRAP WOULDN'T HAVE WORKED WITHOUT QUITE A FEW PEOPLE KNOWING ABOUT IT BEFORE-HAND.
I THINK THE ONLY ONES WHO KNEW...
...WERE THE SURVIVORS FROM FIVE YEARS AGO.
OR, I'D LIKE TO THINK THAT.
I GET IT. YEAH, THAT HAS TO BE IT. SEE, EREN? THAT'S WHAT IT IS.
RIGHT! THEY HAD TO DO IT THAT WAY.
THEY MUST HAVE ASSUMED THAT THE SPY STARTED WORKING ON THE "INSIDE" WHEN THE WALL WAS DESTROYED, FIVE YEARS AGO...
SO THE COMMANDER NARROWED DOWN THE SUSPECTS TO ANYONE WHO JOINED AFTER THAT.
FIVE YEARS ...
IS THERE REALLY A SPY?
I WONDER IF THAT'S WHO...
...KILLED SONNY AND BEAN.
OH ...!
THAT'S WHEN THE COMMANDER ASKED ME THAT QUESTION...

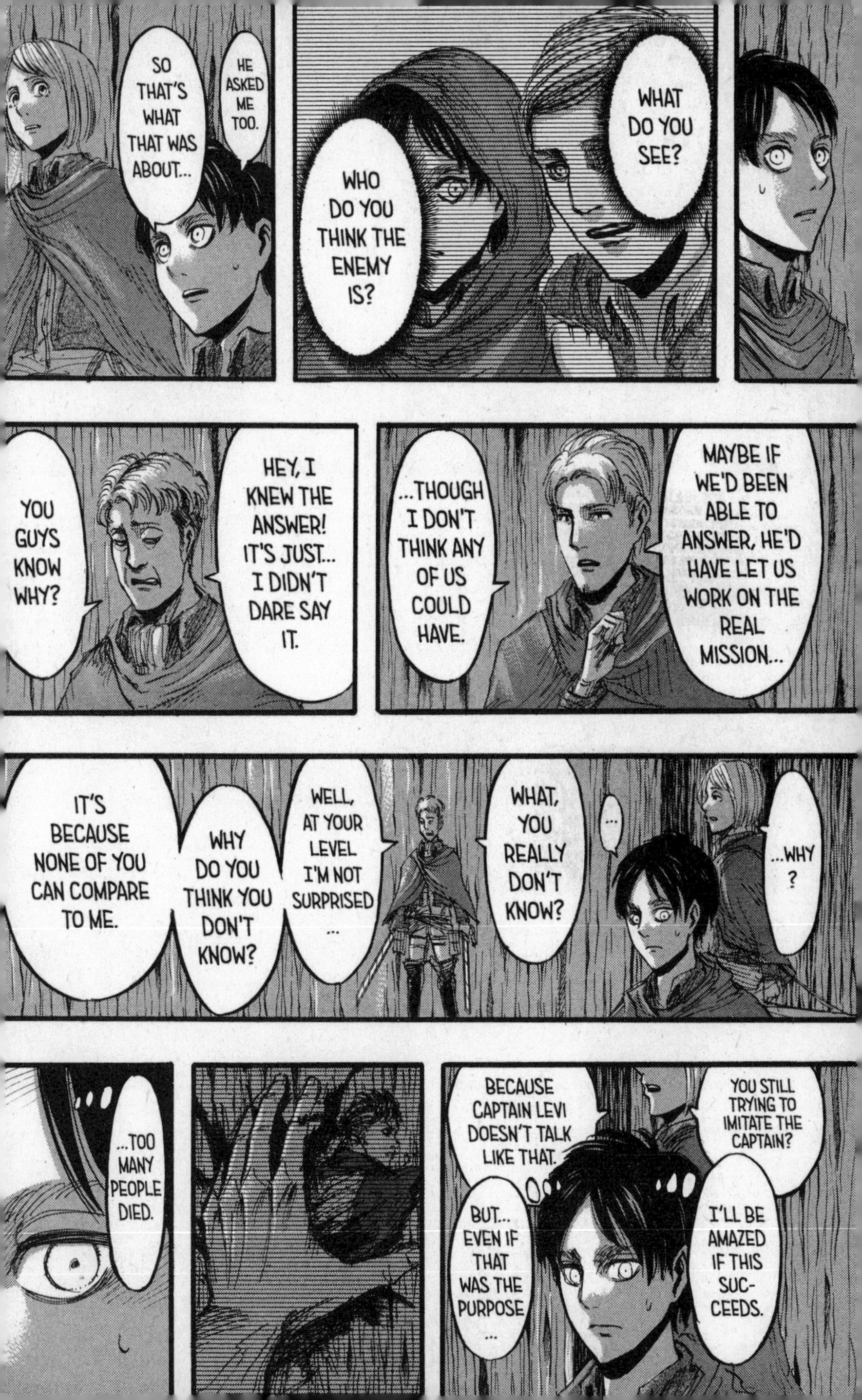
WHAT DO YOU SEE?
WHO DO YOU THINK THE ENEMY IS?
HE ASKED ME TOO.
SO THAT'S WHAT THAT WAS ABOUT...
MAYBE IF WE'D BEEN ABLE TO ANSWER, HE'D HAVE LET US WORK ON THE REAL MISSION...
...THOUGH I DON'T THINK ANY OF US COULD HAVE.
HEY, I KNEW THE ANSWER! IT'S JUST... I DIDN'T DARE SAY IT.
YOU GUYS KNOW WHY?
...WHY ?
...
WHAT, YOU REALLY DON'T KNOW?
WELL, AT YOUR LEVEL I'M NOT SURPRISED ...
WHY DO YOU THINK YOU DON'T KNOW?
IT'S BECAUSE NONE OF YOU CAN COMPARE TO ME.
YOU STILL TRYING TO IMITATE THE CAPTAIN?
BECAUSE CAPTAIN LEVI DOESN'T TALK LIKE THAT.
I'LL BE AMAZED IF THIS SUC-CEEDS.
BUT... EVEN IF THAT WAS THE PURPOSE ...
...TOO MANY PEOPLE DIED.

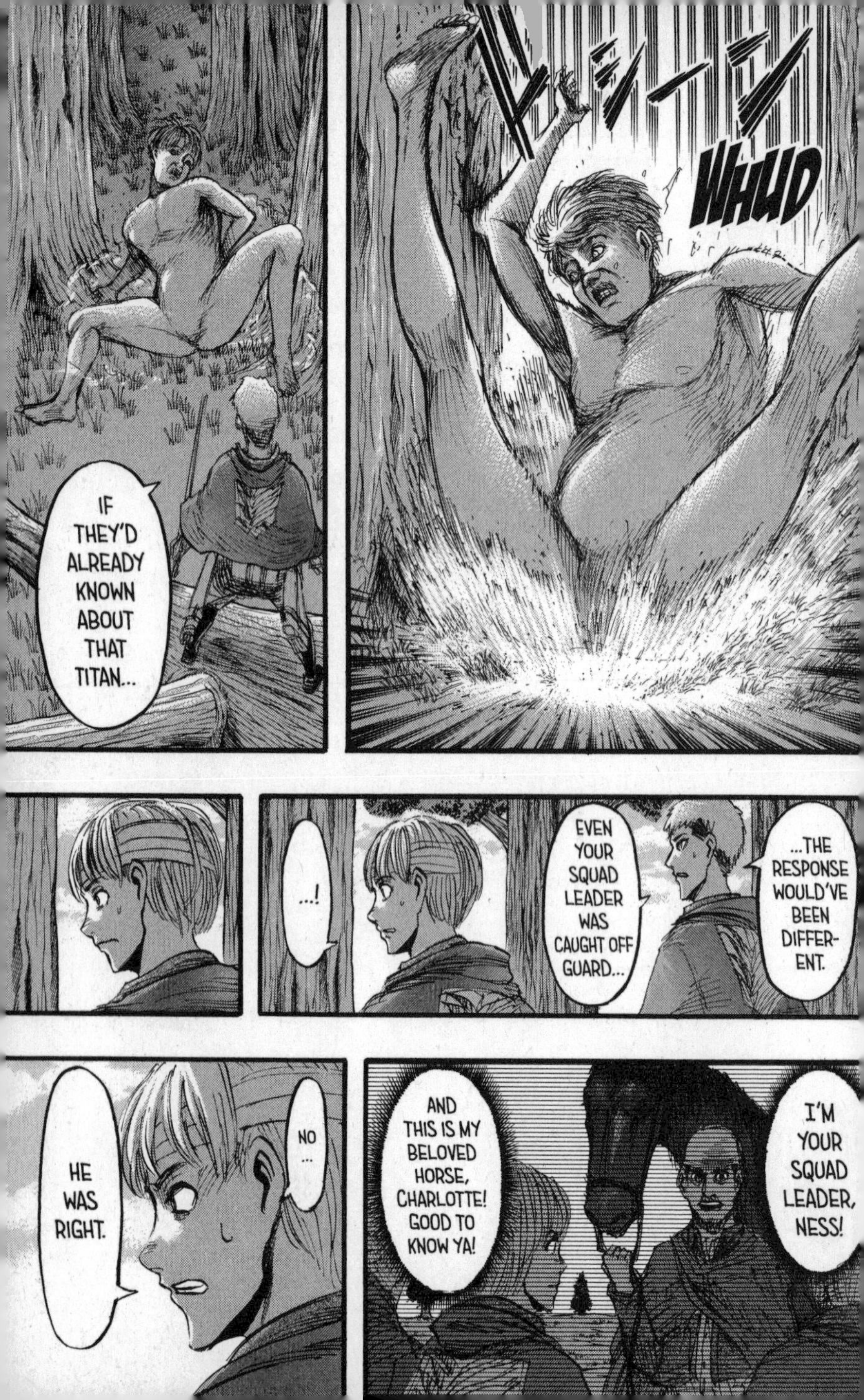
WHUD
IF THEY'D ALREADY KNOWN ABOUT THAT TITAN...
...THE RESPONSE WOULD'VE BEEN DIFFER-ENT.
EVEN YOUR SQUAD LEADER WAS CAUGHT OFF GUARD...
...!
I'M YOUR SQUAD LEADER, NESS!
AND THIS IS MY BELOVED HORSE, CHARLOTTE! GOOD TO KNOW YA!
NO ...
HE WAS RIGHT.

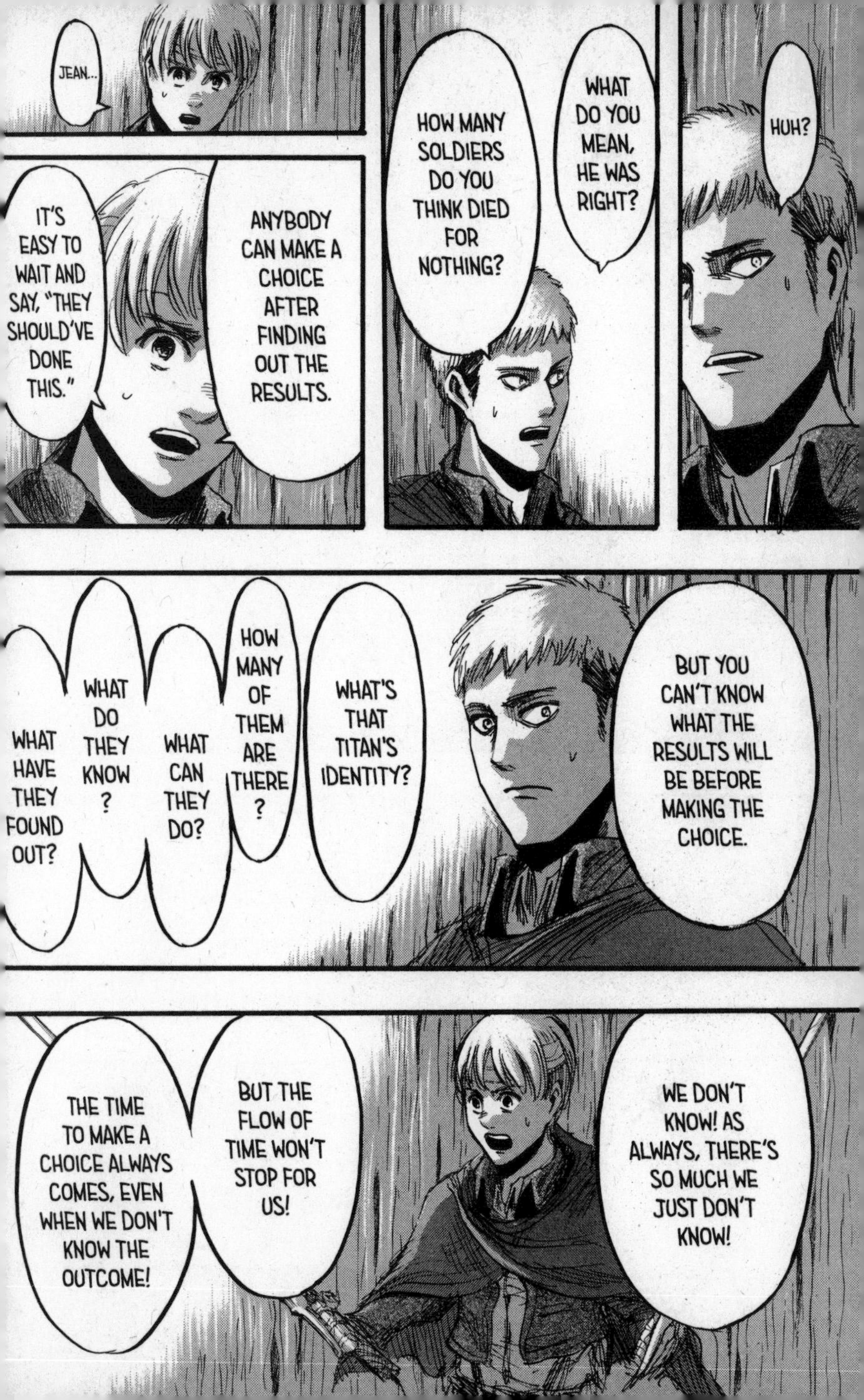
HUH?
WHAT DO YOU MEAN, HE WAS RIGHT?
HOW MANY SOLDIERS DO YOU THINK DIED FOR NOTHING?
JEAN...
ANYBODY CAN MAKE A CHOICE AFTER FINDING OUT THE RESULTS.
IT'S EASY TO WAIT AND SAY, "THEY SHOULD'VE DONE THIS."
BUT YOU CAN'T KNOW WHAT THE RESULTS WILL BE BEFORE MAKING THE CHOICE.
WHAT'S THAT TITAN'S IDENTITY?
HOW MANY OF THEM ARE THERE?
WHAT CAN THEY DO?
WHAT DO THEY KNOW?
WHAT HAVE THEY FOUND OUT?
WE DON'T KNOW! AS ALWAYS, THERE'S SO MUCH WE JUST DON'T KNOW!
BUT THE FLOW OF TIME WON'T STOP FOR US!
THE TIME TO MAKE A CHOICE ALWAYS COMES, EVEN WHEN WE DON'T KNOW THE OUTCOME!

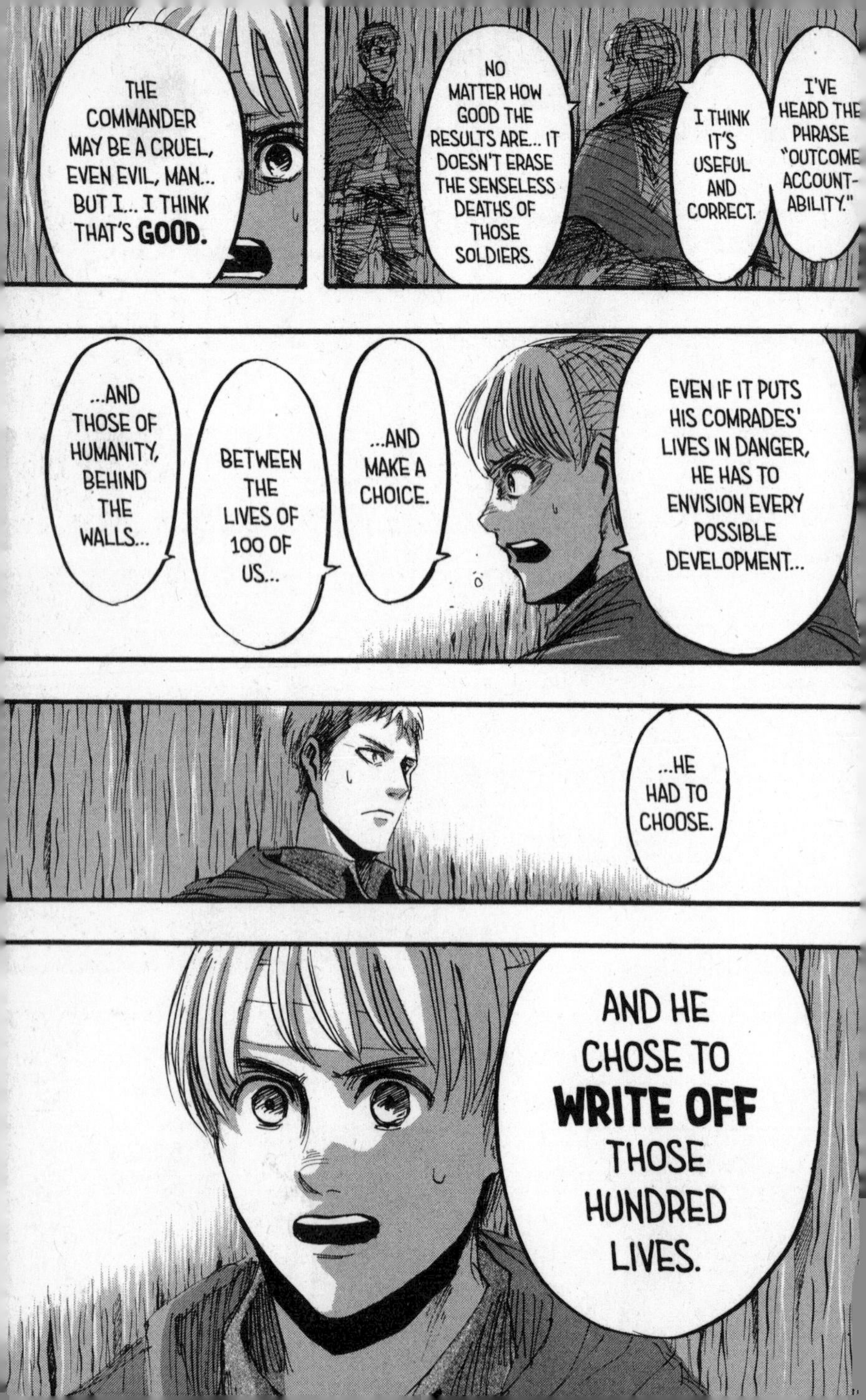
I'VE HEARD THE PHRASE "OUTCOME ACCOUNTABILITY."
I THINK IT'S USEFUL AND CORRECT.
NO MATTER HOW GOOD THE RESULTS ARE... IT DOESN'T ERASE THE SENSELESS DEATHS OF THOSE SOLDIERS.
THE COMMANDER MAY BE A CRUEL, EVEN EVIL, MAN... BUT I... I THINK THAT'S **GOOD.**
EVEN IF IT PUTS HIS COMRADES' LIVES IN DANGER, HE HAS TO ENVISION EVERY POSSIBLE DEVELOPMENT...
...AND MAKE A CHOICE.
BETWEEN THE LIVES OF 100 OF US...
...AND THOSE OF HUMANITY, BEHIND THE WALLS...
...HE HAD TO CHOOSE.
AND HE CHOSE TO **WRITE OFF** THOSE HUNDRED LIVES.

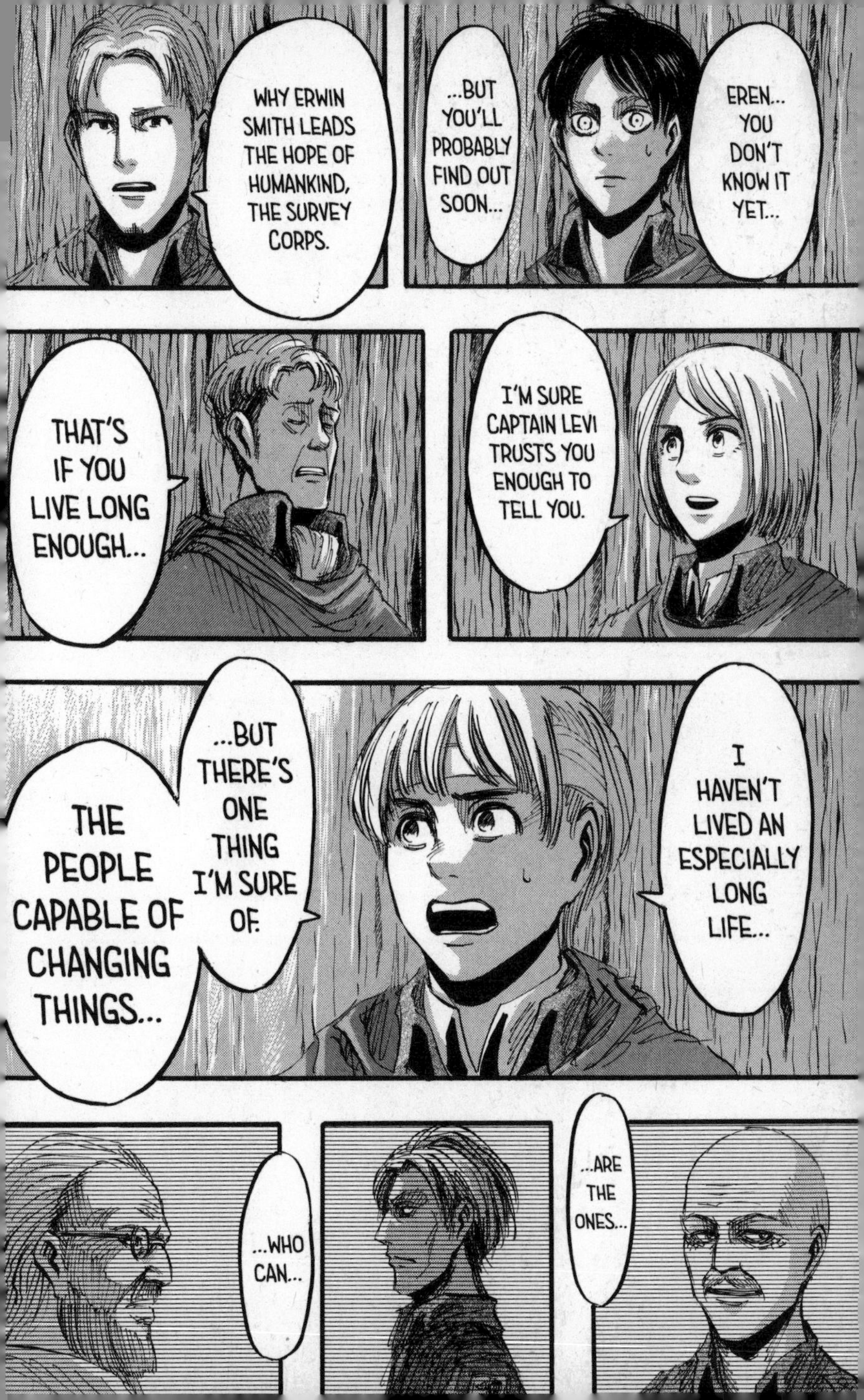
EREN... YOU DON'T KNOW IT YET...
...BUT YOU'LL PROBABLY FIND OUT SOON...
WHY ERWIN SMITH LEADS THE HOPE OF HUMANKIND, THE SURVEY CORPS.
I'M SURE CAPTAIN LEVI TRUSTS YOU ENOUGH TO TELL YOU.
THAT'S IF YOU LIVE LONG ENOUGH...
I HAVEN'T LIVED AN ESPECIALLY LONG LIFE...
...BUT THERE'S ONE THING I'M SURE OF.
THE PEOPLE CAPABLE OF CHANGING THINGS...
...ARE THE ONES...
...WHO CAN...

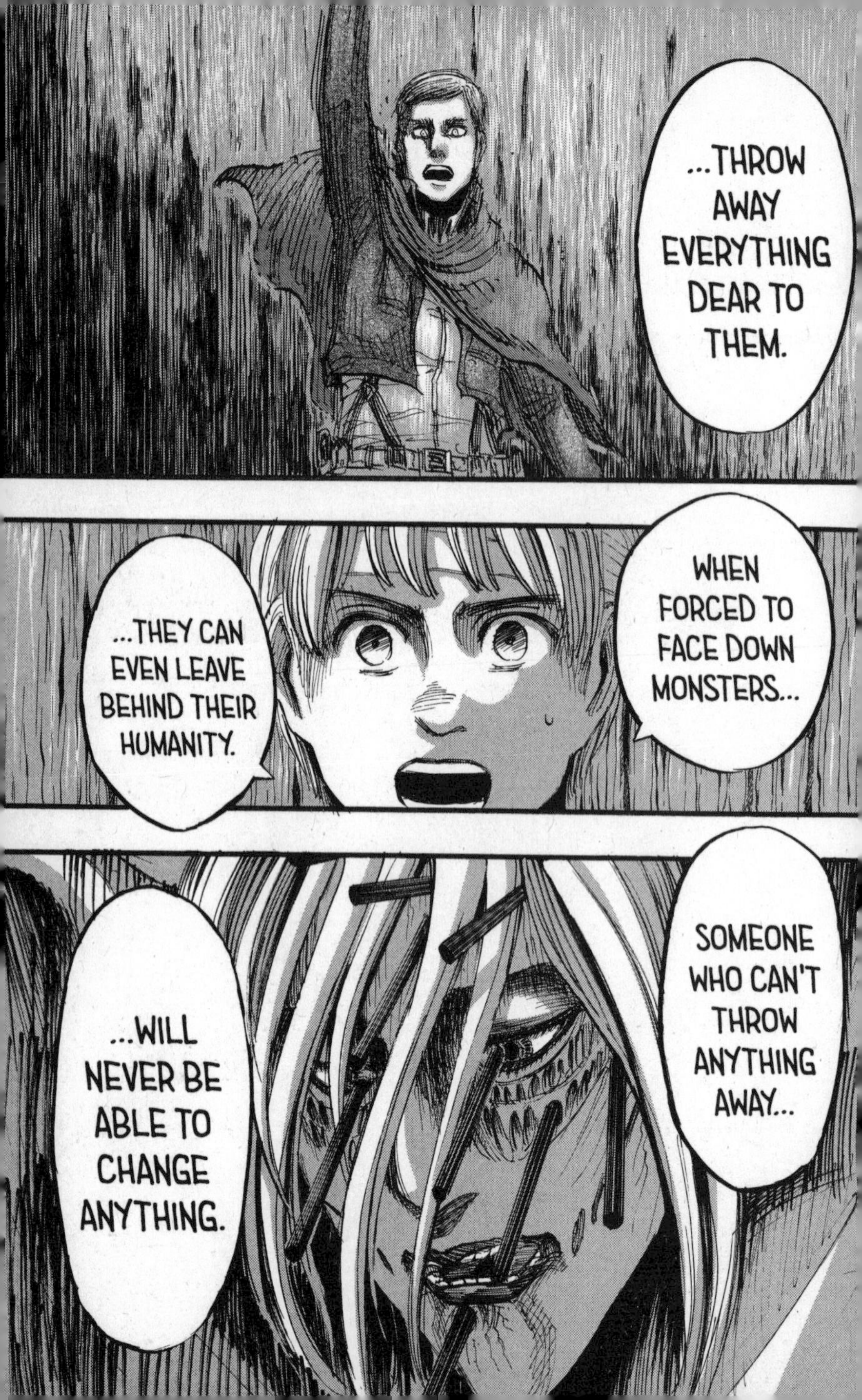
...THROW AWAY EVERYTHING DEAR TO THEM.
WHEN FORCED TO FACE DOWN MONSTERS...
...THEY CAN EVEN LEAVE BEHIND THEIR HUMANITY.
SOMEONE WHO CAN'T THROW ANYTHING AWAY...
...WILL NEVER BE ABLE TO CHANGE ANYTHING.

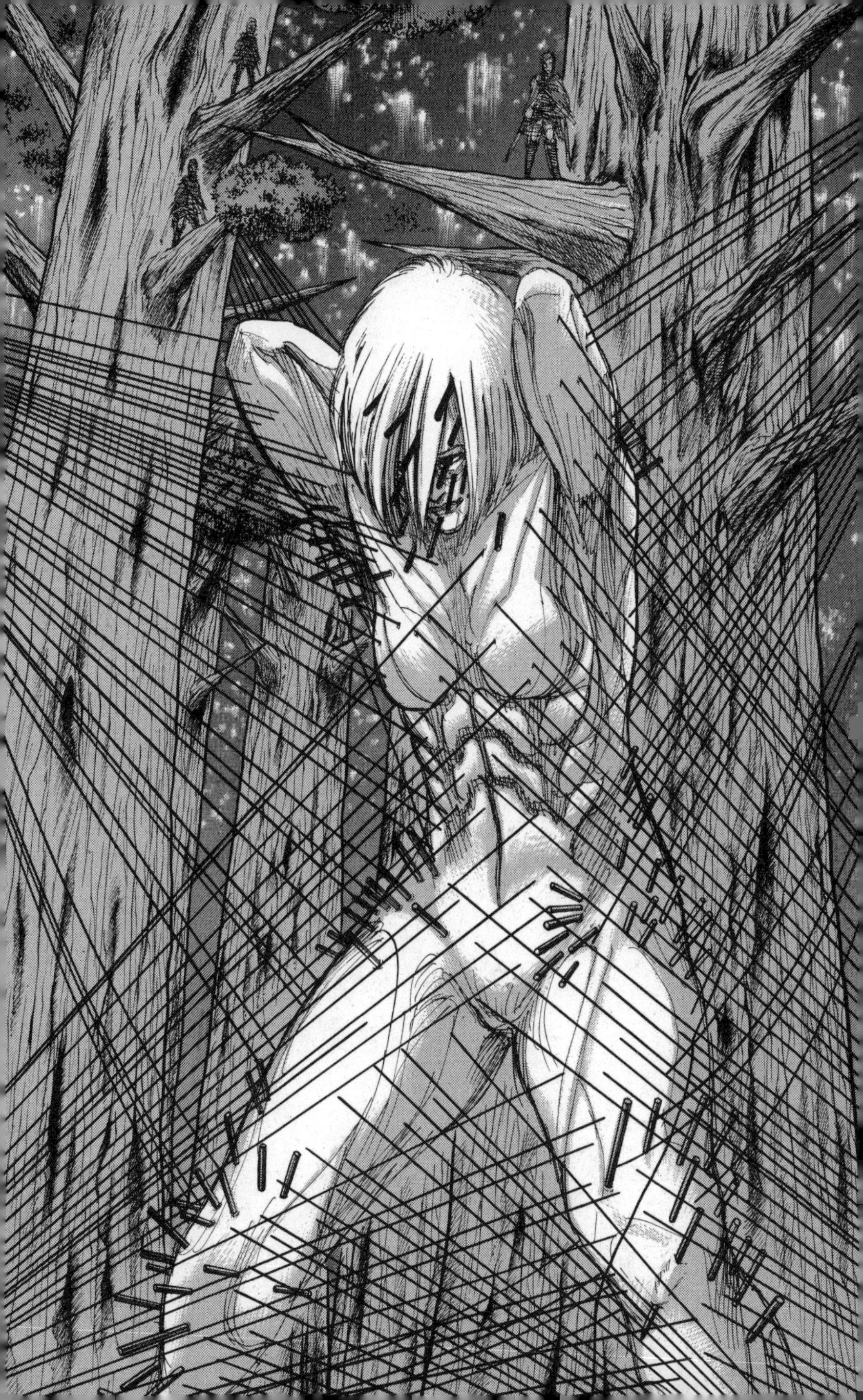

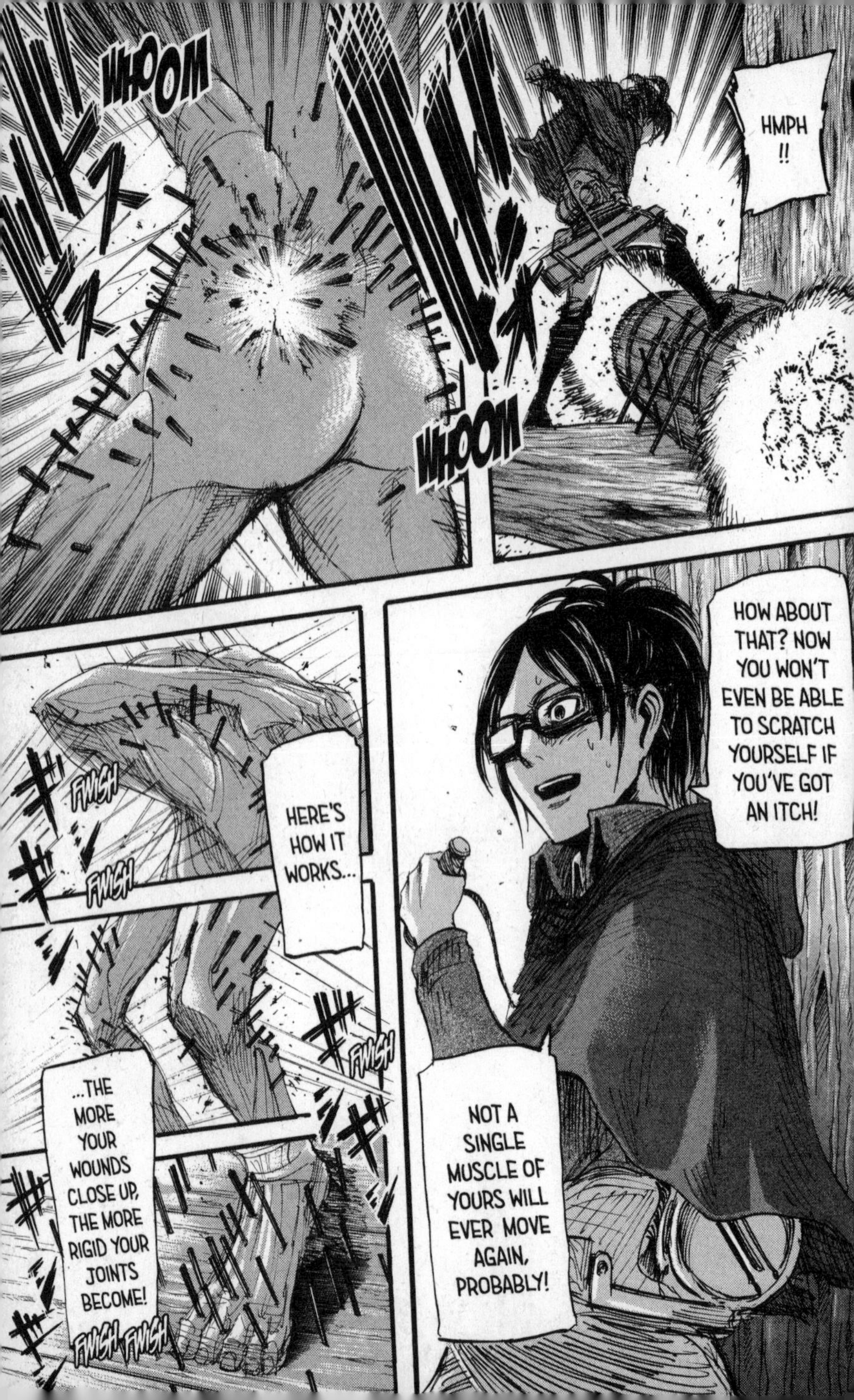
HMPH !!
WHOOM
WHOOM
HOW ABOUT THAT? NOW YOU WON'T EVEN BE ABLE TO SCRATCH YOURSELF IF YOU'VE GOT AN ITCH!
NOT A SINGLE MUSCLE OF YOURS WILL EVER MOVE AGAIN, PROBABLY!
HERE'S HOW IT WORKS...
FWISH
FWISH
...THE MORE YOUR WOUNDS CLOSE UP, THE MORE RIGID YOUR JOINTS BECOME!
FWISH
FWISH FWISH

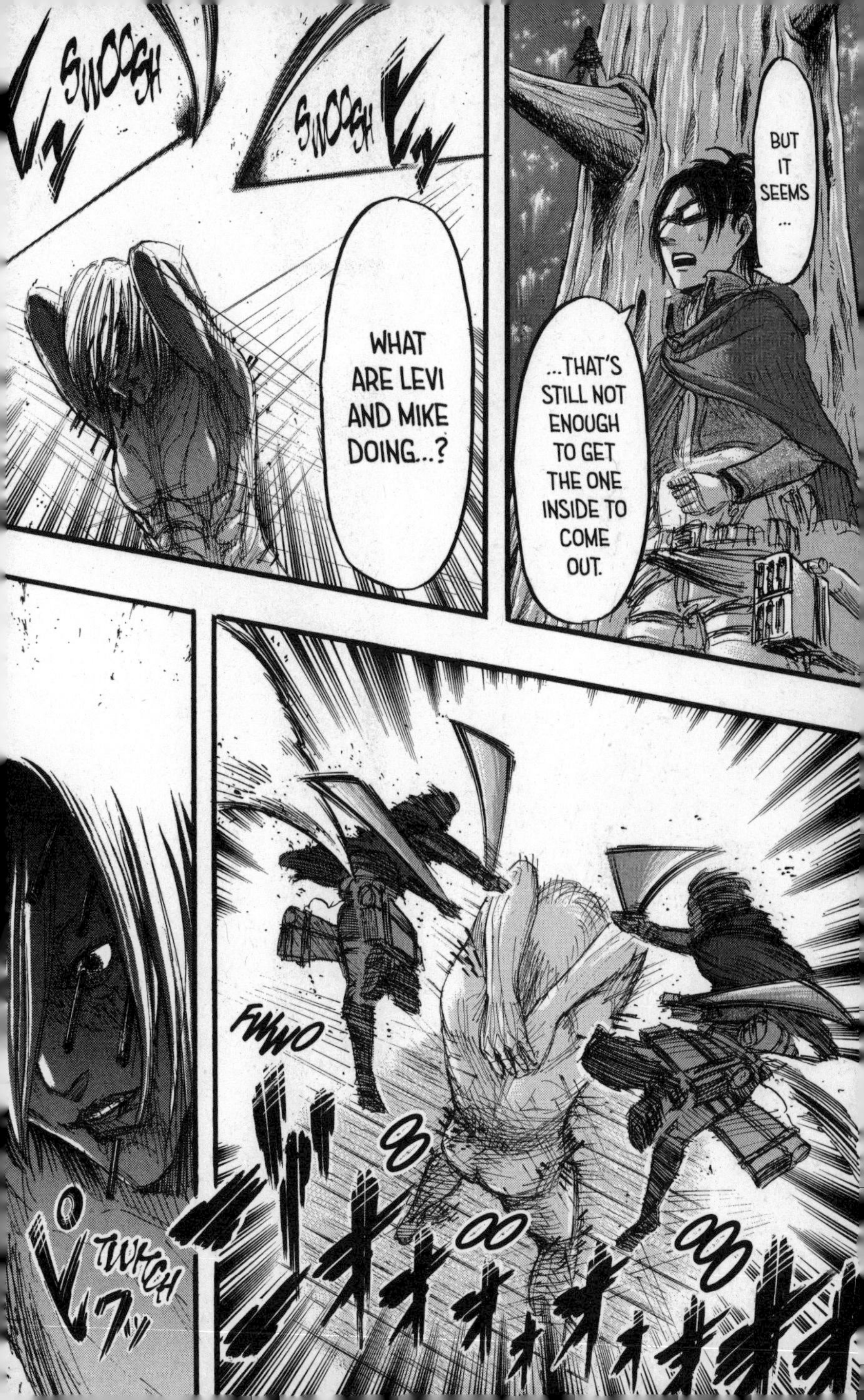
BUT IT SEEMS...
...THAT'S STILL NOT ENOUGH TO GET THE ONE INSIDE TO COME OUT.
SWOOSH
WHAT ARE LEVI AND MIKE DOING...?
SWOOSH
FWWO
TWITCH

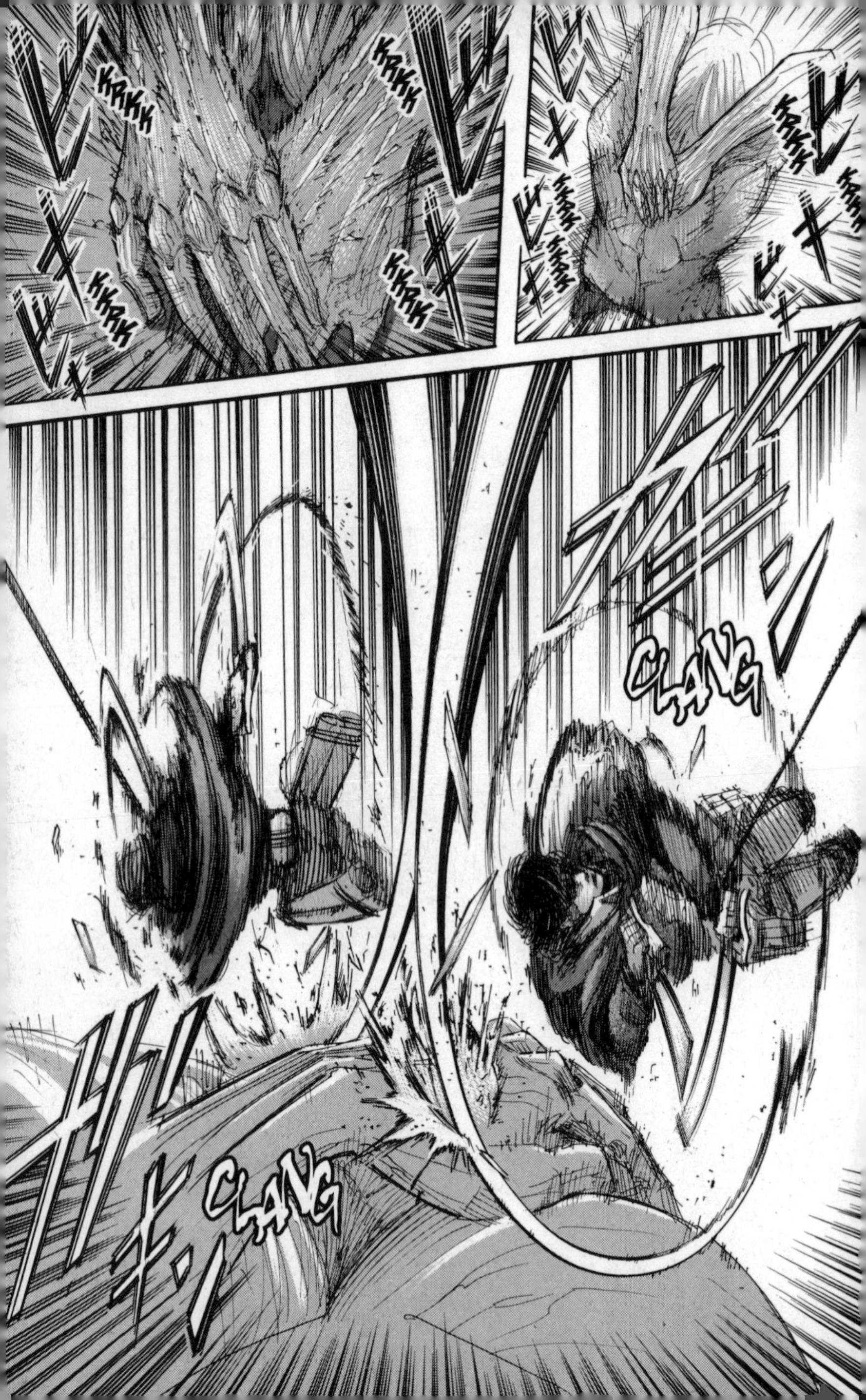
KRRKK
KRRKK
KRRKK
KRKKK
KRKKK
KKRKK
KKRKK
CLANG
CLANG

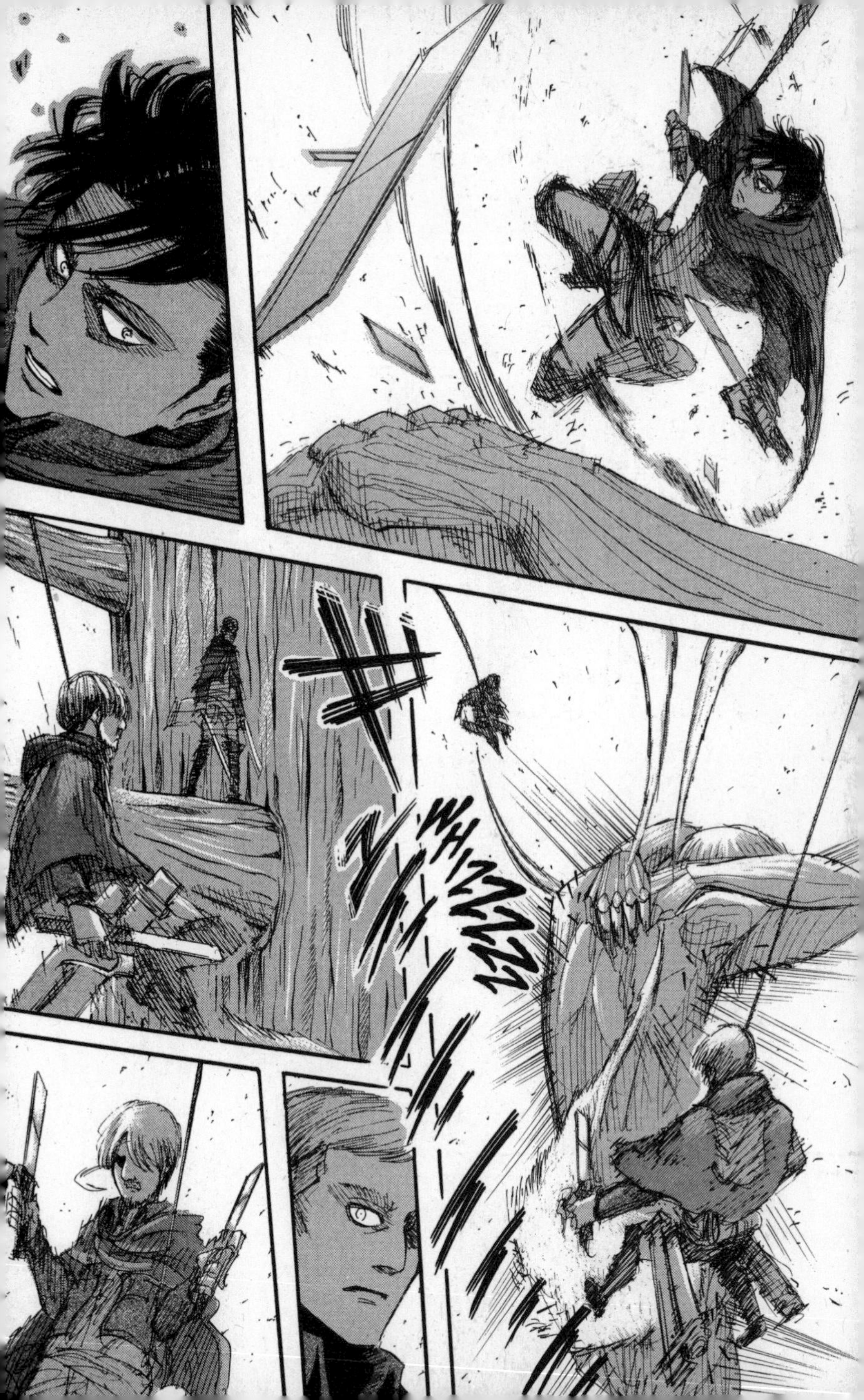
WHIZZZZZZ

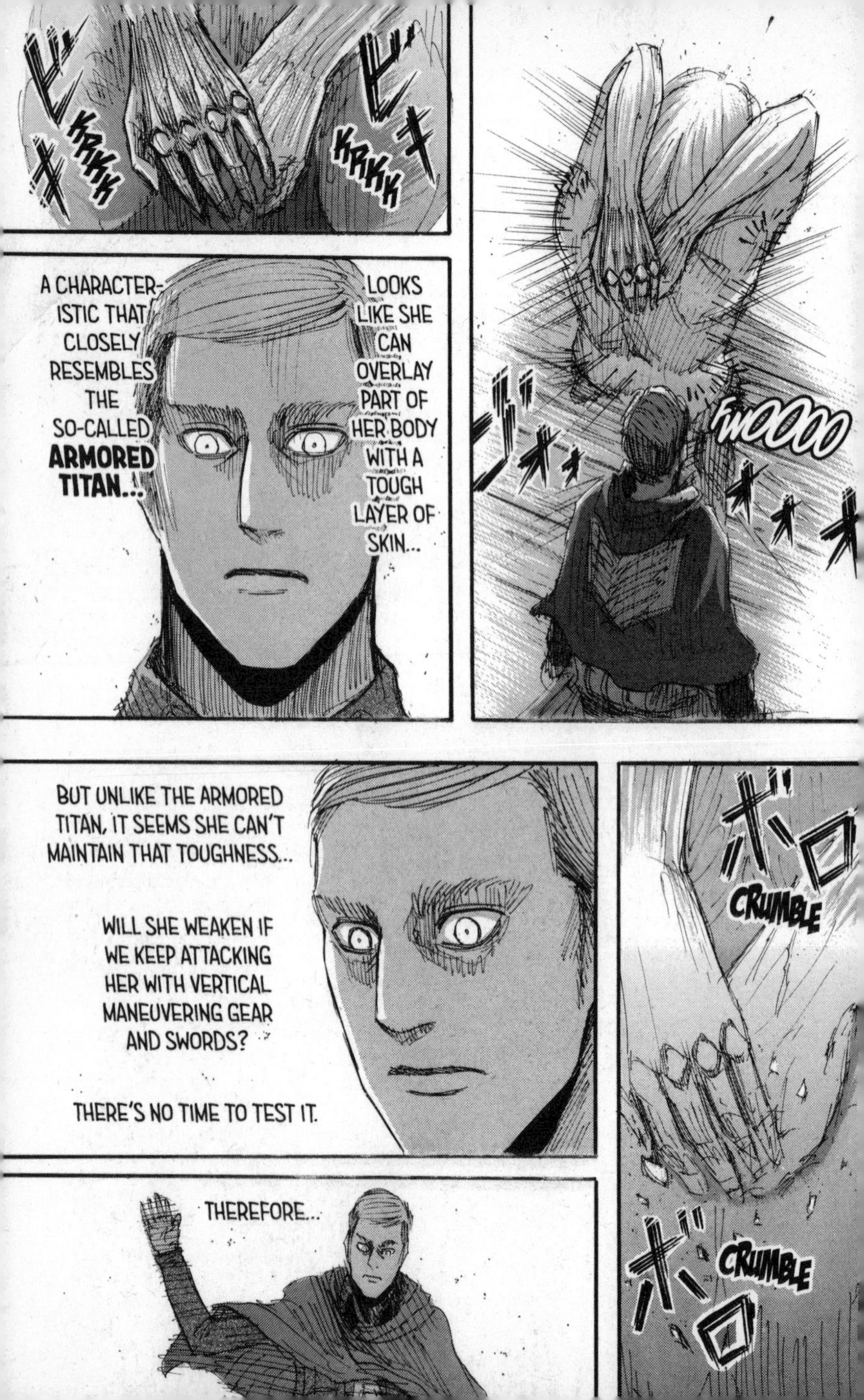

FWOOOO
KRKK
KRKK
LOOKS LIKE SHE CAN OVERLAY PART OF HER BODY WITH A TOUGH LAYER OF SKIN...
A CHARACTERISTIC THAT CLOSELY RESEMBLES THE SO-CALLED **ARMORED TITAN...**
CRUMBLE
CRUMBLE
BUT UNLIKE THE ARMORED TITAN, IT SEEMS SHE CAN'T MAINTAIN THAT TOUGHNESS...
WILL SHE WEAKEN IF WE KEEP ATTACKING HER WITH VERTICAL MANEUVERING GEAR AND SWORDS?
THERE'S NO TIME TO TEST IT.
THEREFORE...

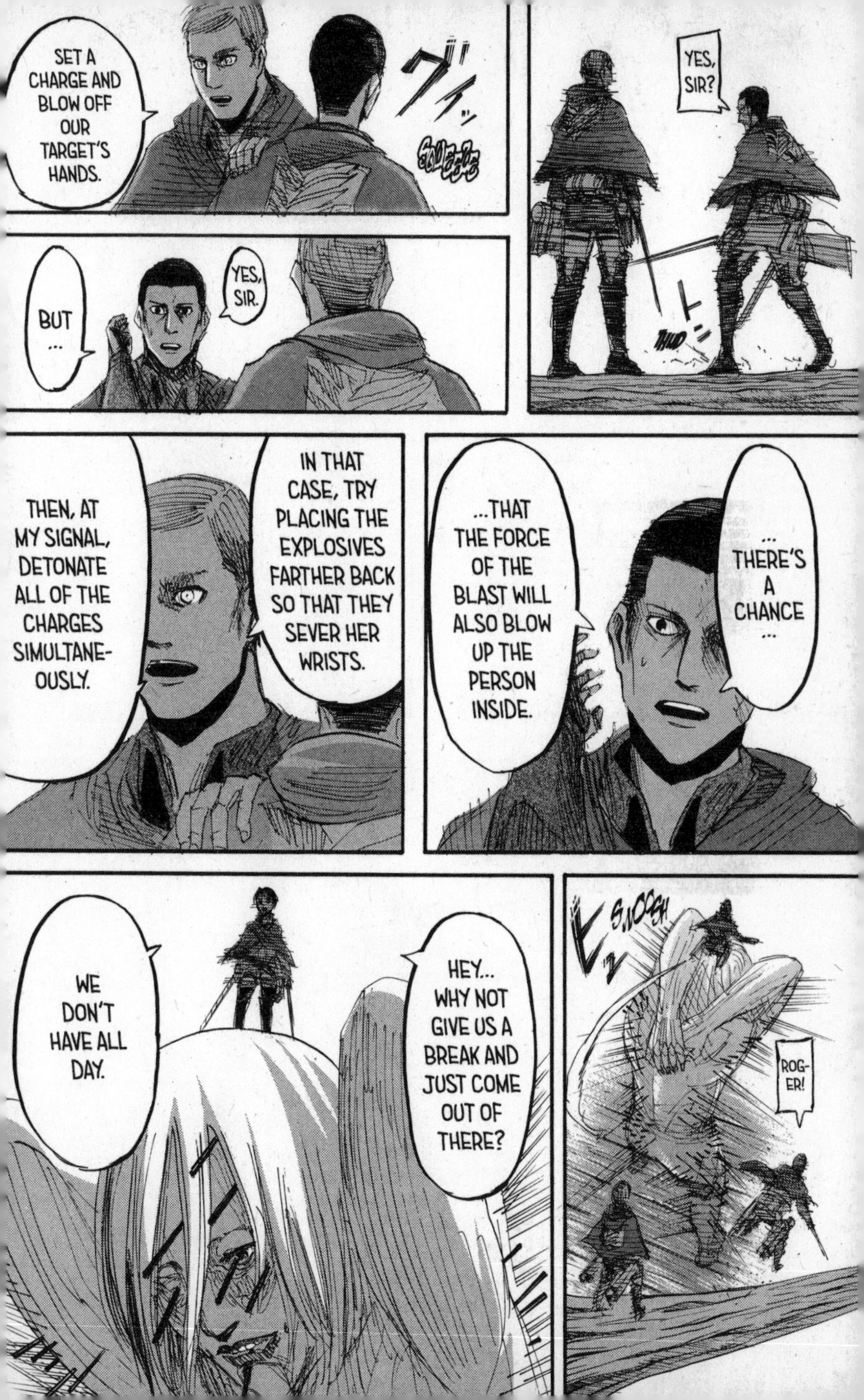
YES, SIR?
THUD
SET A CHARGE AND BLOW OFF OUR TARGET'S HANDS.
YES, SIR.
BUT ...
... THERE'S A CHANCE ...
...THAT THE FORCE OF THE BLAST WILL ALSO BLOW UP THE PERSON INSIDE.
IN THAT CASE, TRY PLACING THE EXPLOSIVES FARTHER BACK SO THAT THEY SEVER HER WRISTS.
THEN, AT MY SIGNAL, DETONATE ALL OF THE CHARGES SIMULTANE-OUSLY.
SWOOSH
ROG-ER!
HEY... WHY NOT GIVE US A BREAK AND JUST COME OUT OF THERE?
WE DON'T HAVE ALL DAY.

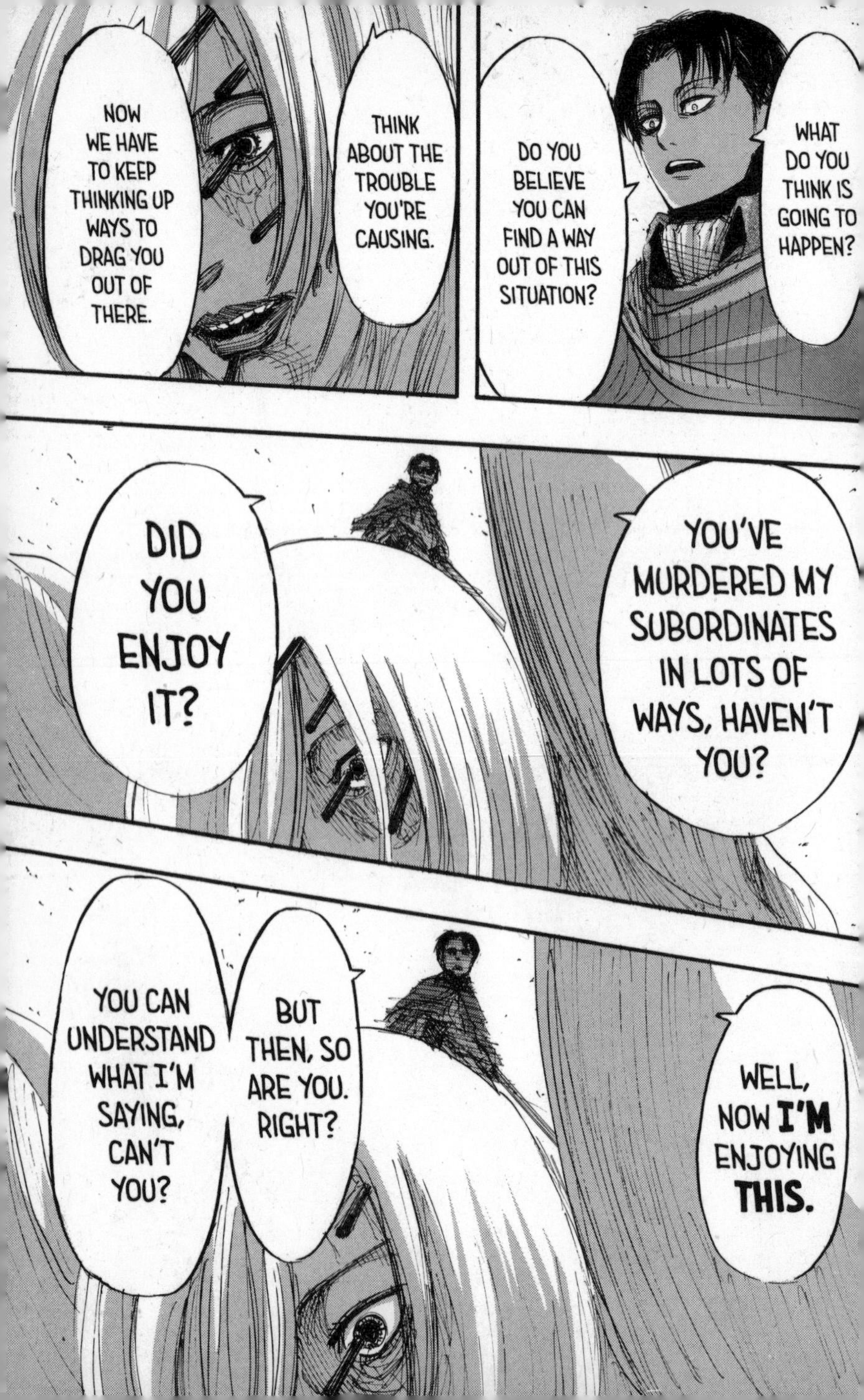
WHAT DO YOU THINK IS GOING TO HAPPEN?
DO YOU BELIEVE YOU CAN FIND A WAY OUT OF THIS SITUATION?
THINK ABOUT THE TROUBLE YOU'RE CAUSING.
NOW WE HAVE TO KEEP THINKING UP WAYS TO DRAG YOU OUT OF THERE.
YOU'VE MURDERED MY SUBORDINATES IN LOTS OF WAYS, HAVEN'T YOU?
DID YOU ENJOY IT?
WELL, NOW **I'M** ENJOYING **THIS.**
BUT THEN, SO ARE YOU. RIGHT?
YOU CAN UNDERSTAND WHAT I'M SAYING, CAN'T YOU?

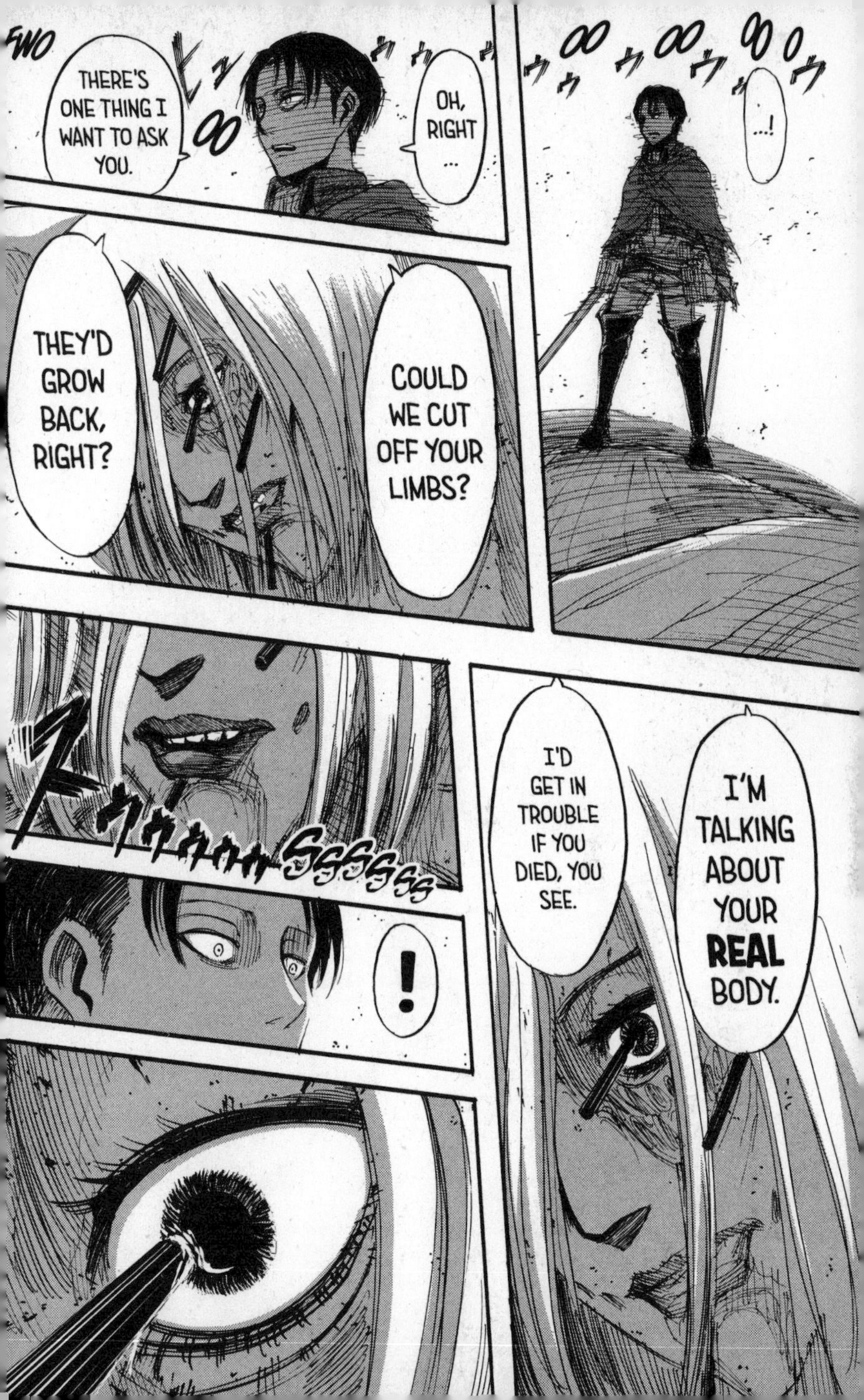
OO OO OO O
…!
OH, RIGHT …
FWO
OO
THERE'S ONE THING I WANT TO ASK YOU.
COULD WE CUT OFF YOUR LIMBS?
THEY'D GROW BACK, RIGHT?
I'M TALKING ABOUT YOUR **REAL** BODY.
I'D GET IN TROUBLE IF YOU DIED, YOU SEE.
SSSSSS
!

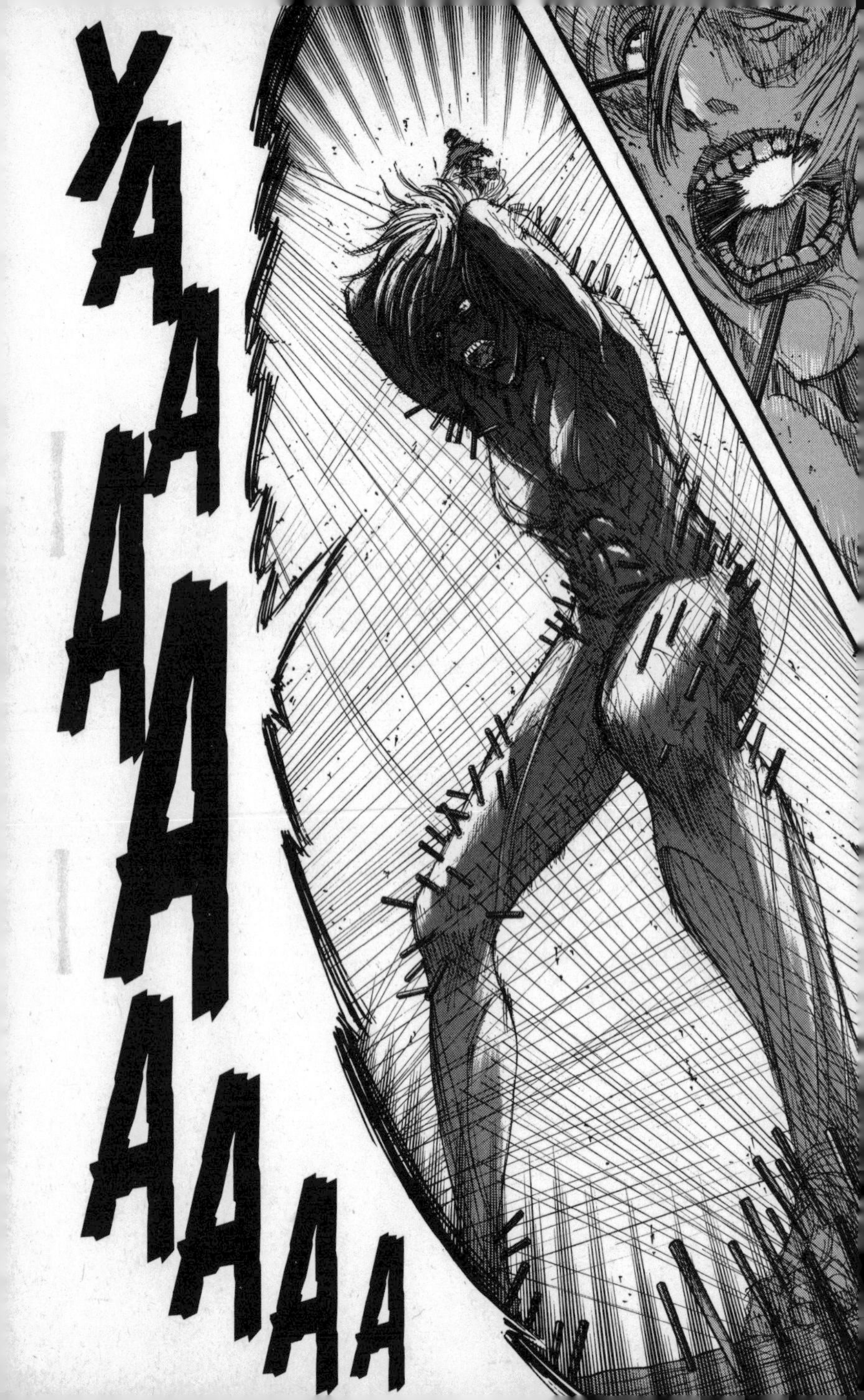
YAAAAAAAAAAA

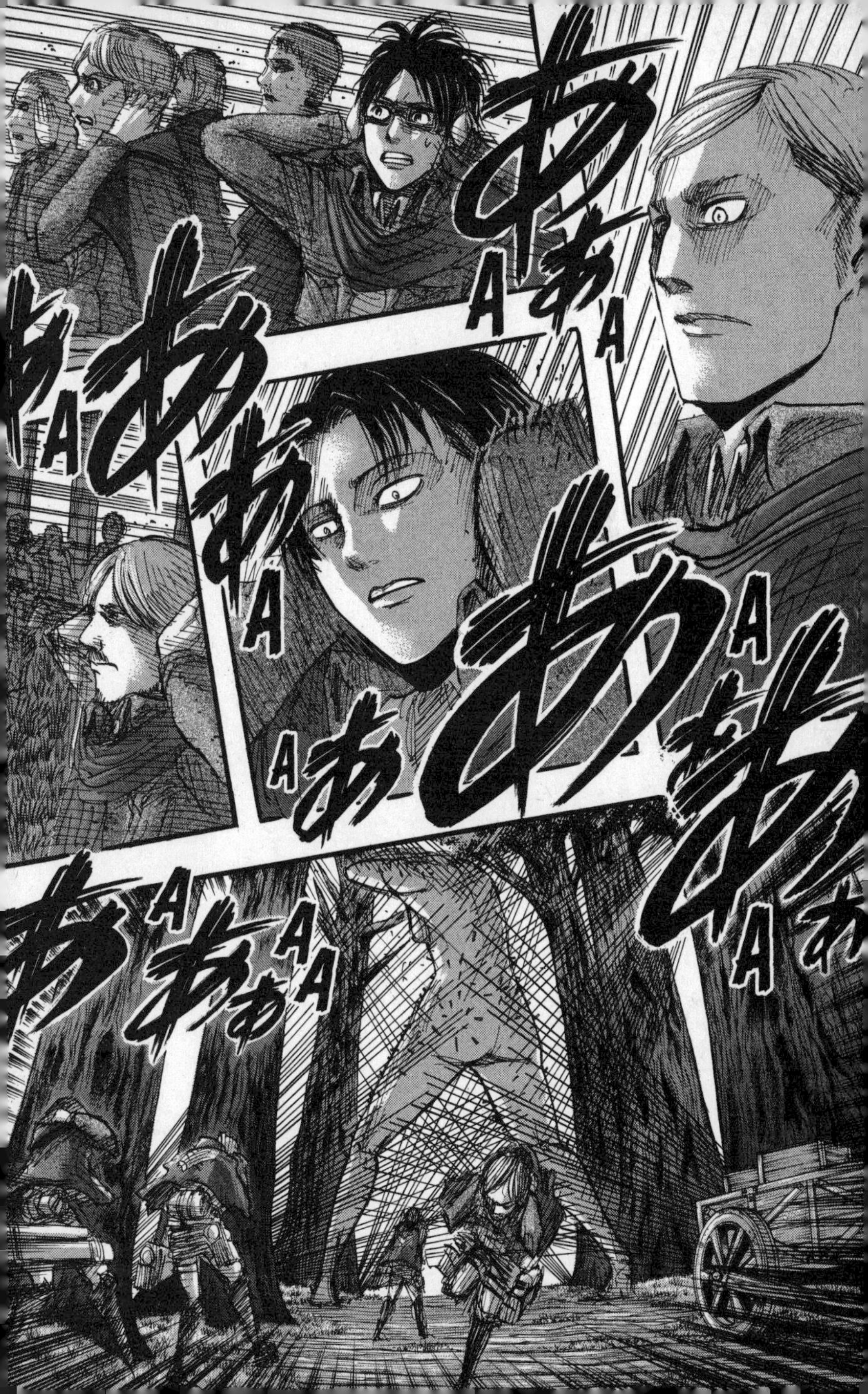

あ
A
あ
A
あ
A
あ
A
あ
A
あ
A
あ
A
あ
A
あ
A
あ
あ
A
A
A

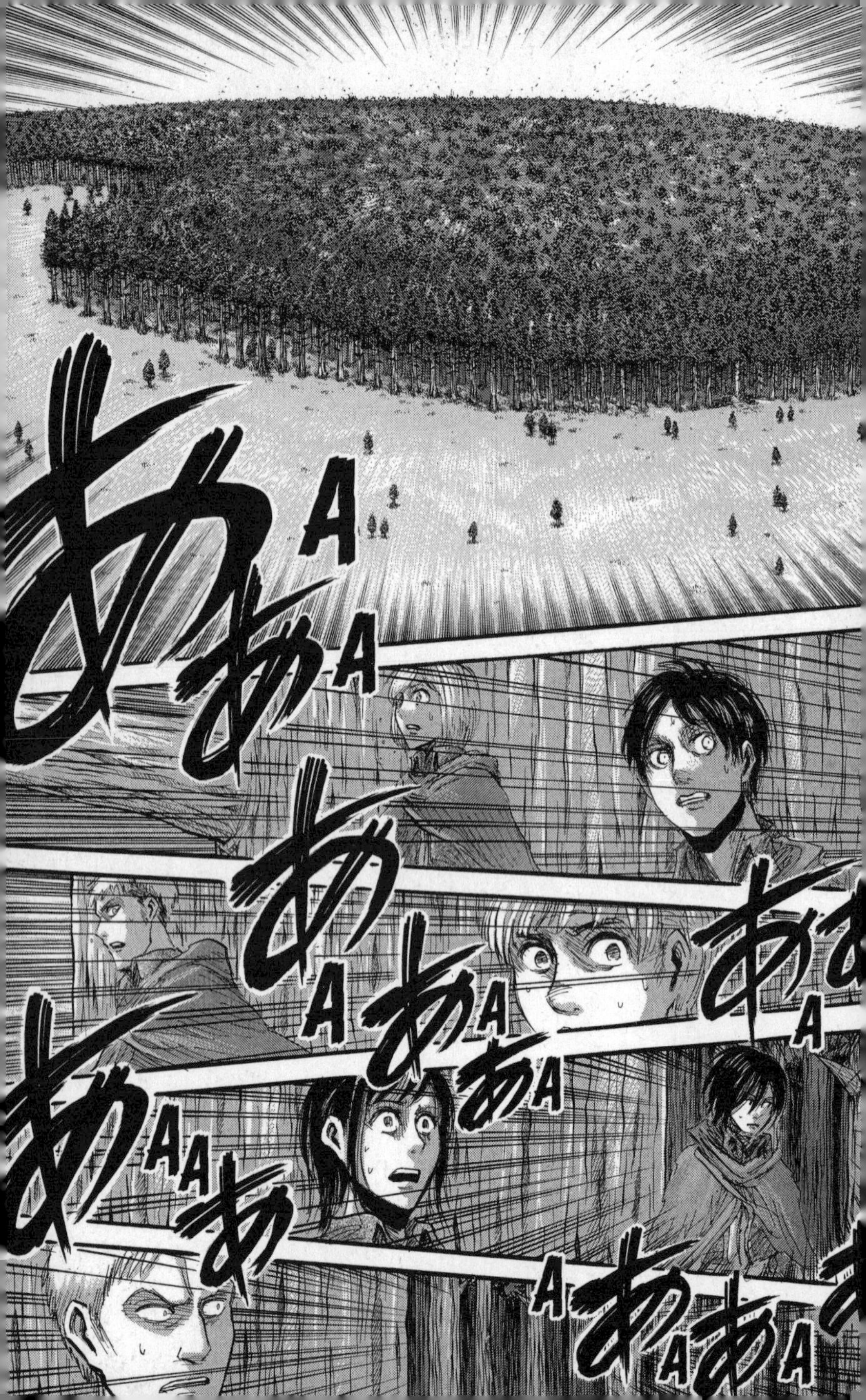
あAあA
あAあAあA
あA
あAAあ
AあAあA

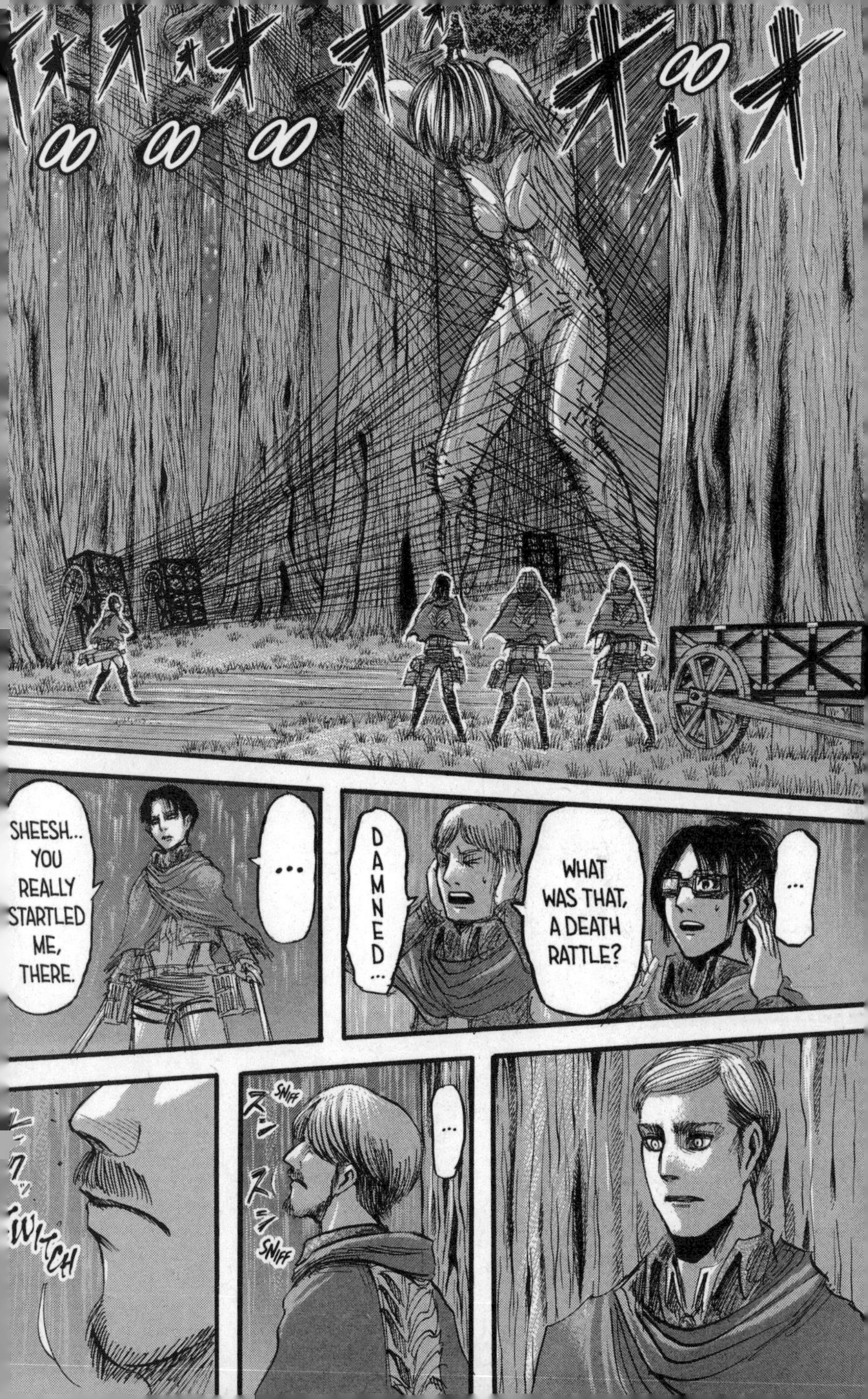
OO
OO
OO
OO
...
WHAT WAS THAT, A DEATH RATTLE?
DAMNED...
...
SHEESH... YOU REALLY STARTLED ME, THERE.
...
SNIFF
SNIFF
TWITCH

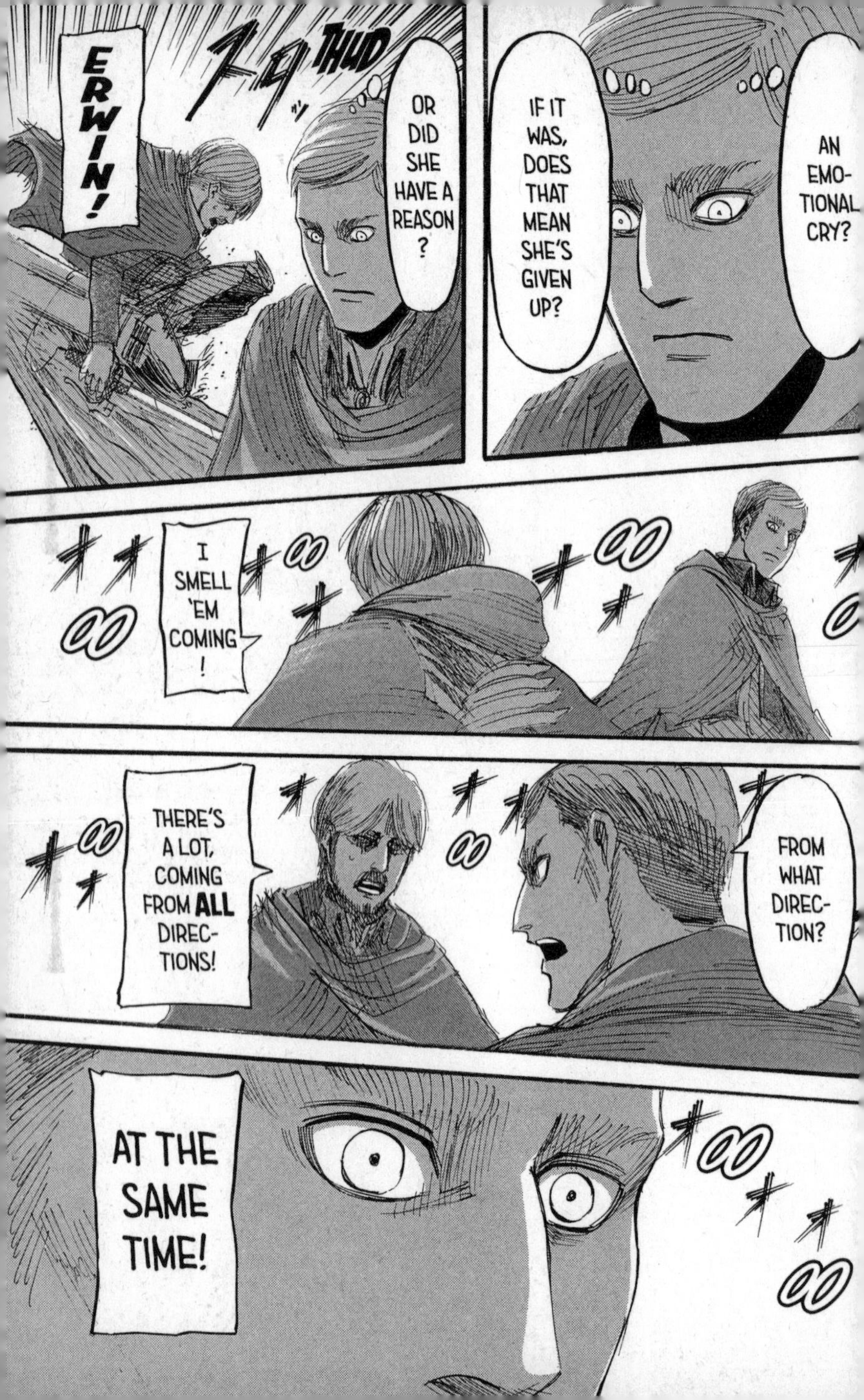
AN EMOTIONAL CRY?
IF IT WAS, DOES THAT MEAN SHE'S GIVEN UP?
OR DID SHE HAVE A REASON?
THUD
ERWIN!
I SMELL 'EM COMING!
FROM WHAT DIRECTION?
THERE'S A LOT, COMING FROM ALL DIRECTIONS!
AT THE SAME TIME!

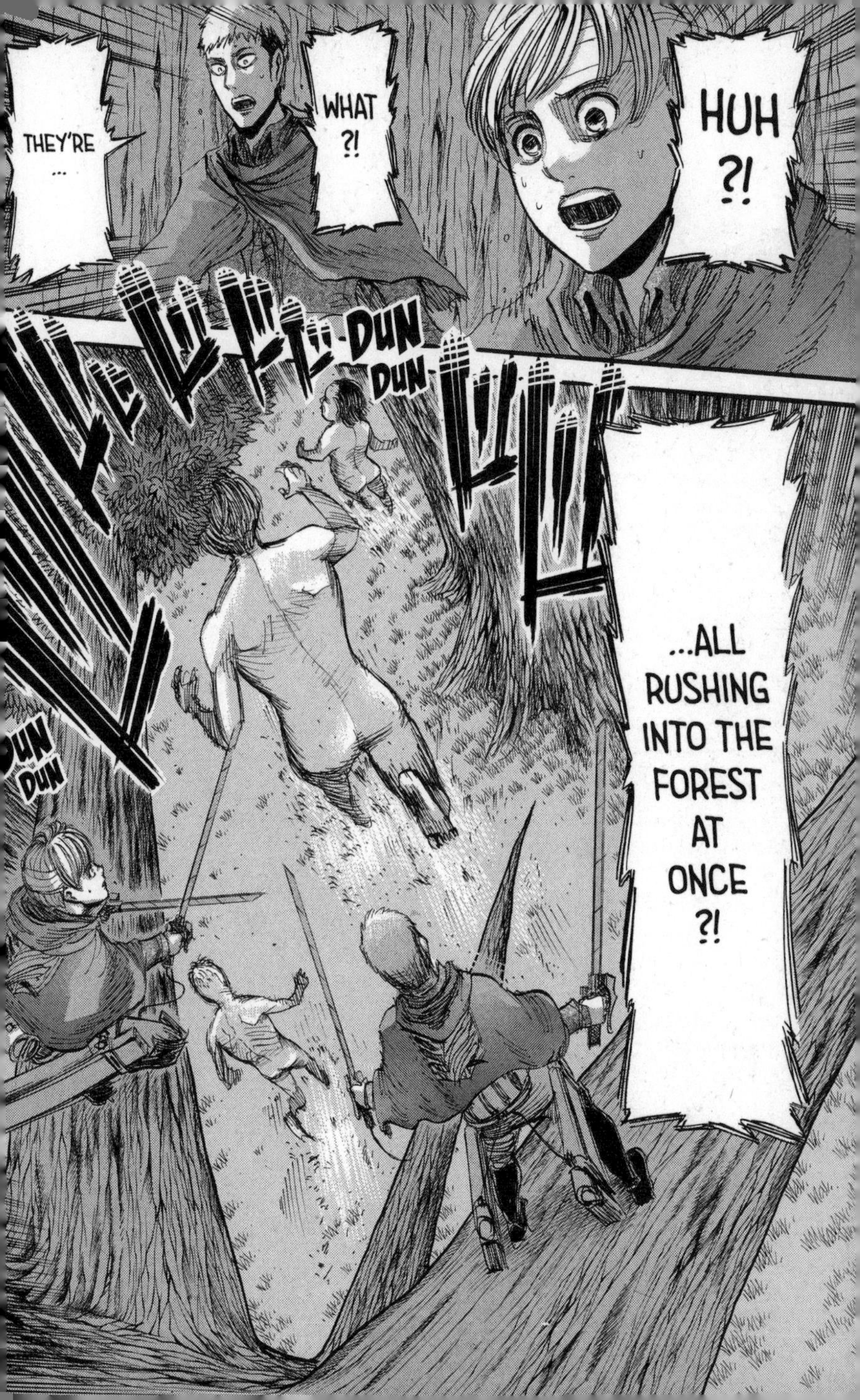
HUH ?!
WHAT ?!
THEY'RE ...
DUN DUN
...ALL RUSHING INTO THE FOREST AT ONCE ?!
DUN DUN

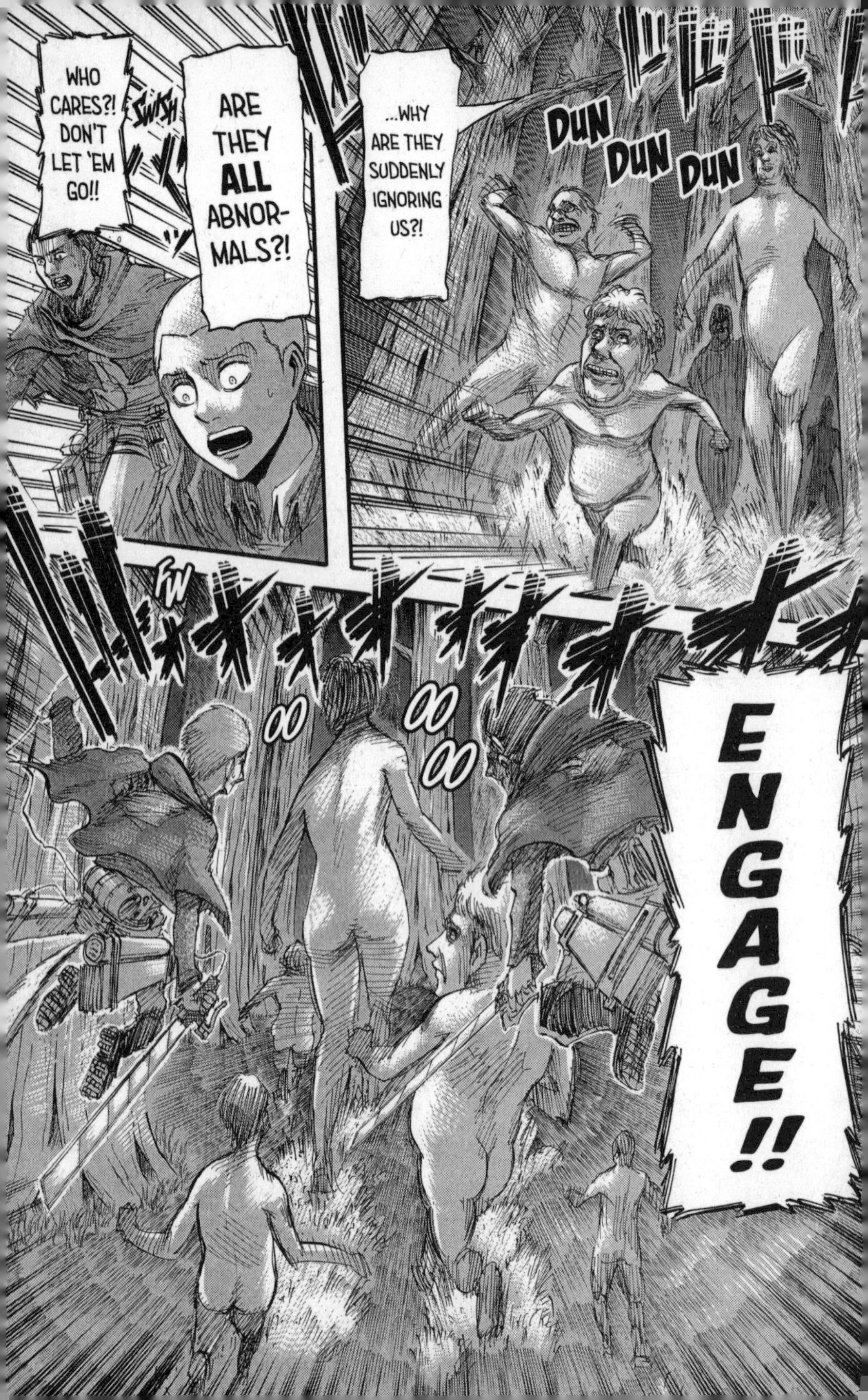

...WHY ARE THEY SUDDENLY IGNORING US?!
DUN DUN DUN
ARE THEY **ALL** ABNORMALS?!
SWISH
WHO CARES?! DON'T LET 'EM GO!!
ENGAGE!!
FW

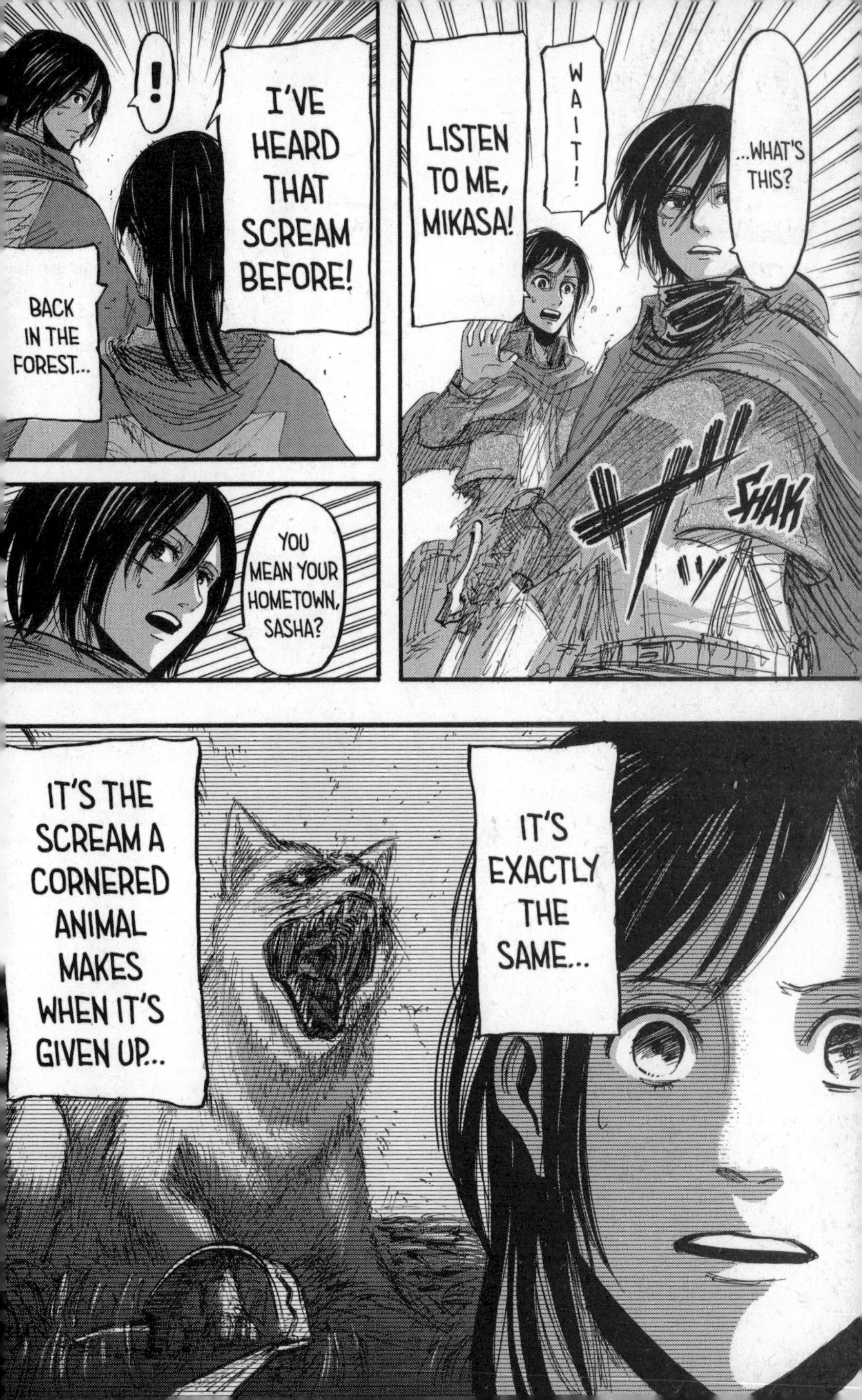
...WHAT'S THIS?
WAIT!
LISTEN TO ME, MIKASA!
SHAK
I'VE HEARD THAT SCREAM BEFORE!
!
BACK IN THE FOREST...
YOU MEAN YOUR HOMETOWN, SASHA?
IT'S EXACTLY THE SAME...
IT'S THE SCREAM A CORNERED ANIMAL MAKES WHEN IT'S GIVEN UP...

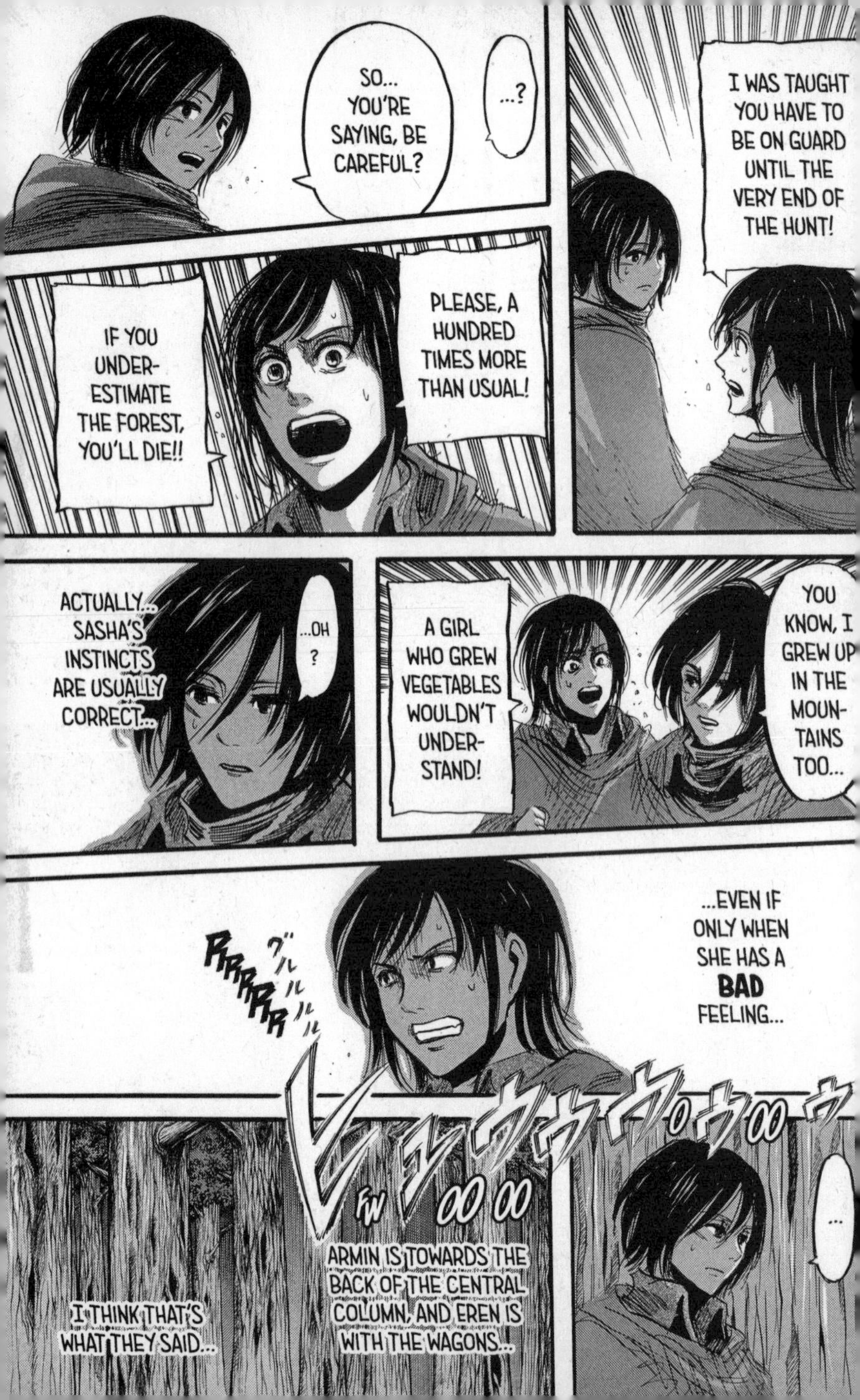
I WAS TAUGHT YOU HAVE TO BE ON GUARD UNTIL THE VERY END OF THE HUNT!
...?
SO... YOU'RE SAYING, BE CAREFUL?
PLEASE, A HUNDRED TIMES MORE THAN USUAL!
IF YOU UNDER-ESTIMATE THE FOREST, YOU'LL DIE!!
YOU KNOW, I GREW UP IN THE MOUNTAINS TOO...
A GIRL WHO GREW VEGETABLES WOULDN'T UNDER-STAND!
...OH?
ACTUALLY... SASHA'S INSTINCTS ARE USUALLY CORRECT...
...EVEN IF ONLY WHEN SHE HAS A **BAD** FEELING...
ヴルルル
RRRRRR
...
ヒュウウウウ
FW OO OO
ARMIN IS TOWARDS THE BACK OF THE CENTRAL COLUMN, AND EREN IS WITH THE WAGONS...
I THINK THAT'S WHAT THEY SAID...

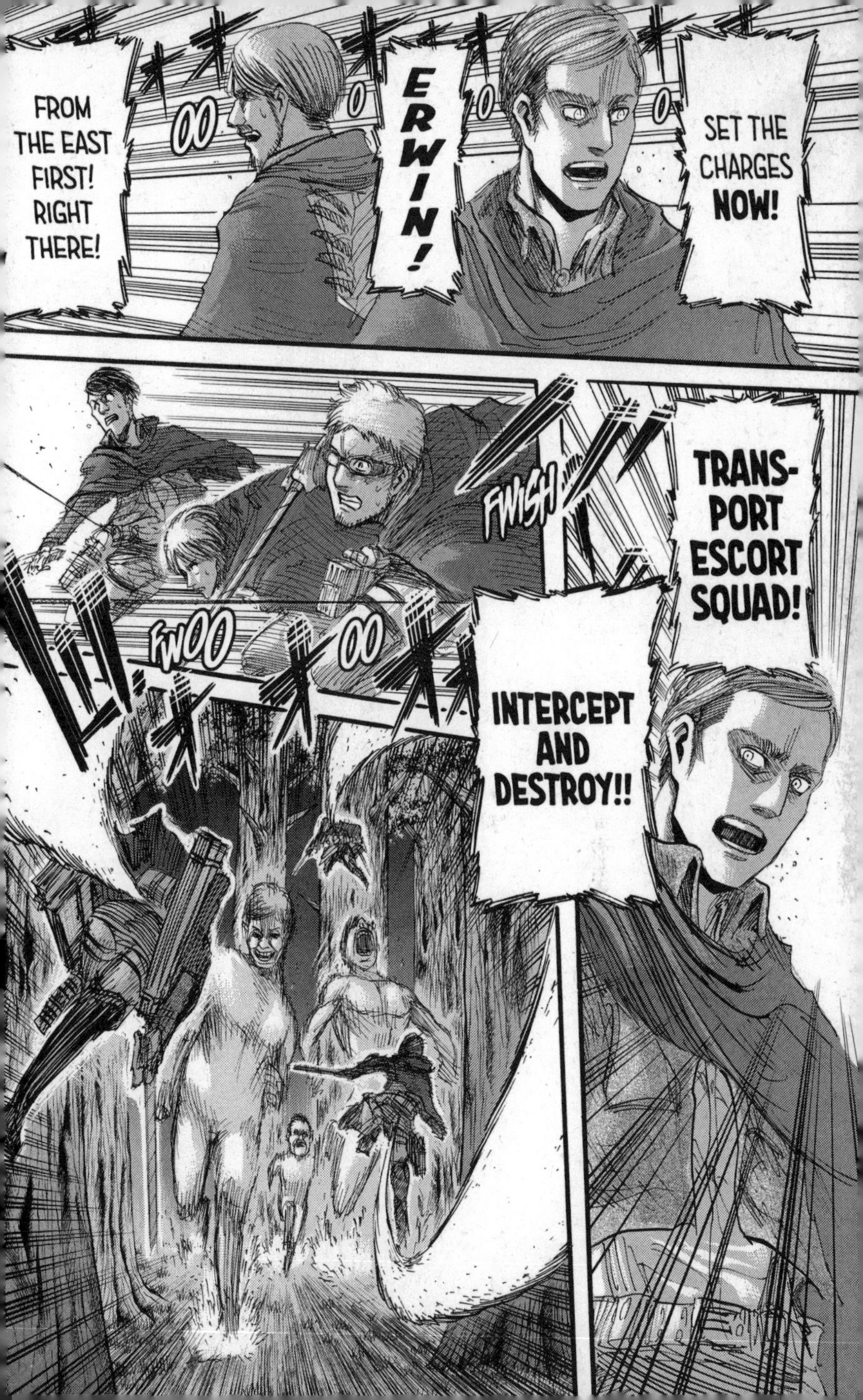
SET THE CHARGES **NOW!**
ERWIN!
OO
FROM THE EAST FIRST! RIGHT THERE!
TRANS-PORT ESCORT SQUAD!
INTERCEPT AND DESTROY!!
FWISH
FWOO
OO

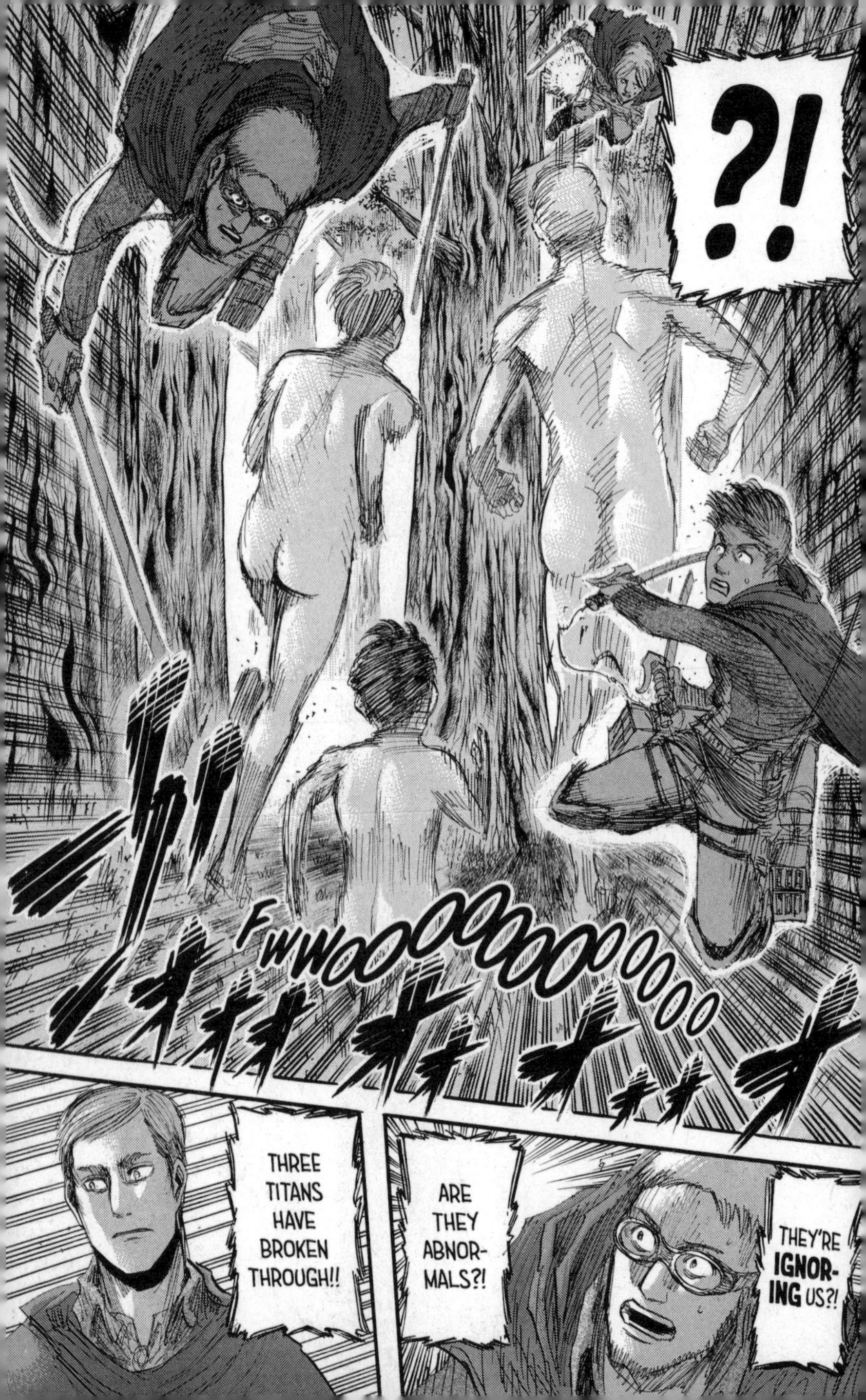
?!
FWWOOOOOOOOOOOOOOO
THEY'RE IGNORING US?!
ARE THEY ABNORMALS?!
THREE TITANS HAVE BROKEN THROUGH!!

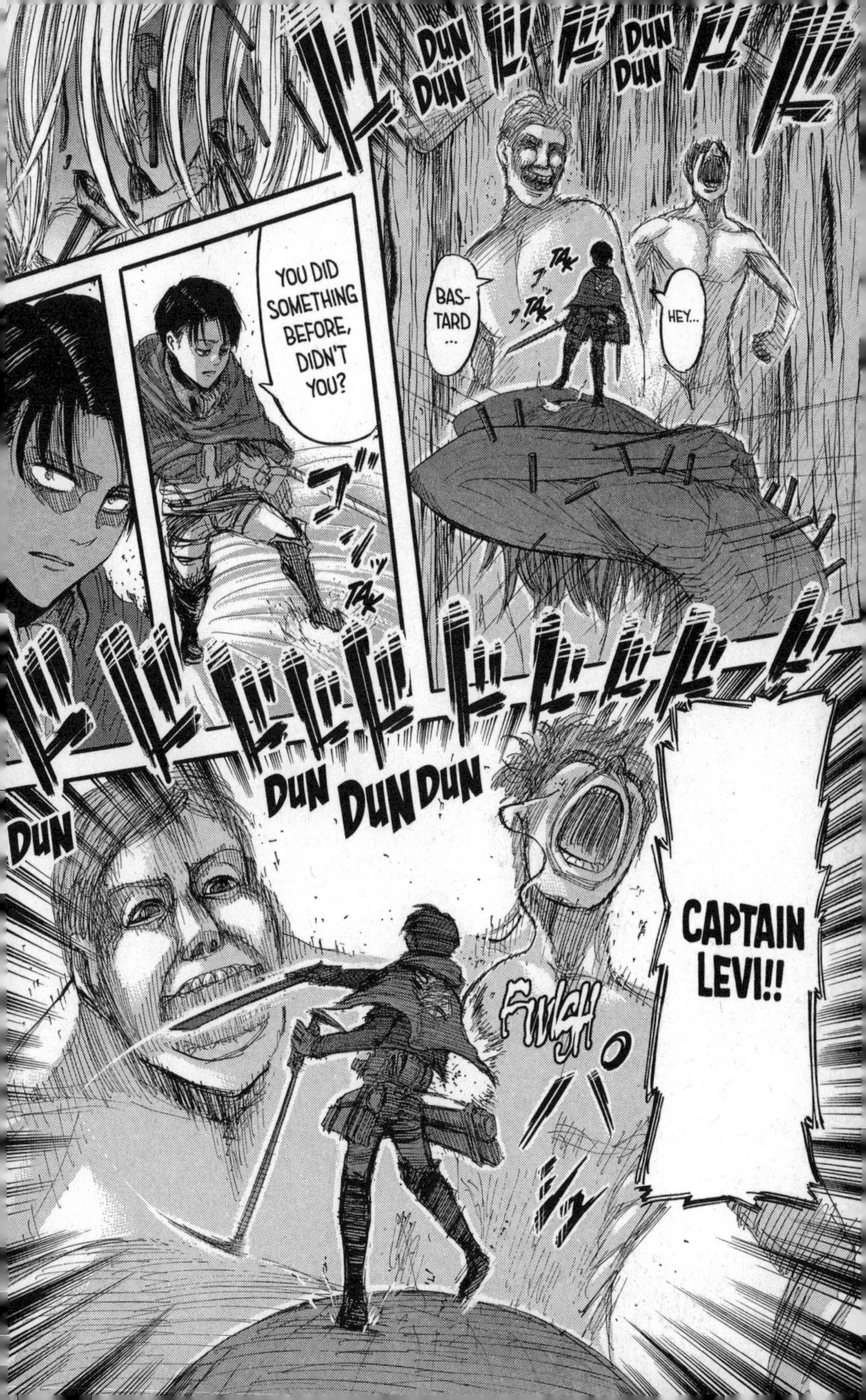
DUN DUN
DUN DUN
HEY...
BAS-TARD ...
TAK TAK
YOU DID SOMETHING BEFORE, DIDN'T YOU?
TAK
CAPTAIN LEVI!!
DUN DUN DUN
DUN
FWUSH

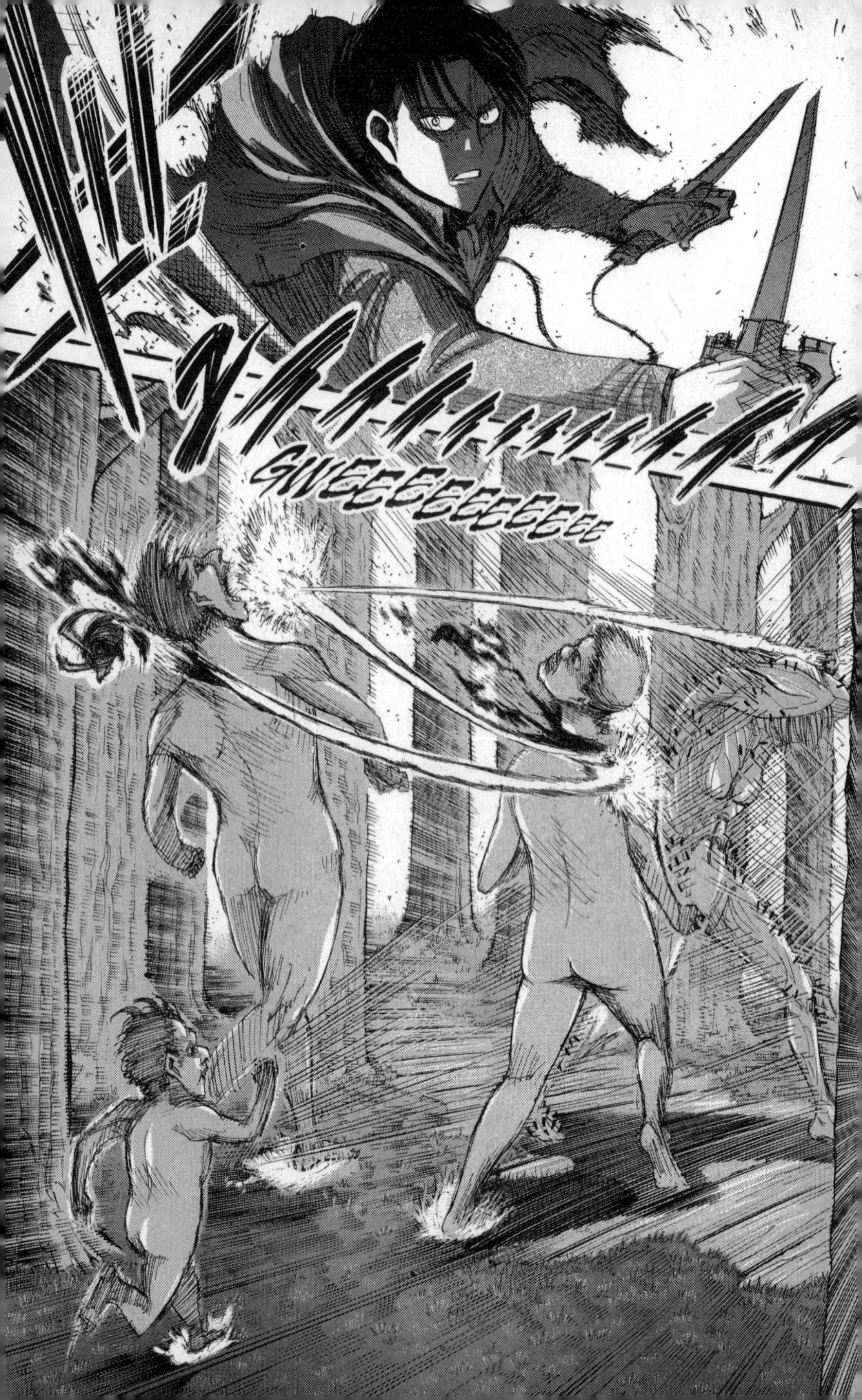
GWEEEEEEEEEEEEEE

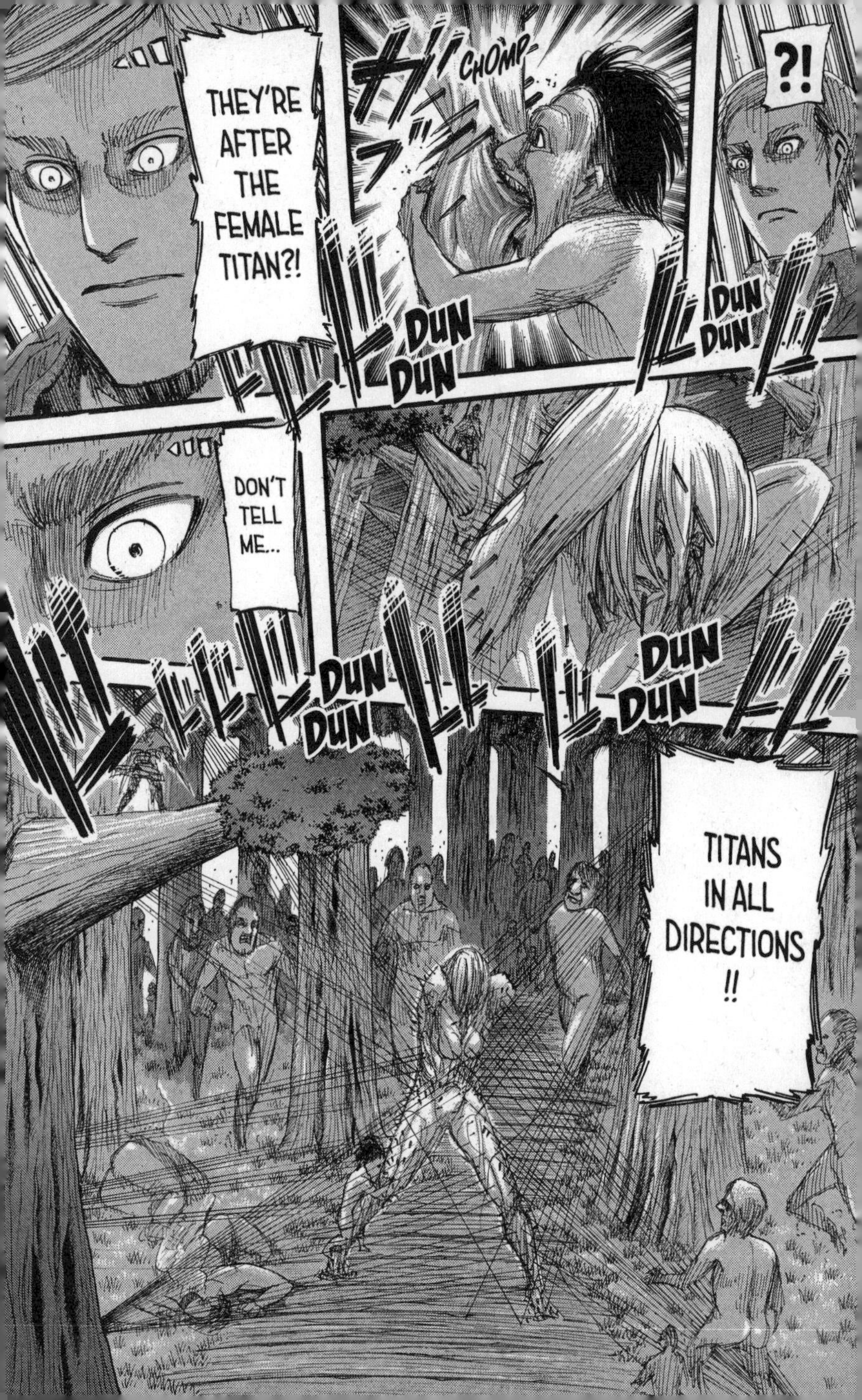
?!
DUN DUN
CHOMP
DUN DUN
THEY'RE AFTER THE FEMALE TITAN?!
DUN DUN
DON'T TELL ME...
DUN DUN
TITANS IN ALL DIRECTIONS !!

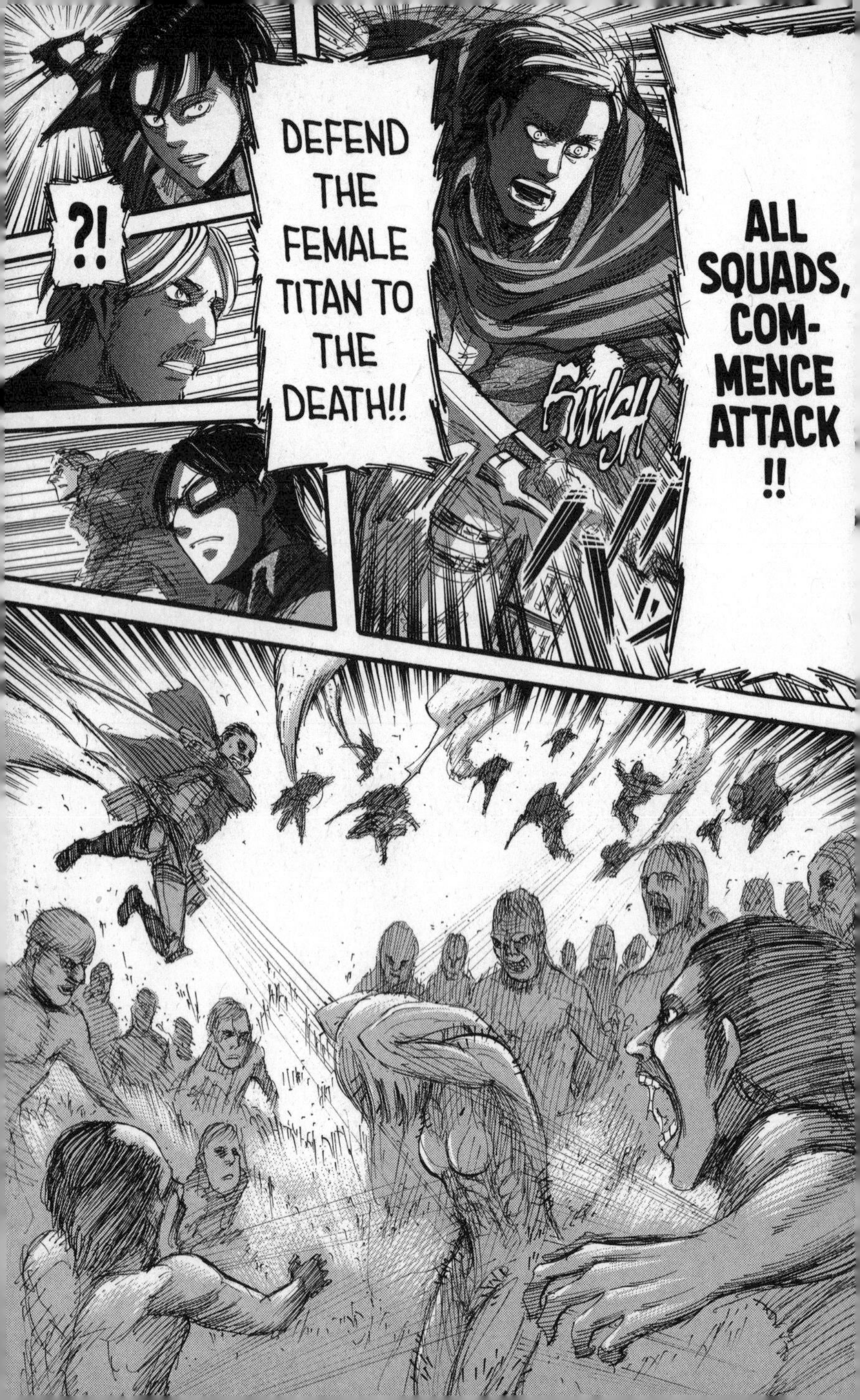
ALL SQUADS, COMMENCE ATTACK!!
Fwish
DEFEND THE FEMALE TITAN TO THE DEATH!!
?!

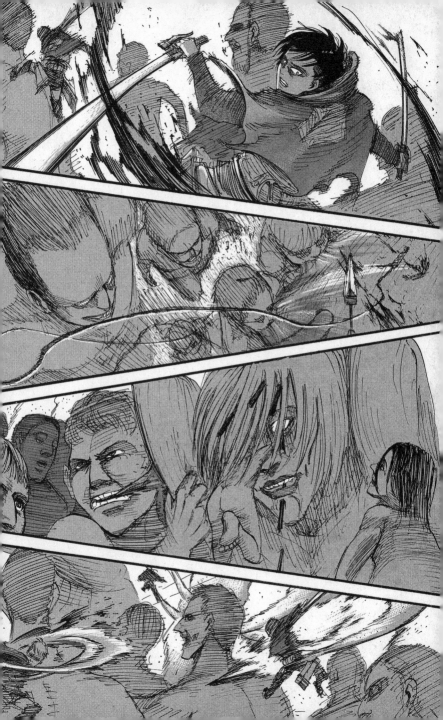

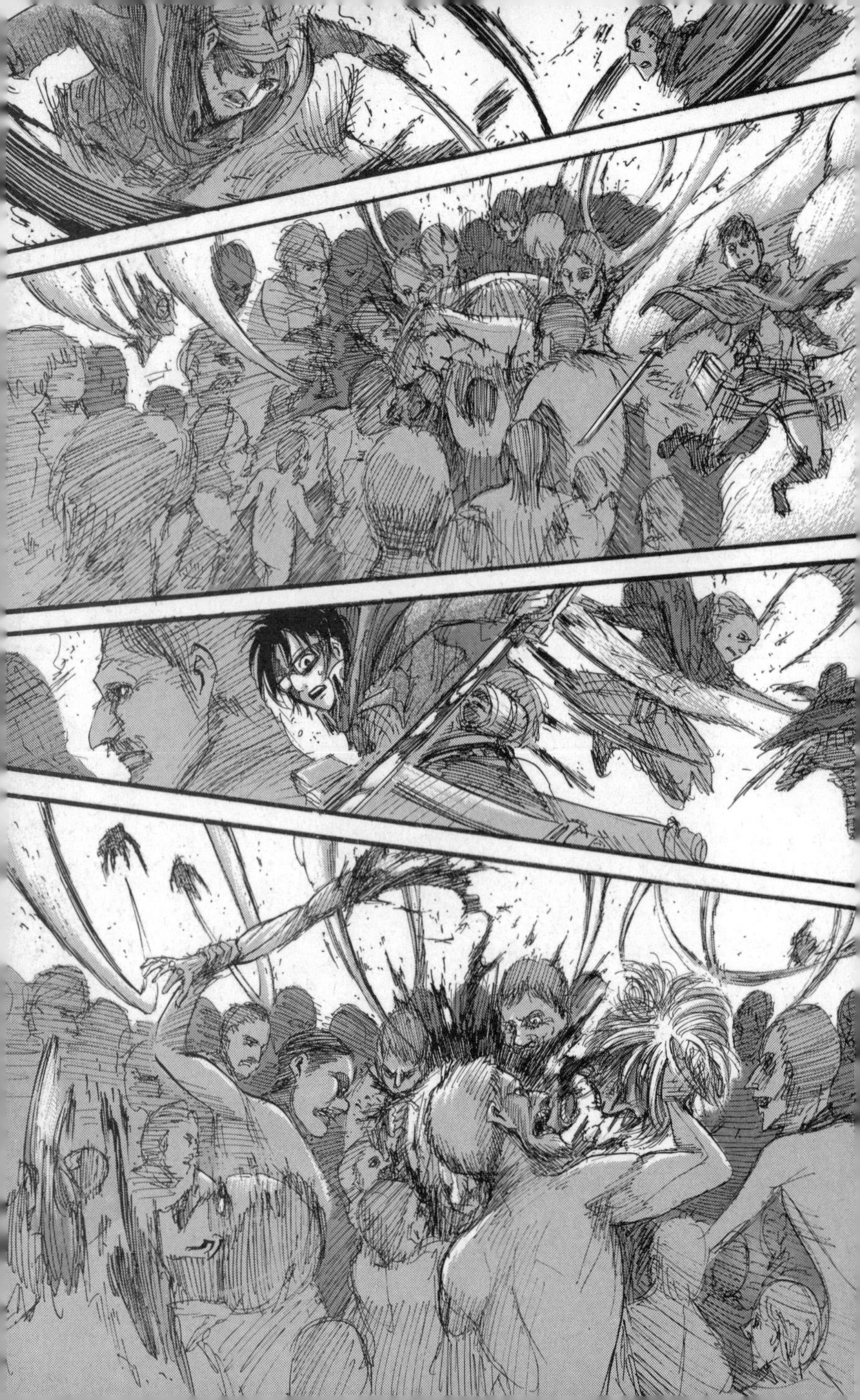

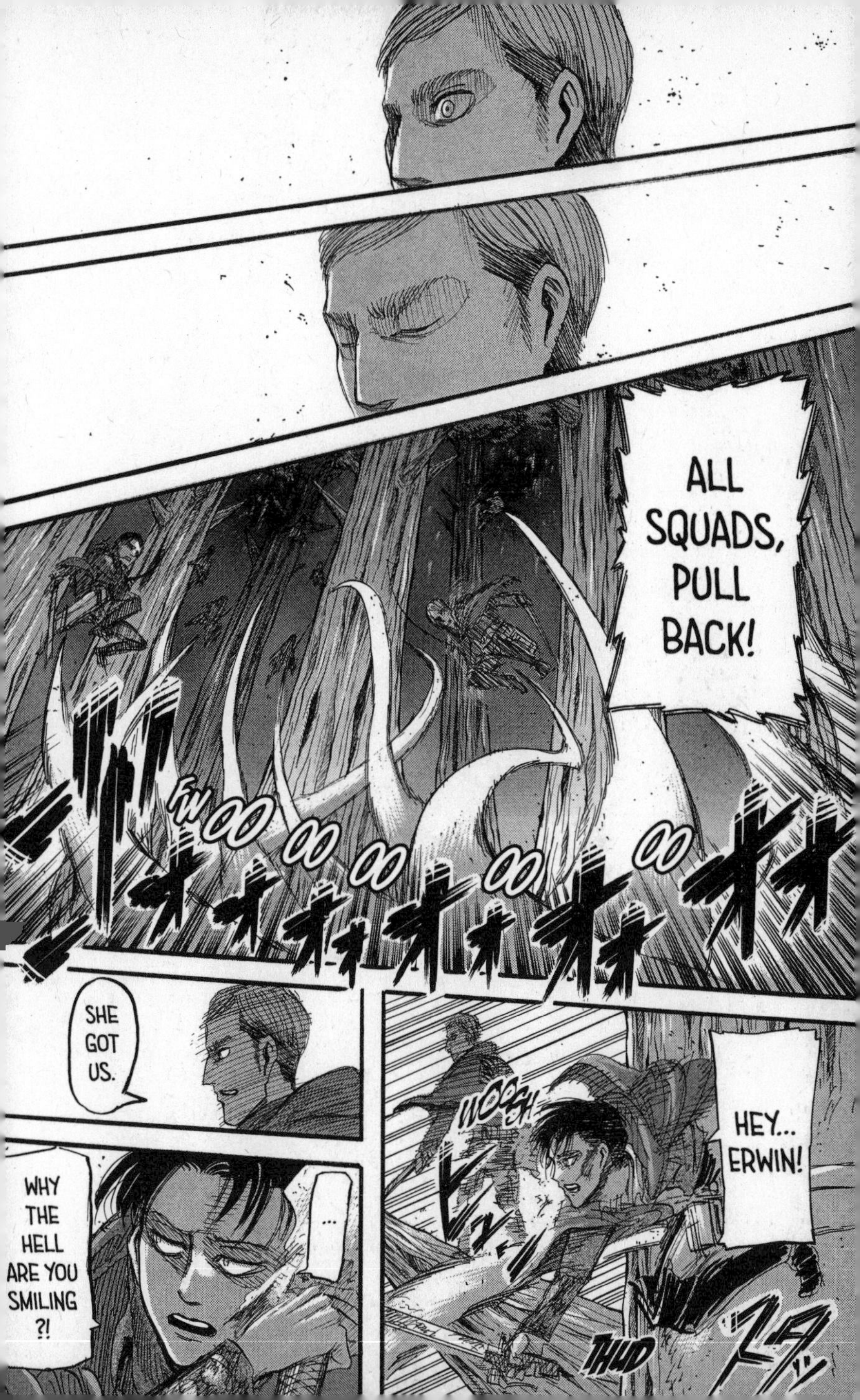
ALL SQUADS, PULL BACK!
FWOO OO OO OO OO
HEY... ERWIN!
WOOSH
THUD
SHE GOT US.
WHY THE HELL ARE YOU SMILING?!
...

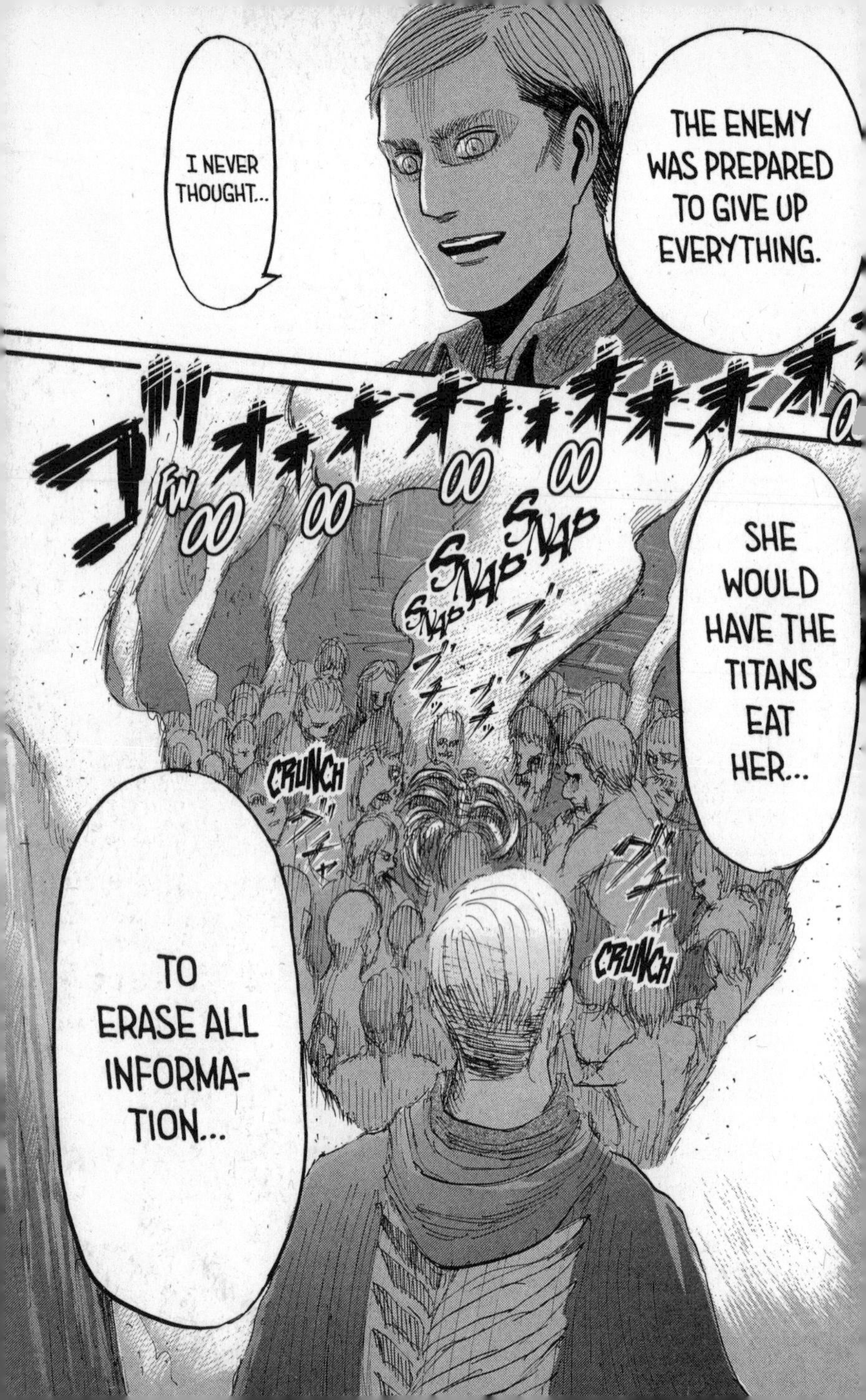
THE ENEMY WAS PREPARED TO GIVE UP EVERYTHING.
I NEVER THOUGHT...
FWOOOOOO
SNAP SNAP SNAP
SHE WOULD HAVE THE TITANS EAT HER...
CRUNCH
CRUNCH
TO ERASE ALL INFORMATION...

13. Special Target Restraining Weapons

HE SURVEY CORPS HAS DEVELOPED A NEW WEAPON IN ORDER TO RESTRAIN SPECIFIC TITANS. TO THE NTRAINED EYE, IT LOOKS LIKE A NORMAL WAGON CARRYING BARRELS, BUT INSIDE EACH BARREL ARE EVEN IRON TUBES CONTAINING COILED WIRES WITH ARROWHEADS ATTACHED AT BOTH ENDS.

HE WIRES ARE STRONG AND SPECIALLY MADE TO BECOME ELASTIC AFTER BEING EJECTED FROM HE BARRELS. WHEN THE DEVICE IS ACTIVATED, ARROWHEADS ARE FIRED FROM BOTH ENDS OF THE UBES. THE ARROWHEADS ON ONE SIDE HEAD FOR THE TARGETED TITAN, WHILE THE ONES AT THE THER SIDE BECOME LODGED IN A TREE RUNK, SO IF THE TIP PIERCES THE TITAN'S LESH, IT'S POSSIBLE TO TETHER THE ITAN TO THE TREE WITH THE WIRE. HE PURPOSE OF THIS WEAPON IS TO IMOBILIZE THE TARGET, ANCHORING IT ITH HUNDREDS OF ARROWHEADS FIRED ROM SEVERAL DIRECTIONS AND WIRES ITH GREAT TENSILE STRENGTH.

EVELOPMENT OF THIS WEAPON REQUIRED SIGNIFICANT CAPITAL OUTLAY, SO THE URVEY CORPS HAD TO GUARANTEE OSITIVE RESULTS BEFORE INVESTORS OULD CONTRIBUTE THE MONEY. TO THAT ND, THE CONTINUED EXISTENCE OF THE URVEY CORPS ITSELF IS AT LEAST ARTIALLY DEPENDENT ON THE RESULTS F THEIR CURRENT MISSION.

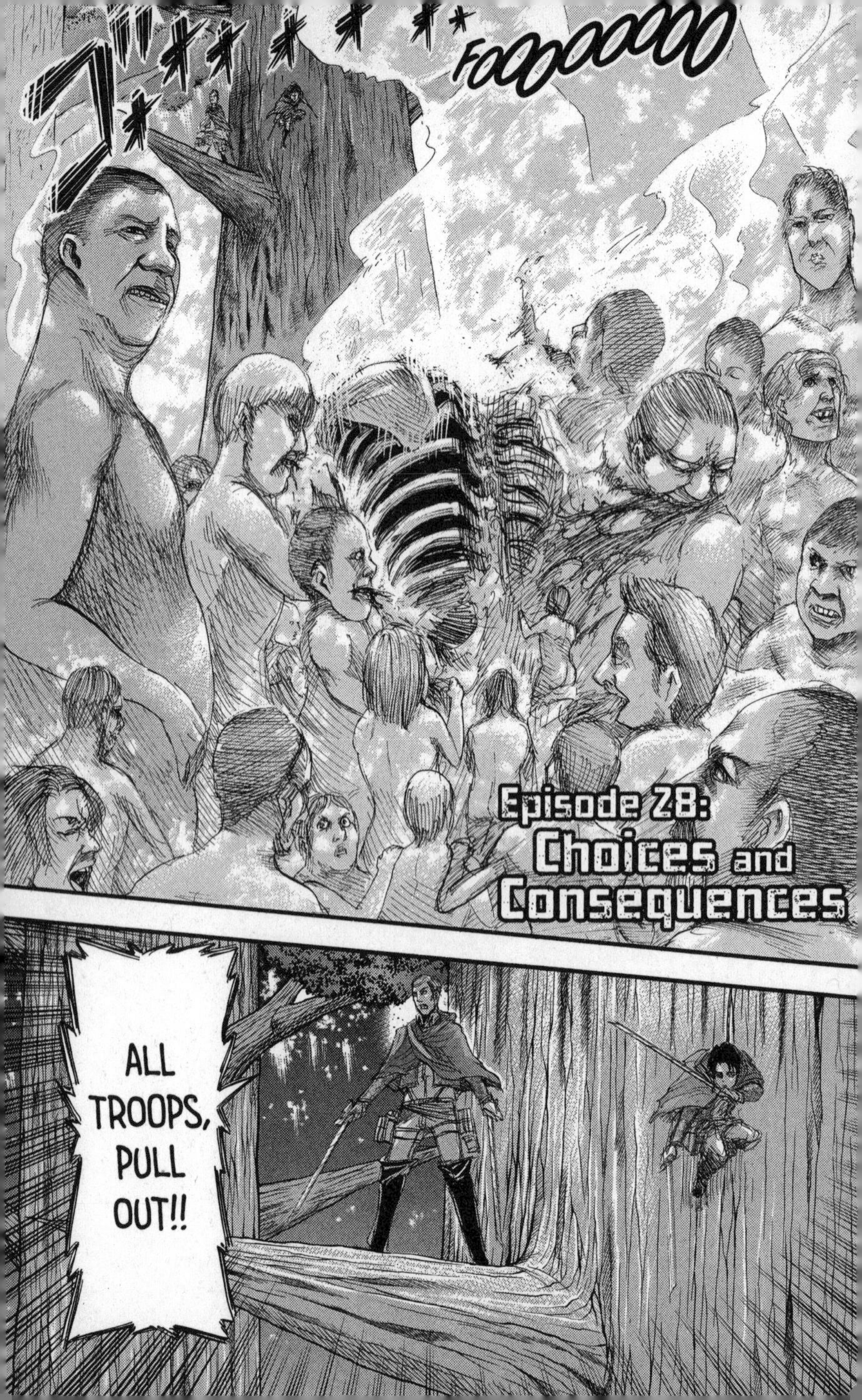
FOOOOOOOO
Episode 28:
Choices and Consequences
ALL TROOPS, PULL OUT!!

GET TO YOUR HORSES WHILE THE TITANS ARE FOCUSED ON HER REMAINS!
WE'RE LEAVING ALL THE WAGONS BEHIND!

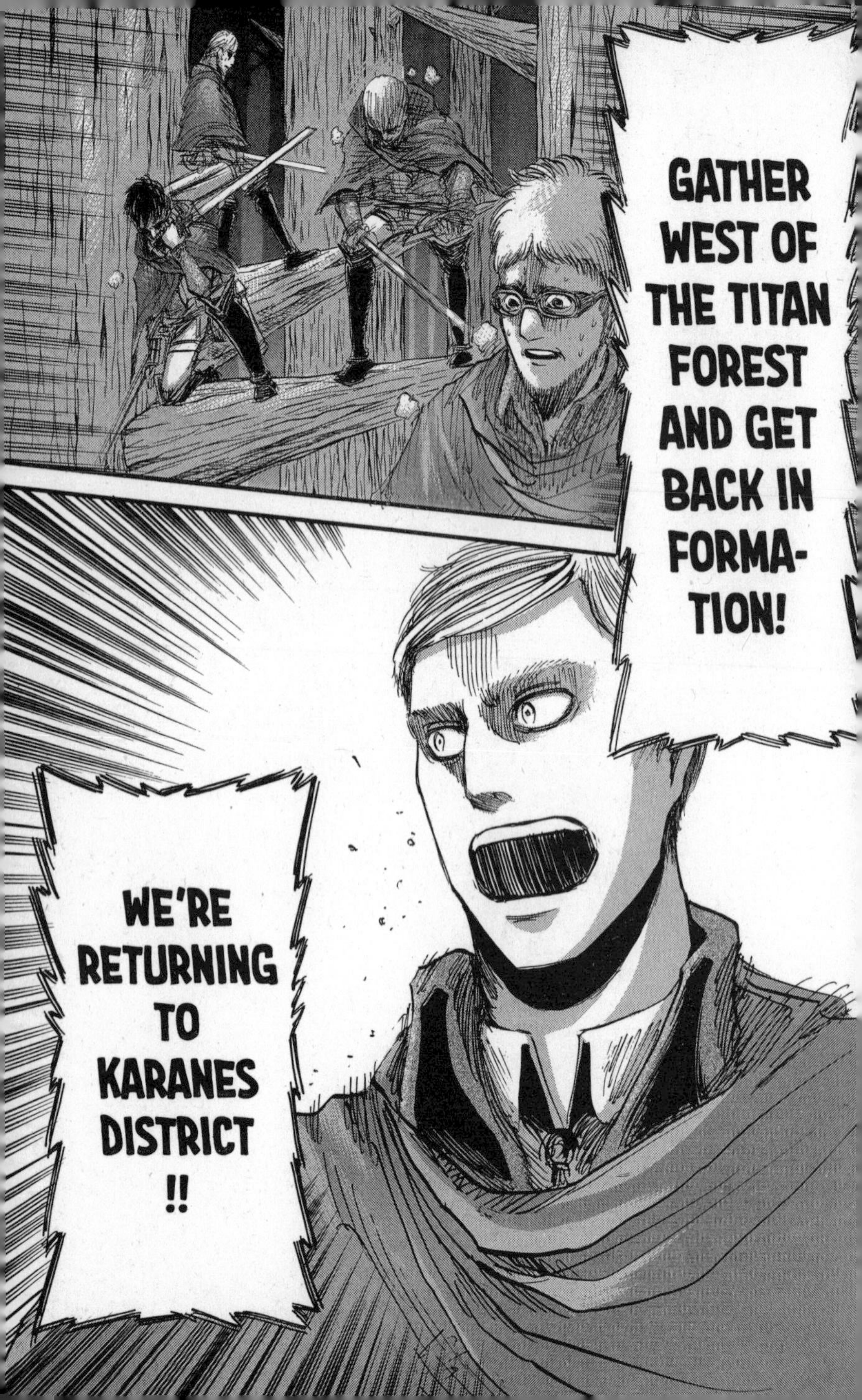
GATHER WEST OF THE TITAN FOREST AND GET BACK IN FORMA-TION!
WE'RE RETURNING TO KARANES DISTRICT !!

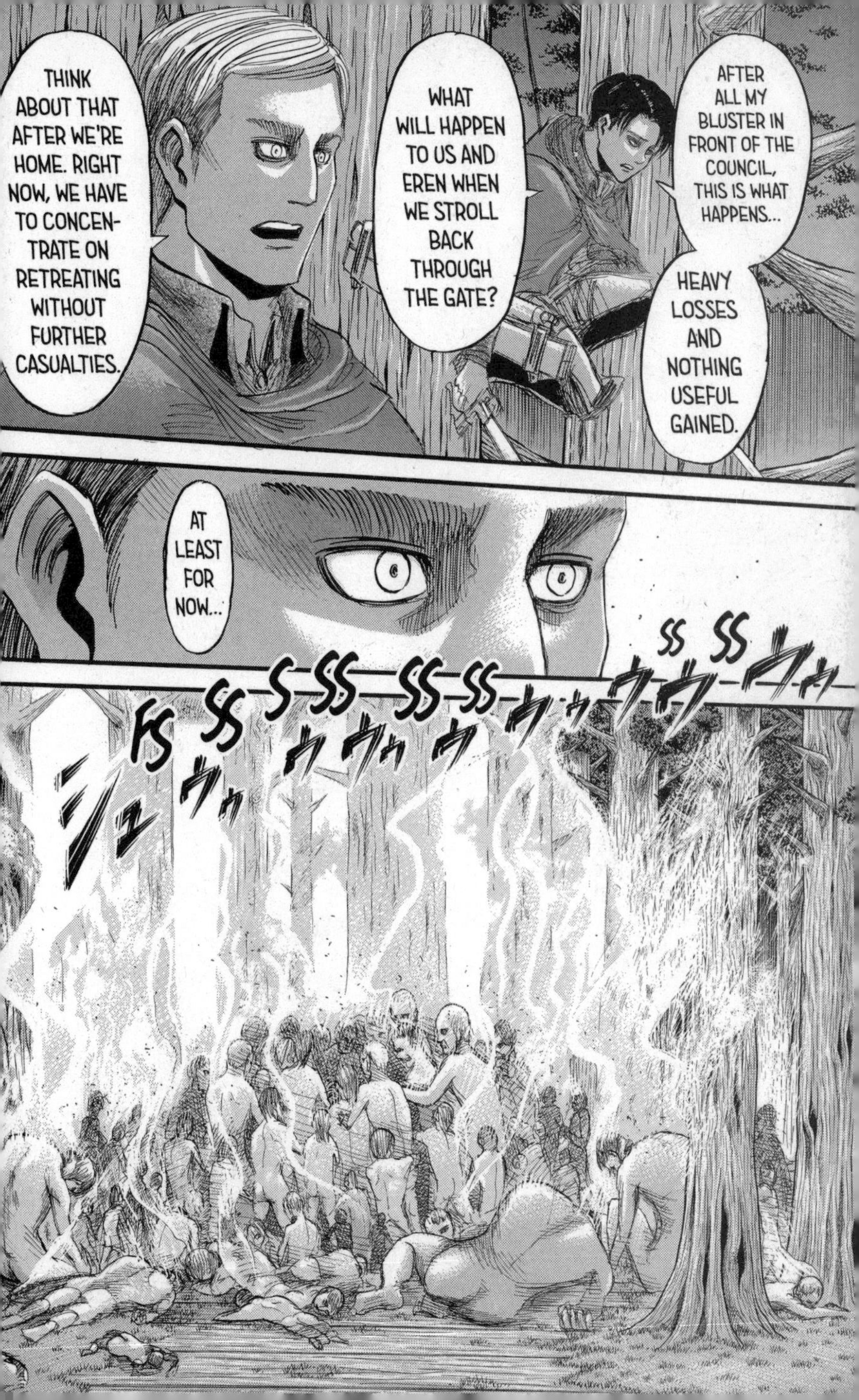
AFTER ALL MY BLUSTER IN FRONT OF THE COUNCIL, THIS IS WHAT HAPPENS...
HEAVY LOSSES AND NOTHING USEFUL GAINED.
WHAT WILL HAPPEN TO US AND EREN WHEN WE STROLL BACK THROUGH THE GATE?
THINK ABOUT THAT AFTER WE'RE HOME. RIGHT NOW, WE HAVE TO CONCENTRATE ON RETREATING WITHOUT FURTHER CASUALTIES.
AT LEAST FOR NOW...
FSSSSSSSSSSSSSS

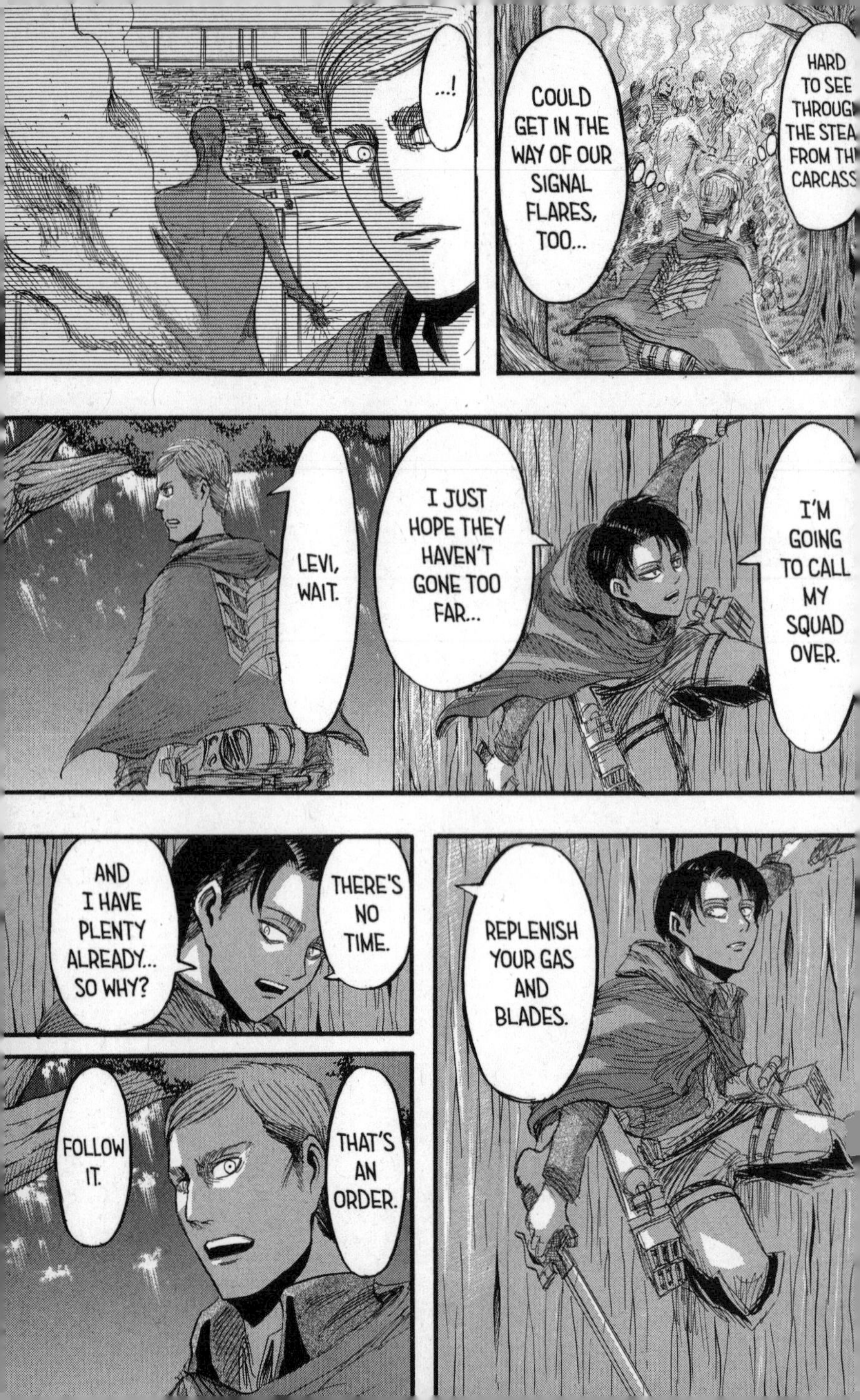
HARD TO SEE THROUG THE STEA FROM TH CARCASS
COULD GET IN THE WAY OF OUR SIGNAL FLARES, TOO...
...!
I'M GOING TO CALL MY SQUAD OVER.
I JUST HOPE THEY HAVEN'T GONE TOO FAR...
LEVI, WAIT.
REPLENISH YOUR GAS AND BLADES.
THERE'S NO TIME.
AND I HAVE PLENTY ALREADY... SO WHY?
THAT'S AN ORDER.
FOLLOW IT.

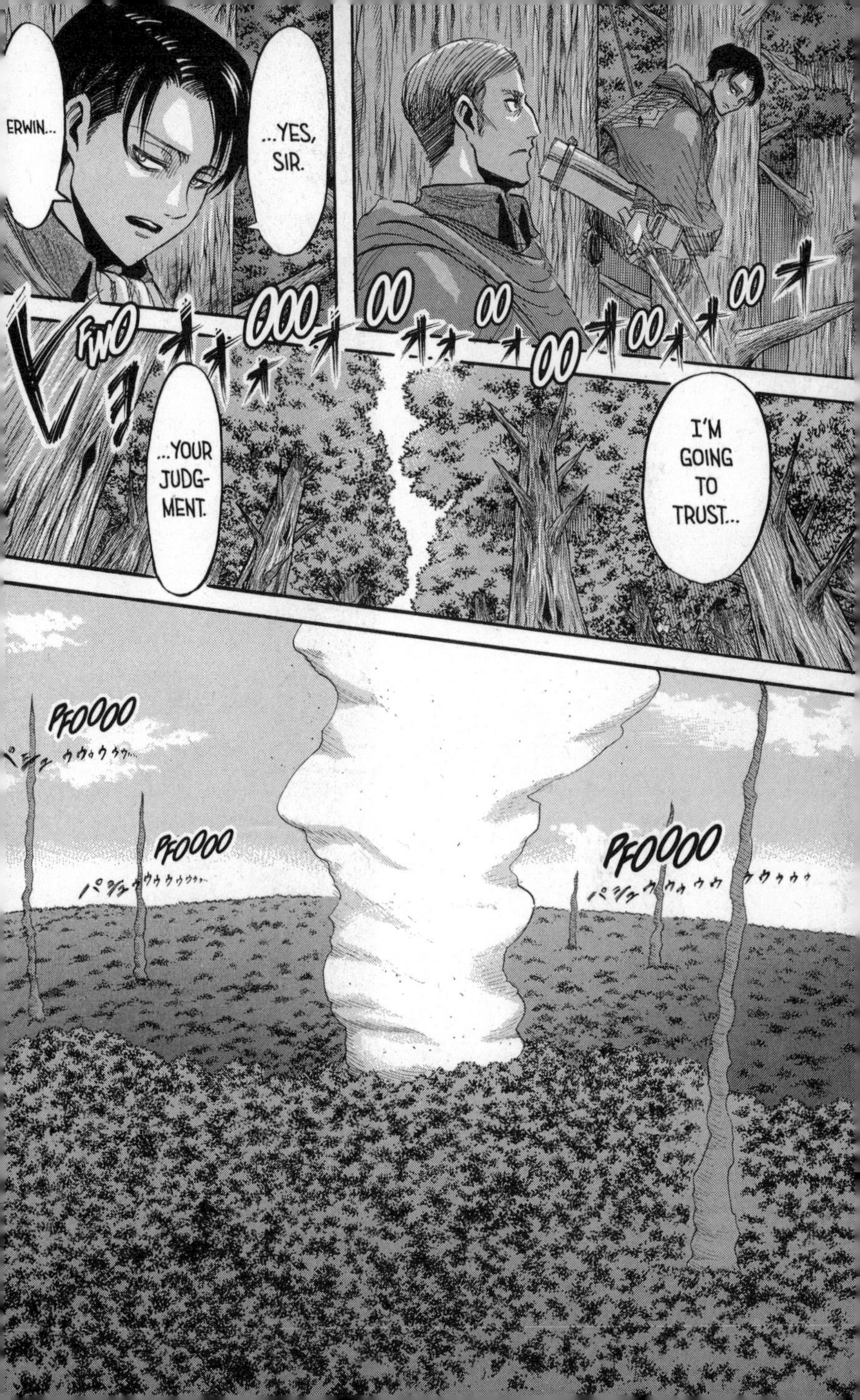
...YES, SIR.
ERWIN...
FWO OOO OO OO OO OO OO
I'M GOING TO TRUST...
...YOUR JUDGMENT.
PFOOOO
PFOOOO
PFOOOO

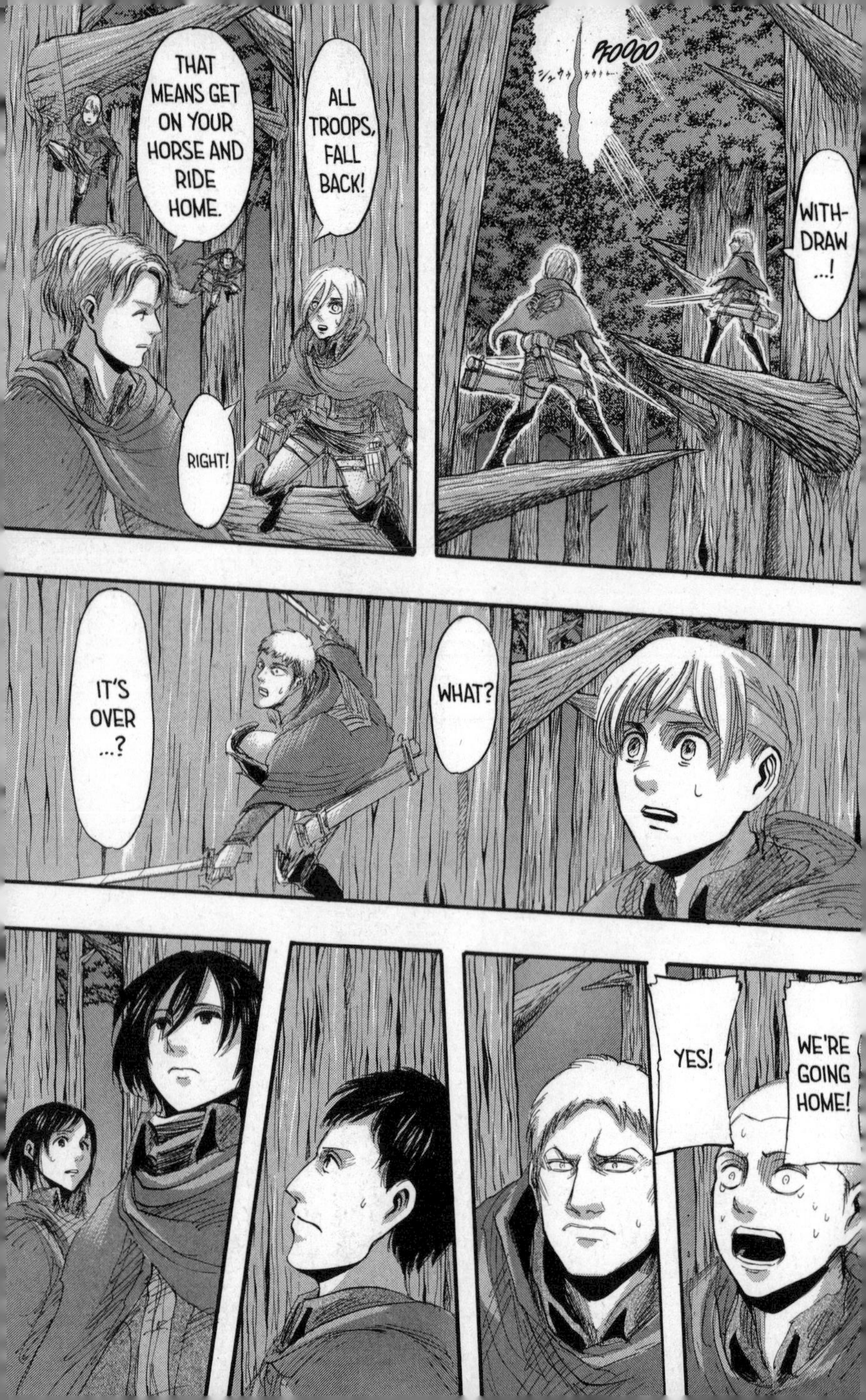
PFOOOO
WITH-DRAW ...!
ALL TROOPS, FALL BACK!
THAT MEANS GET ON YOUR HORSE AND RIDE HOME.
RIGHT!
WHAT?
IT'S OVER ...?
WE'RE GOING HOME!
YES!

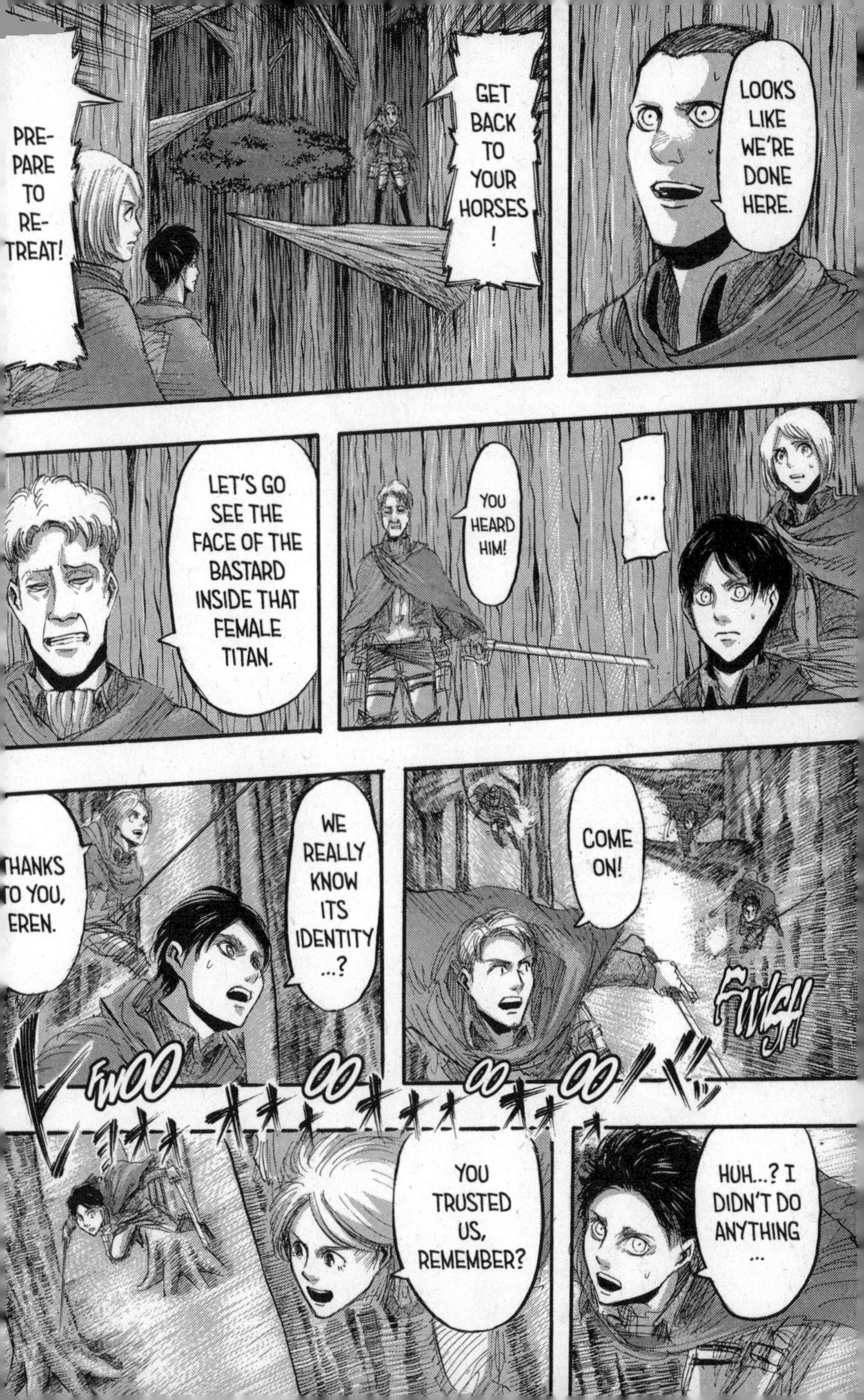
LOOKS LIKE WE'RE DONE HERE.
GET BACK TO YOUR HORSES!
PRE-PARE TO RE-TREAT!
...
YOU HEARD HIM!
LET'S GO SEE THE FACE OF THE BASTARD INSIDE THAT FEMALE TITAN.
COME ON!
FWISH
WE REALLY KNOW ITS IDENTITY ...?
THANKS TO YOU, EREN.
FWOOOOOOOO
HUH...? I DIDN'T DO ANYTHING ...
YOU TRUSTED US, REMEMBER?

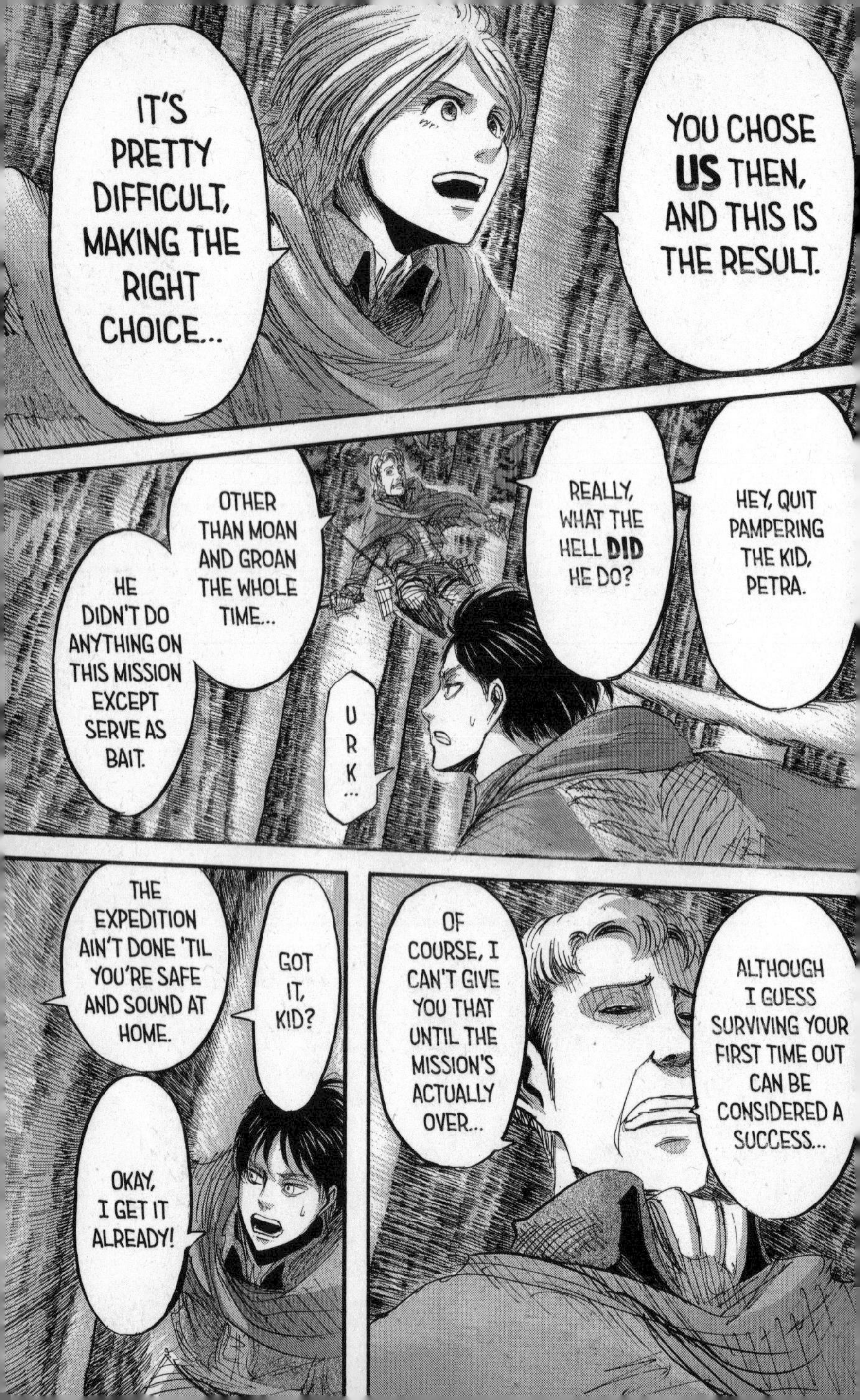
YOU CHOSE **US** THEN, AND THIS IS THE RESULT.
IT'S PRETTY DIFFICULT, MAKING THE RIGHT CHOICE...
HEY, QUIT PAMPERING THE KID, PETRA.
REALLY, WHAT THE HELL **DID** HE DO?
OTHER THAN MOAN AND GROAN THE WHOLE TIME...
HE DIDN'T DO ANYTHING ON THIS MISSION EXCEPT SERVE AS BAIT.
URK...
ALTHOUGH I GUESS SURVIVING YOUR FIRST TIME OUT CAN BE CONSIDERED A SUCCESS...
OF COURSE, I CAN'T GIVE YOU THAT UNTIL THE MISSION'S ACTUALLY OVER...
THE EXPEDITION AIN'T DONE 'TIL YOU'RE SAFE AND SOUND AT HOME.
GOT IT, KID?
OKAY, I GET IT ALREADY!

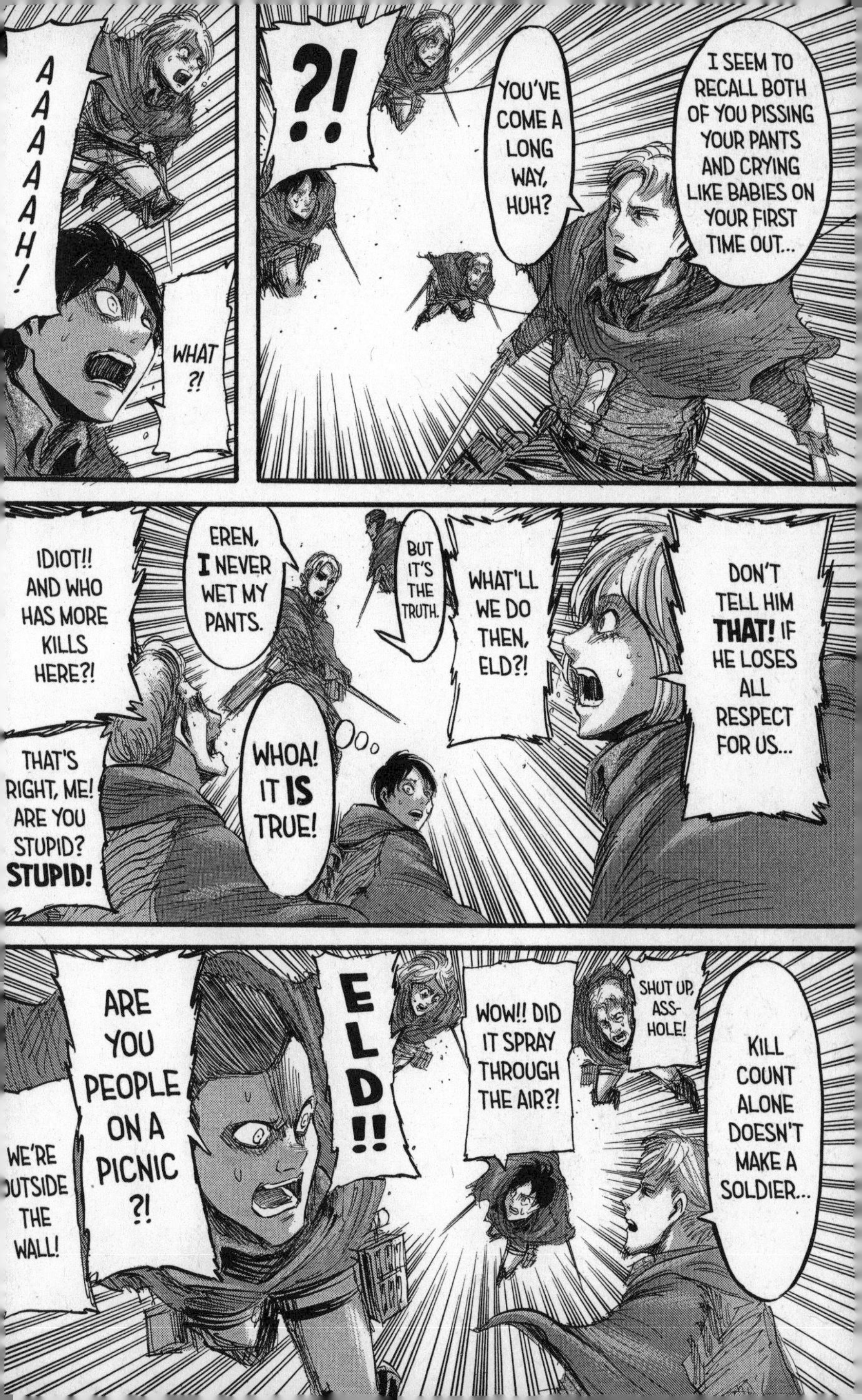
I SEEM TO RECALL BOTH OF YOU PISSING YOUR PANTS AND CRYING LIKE BABIES ON YOUR FIRST TIME OUT...
YOU'VE COME A LONG WAY, HUH?
?!
AAAAAAAH!
WHAT?!
DON'T TELL HIM **THAT!** IF HE LOSES ALL RESPECT FOR US...
WHAT'LL WE DO THEN, ELD?!
BUT IT'S THE TRUTH.
EREN, **I** NEVER WET MY PANTS.
IDIOT!! AND WHO HAS MORE KILLS HERE?!
WHOA! IT **IS** TRUE!
THAT'S RIGHT, ME! ARE YOU STUPID? **STUPID!**
KILL COUNT ALONE DOESN'T MAKE A SOLDIER...
SHUT UP, ASS-HOLE!
WOW!! DID IT SPRAY THROUGH THE AIR?!
ELD!!
ARE YOU PEOPLE ON A PICNIC?!
WE'RE OUTSIDE THE WALL!

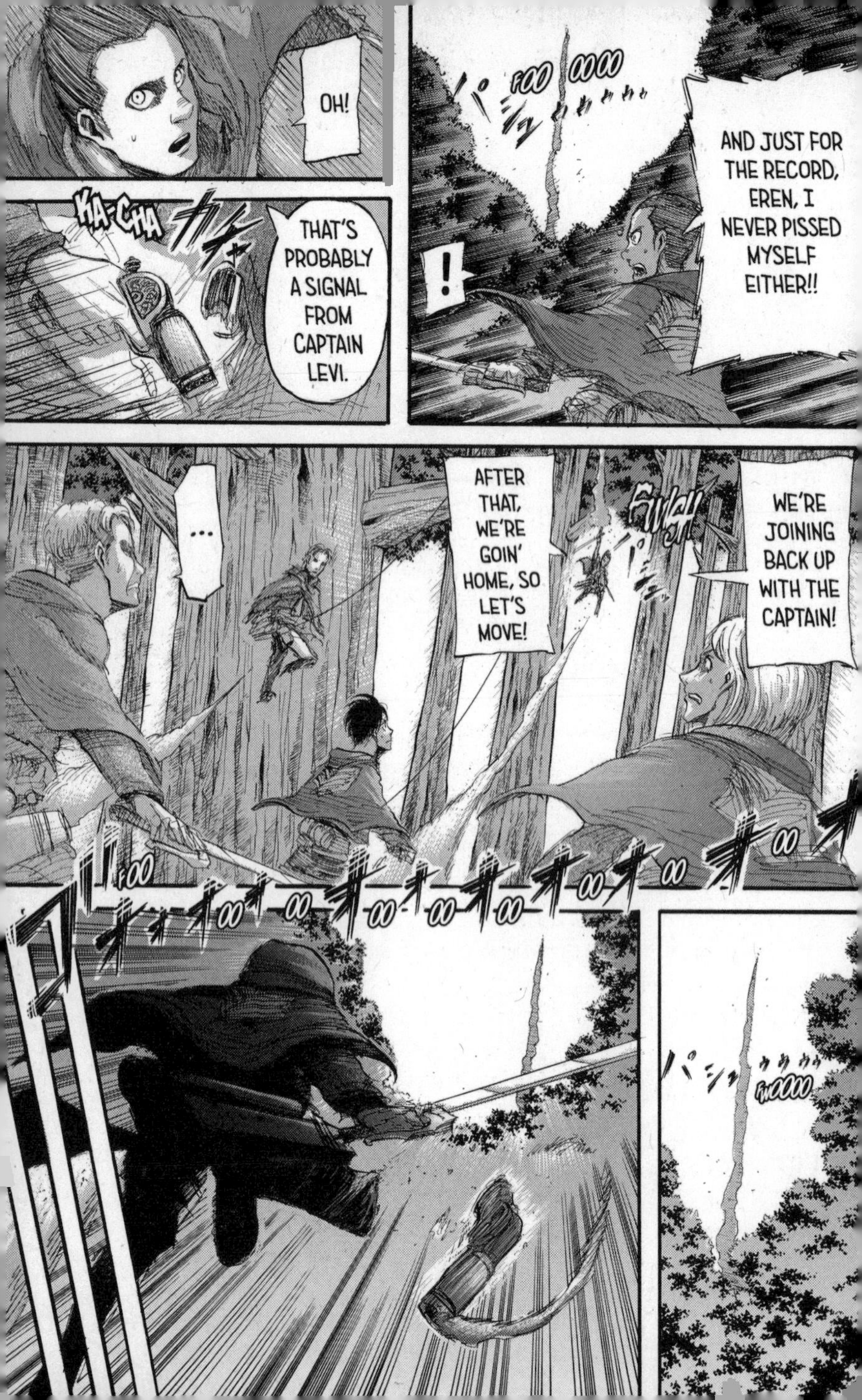
FOO OOOO
!
AND JUST FOR THE RECORD, EREN, I NEVER PISSED MYSELF EITHER!!
OH!
KA-CHA
THAT'S PROBABLY A SIGNAL FROM CAPTAIN LEVI.
WE'RE JOINING BACK UP WITH THE CAPTAIN!
FWISH
AFTER THAT, WE'RE GOIN' HOME, SO LET'S MOVE!
...
FWOOOO
FOO OO OO OO OO OO OO OO OO OO OO

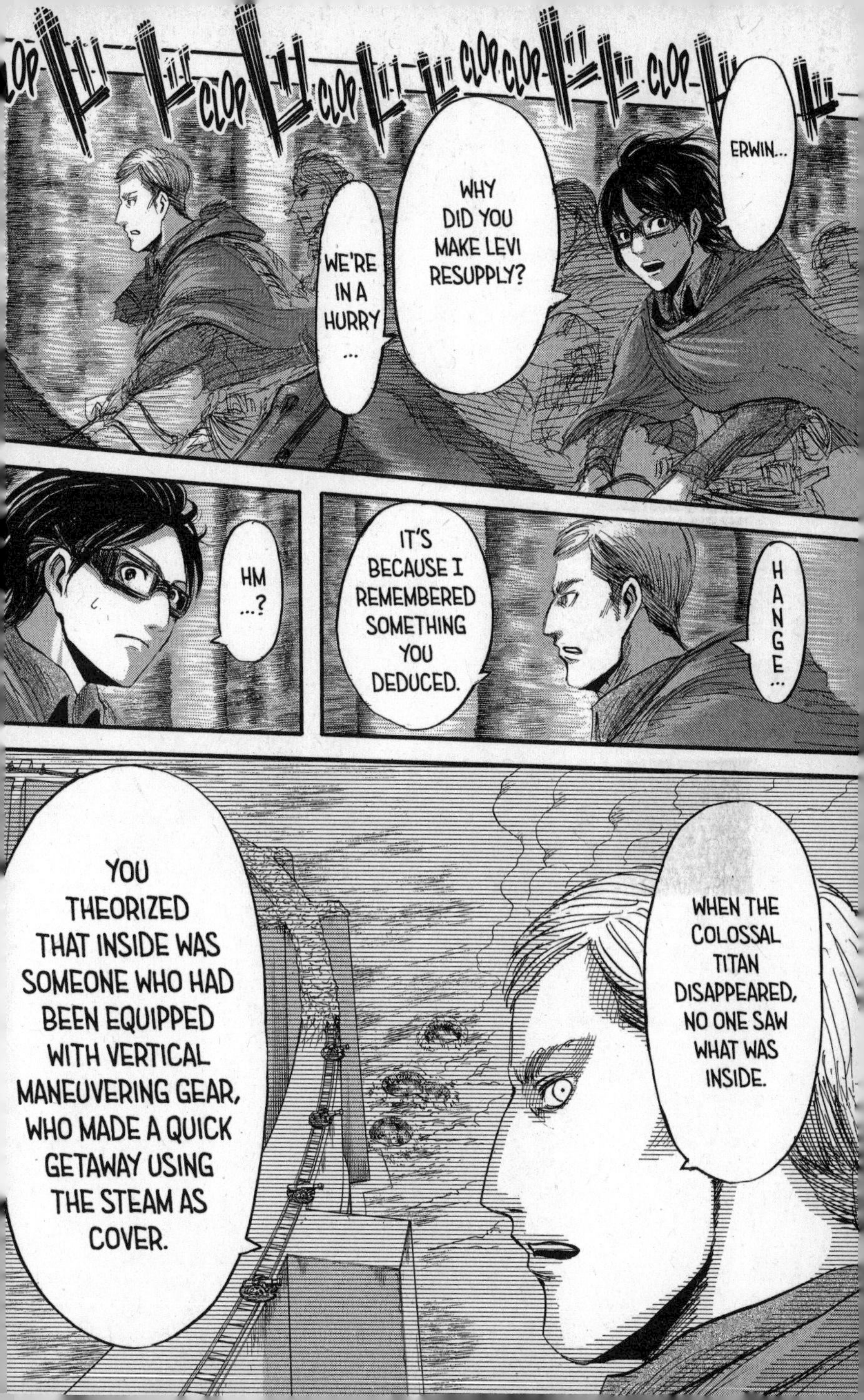
CLOP
CLOP
CLOP
CLOP
CLOP
CLOP
ERWIN...
WHY DID YOU MAKE LEVI RESUPPLY?
WE'RE IN A HURRY ...
HANGE ...
IT'S BECAUSE I REMEMBERED SOMETHING YOU DEDUCED.
HM ...?
WHEN THE COLOSSAL TITAN DISAPPEARED, NO ONE SAW WHAT WAS INSIDE.
YOU THEORIZED THAT INSIDE WAS SOMEONE WHO HAD BEEN EQUIPPED WITH VERTICAL MANEUVERING GEAR, WHO MADE A QUICK GETAWAY USING THE STEAM AS COVER.

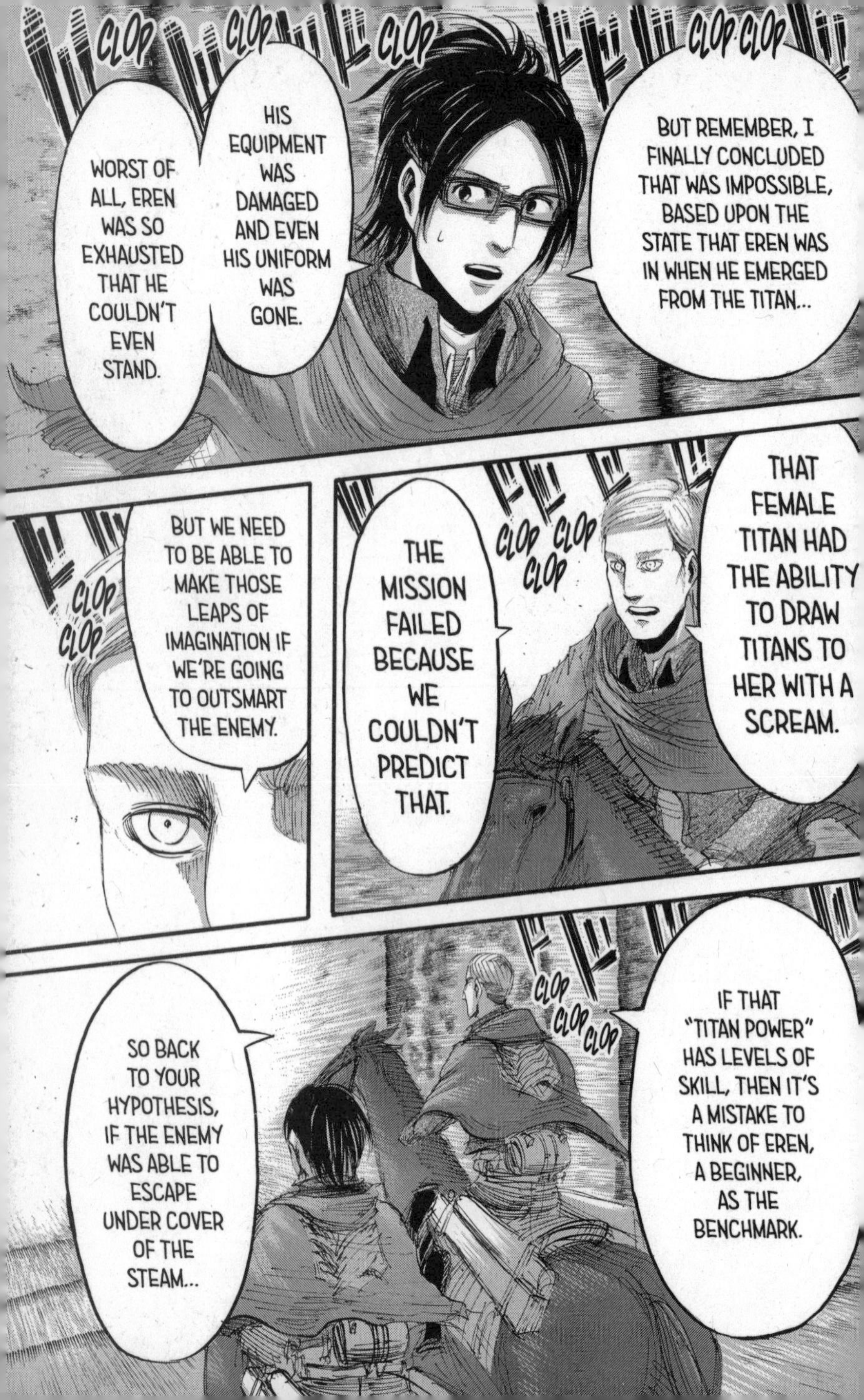
CLOP CLOP
CLOP
CLOP
CLOP
BUT REMEMBER, I FINALLY CONCLUDED THAT WAS IMPOSSIBLE, BASED UPON THE STATE THAT EREN WAS IN WHEN HE EMERGED FROM THE TITAN...
HIS EQUIPMENT WAS DAMAGED AND EVEN HIS UNIFORM WAS GONE.
WORST OF ALL, EREN WAS SO EXHAUSTED THAT HE COULDN'T EVEN STAND.
THAT FEMALE TITAN HAD THE ABILITY TO DRAW TITANS TO HER WITH A SCREAM.
CLOP CLOP CLOP
THE MISSION FAILED BECAUSE WE COULDN'T PREDICT THAT.
BUT WE NEED TO BE ABLE TO MAKE THOSE LEAPS OF IMAGINATION IF WE'RE GOING TO OUTSMART THE ENEMY.
CLOP CLOP
IF THAT "TITAN POWER" HAS LEVELS OF SKILL, THEN IT'S A MISTAKE TO THINK OF EREN, A BEGINNER, AS THE BENCHMARK.
CLOP CLOP CLOP
SO BACK TO YOUR HYPOTHESIS, IF THE ENEMY WAS ABLE TO ESCAPE UNDER COVER OF THE STEAM...

...AND HAD ON THE SAME EQUIPMENT THAT WE DO...
FWOOOOOOOO
!
CAP-TAIN LEVI!
...
WAIT, THAT ISN'T ...
WHO ARE YOU ?
...THEN THEY COULD BLEND IN WITH THE SOLDIERS.
WOOSH

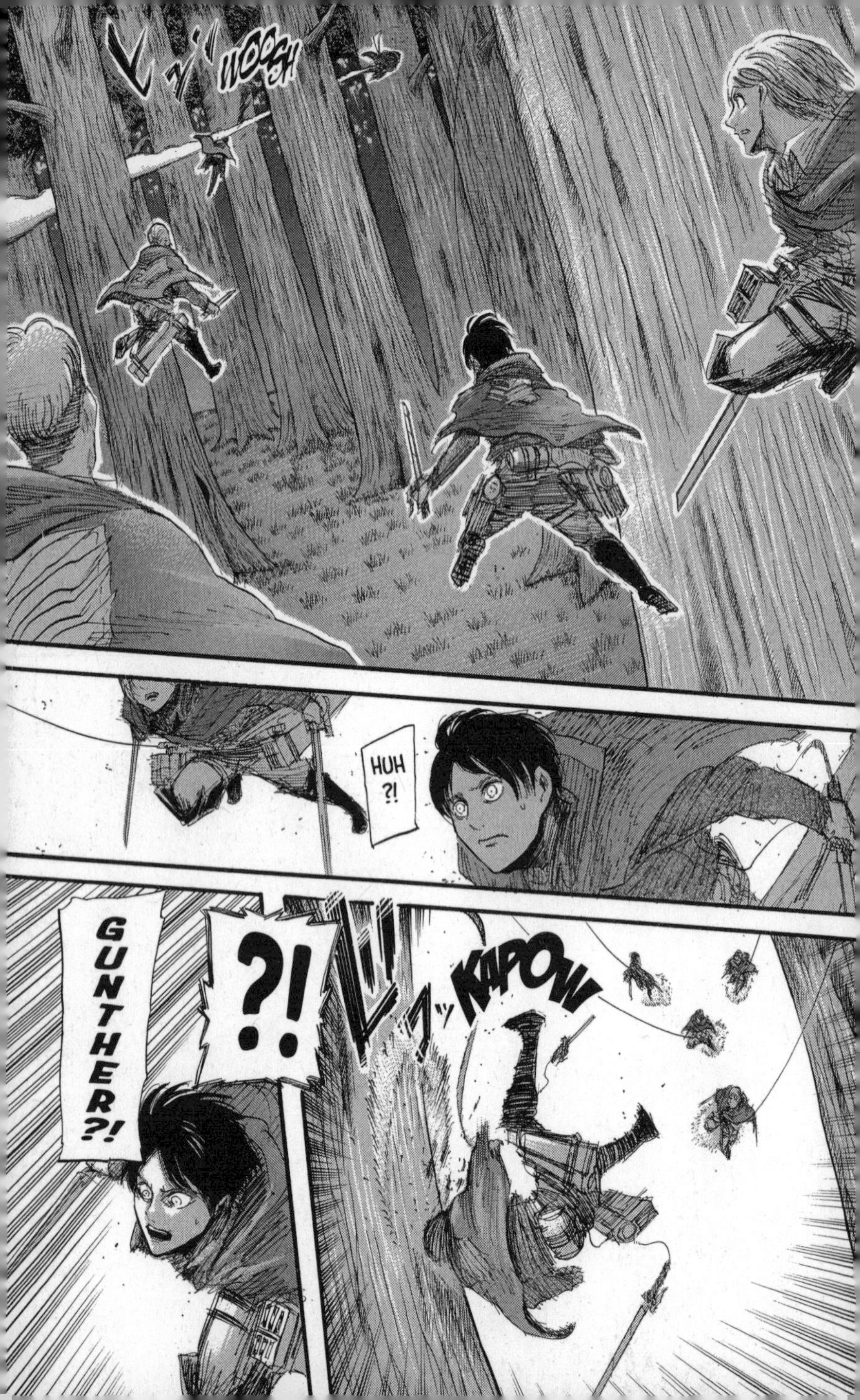
WOOSH
HUH ?!
KAPOW
?!
GUNTHER?!

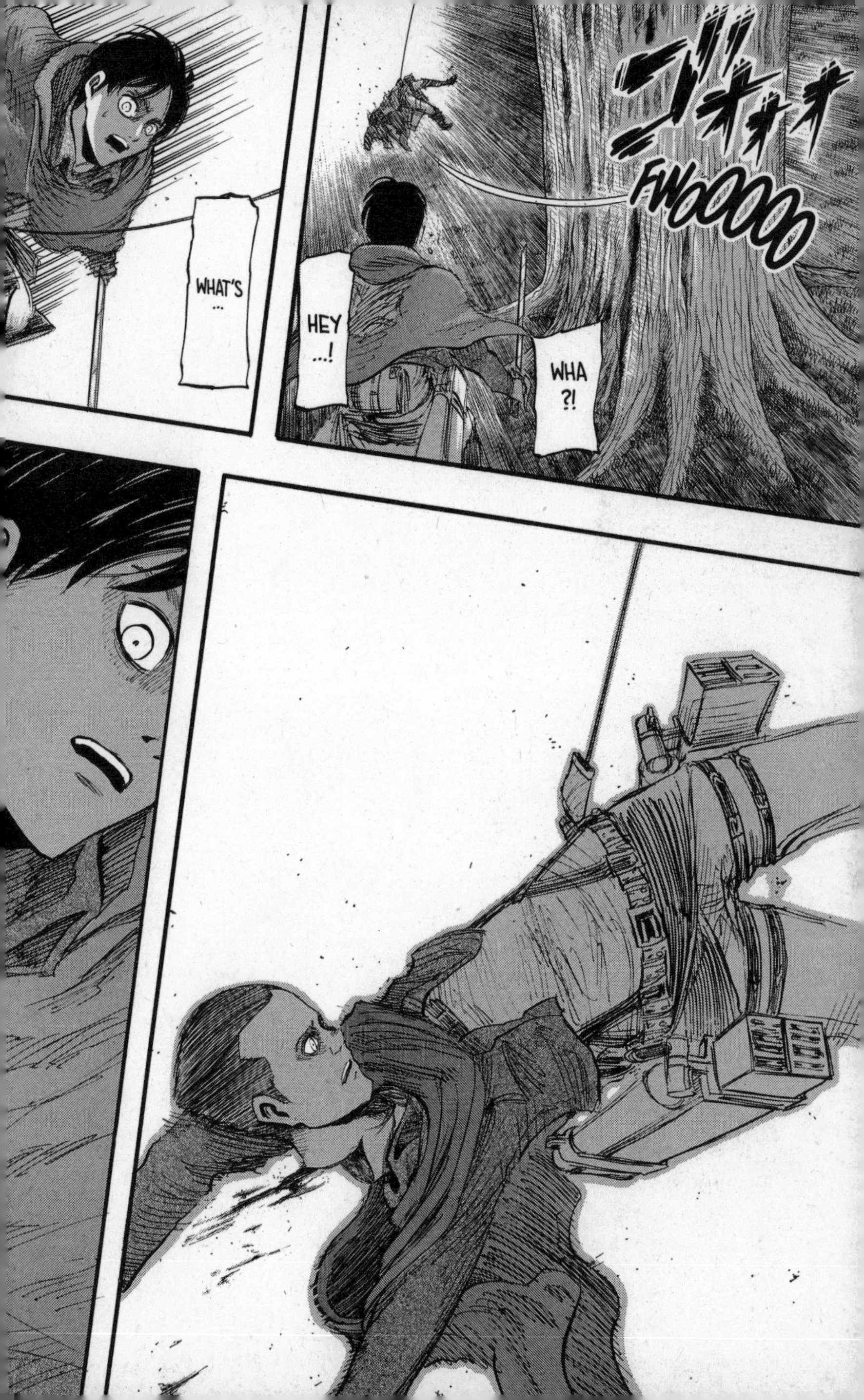
FWOOOO
WHA ?!
HEY ...!
WHAT'S ...

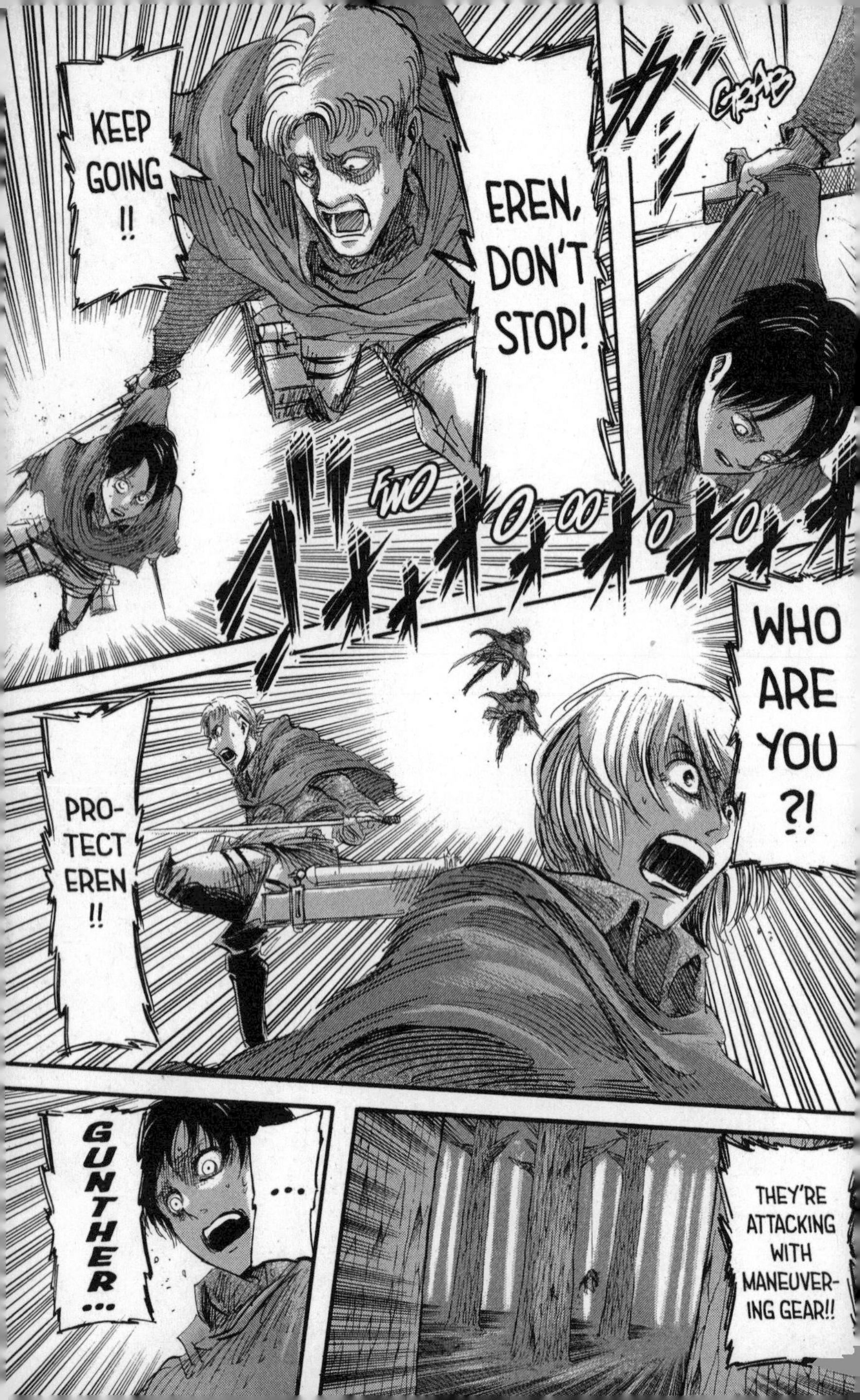
GRAB
EREN, DON'T STOP!
KEEP GOING!!
FWOOOOOOO
WHO ARE YOU?!
PROTECT EREN!!
THEY'RE ATTACKING WITH MANEUVERING GEAR!!
...
GUNTHER...

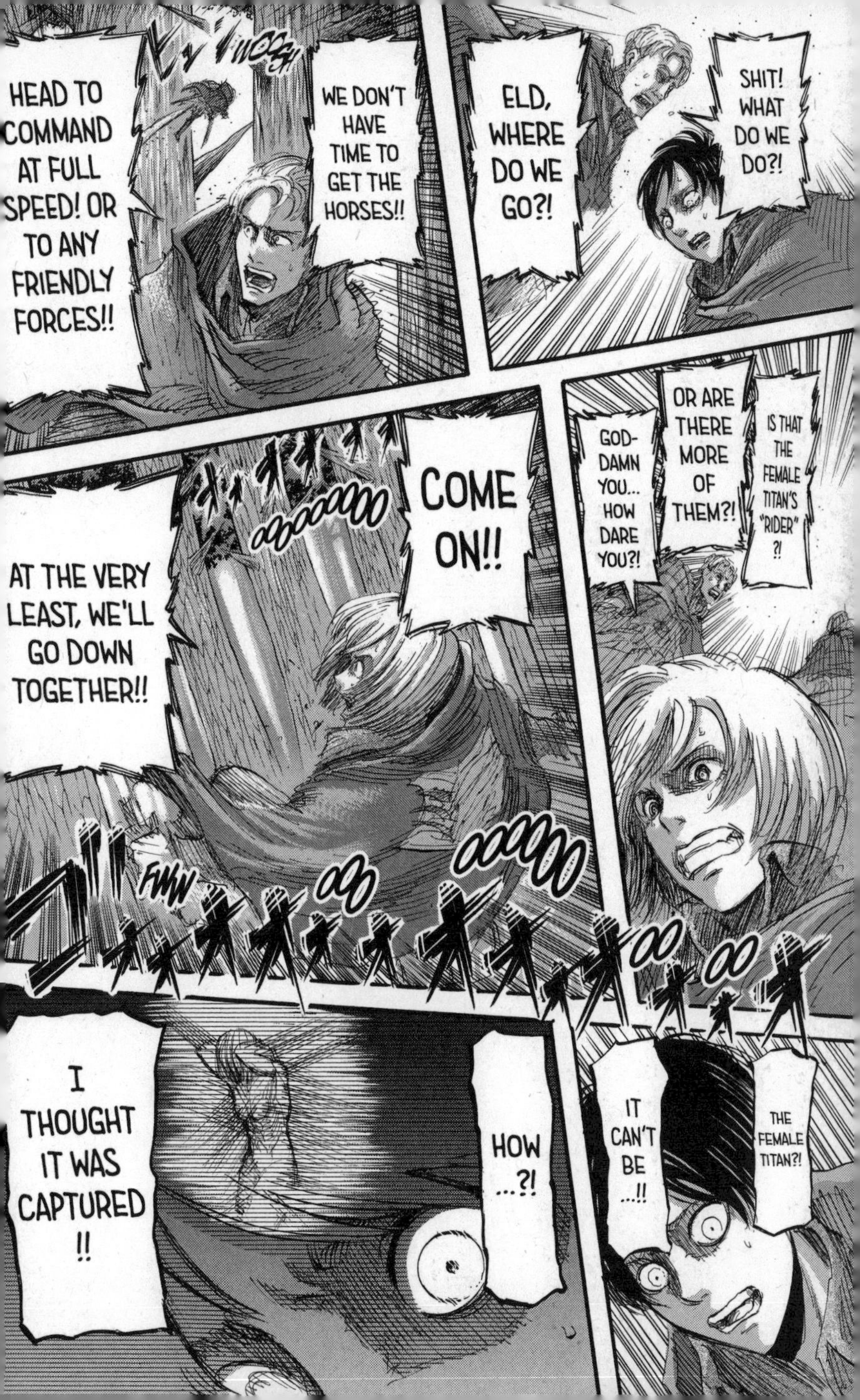
SHIT! WHAT DO WE DO?!
ELD, WHERE DO WE GO?!
WOOSH
WE DON'T HAVE TIME TO GET THE HORSES!!
HEAD TO COMMAND AT FULL SPEED! OR TO ANY FRIENDLY FORCES!!
IS THAT THE FEMALE TITAN'S "RIDER"?!
OR ARE THERE MORE OF THEM?!
GOD-DAMN YOU... HOW DARE YOU?!
COME ON!!
AT THE VERY LEAST, WE'LL GO DOWN TOGETHER!!
FWW
THE FEMALE TITAN?!
IT CAN'T BE ...!!
HOW ...?!
I THOUGHT IT WAS CAPTURED !!

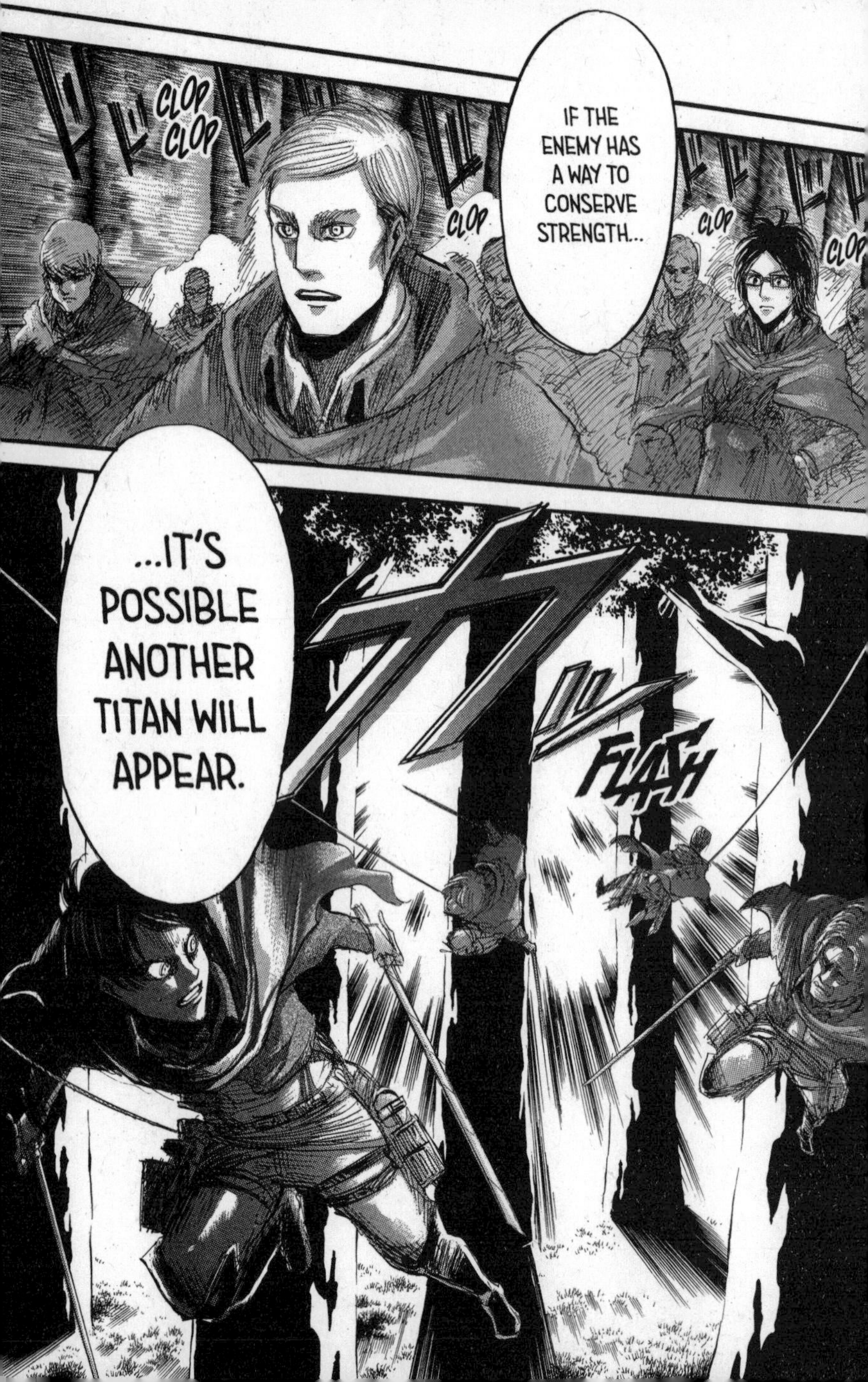
CLOP
CLOP
IF THE ENEMY HAS A WAY TO CONSERVE STRENGTH...
CLOP
CLOP CLOP
...IT'S POSSIBLE ANOTHER TITAN WILL APPEAR.
FLASH

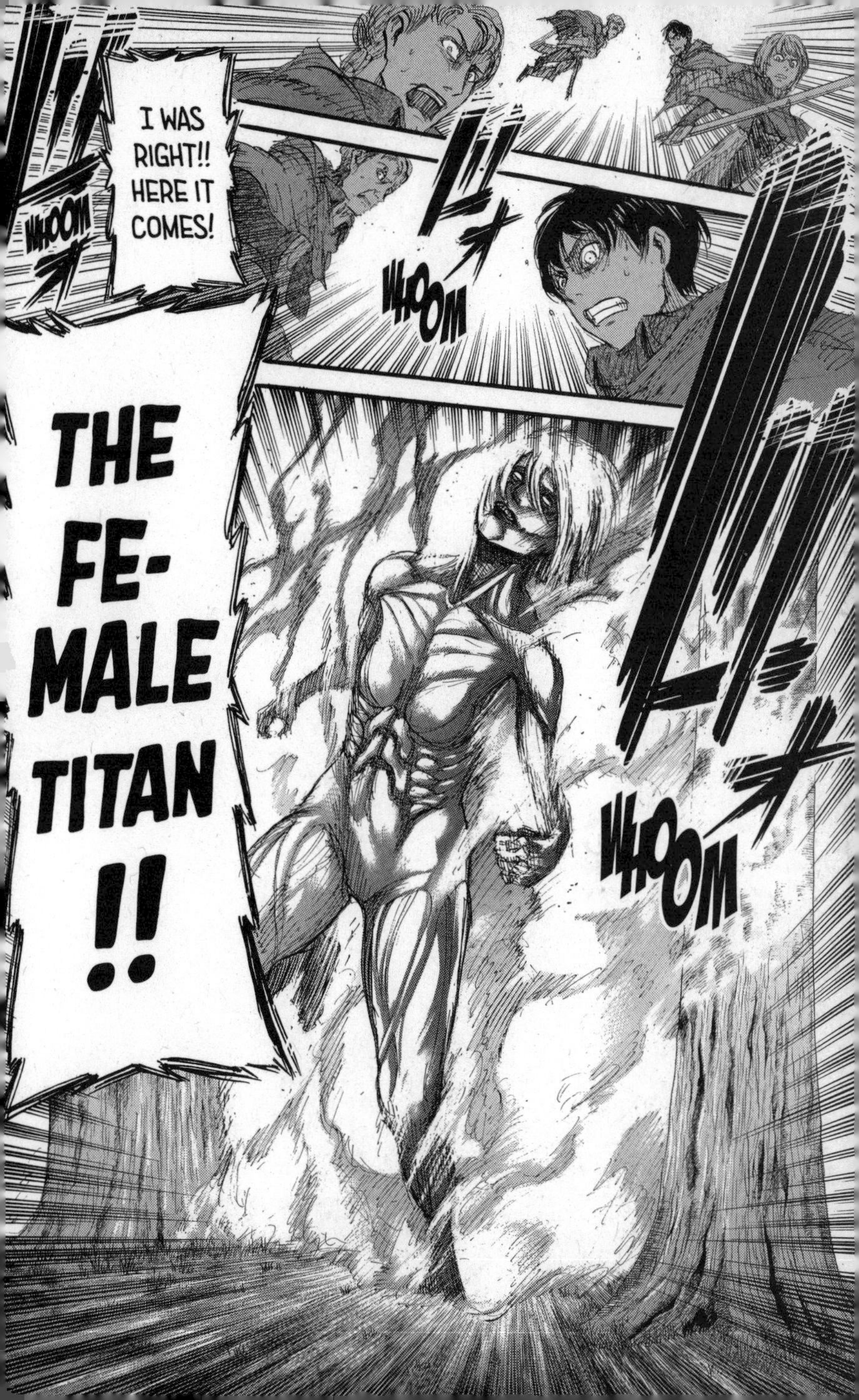
I WAS RIGHT!! HERE IT COMES!
WHOOM
WHOOM
THE FE- MALE TITAN !!
WHOOM

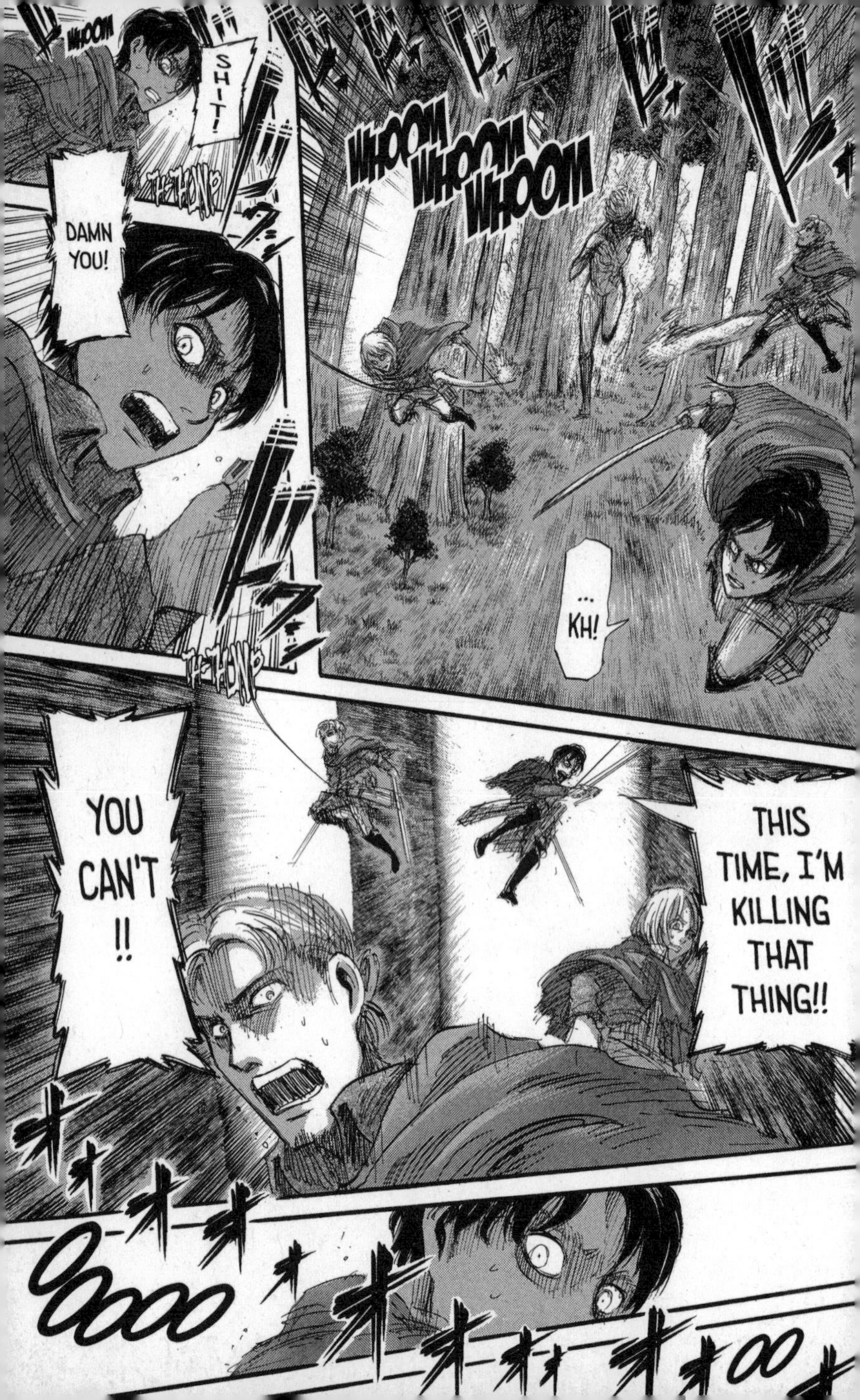
WHOOM WHOOM WHOOM
... KH!
WHOOM
SHIT!
DAMN YOU!
THIS TIME, I'M KILLING THAT THING!!
YOU CAN'T!!
OOOO
OO

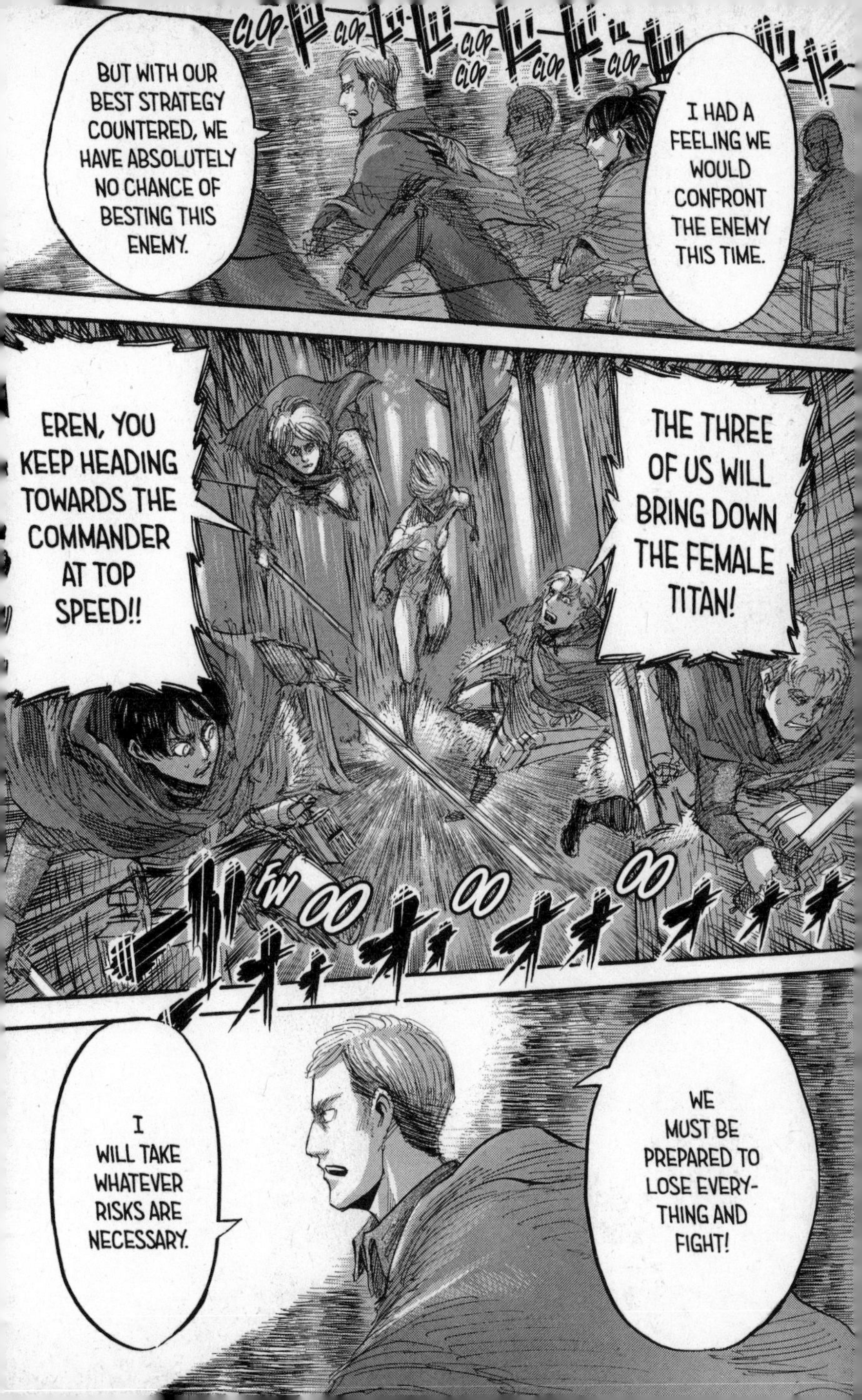
CLOP CLOP CLOP CLOP CLOP CLOP
I HAD A FEELING WE WOULD CONFRONT THE ENEMY THIS TIME.
BUT WITH OUR BEST STRATEGY COUNTERED, WE HAVE ABSOLUTELY NO CHANCE OF BESTING THIS ENEMY.
THE THREE OF US WILL BRING DOWN THE FEMALE TITAN!
EREN, YOU KEEP HEADING TOWARDS THE COMMANDER AT TOP SPEED!!
FWOOOOOO
WE MUST BE PREPARED TO LOSE EVERY-THING AND FIGHT!
I WILL TAKE WHATEVER RISKS ARE NECESSARY.

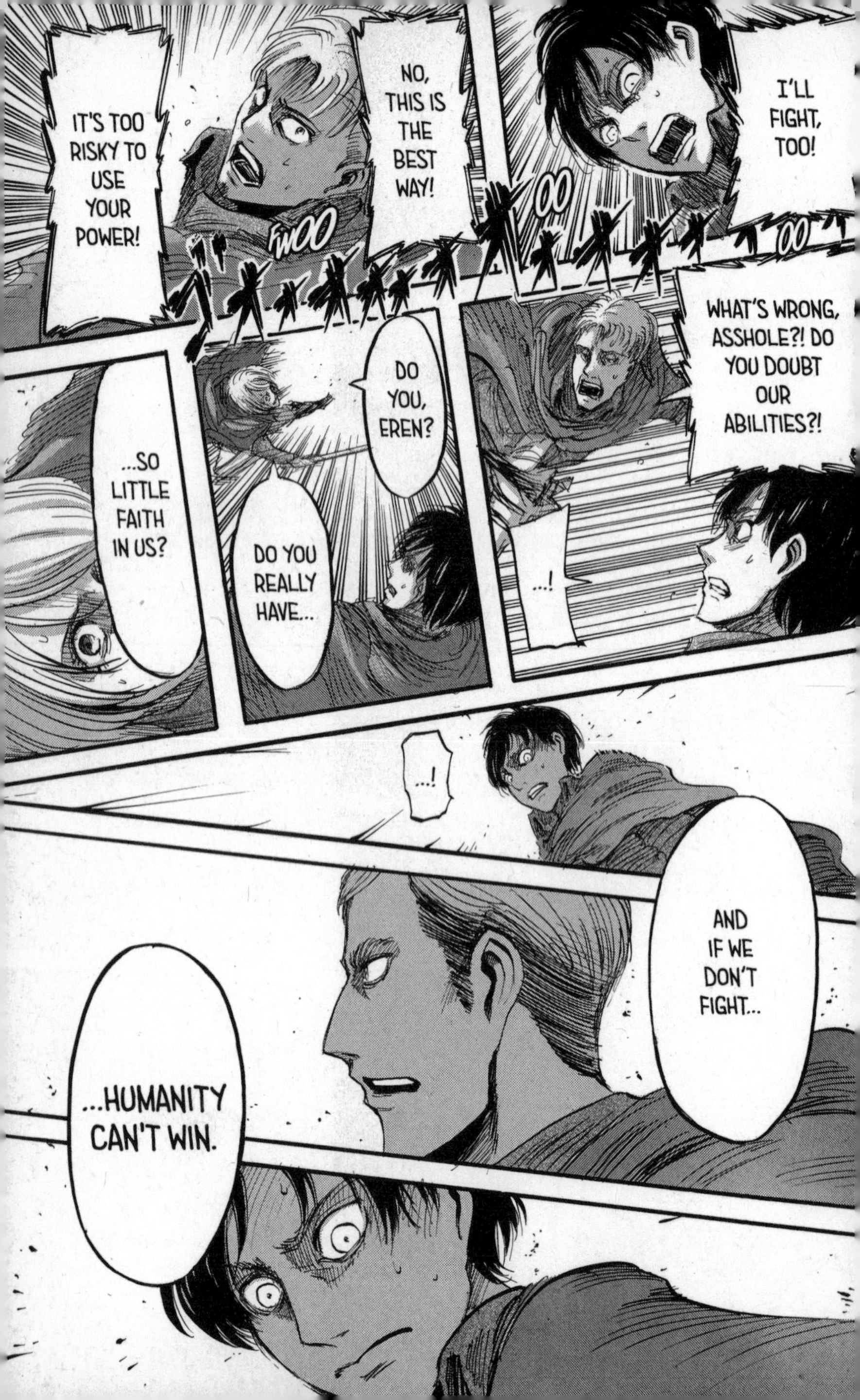

I'LL FIGHT, TOO!
OO
OO
NO, THIS IS THE BEST WAY!
FWOO
IT'S TOO RISKY TO USE YOUR POWER!
WHAT'S WRONG, ASSHOLE?! DO YOU DOUBT OUR ABILITIES?!
...!
DO YOU, EREN?
DO YOU REALLY HAVE...
...SO LITTLE FAITH IN US?
...!
AND IF WE DON'T FIGHT...
...HUMANITY CAN'T WIN.

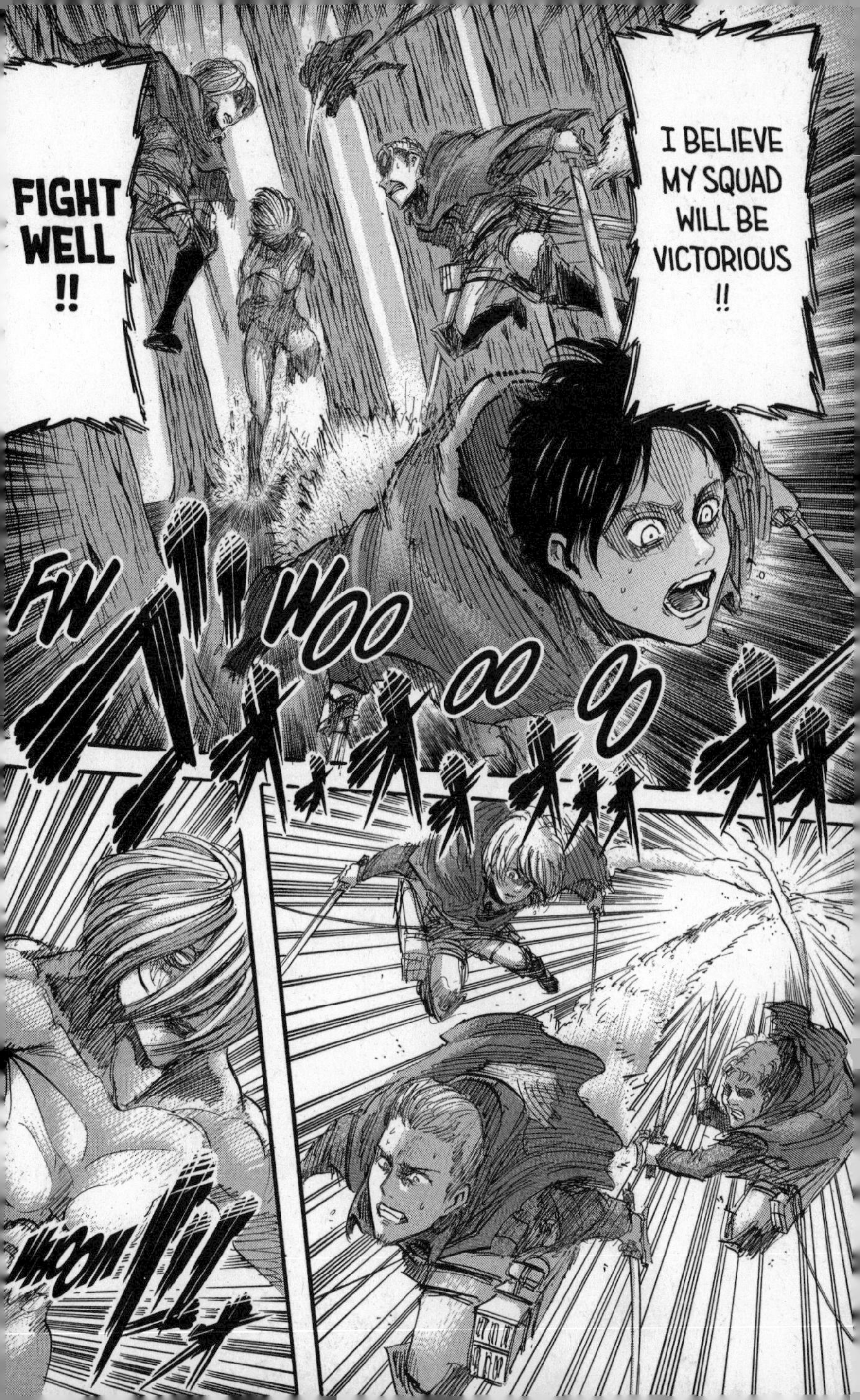
I BELIEVE MY SQUAD WILL BE VICTORIOUS !!
FIGHT WELL !!
FWWOOOOOO
WHOOM

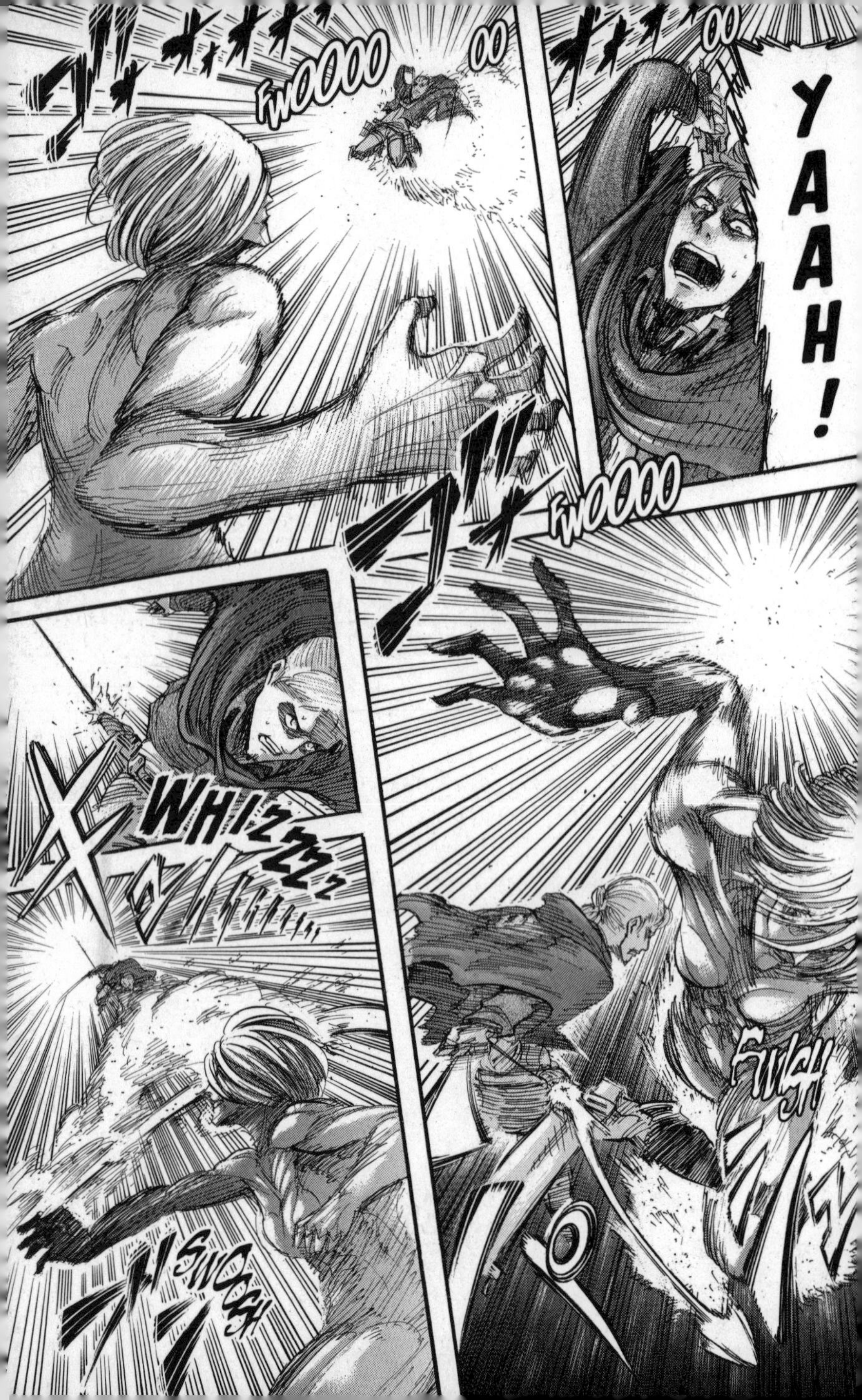
OO
YAAH!
FWOOOO
FWOOOO
OO
FWUGH
WHIZZZZ
SWOOSH

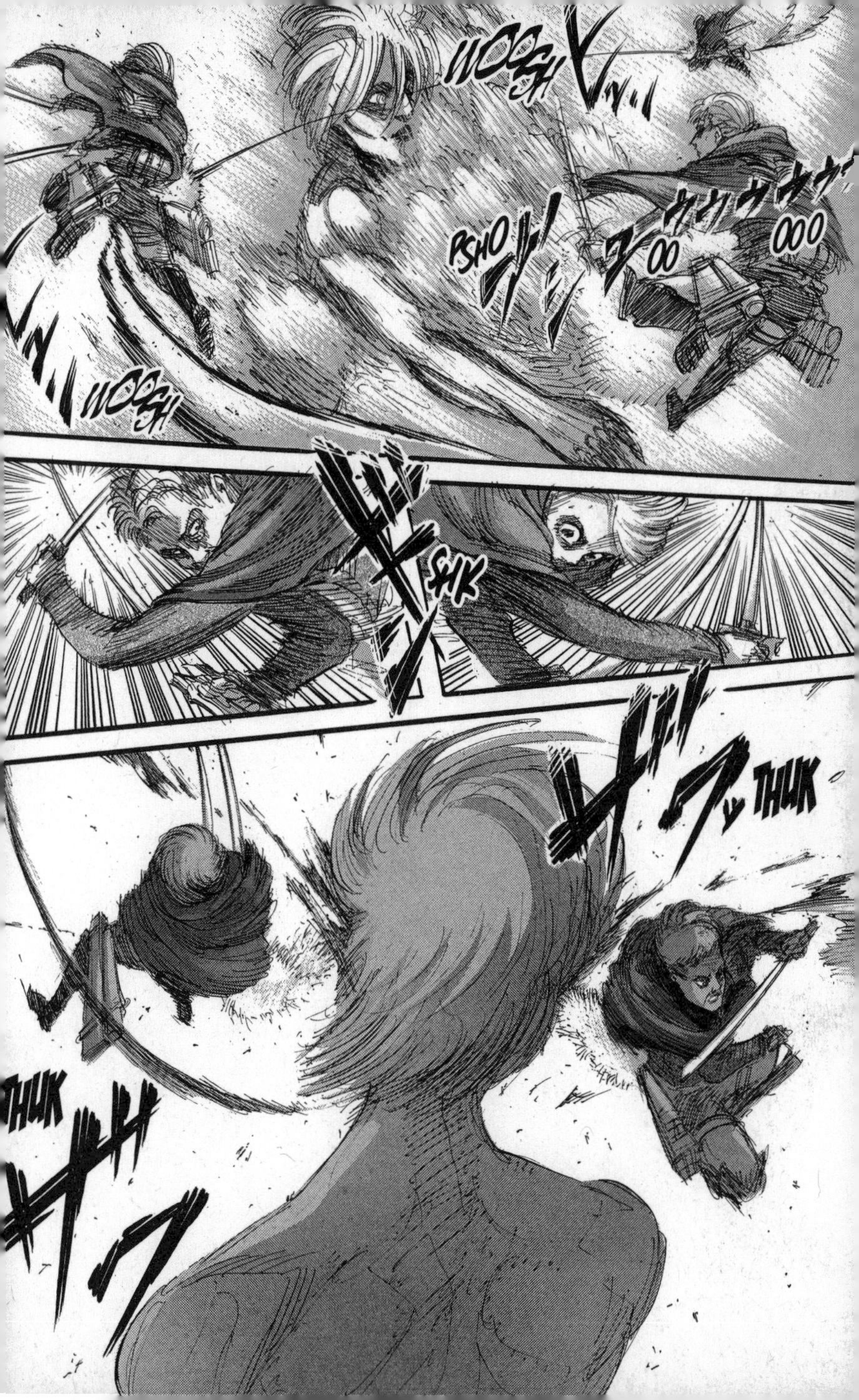
WOOSH
OOO
OO
PSHO
WOOSH
SHK
THUK
THUK

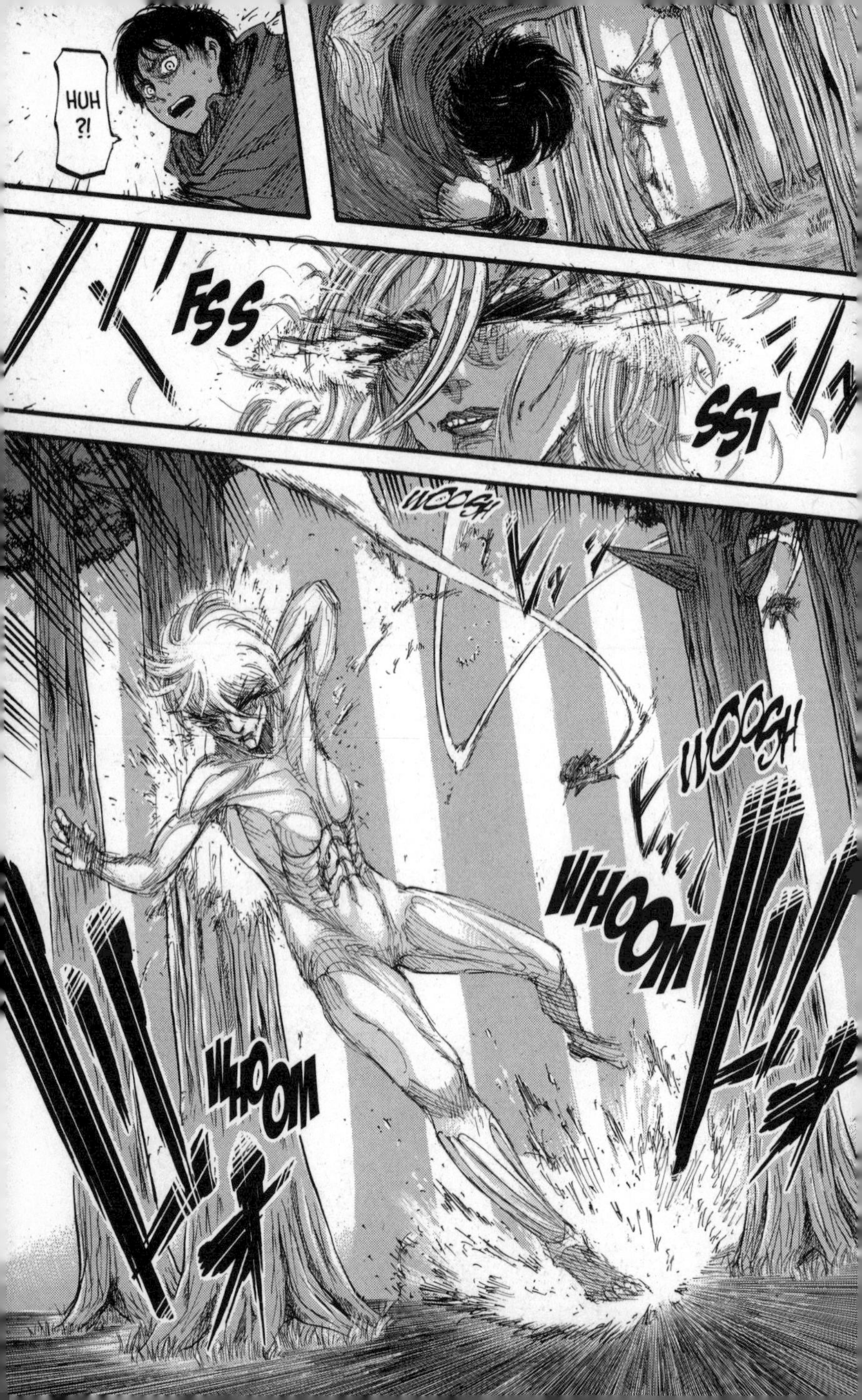

HUH ?!
SST
FSS
WOOSH
WOOSH
WHOOM
WHOOM

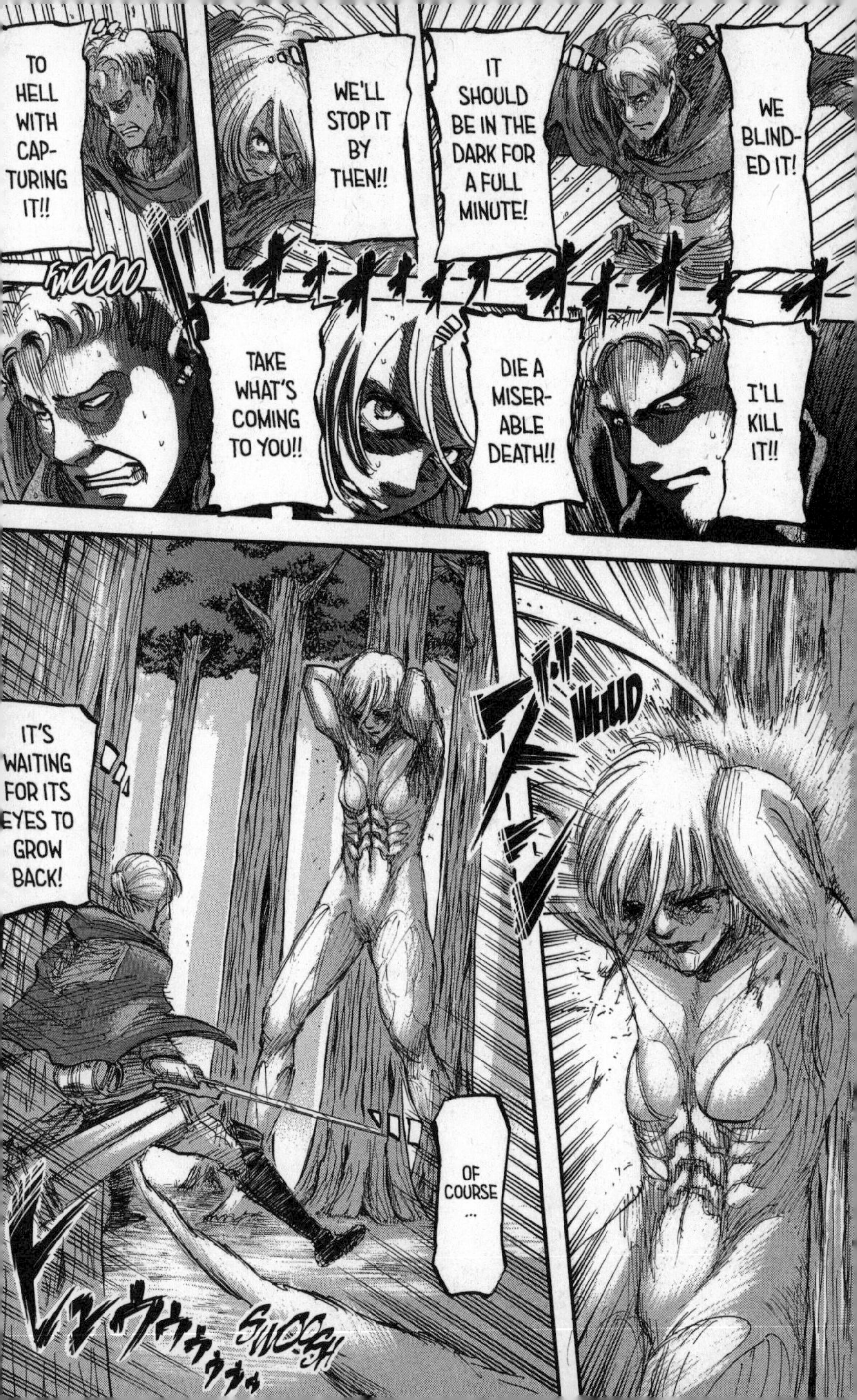
WE BLINDED IT!
IT SHOULD BE IN THE DARK FOR A FULL MINUTE!
WE'LL STOP IT BY THEN!!
TO HELL WITH CAPTURING IT!!
I'LL KILL IT!!
DIE A MISERABLE DEATH!!
TAKE WHAT'S COMING TO YOU!!
FWOOOO
WHUD
IT'S WAITING FOR ITS EYES TO GROW BACK!
OF COURSE ...
SWOOSH

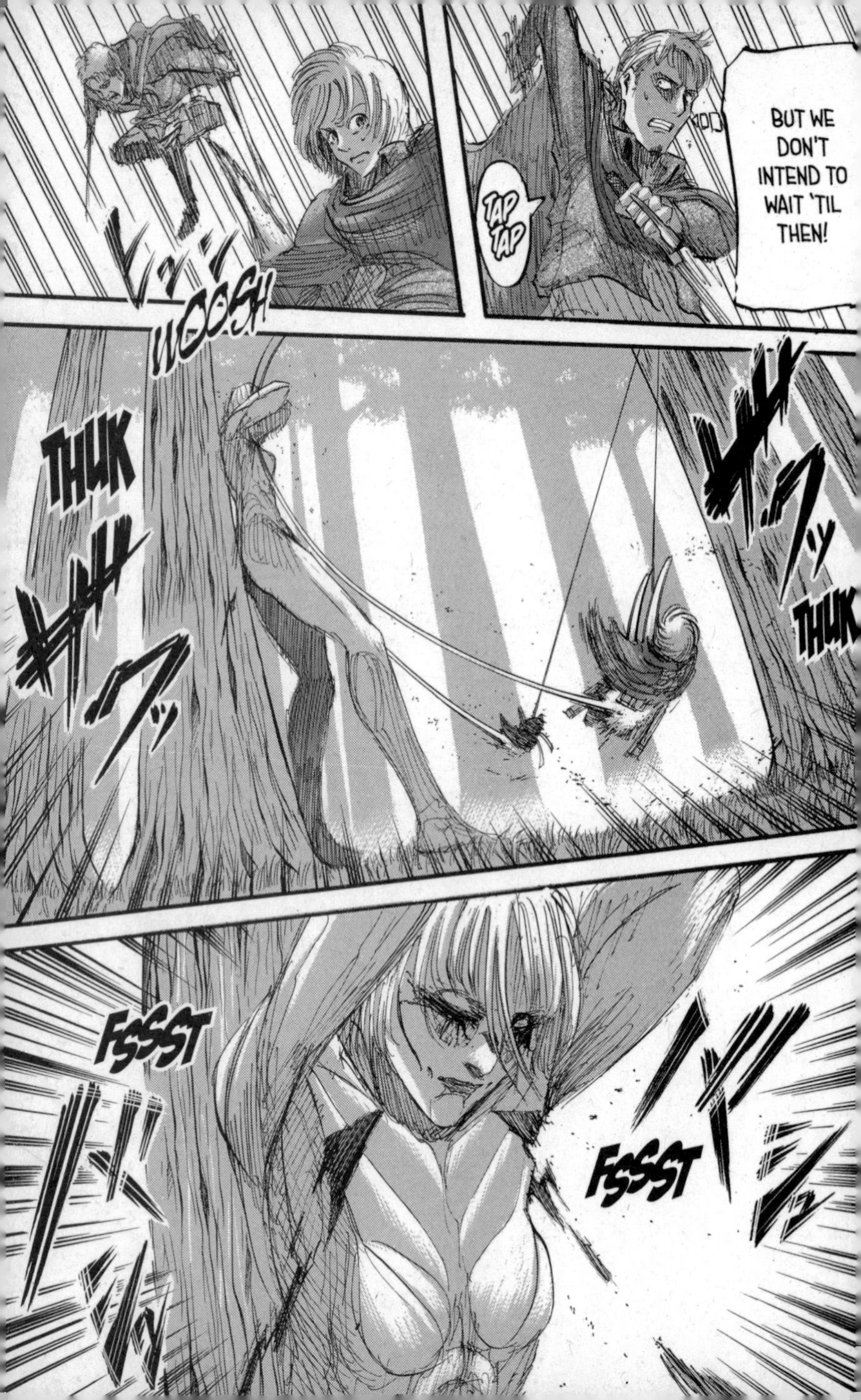
BUT WE DON'T INTEND TO WAIT 'TIL THEN!
TAP TAP
WOOSH
THUK
THUK
FSSST
FSSST

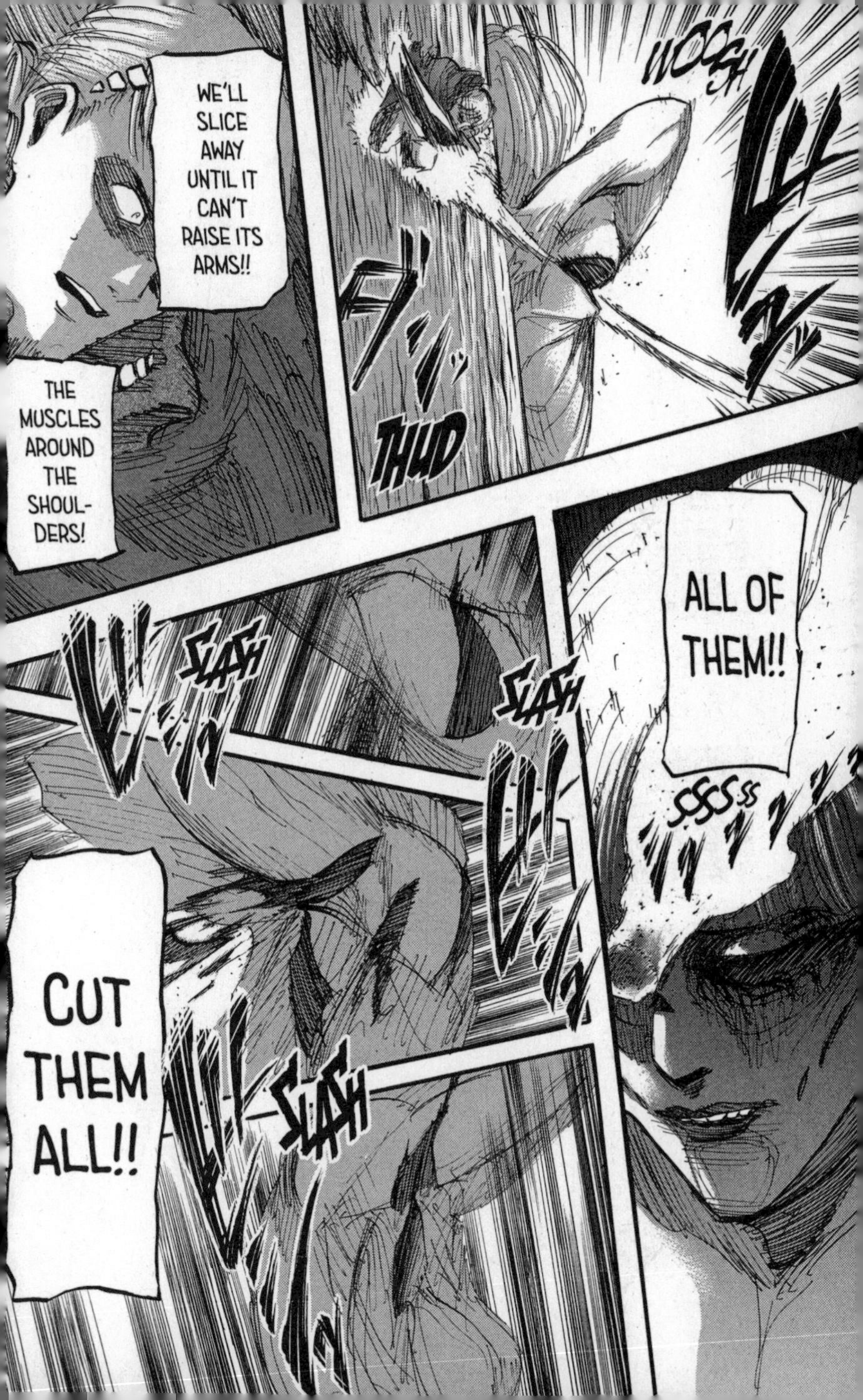
WOOSH
THUD
WE'LL SLICE AWAY UNTIL IT CAN'T RAISE ITS ARMS!!
THE MUSCLES AROUND THE SHOUL-DERS!
ALL OF THEM!!
SSSSS
SLASH
SLASH
CUT THEM ALL!!
SLASH

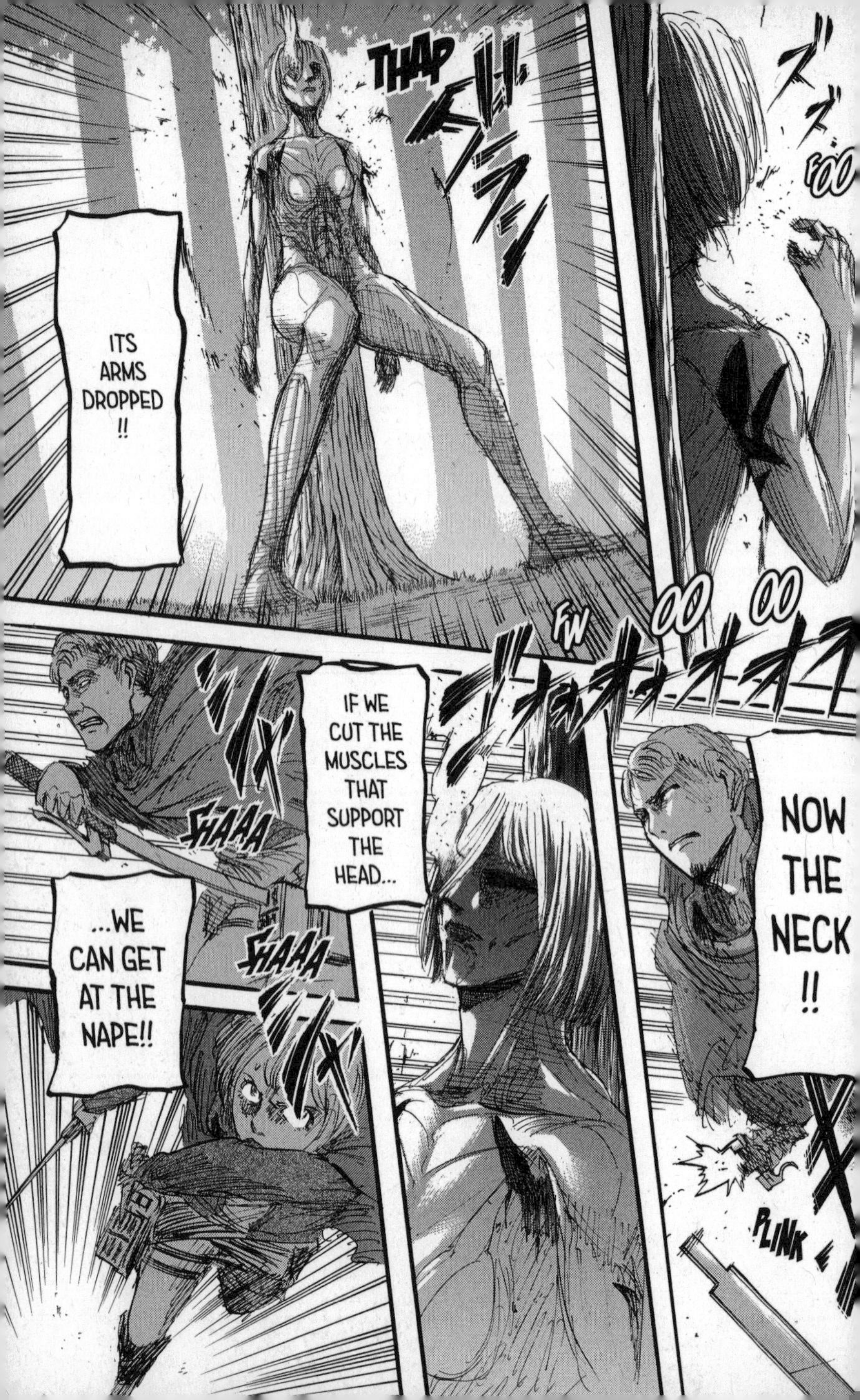
FOO
THAP
ITS ARMS DROPPED !!
FW OO OO
NOW THE NECK !!
PLINK
IF WE CUT THE MUSCLES THAT SUPPORT THE HEAD...
SHAAA
SHAAA
...WE CAN GET AT THE NAPE!!

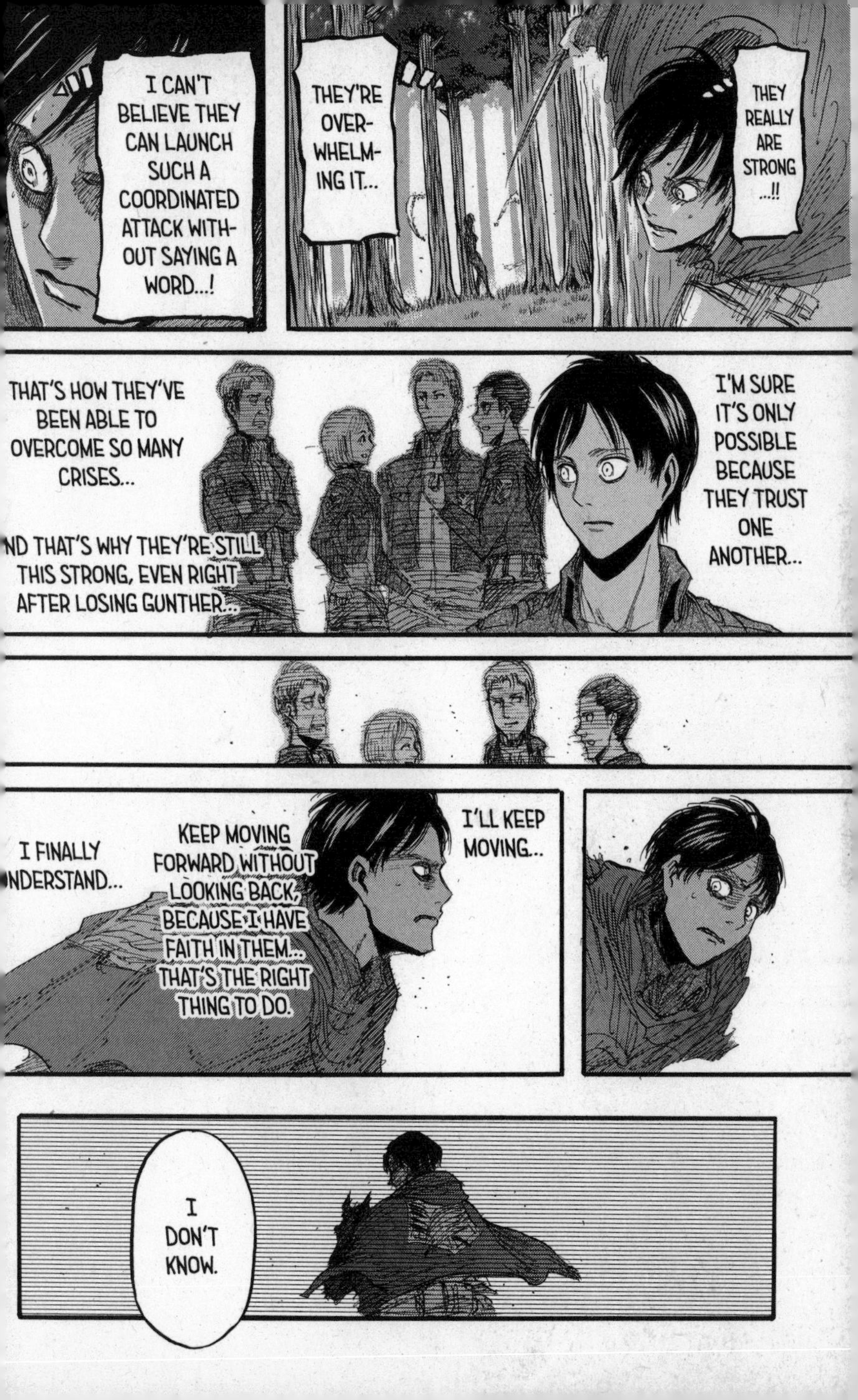
THEY REALLY ARE STRONG ...!!
THEY'RE OVER-WHELMING IT...
I CAN'T BELIEVE THEY CAN LAUNCH SUCH A COORDINATED ATTACK WITHOUT SAYING A WORD...!
I'M SURE IT'S ONLY POSSIBLE BECAUSE THEY TRUST ONE ANOTHER...
THAT'S HOW THEY'VE BEEN ABLE TO OVERCOME SO MANY CRISES...
ND THAT'S WHY THEY'RE STILL THIS STRONG, EVEN RIGHT AFTER LOSING GUNTHER...
I'LL KEEP MOVING...
KEEP MOVING FORWARD WITHOUT LOOKING BACK, BECAUSE I HAVE FAITH IN THEM... THAT'S THE RIGHT THING TO DO.
I FINALLY NDERSTAND...
I DON'T KNOW.

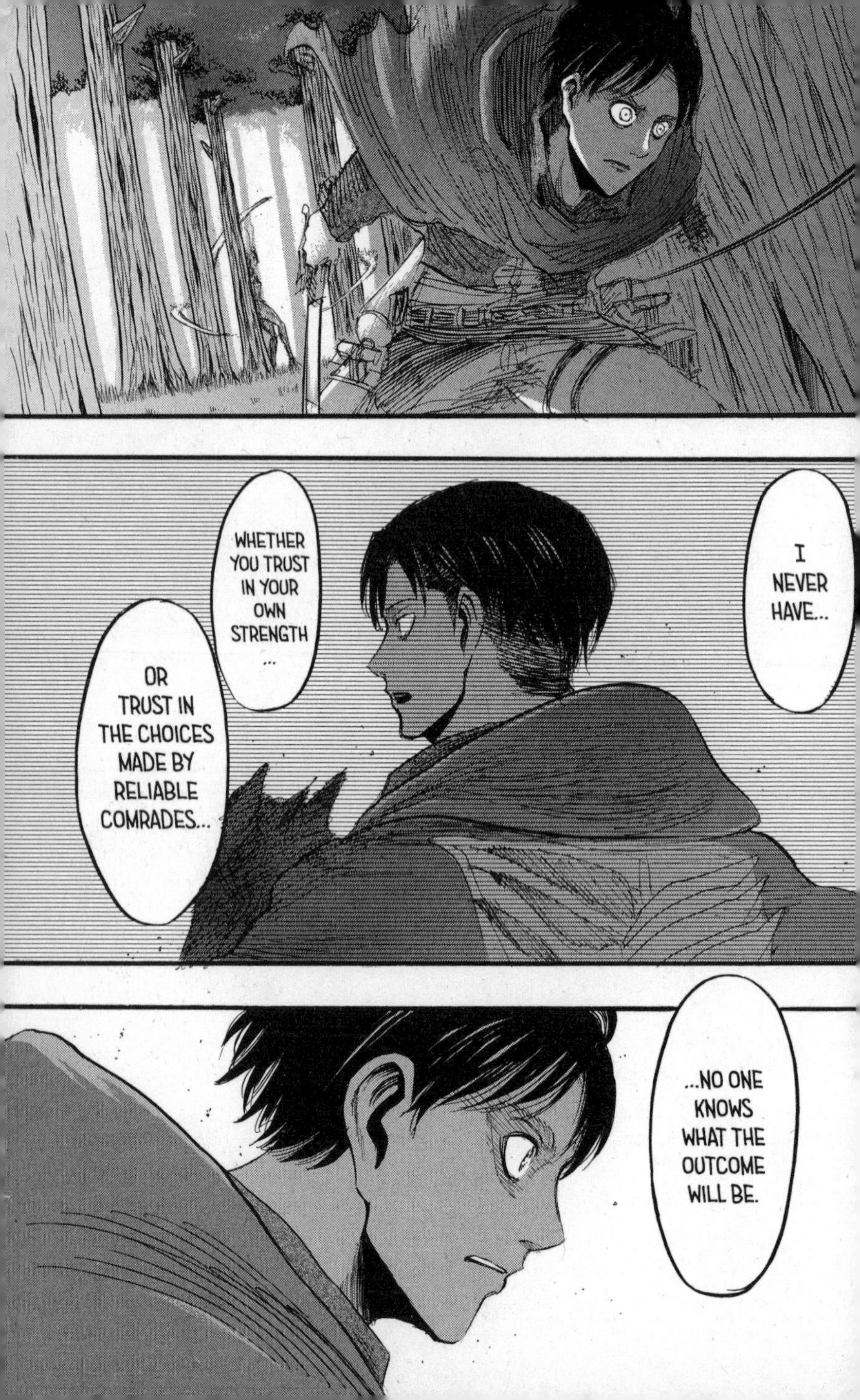
I NEVER HAVE...
WHETHER YOU TRUST IN YOUR OWN STRENGTH...
OR TRUST IN THE CHOICES MADE BY RELIABLE COMRADES...
...NO ONE KNOWS WHAT THE OUTCOME WILL BE.

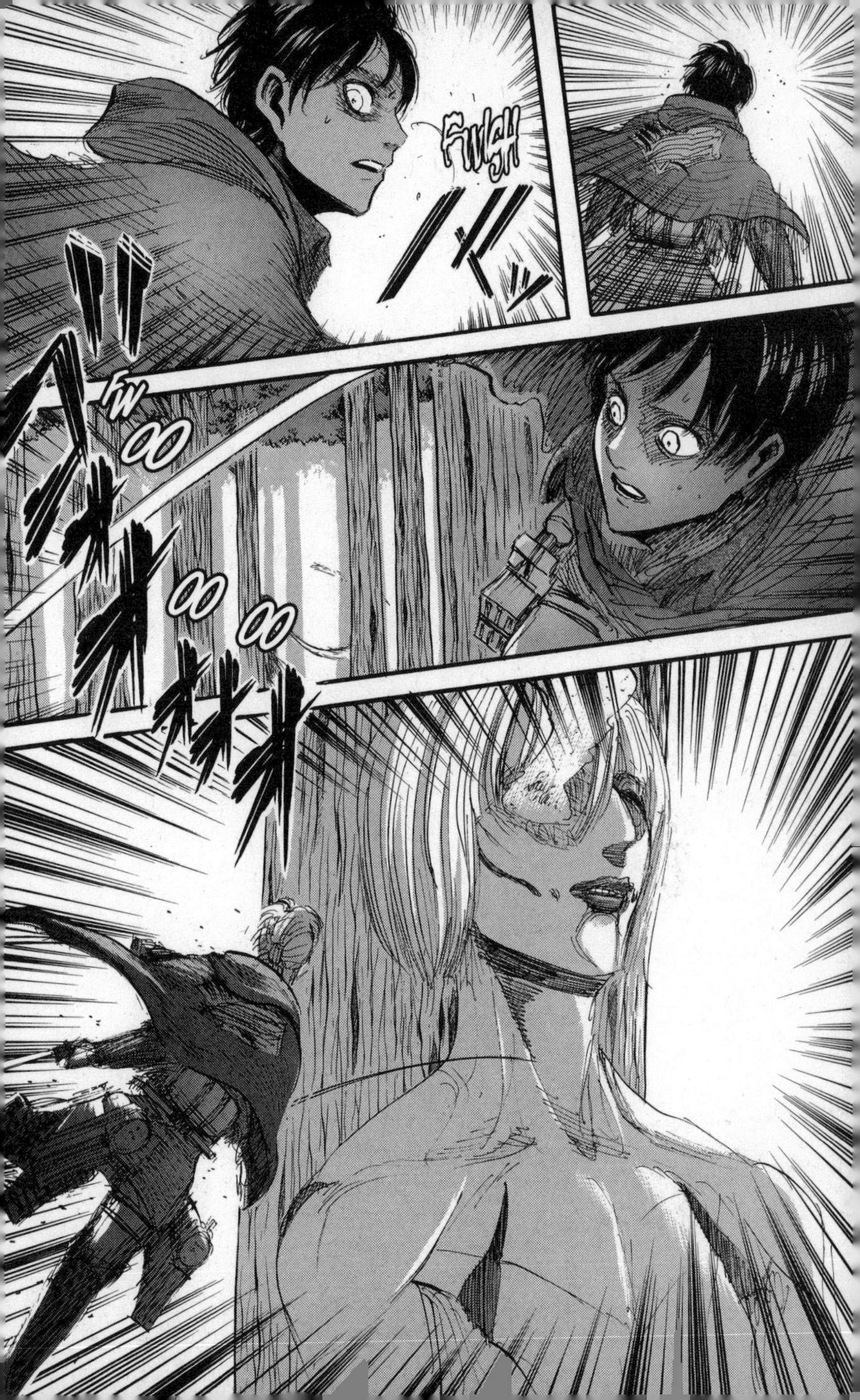
FWISH
FWOOOOOO

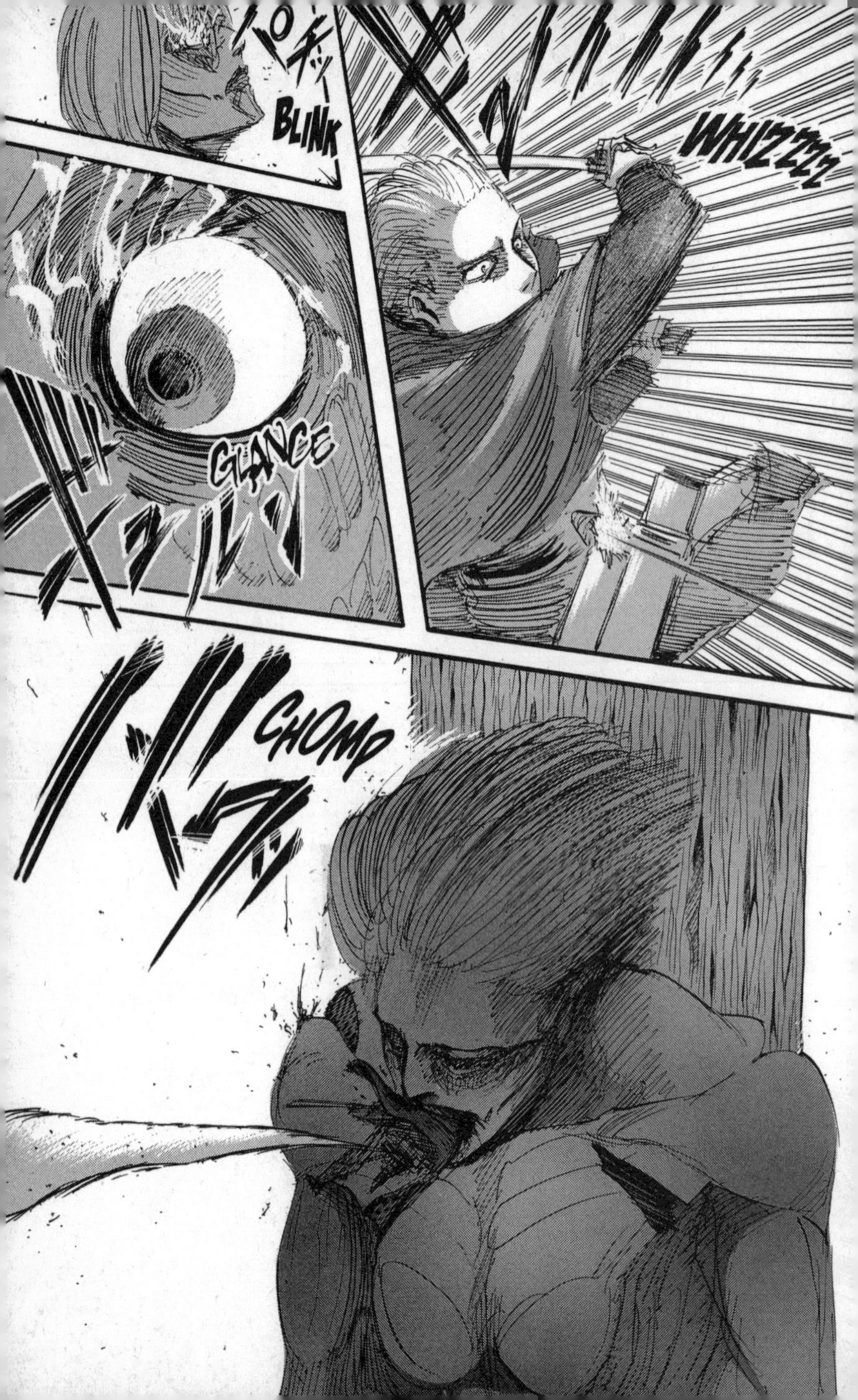
WHIZZZZ
BLINK
GLANCE
CHOMP

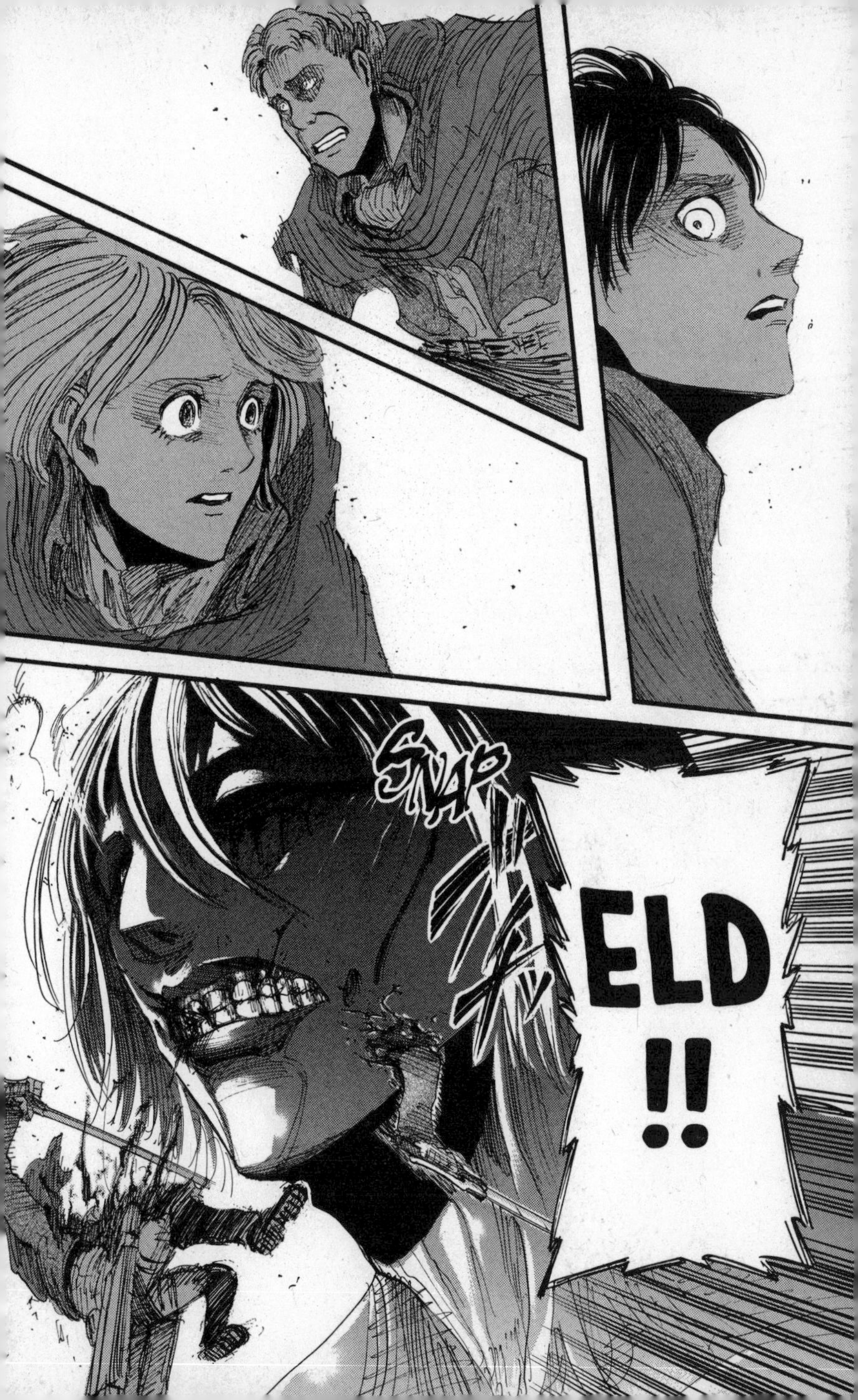
ELD!!
SNAP

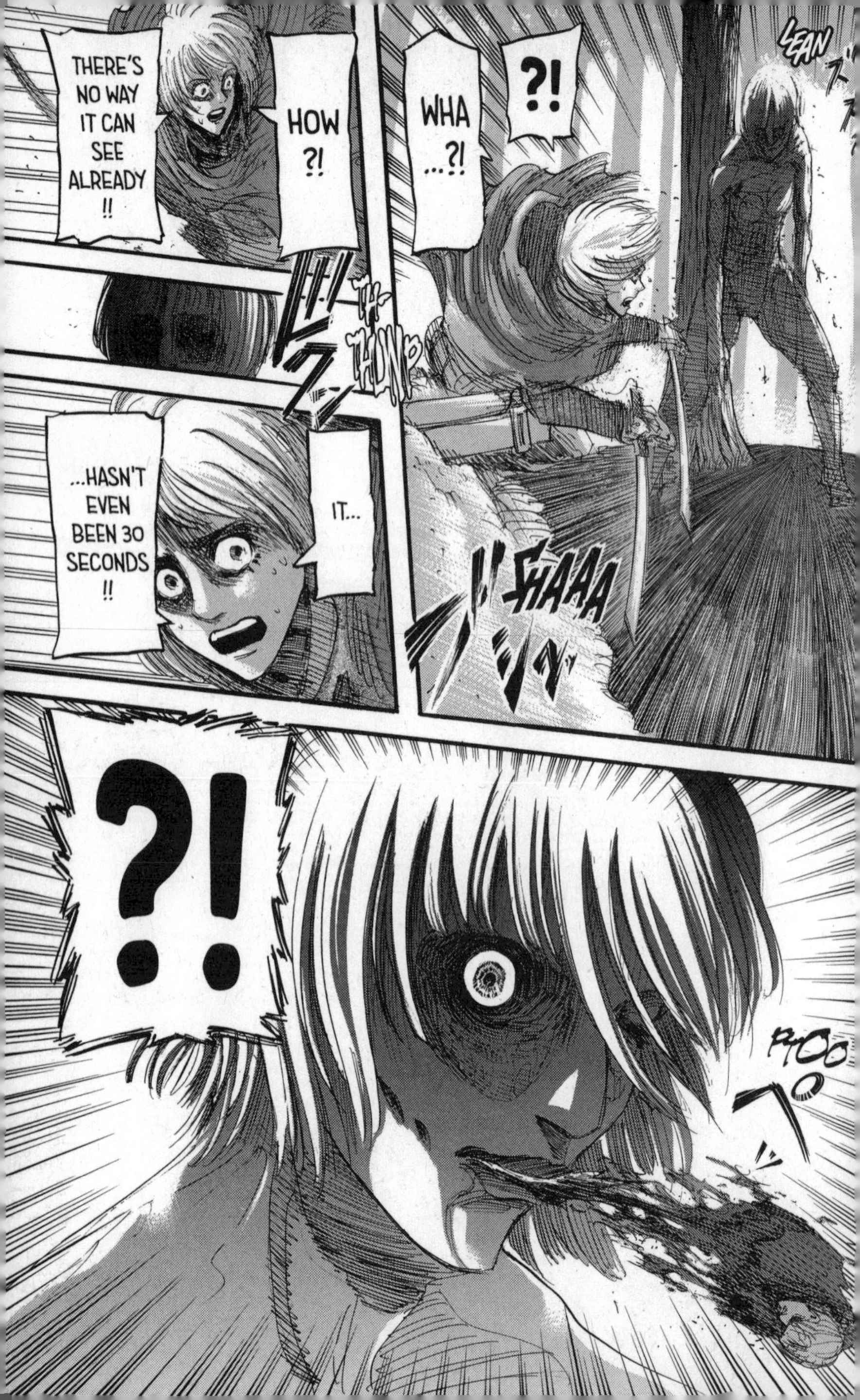

LEAN
?!
WHA ...?!
SHAAA
HOW ?!
THERE'S NO WAY IT CAN SEE ALREADY !!
TH-THUMP
IT...
...HASN'T EVEN BEEN 30 SECONDS !!
?!
PTOOO

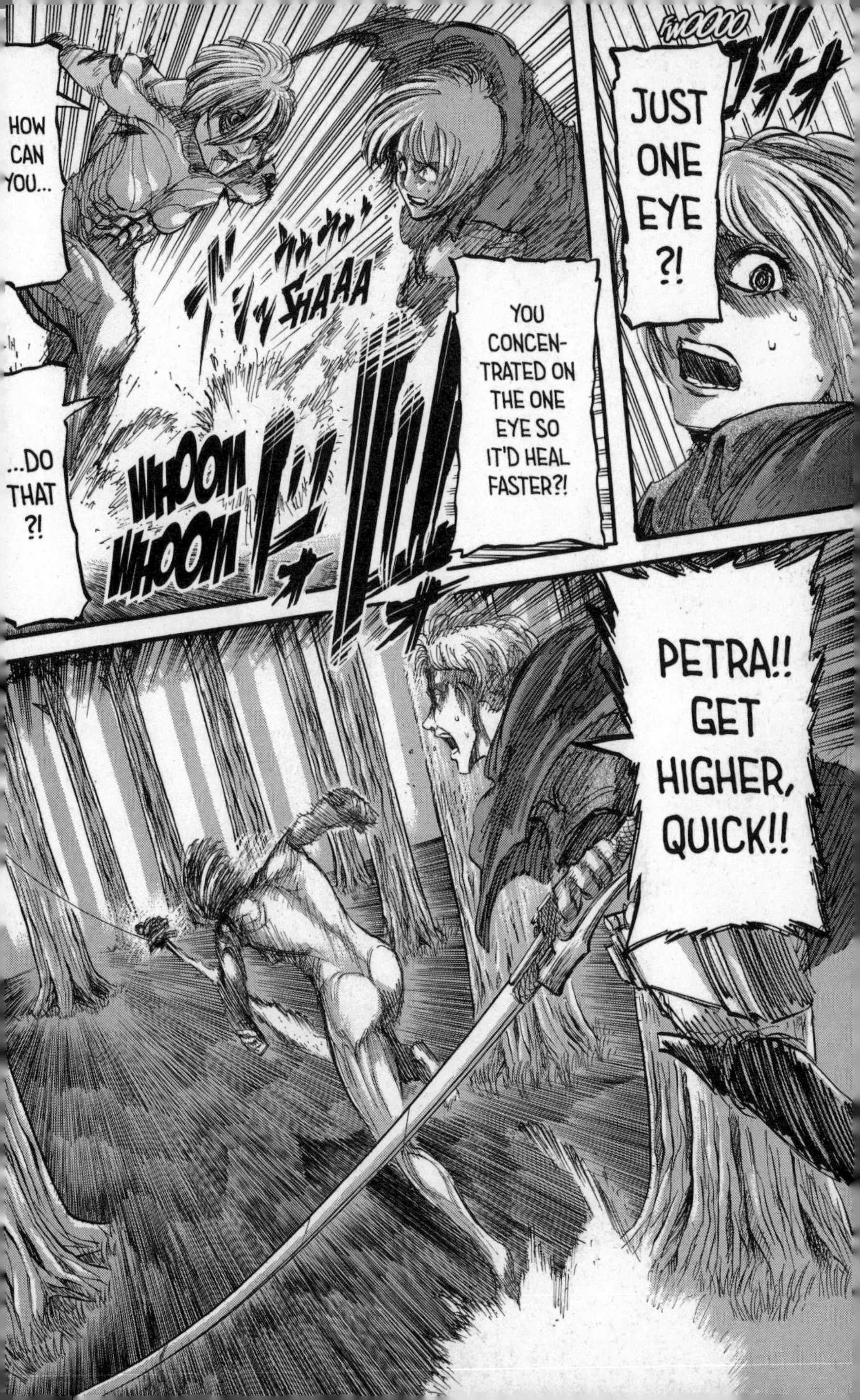
FWOOOO
JUST ONE EYE?!
YOU CONCENTRATED ON THE ONE EYE SO IT'D HEAL FASTER?!
SHAAA
HOW CAN YOU...
...DO THAT?!
WHOOM WHOOM
PETRA!! GET HIGHER, QUICK!!

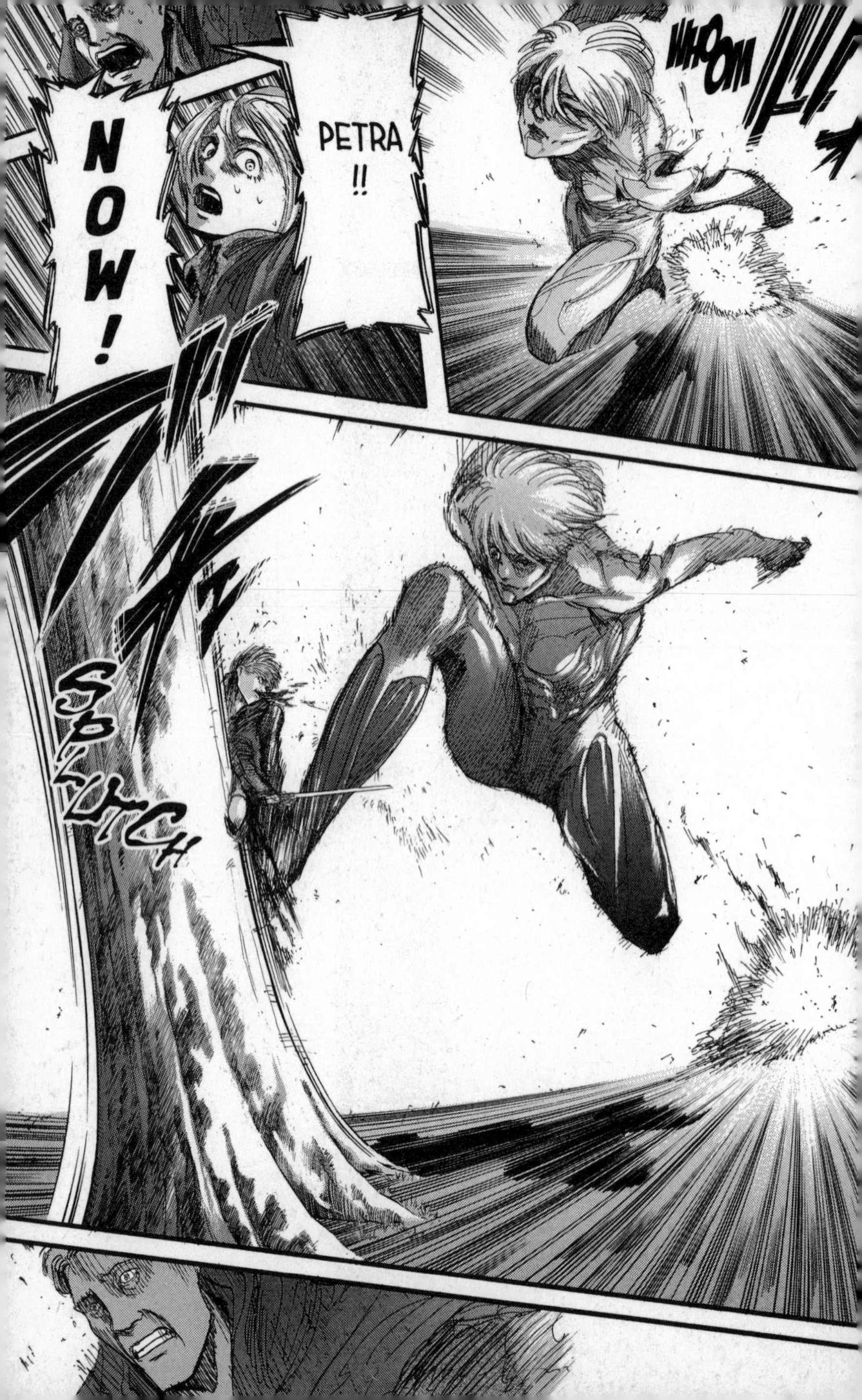
WHOOM
PETRA !!
NOW!
SPLLTCH

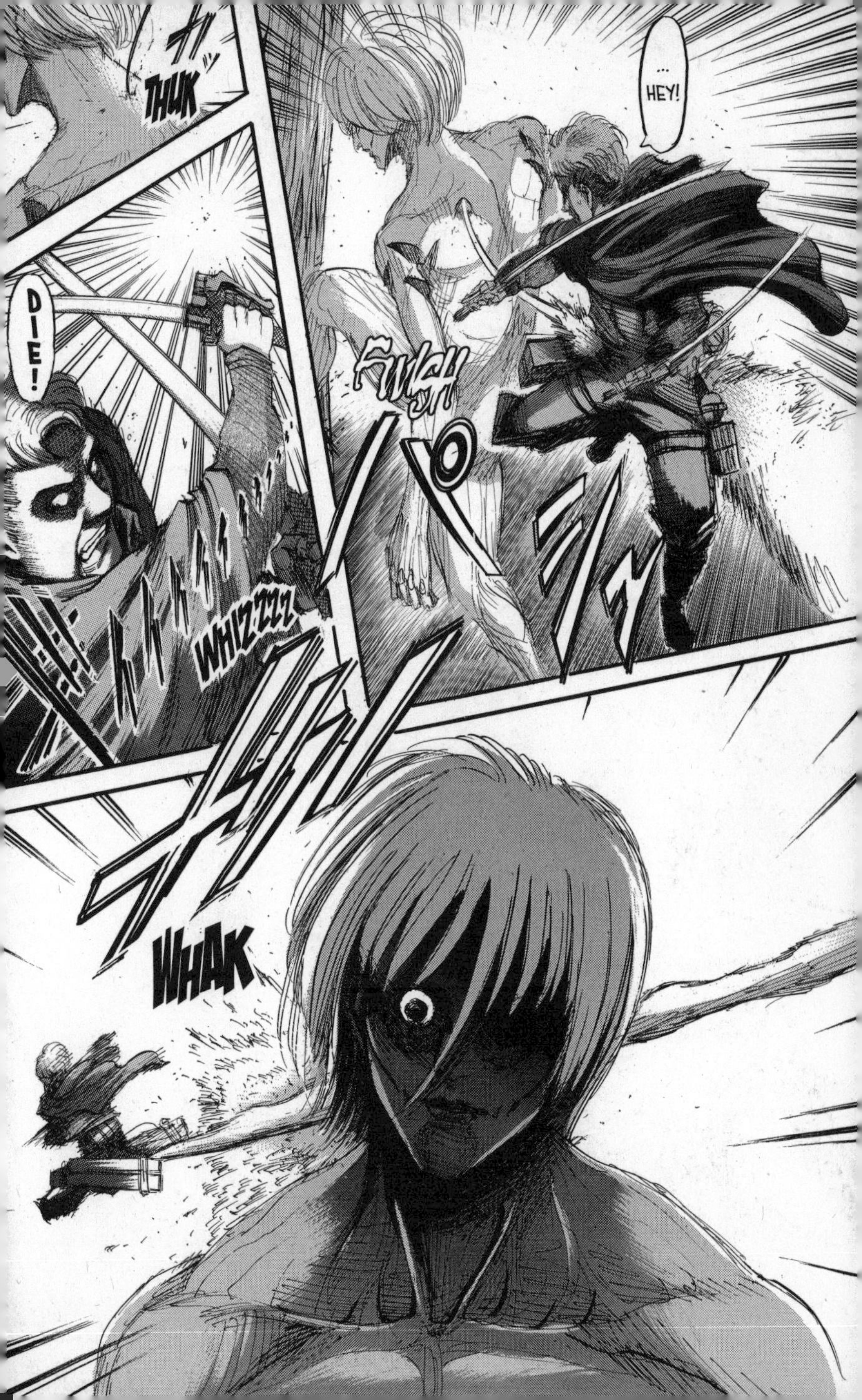

THUK
... HEY!
FWISH
DIE!
WHIZZZZ
WHAK

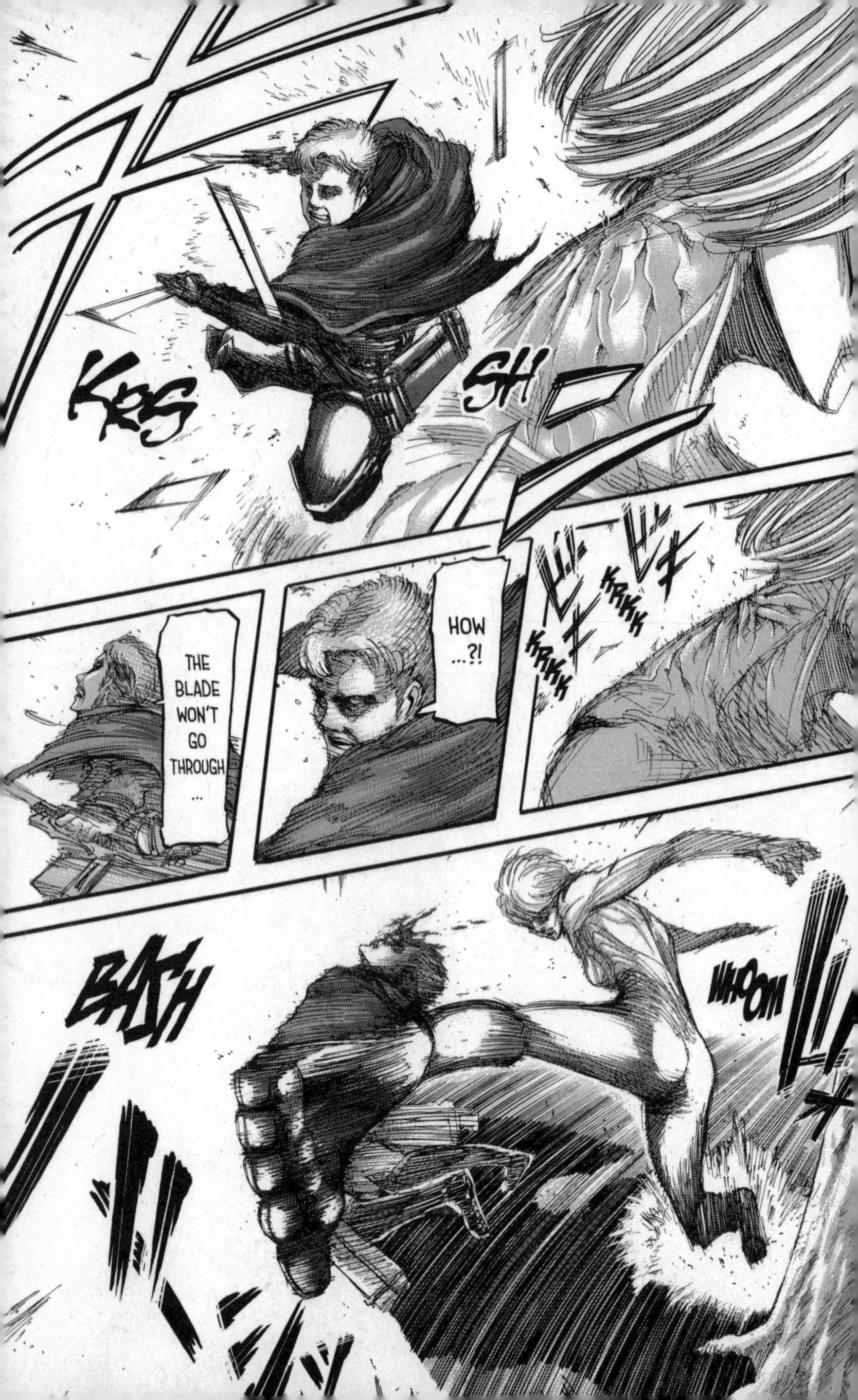
SH
KRS
KRKK
KRKK
HOW ...?!
THE BLADE WON'T GO THROUGH ...
WHOOM
BASH

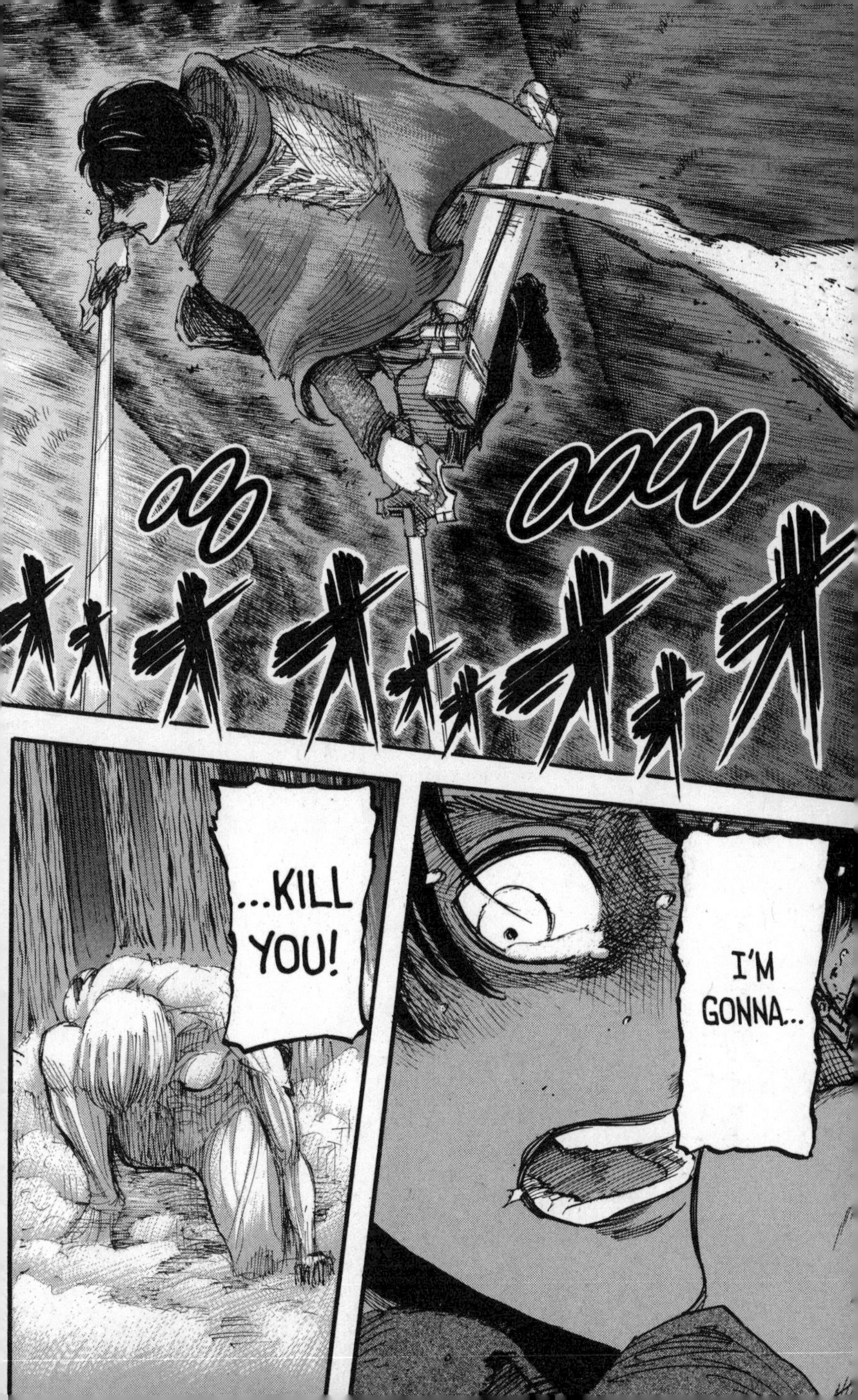
OOOO
OO
I'M GONNA...
...KILL YOU!

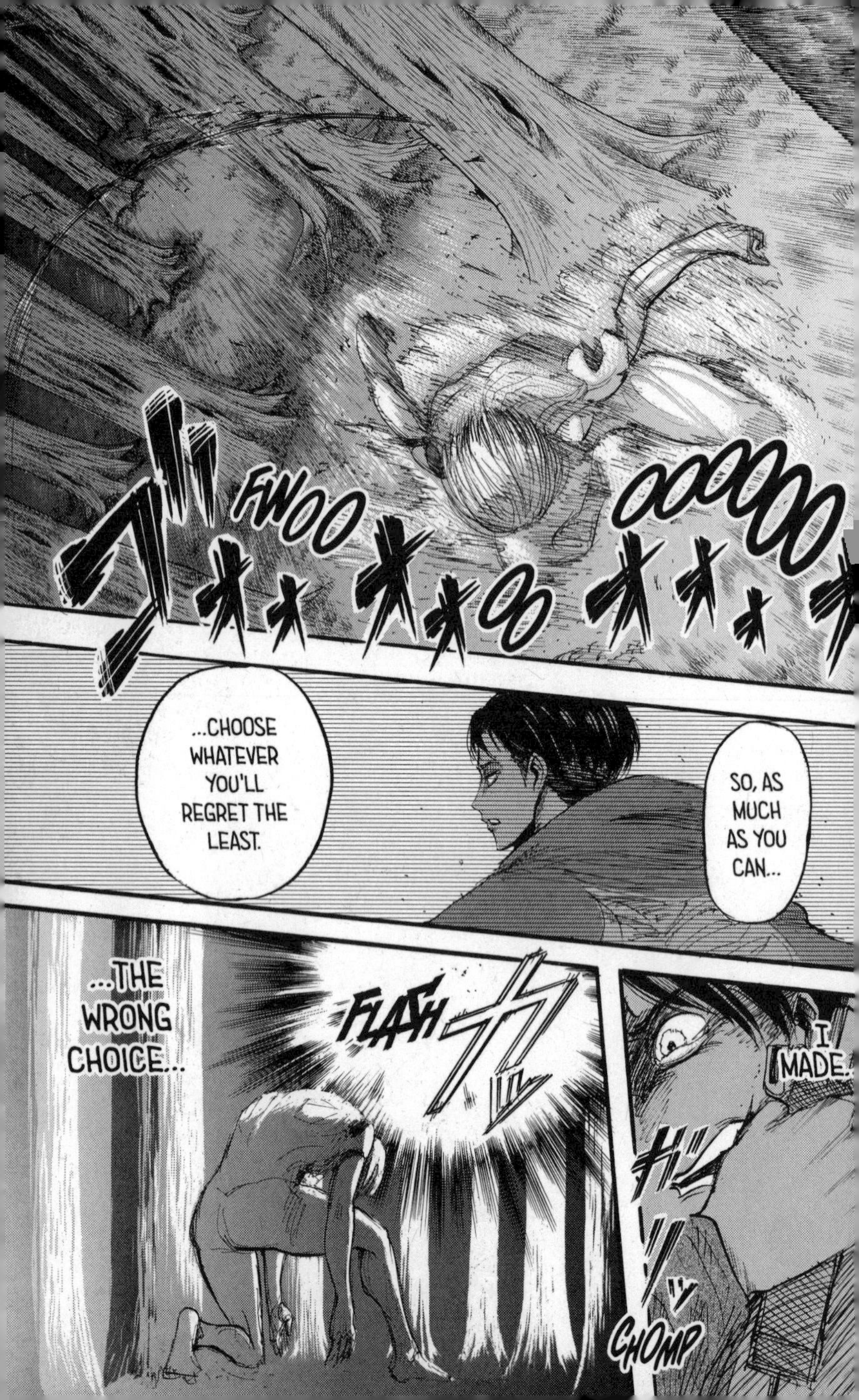
FWOO
OOOOOO
SO, AS MUCH AS YOU CAN...
...CHOOSE WHATEVER YOU'LL REGRET THE LEAST.
I MADE...
CHOMP
...THE WRONG CHOICE...
FLASH

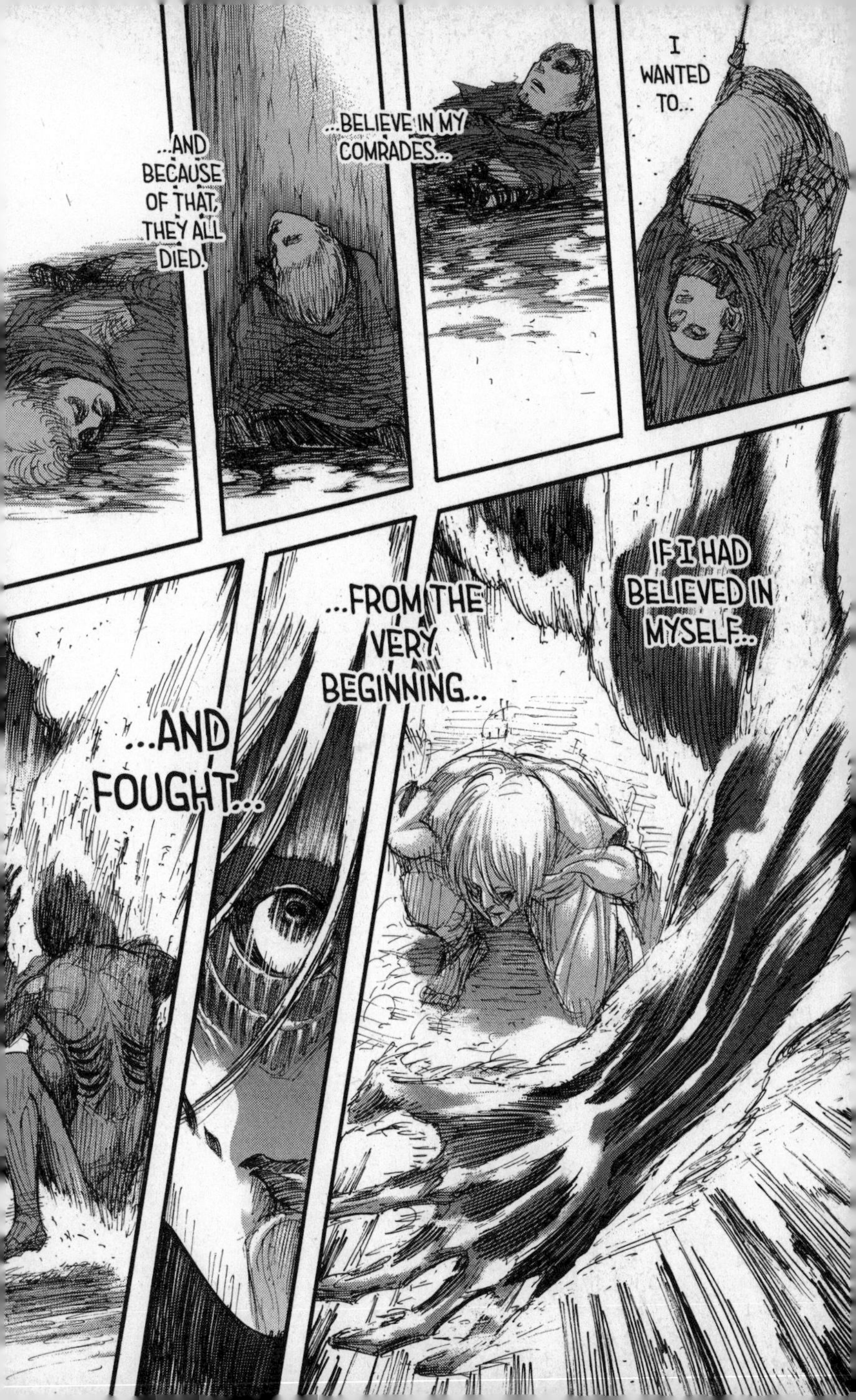
I WANTED TO...
...BELIEVE IN MY COMRADES...
...AND BECAUSE OF THAT, THEY ALL DIED.
IF I HAD BELIEVED IN MYSELF...
...FROM THE VERY BEGINNING...
...AND FOUGHT...

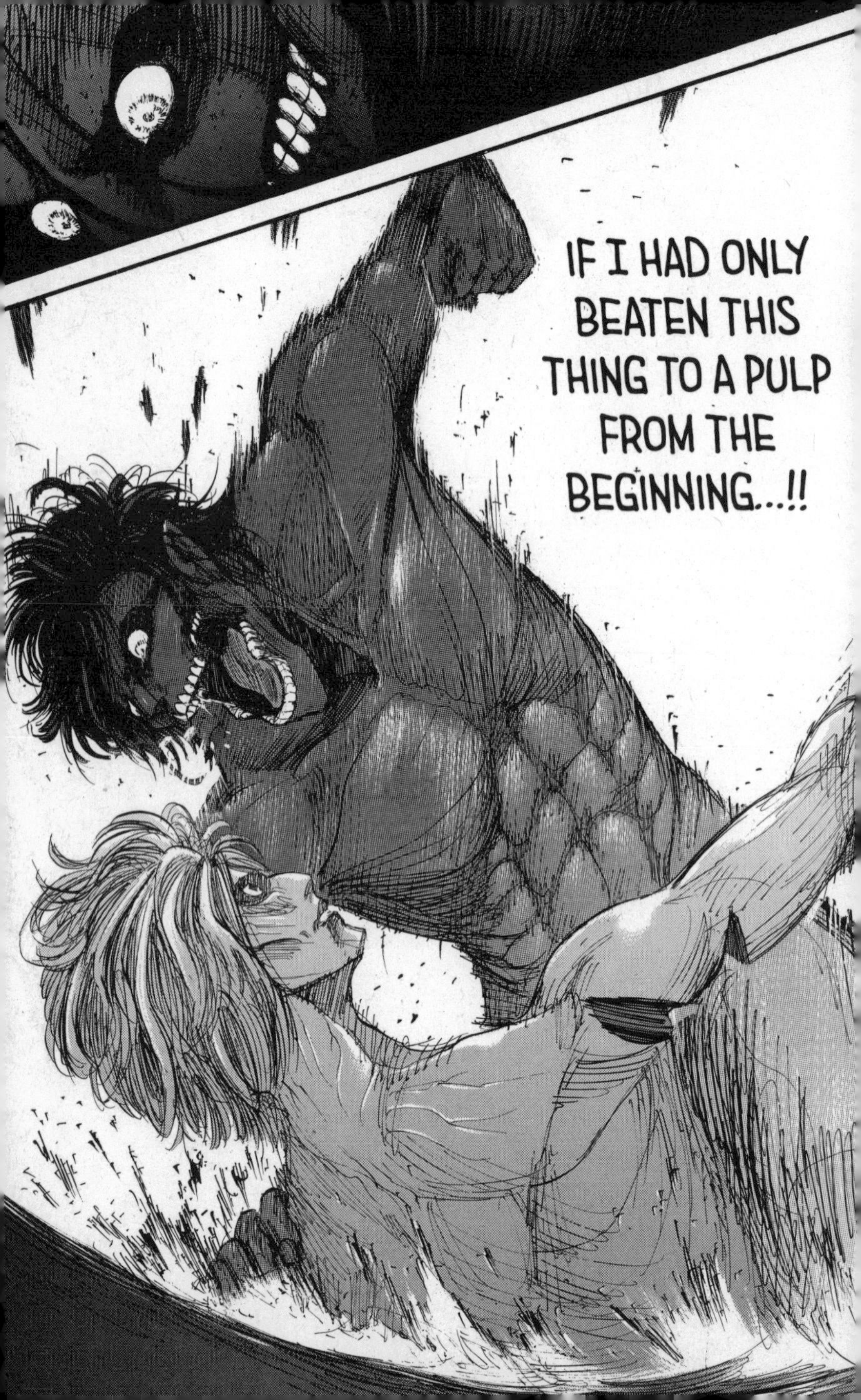
IF I HAD ONLY BEATEN THIS THING TO A PULP FROM THE BEGINNING...!!

ATTACK on TITAN

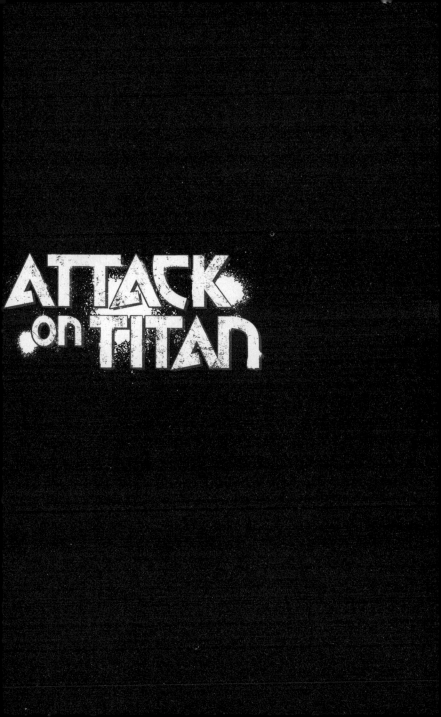

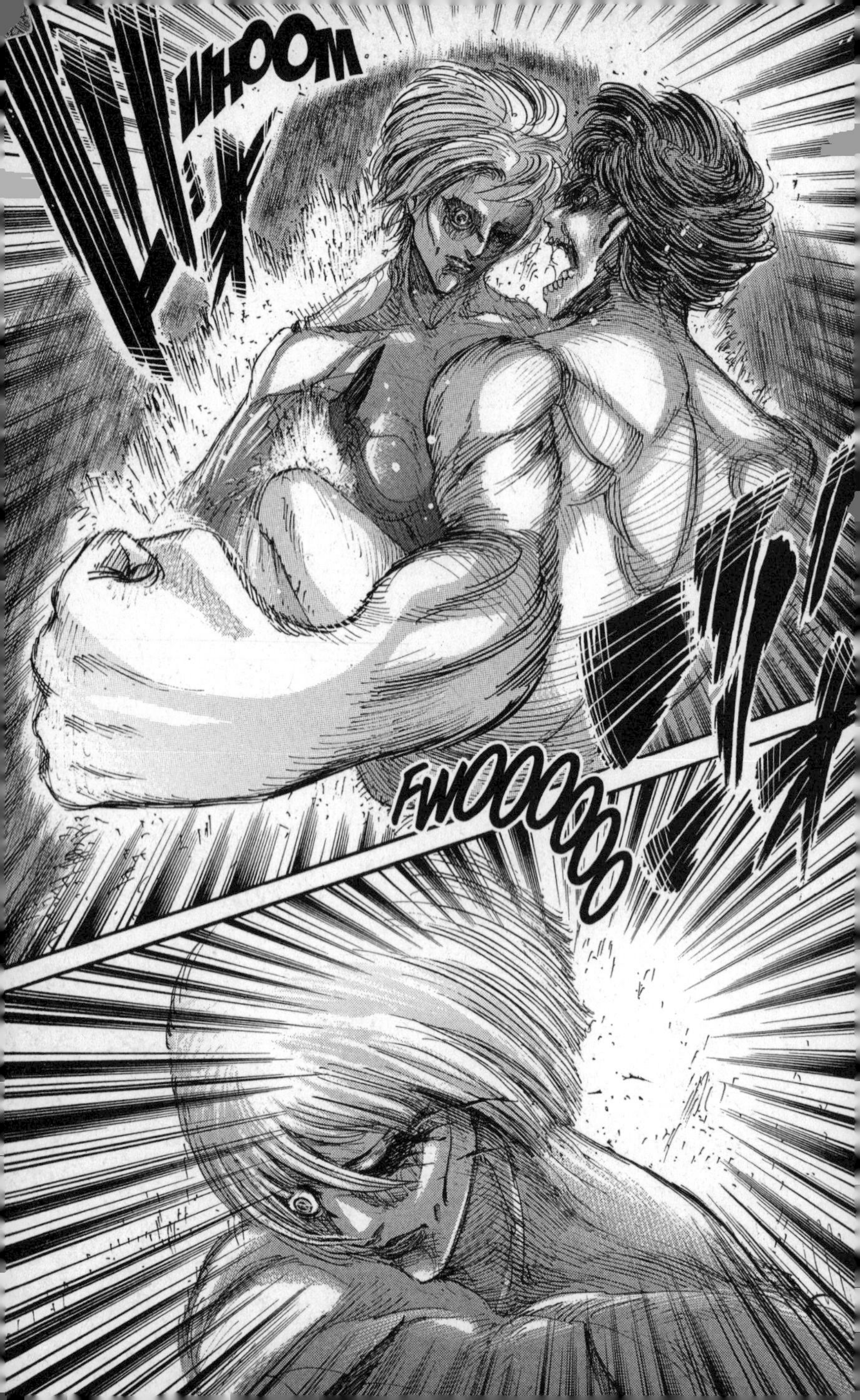
WHOOM
FWOOOOOO

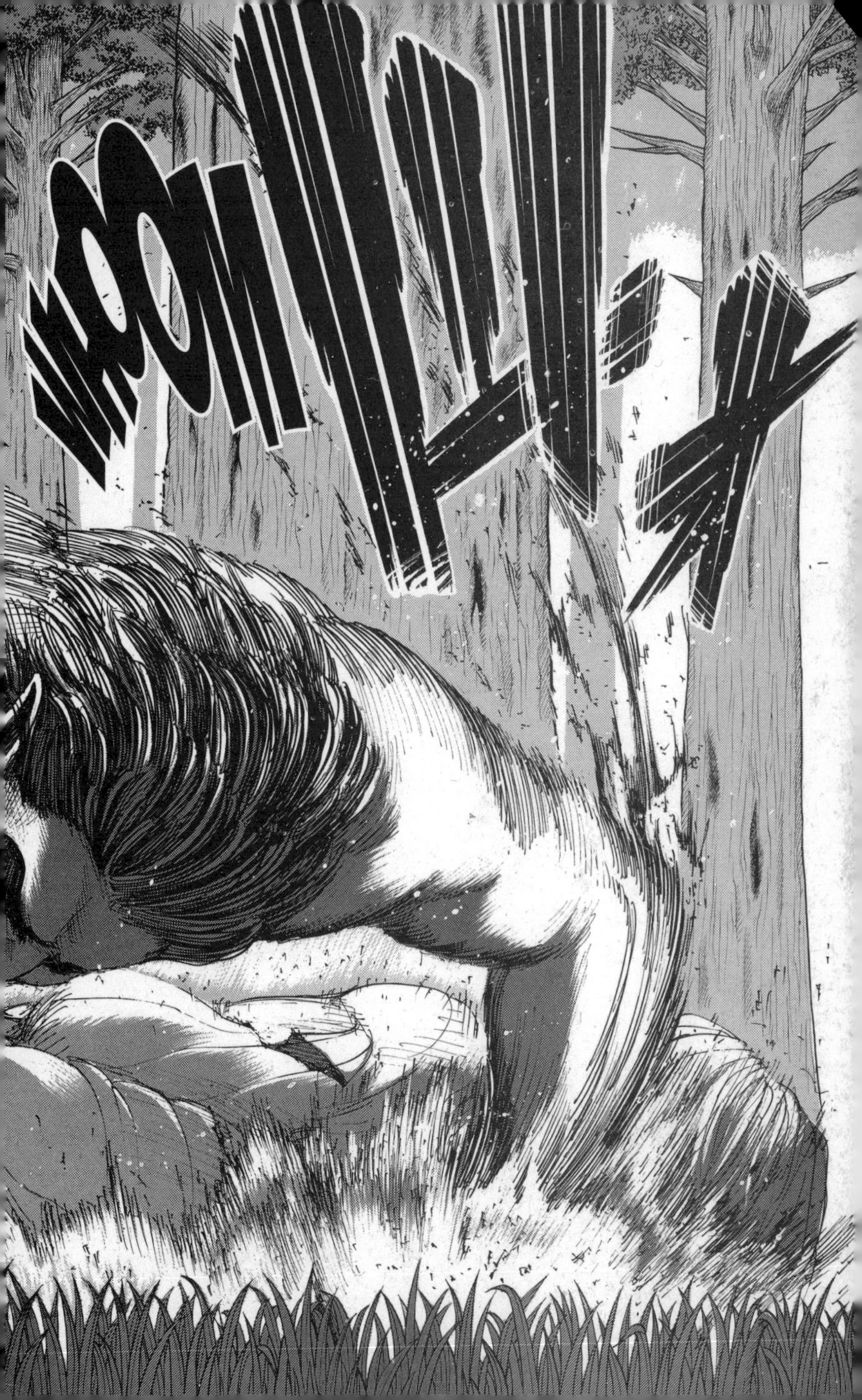
WHOOM

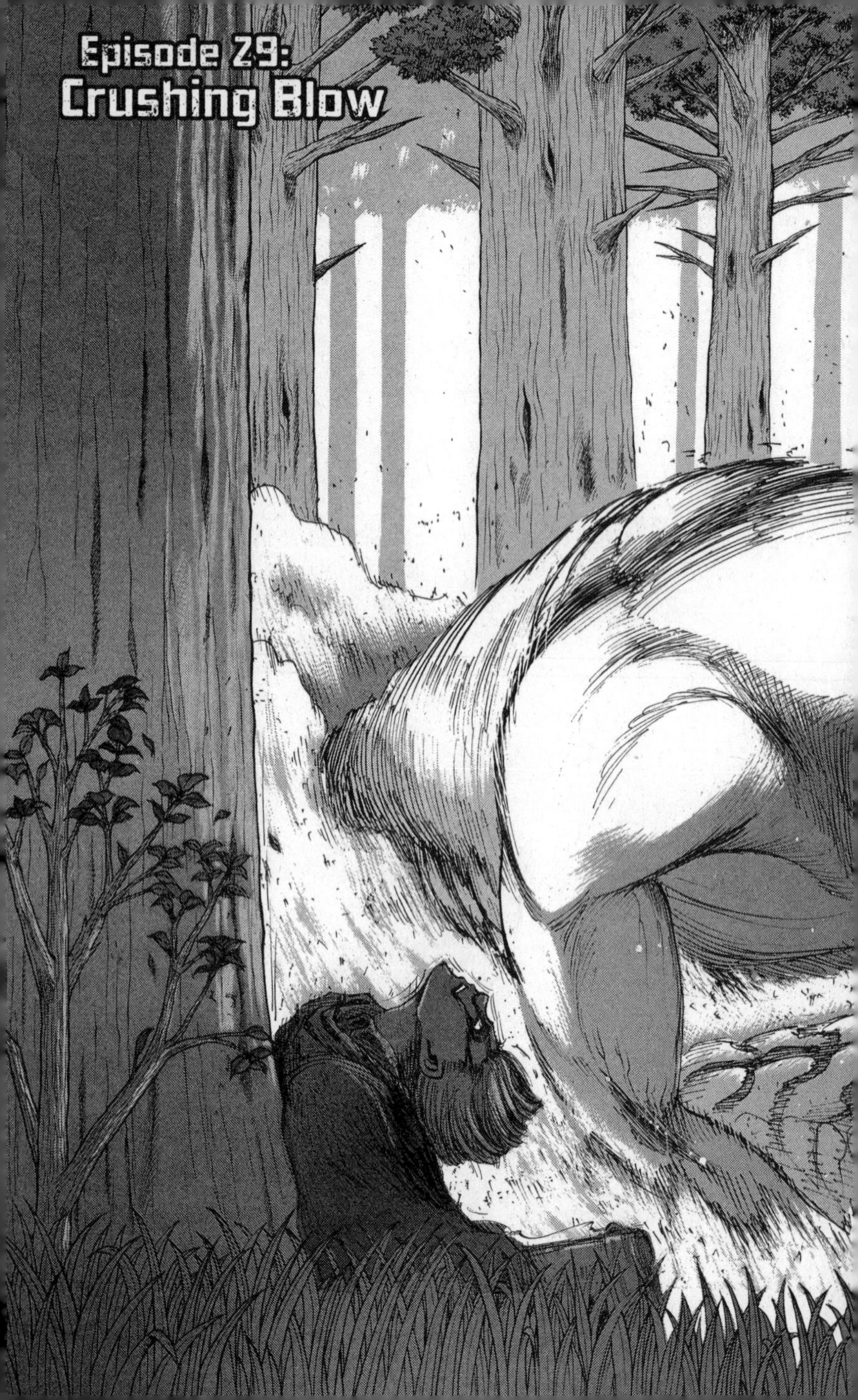
Episode 29:
Crushing Blow

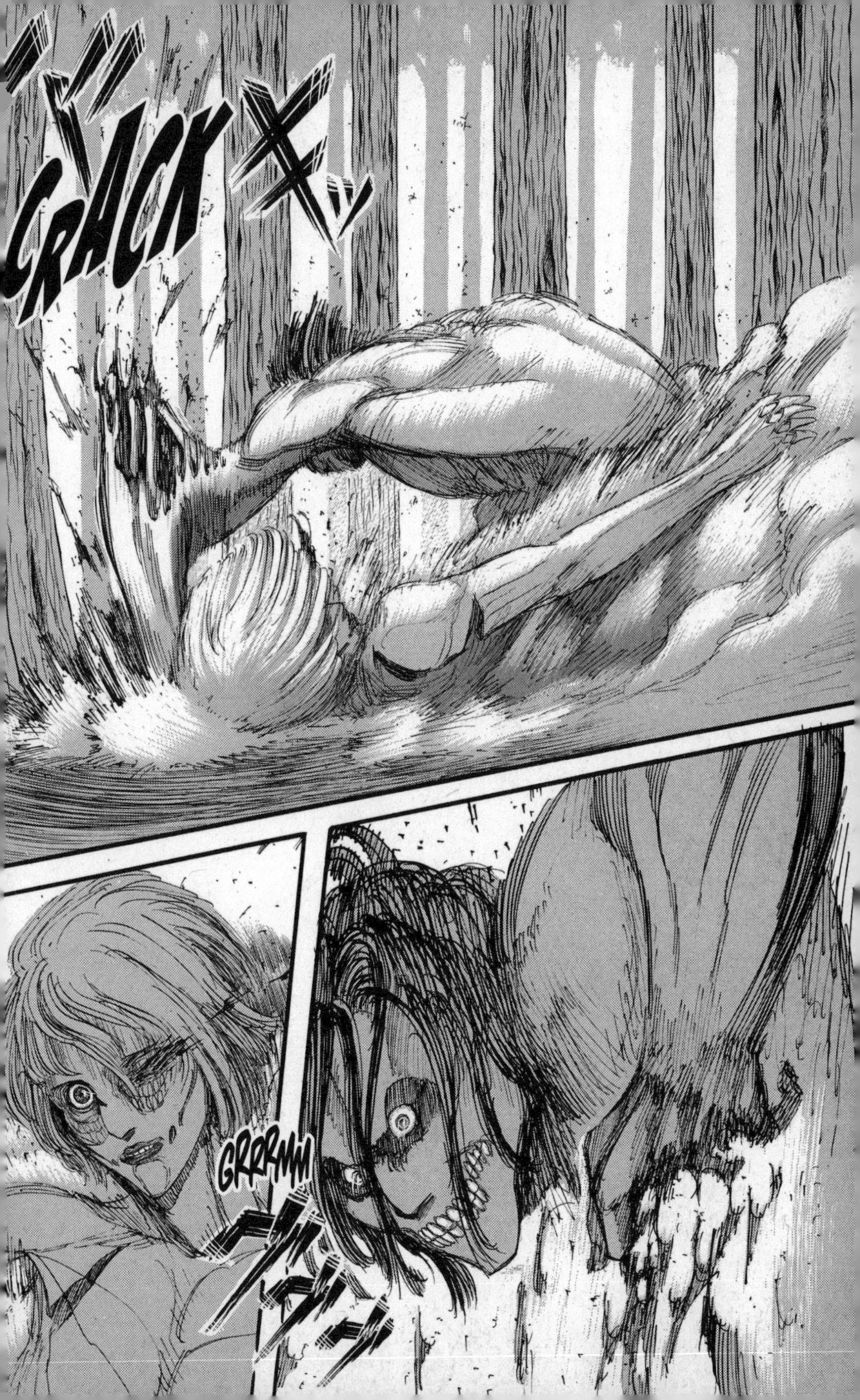
CRACK
GRRRMM

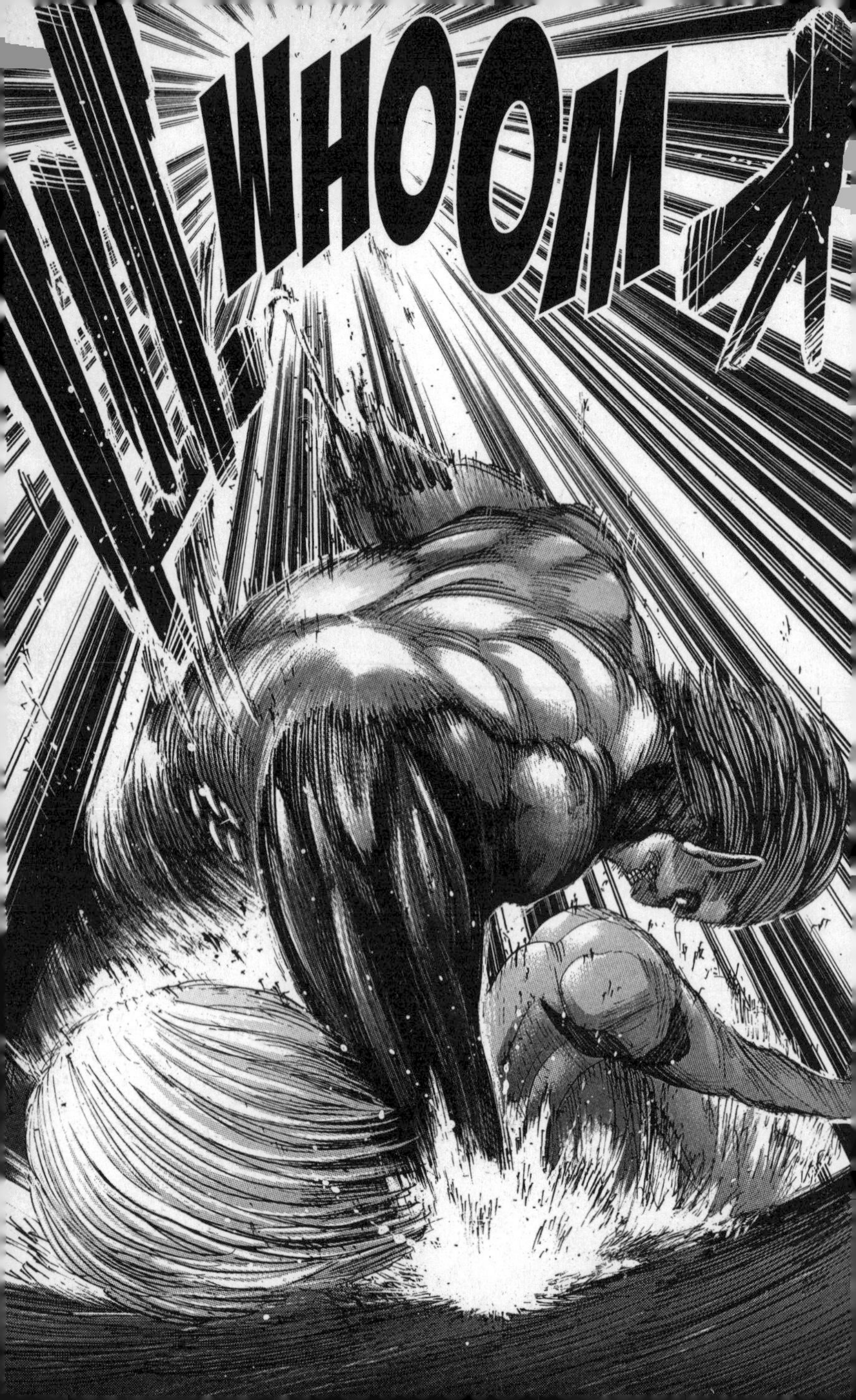
WHOOM

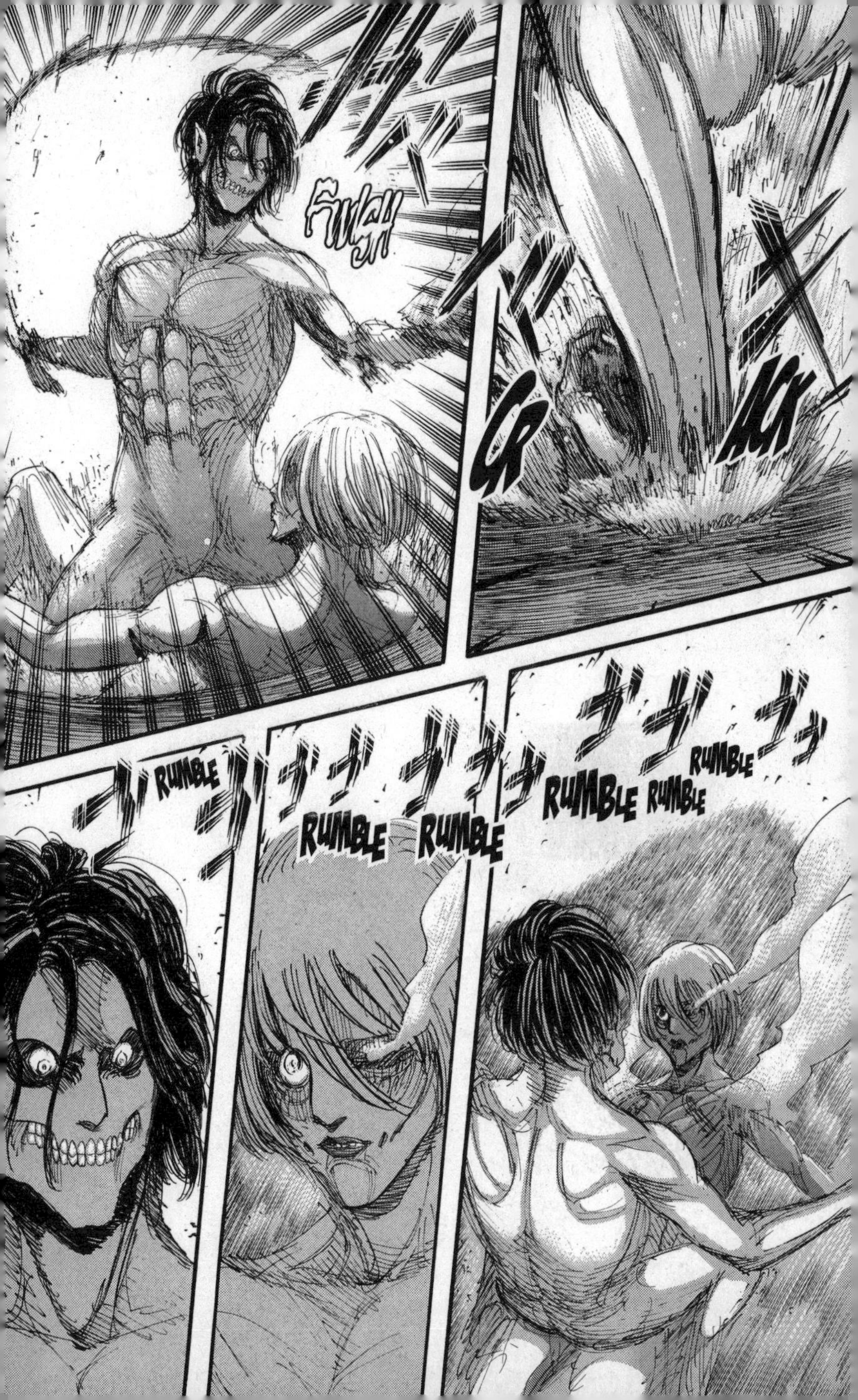
CRACK
FWAGH!
RUMBLE
RUMBLE
RUMBLE
RUMBLE
RUMBLE
RUMBLE

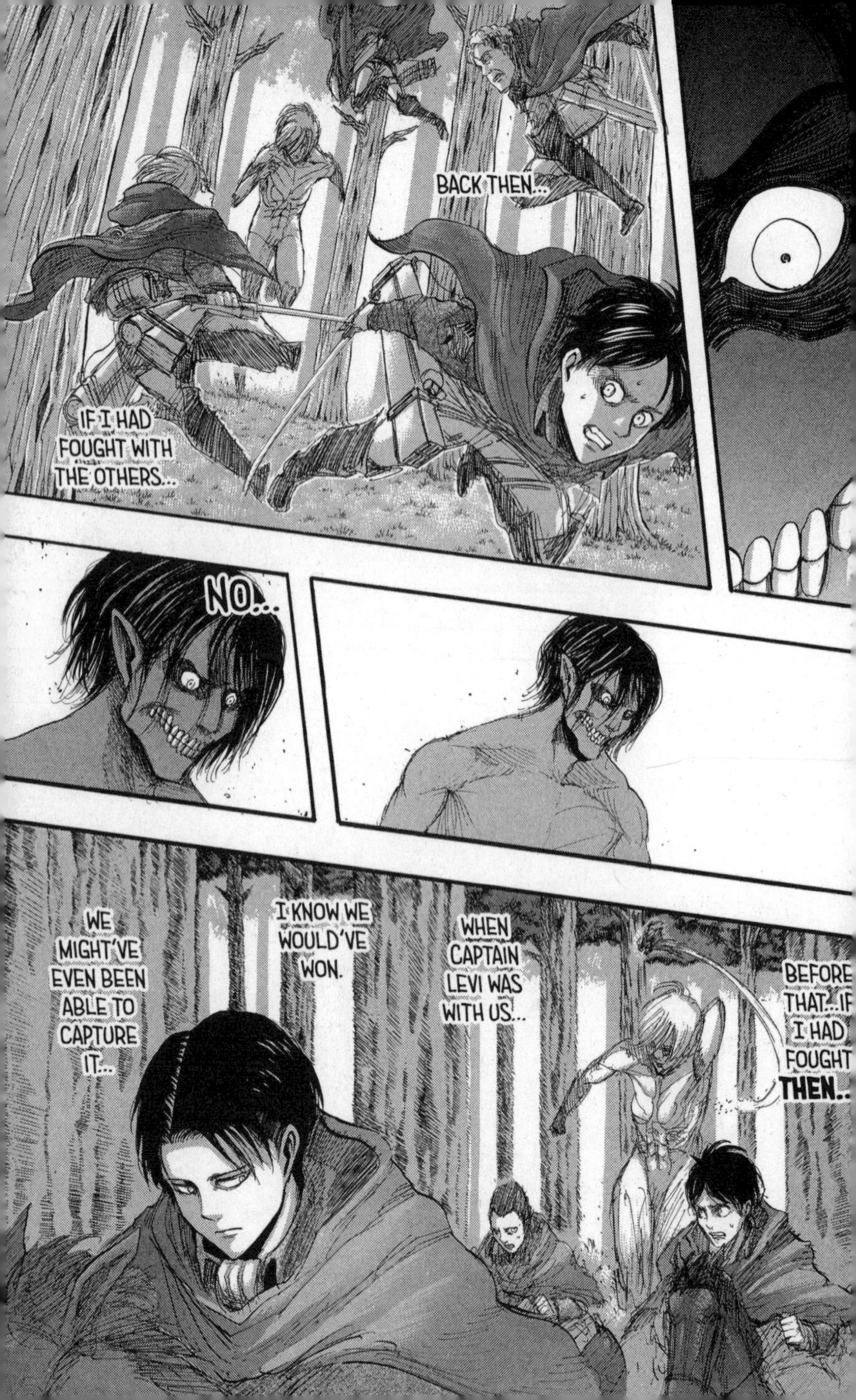
BACK THEN...
IF I HAD FOUGHT WITH THE OTHERS...
NO...
BEFORE THAT...IF I HAD FOUGHT THEN...
WHEN CAPTAIN LEVI WAS WITH US...
I KNOW WE WOULD'VE WON.
WE MIGHT'VE EVEN BEEN ABLE TO CAPTURE IT...

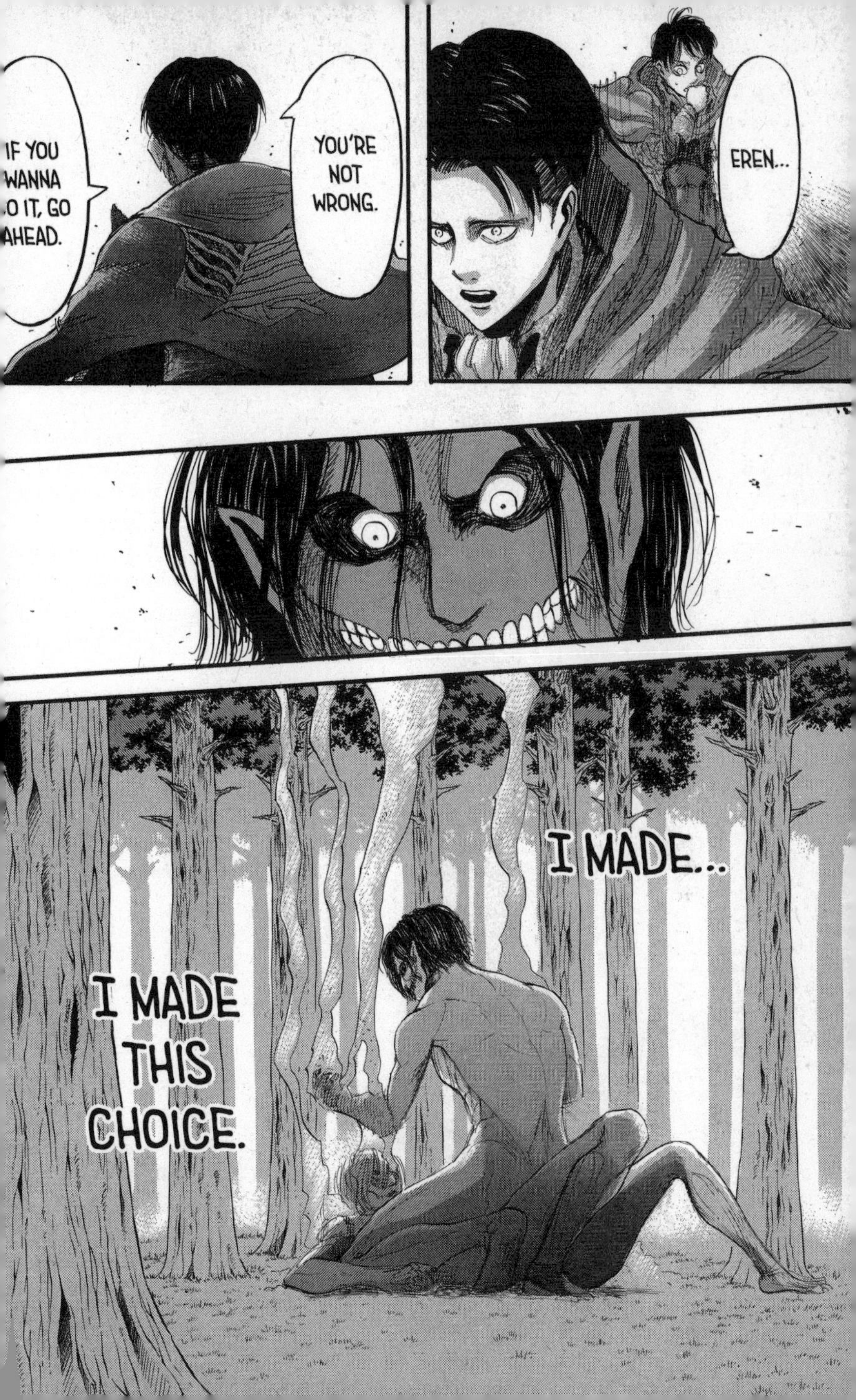

EREN...
YOU'RE NOT WRONG.
IF YOU WANNA O IT, GO AHEAD.
I MADE...
I MADE THIS CHOICE.

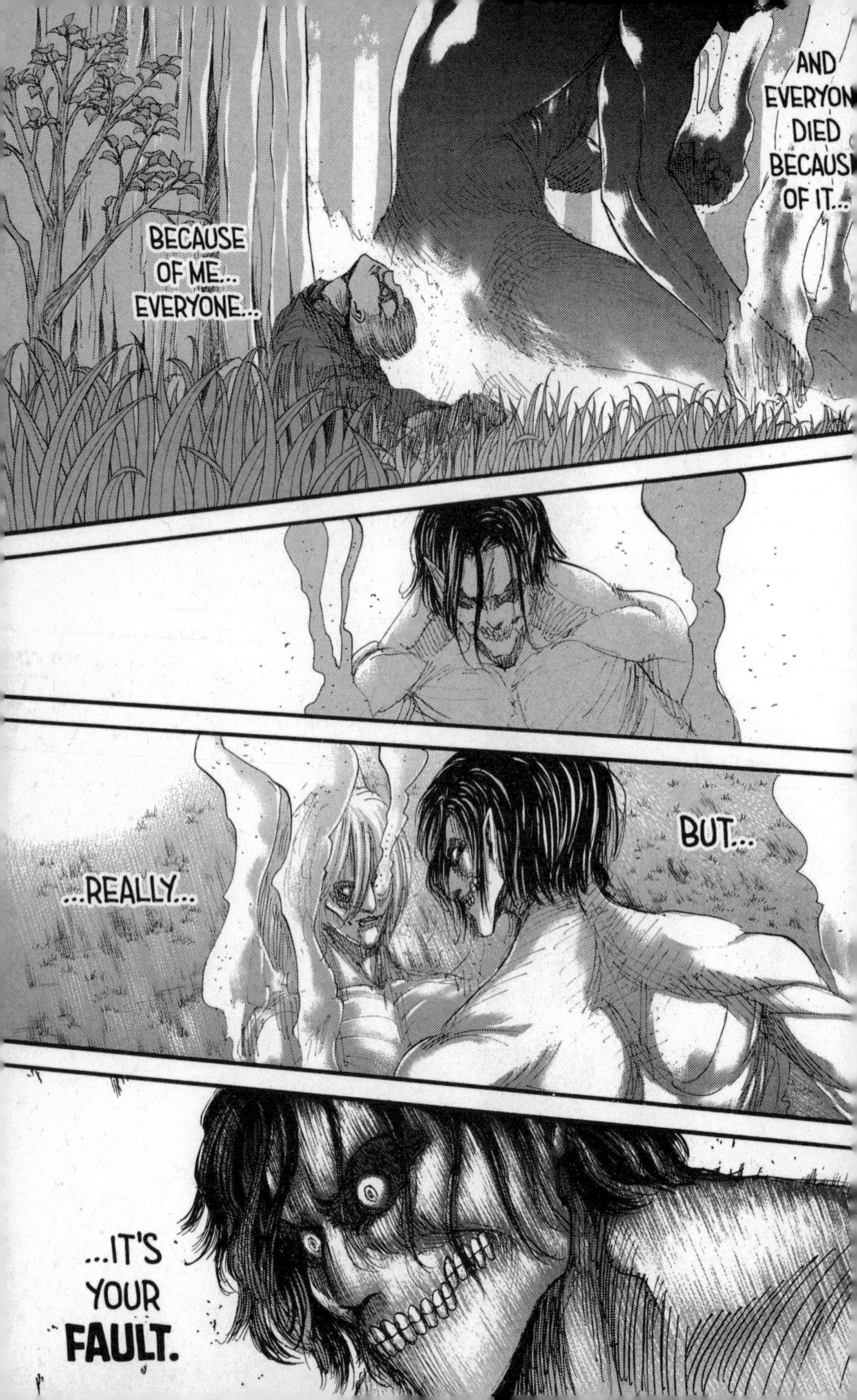
AND EVERYON DIED BECAUS OF IT...
BECAUSE OF ME... EVERYONE...
BUT...
...REALLY...
...IT'S YOUR FAULT.

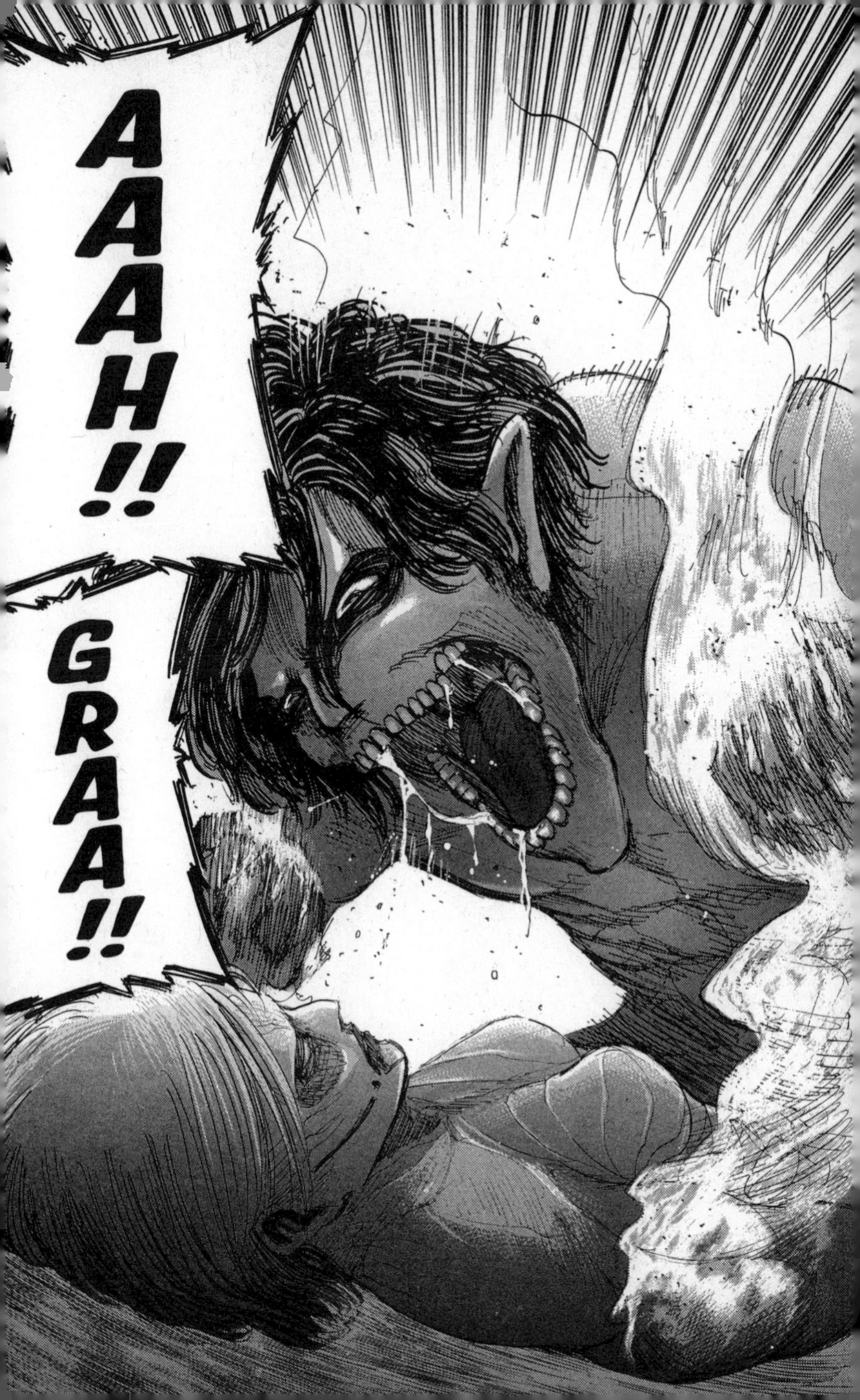

AAAH!!
GRAA!!

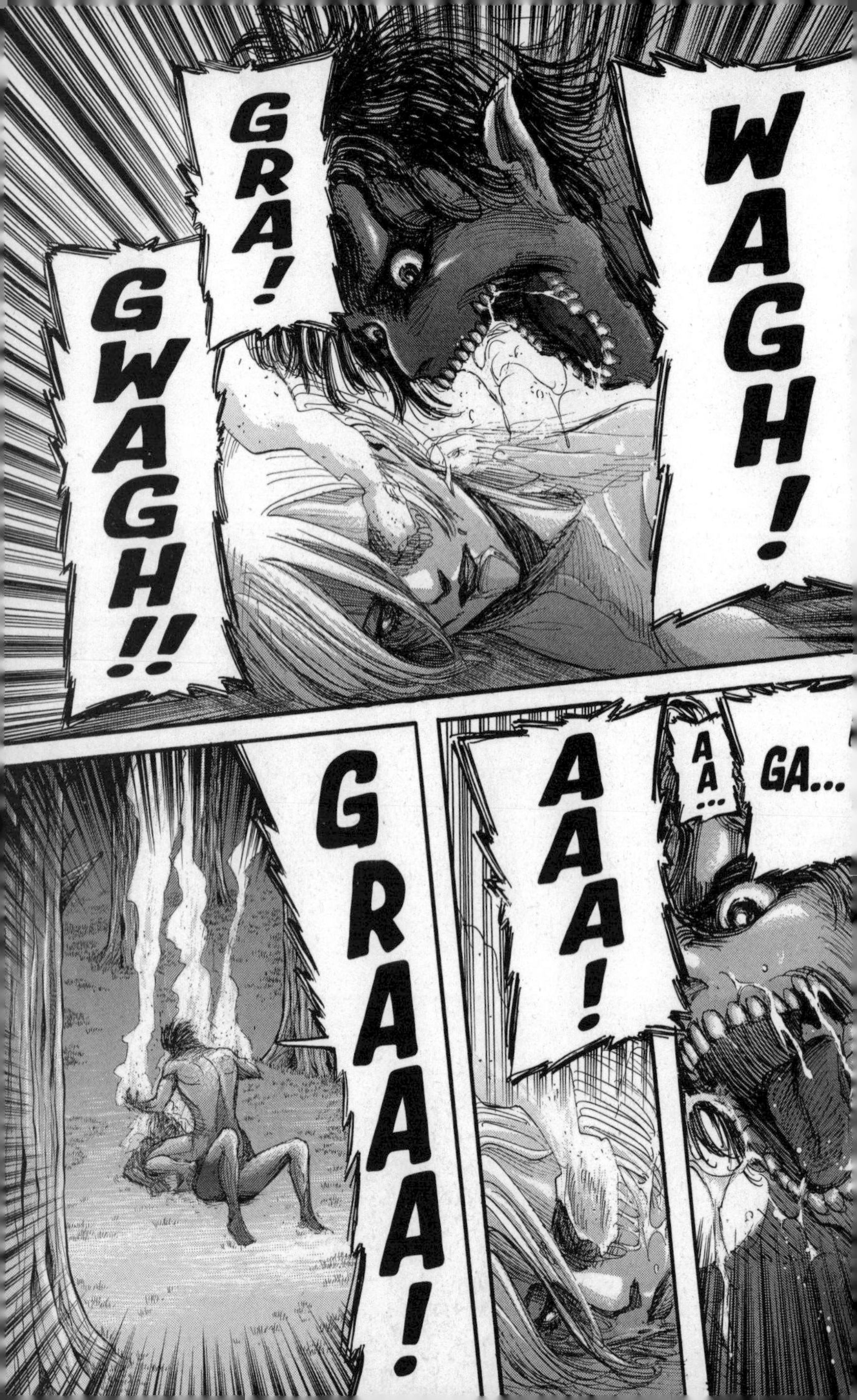
WAGH!
GRA!
GWAGH!!
GA...
AA...
AAA!
GRAAAA!

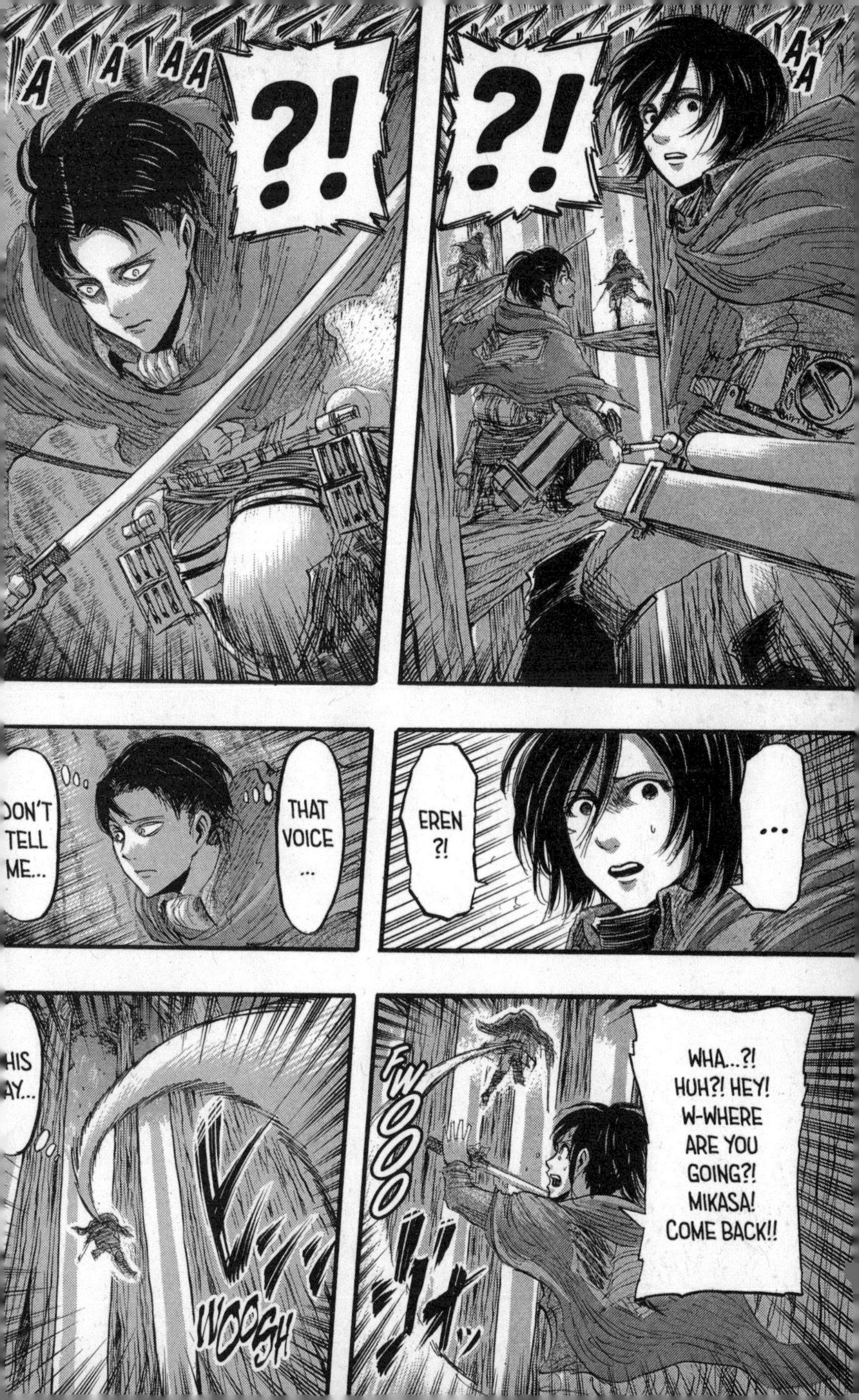

AAA
?!
AAAAA
?!
...
EREN ?!
THAT VOICE ...
DON'T TELL ME...
WHA...?! HUH?! HEY! W-WHERE ARE YOU GOING?! MIKASA! COME BACK!!
FWOOOO
HIS AY...
WOOSH

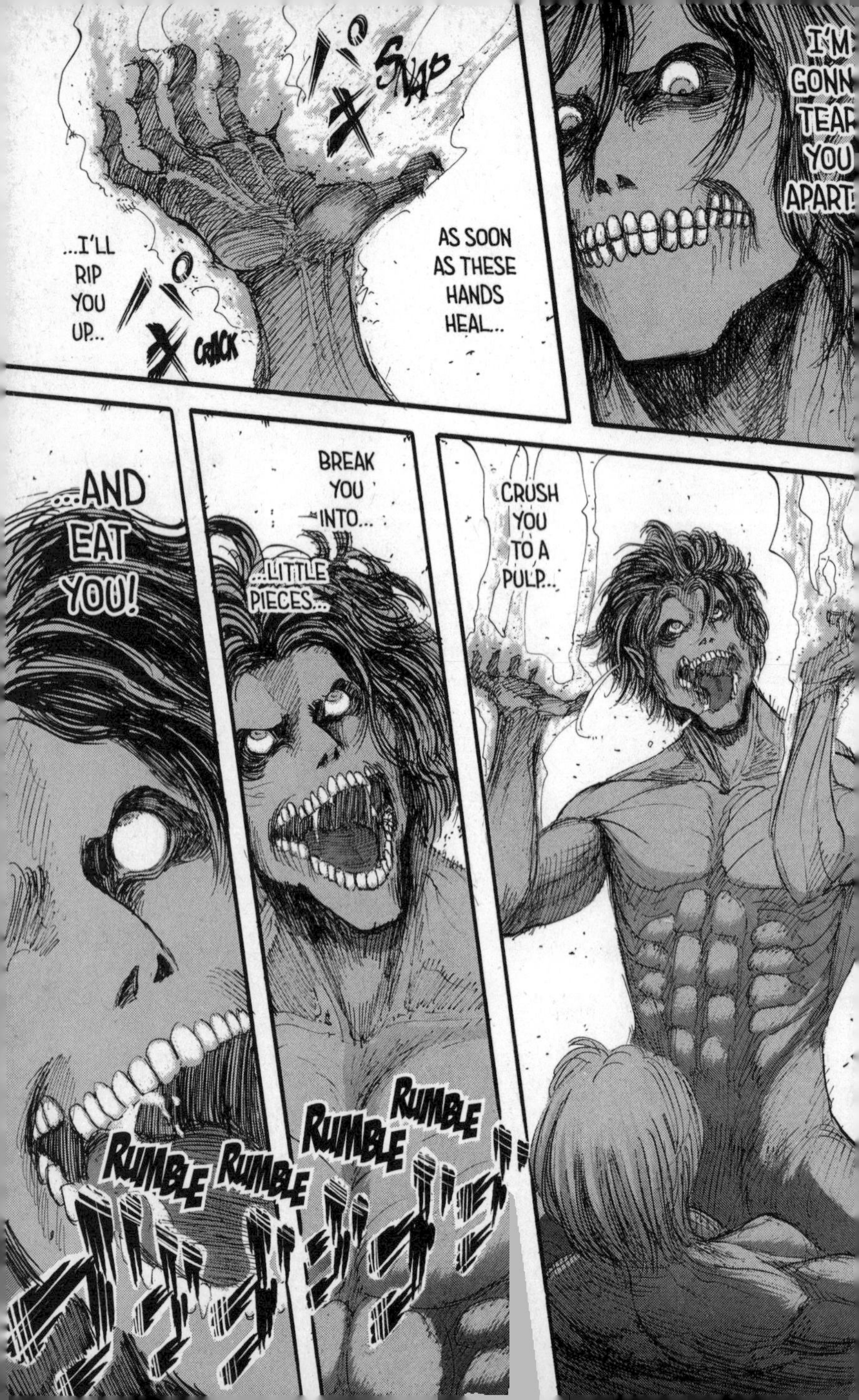
I'M GONN TEAR YOU APART
SNAP
AS SOON AS THESE HANDS HEAL...
...I'LL RIP YOU UP...
CRACK
CRUSH YOU TO A PULP...
BREAK YOU INTO...
...LITTLE PIECES...
...AND EAT YOU!
RUMBLE
RUMBLE
RUMBLE
RUMBLE

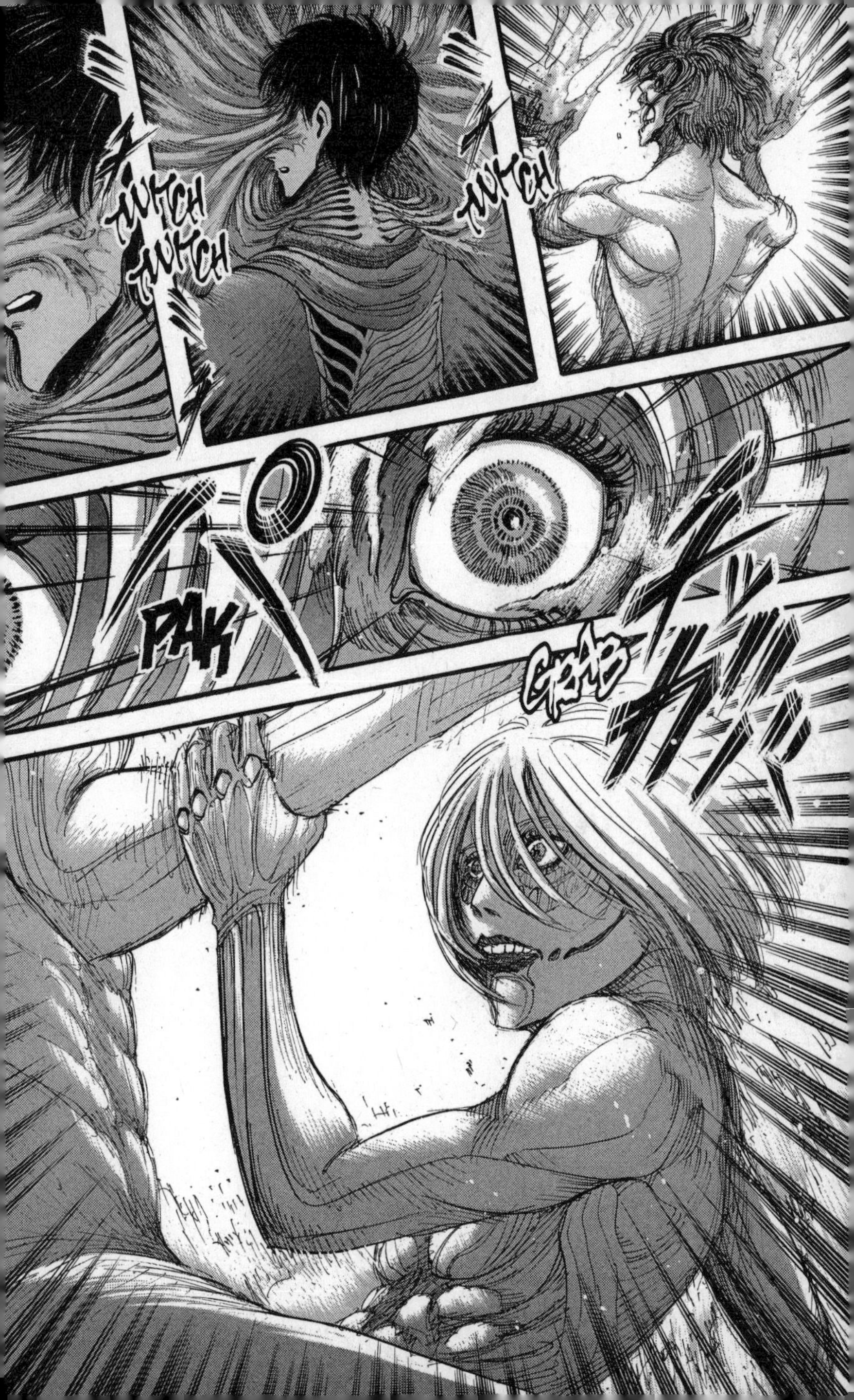
TWITCH
TWITCH
TWITCH
PAK
GRAB

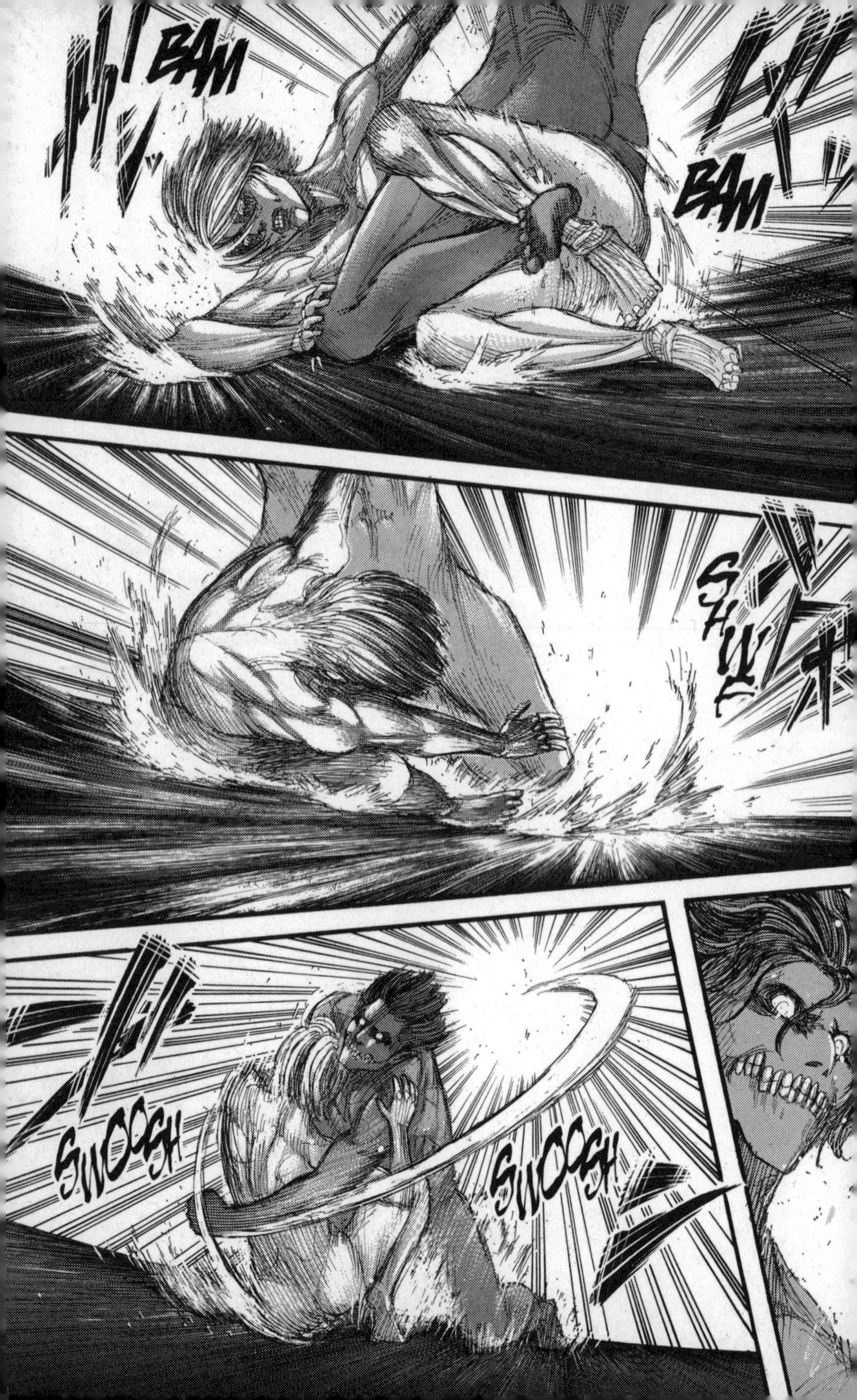
BAM
BAM
SHWF
SWOOSH
SWOOSH

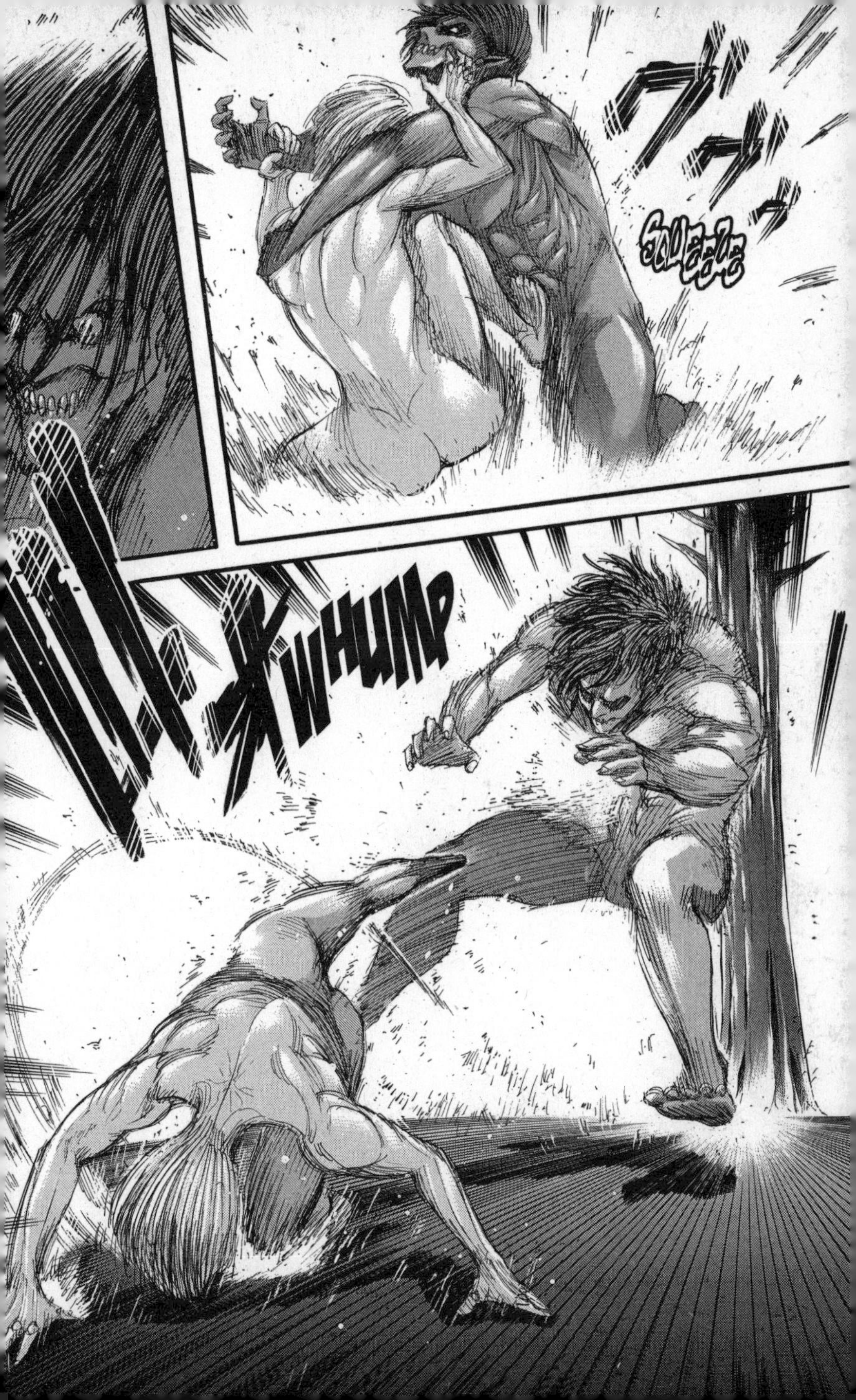
SQUEEZE
WHUMP

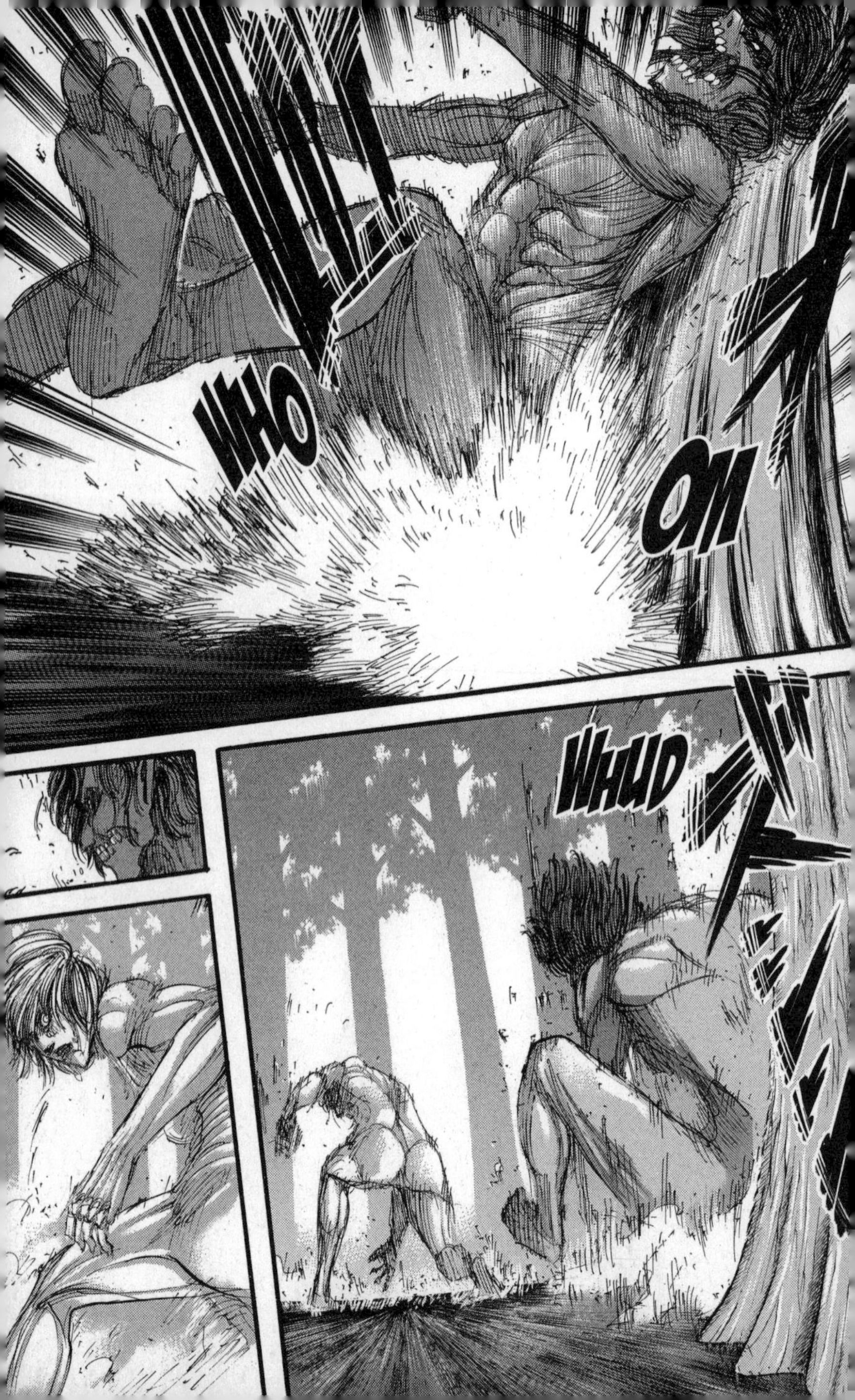
WHO
OM
WHUD

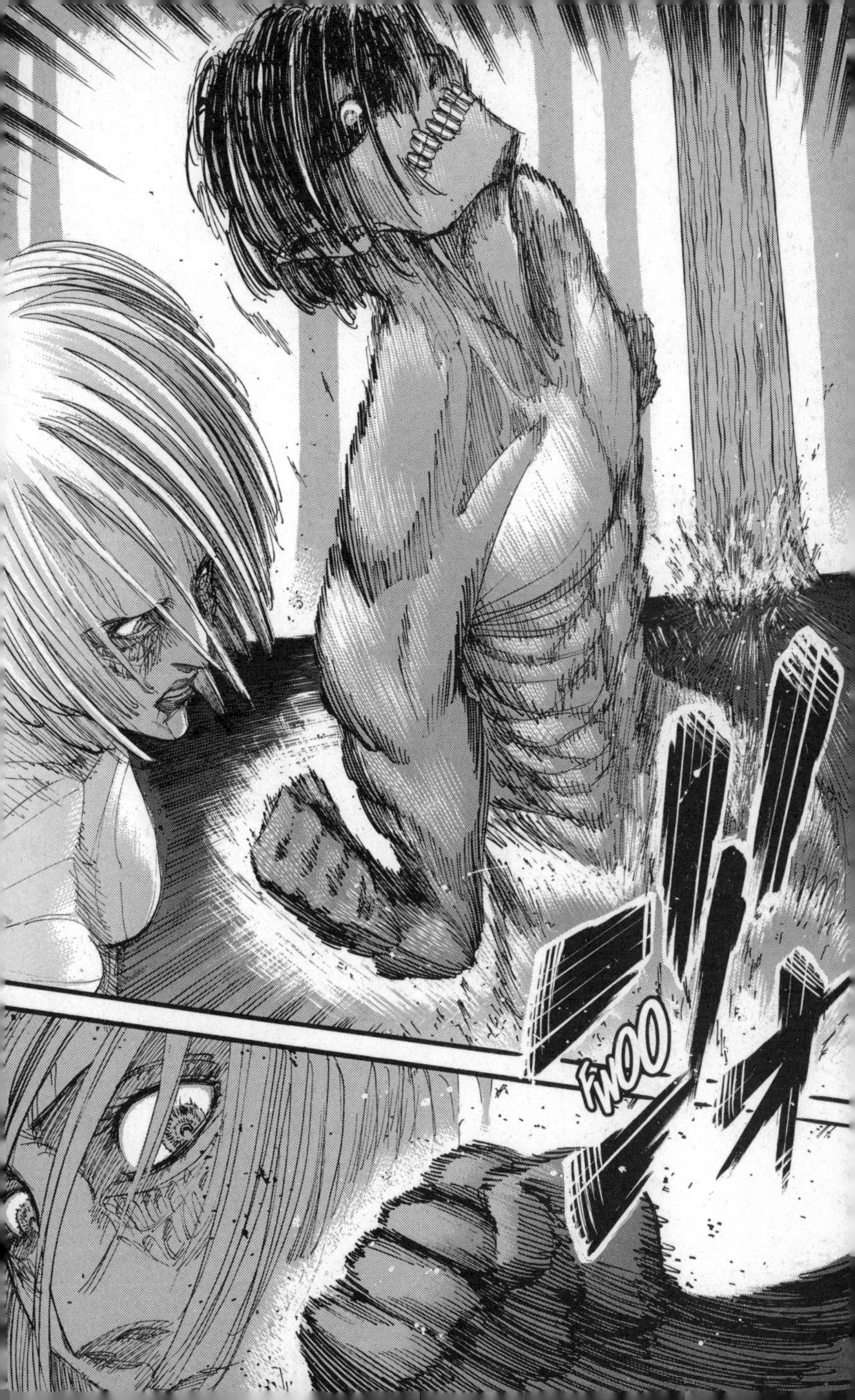
FWOO

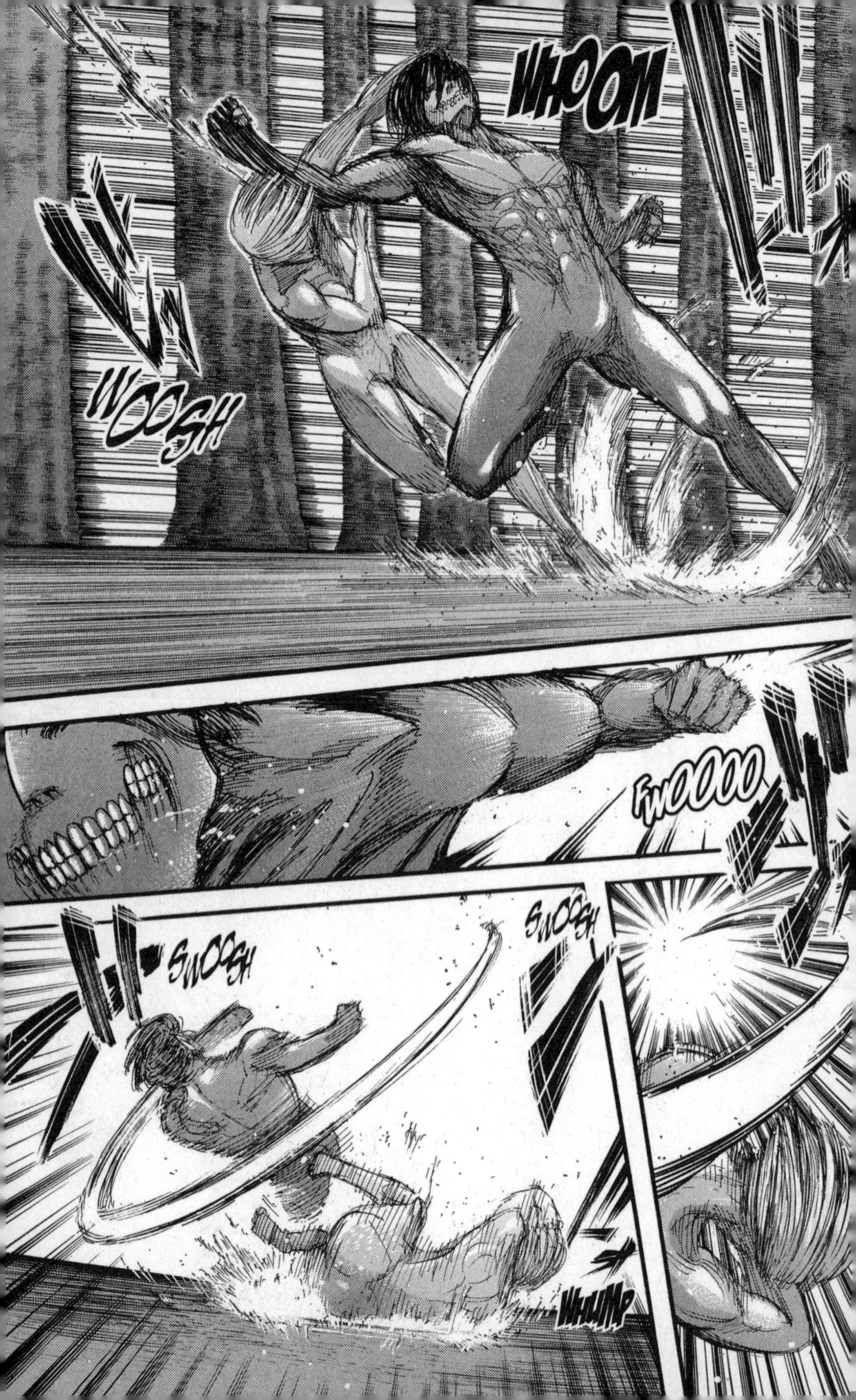
WHOOM
WOOSH
FWOOOO
SWOOSH
SWOOSH
WHUMP

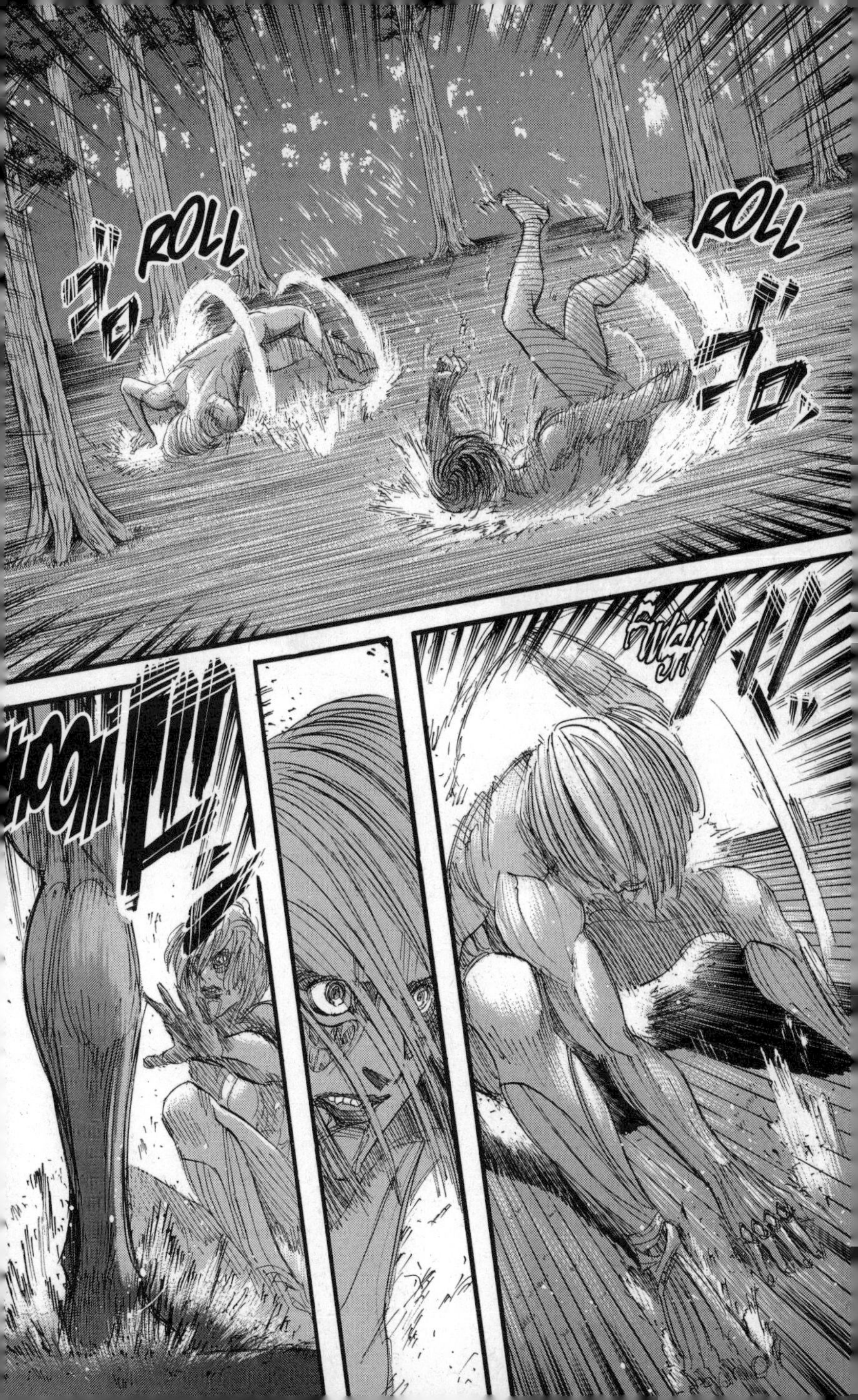
ROLL
ゴロ
ROLL
ゴロ
HOOM

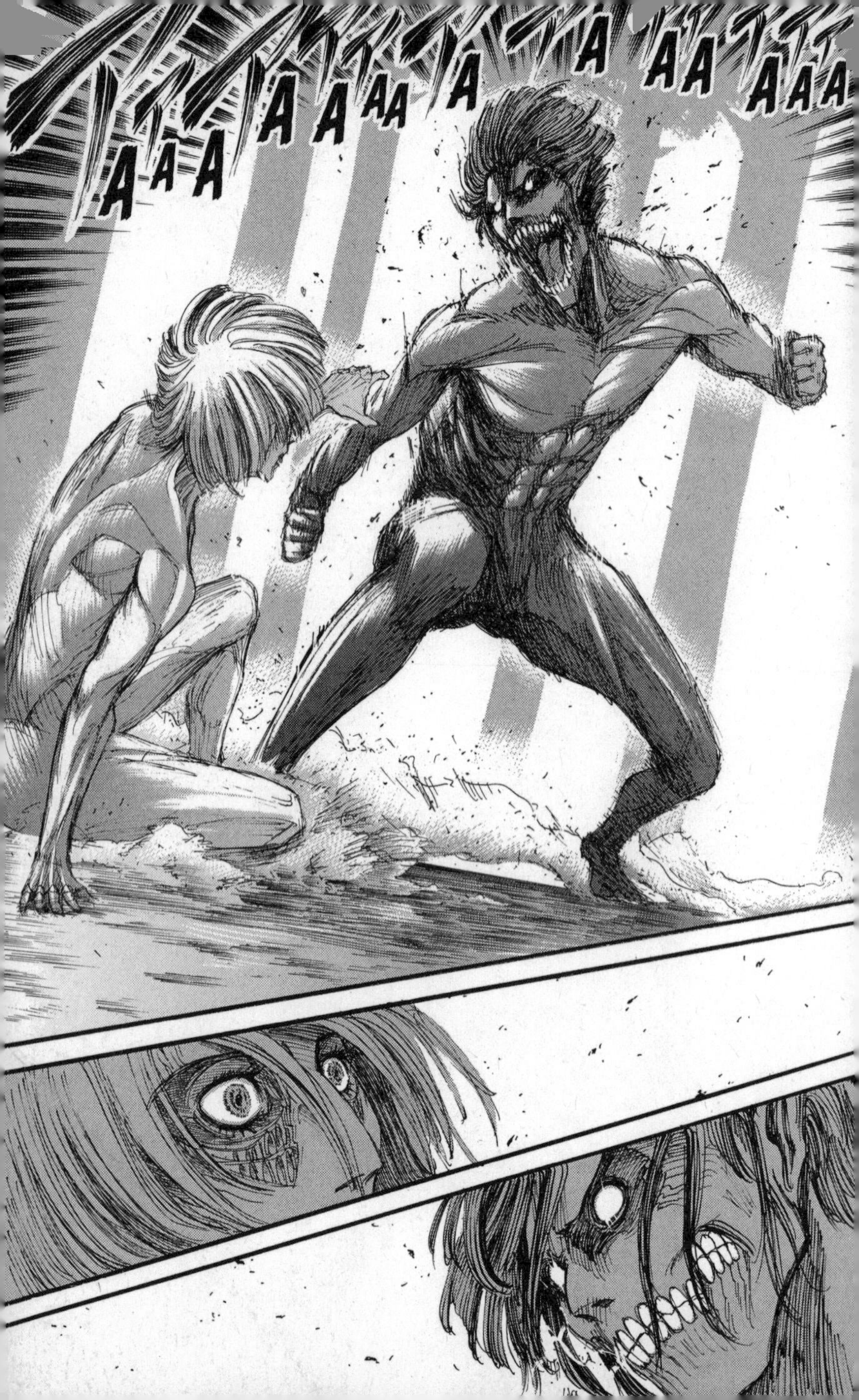
AAAAAAAAAAAAAA

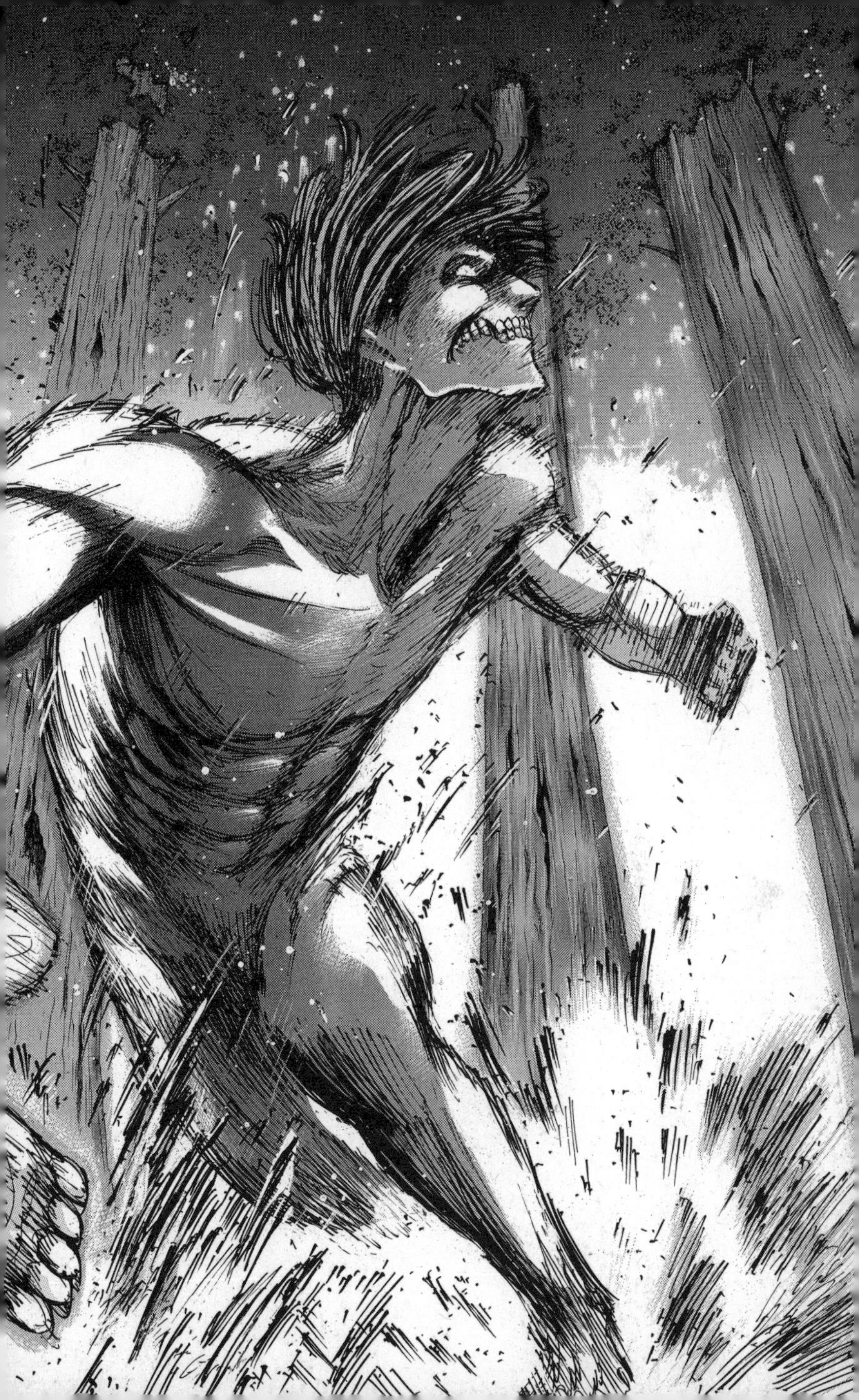

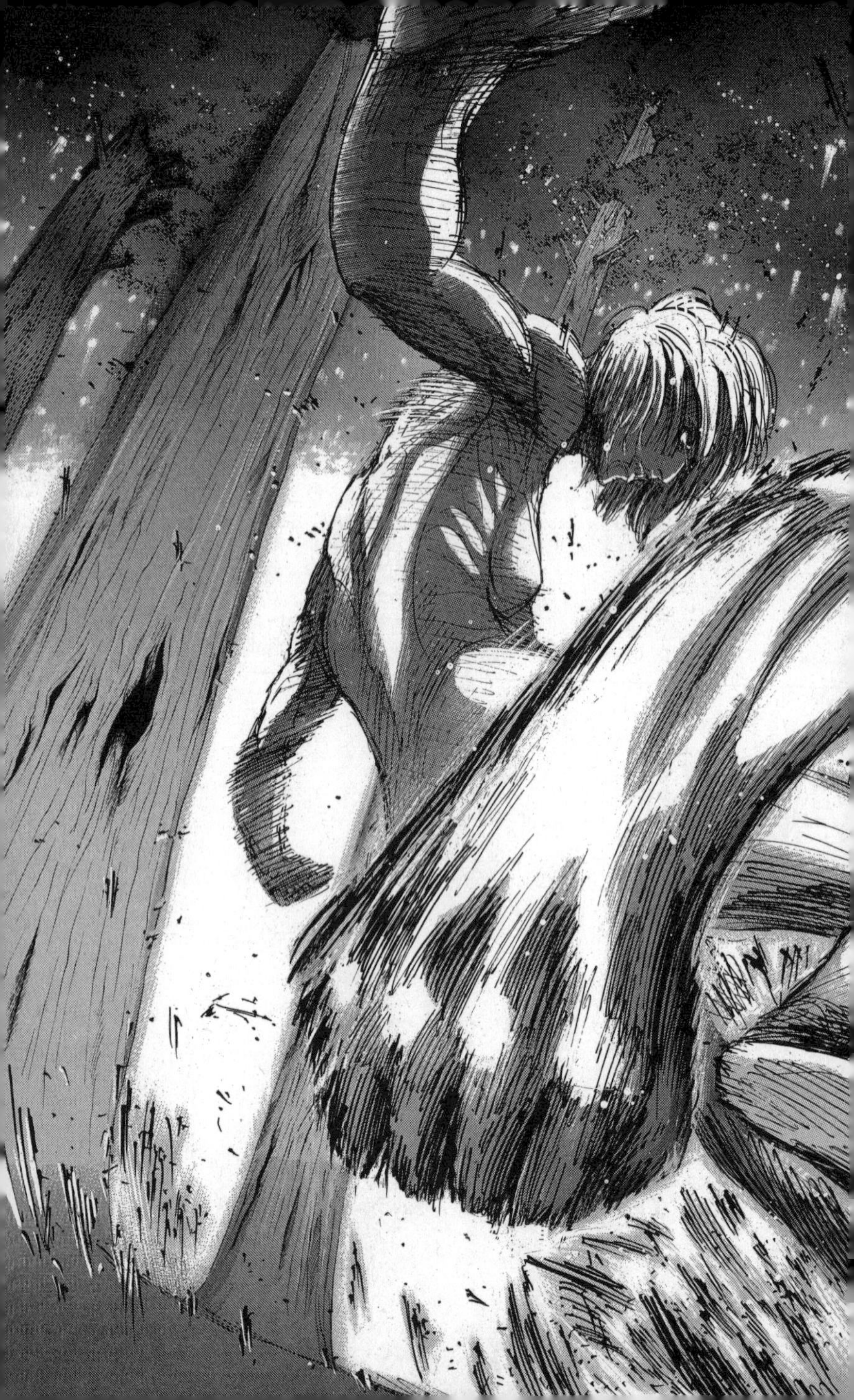

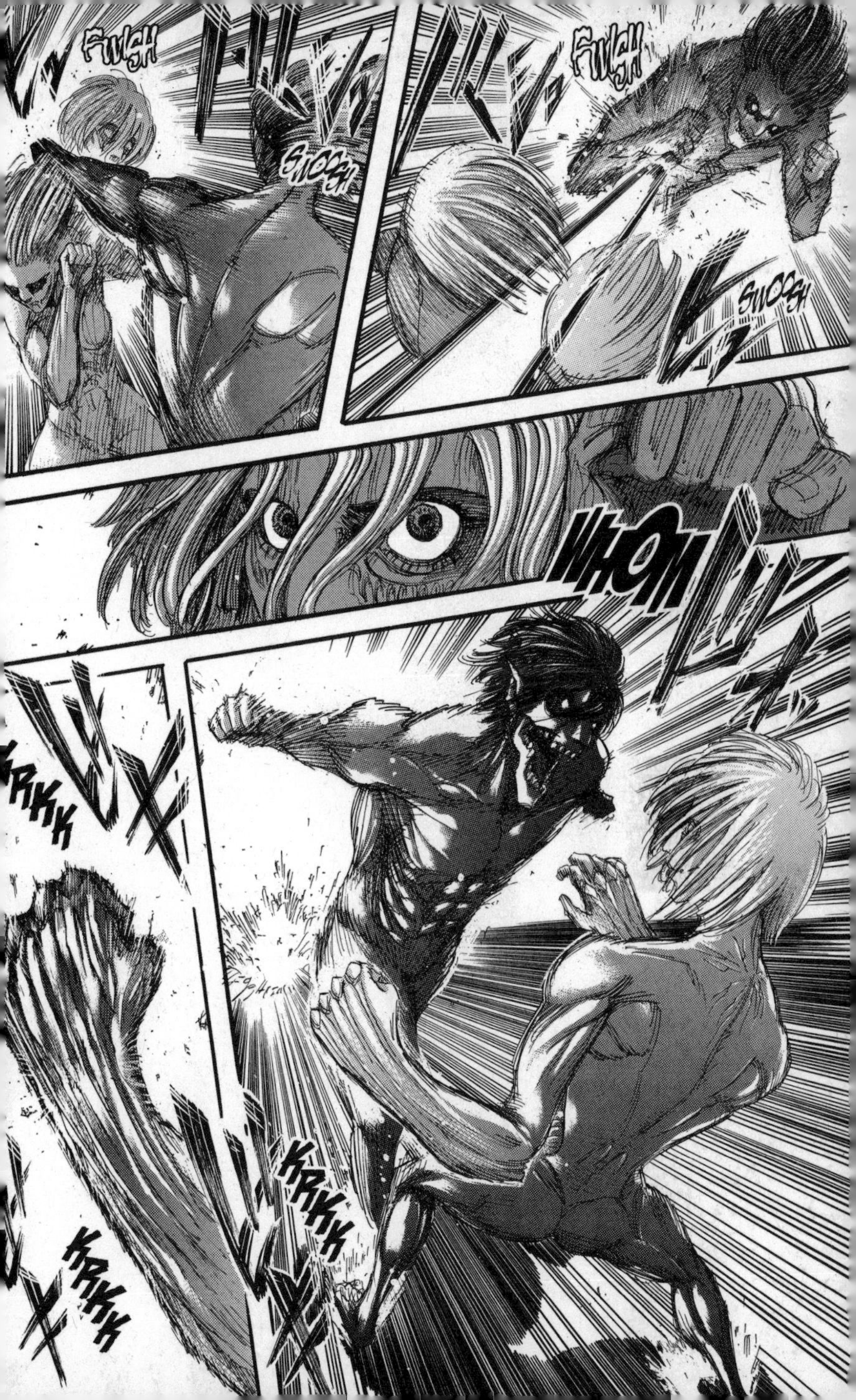
FWISH
SWOOSH
FWISH
SWOOSH
WHON
KRKKK
KRKKK
KRKKK

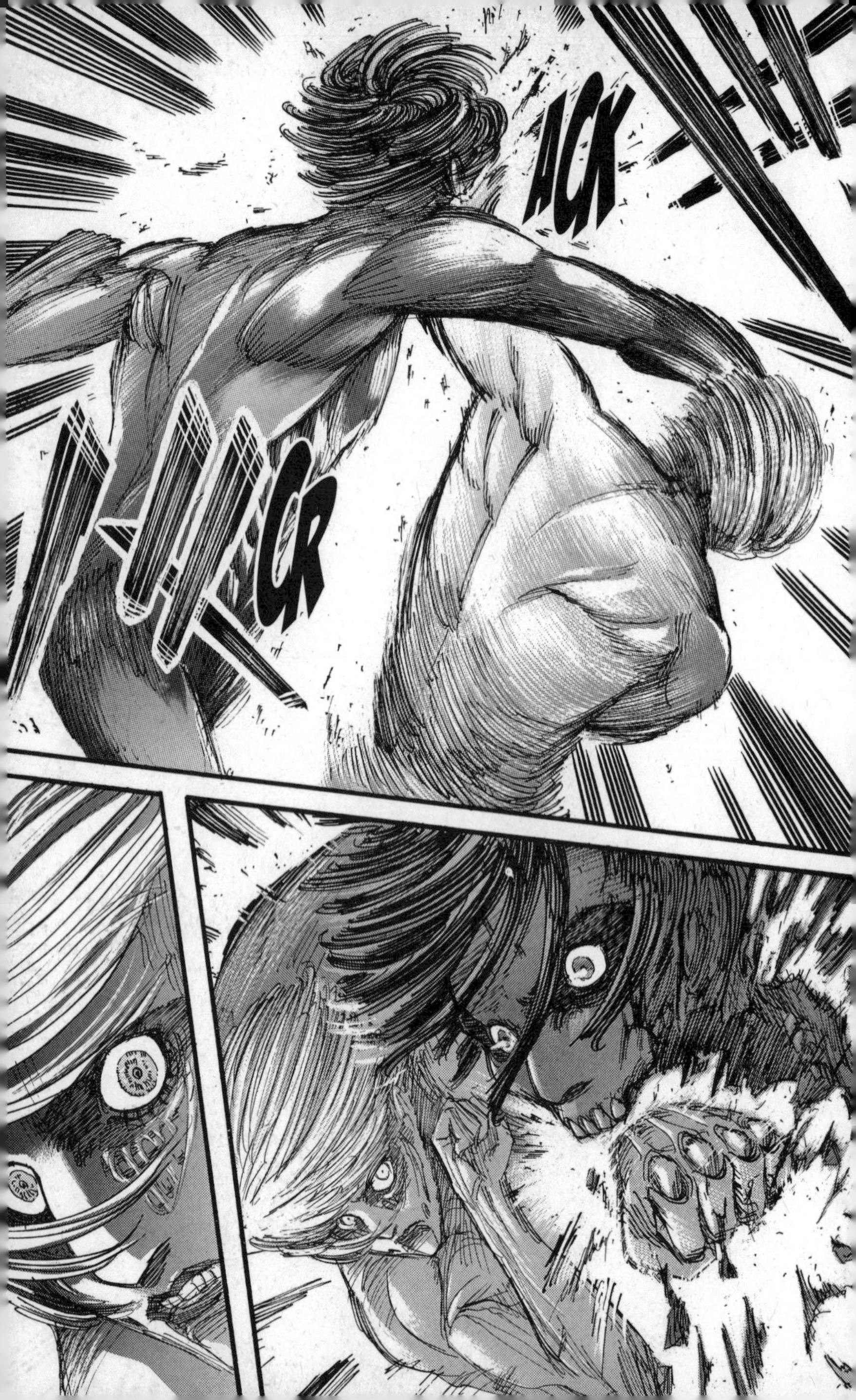
ACK
GR

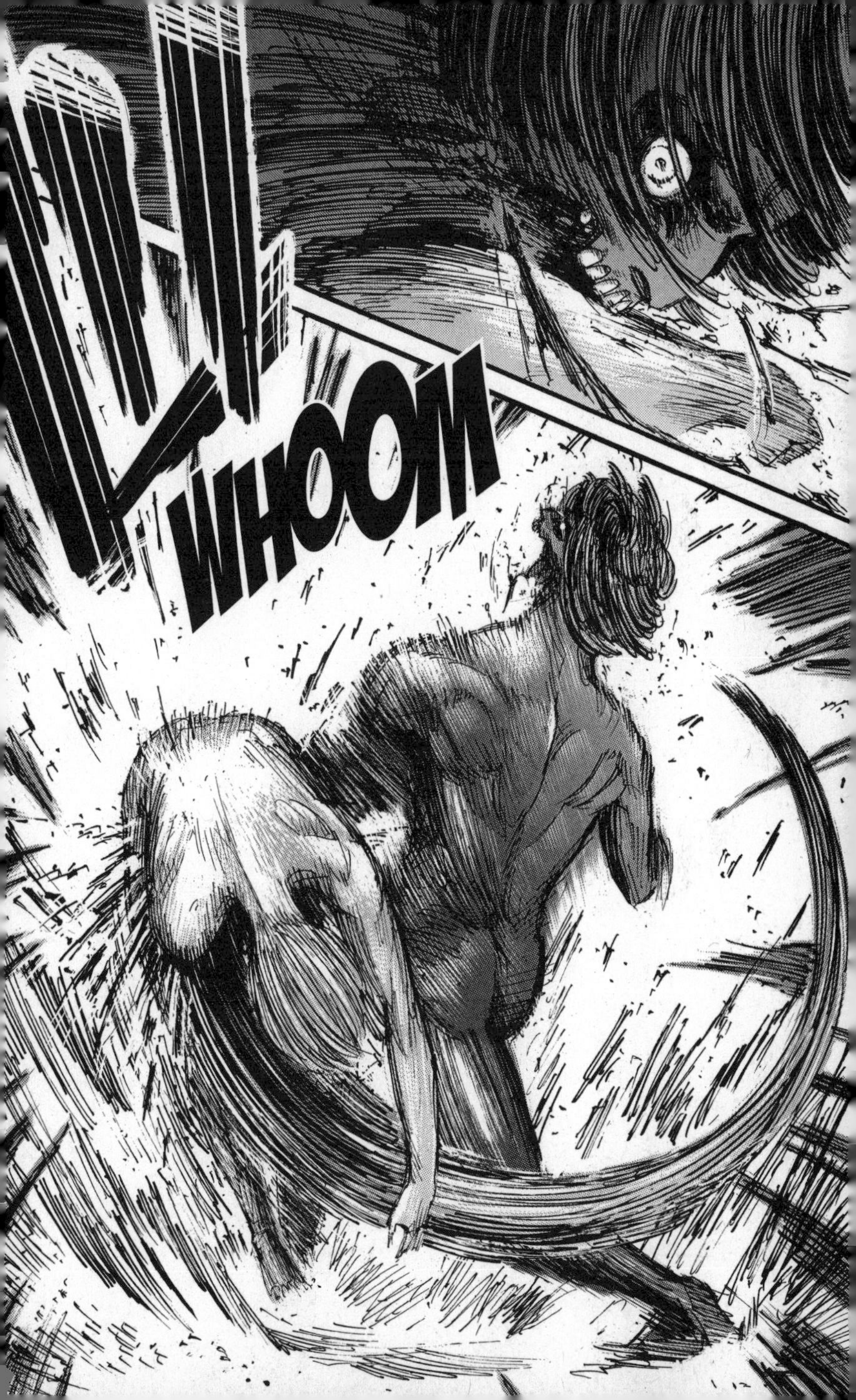
WHOOM

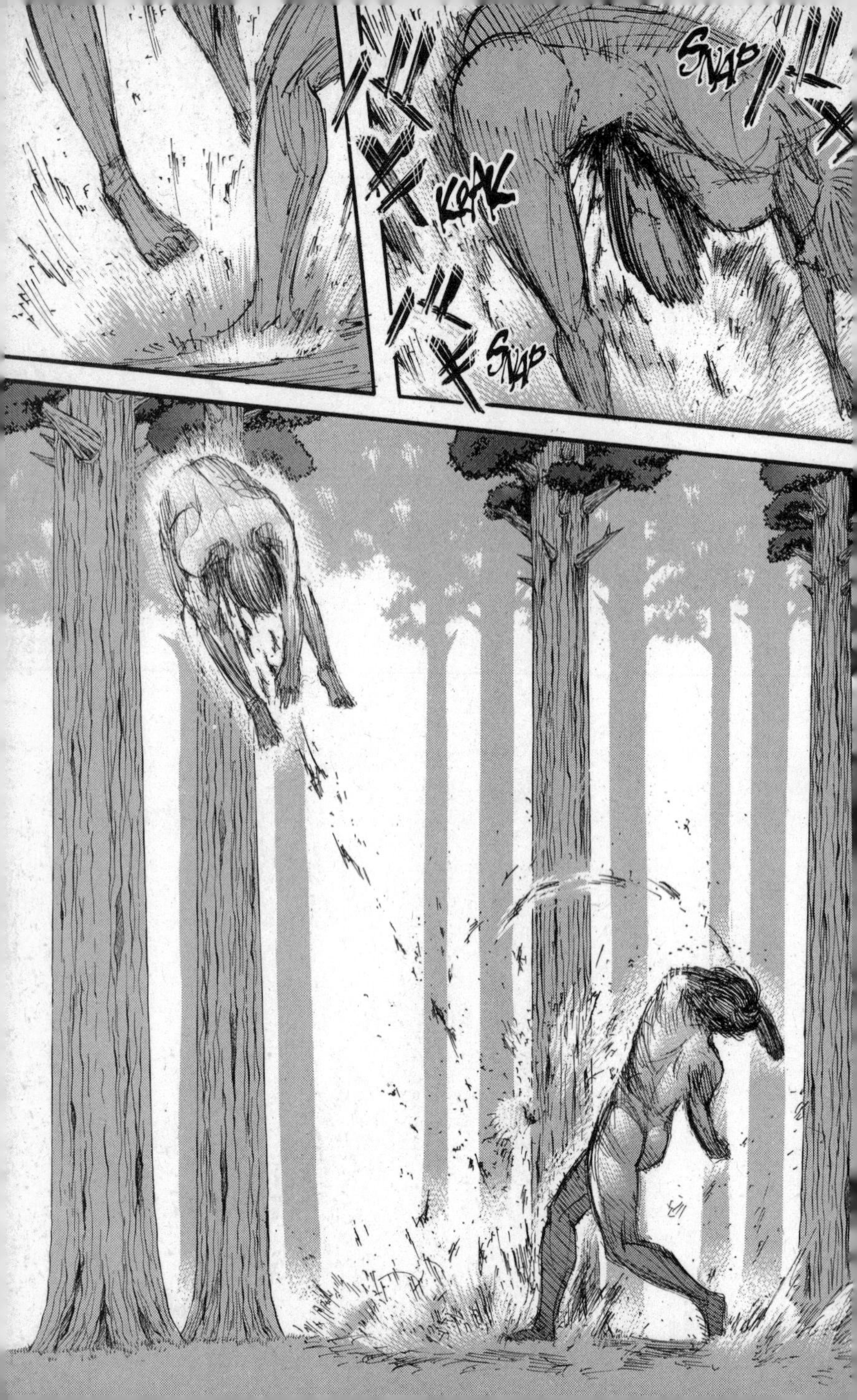
SNAP
KRAK
SNAP

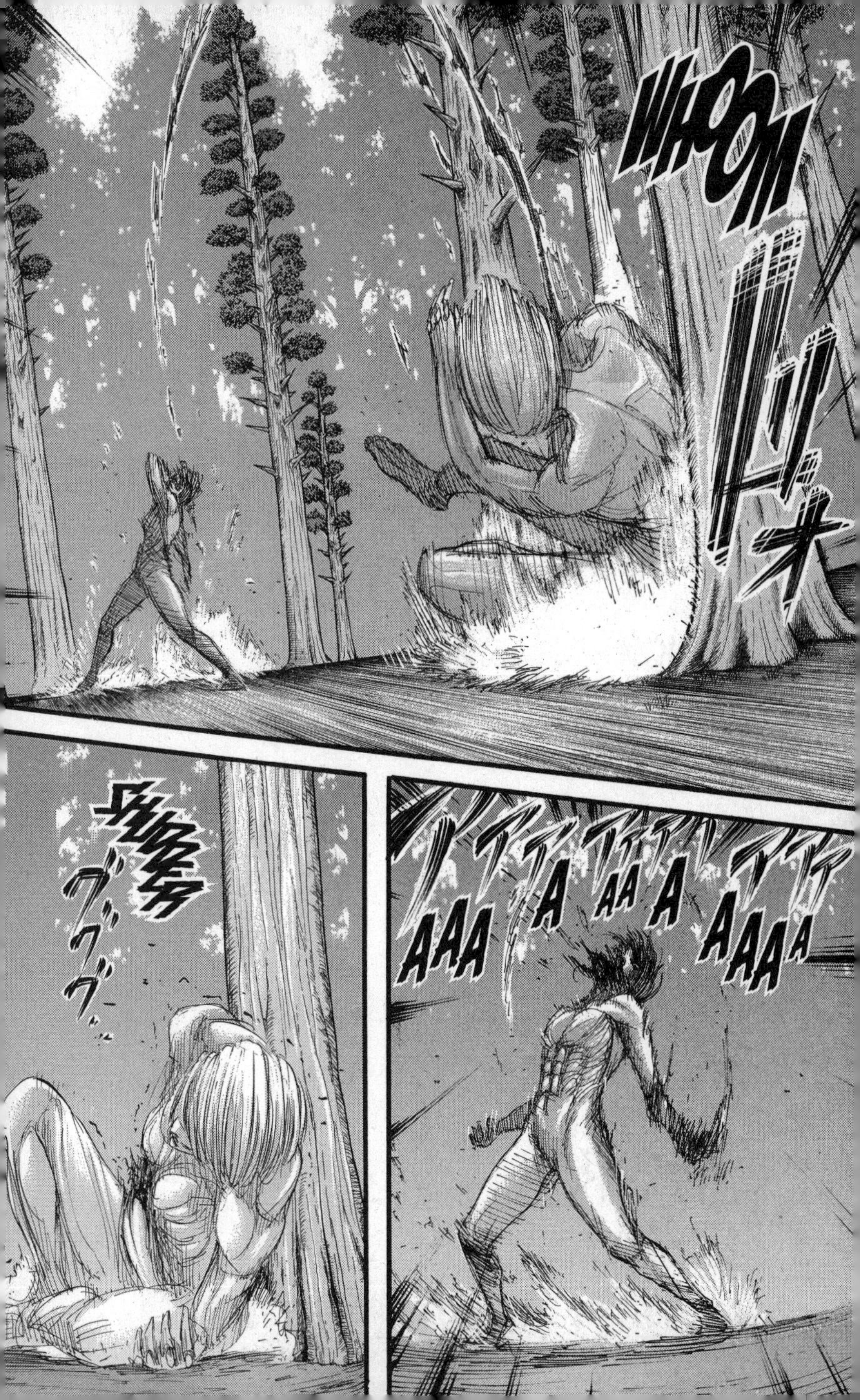
WHOOM
グググ

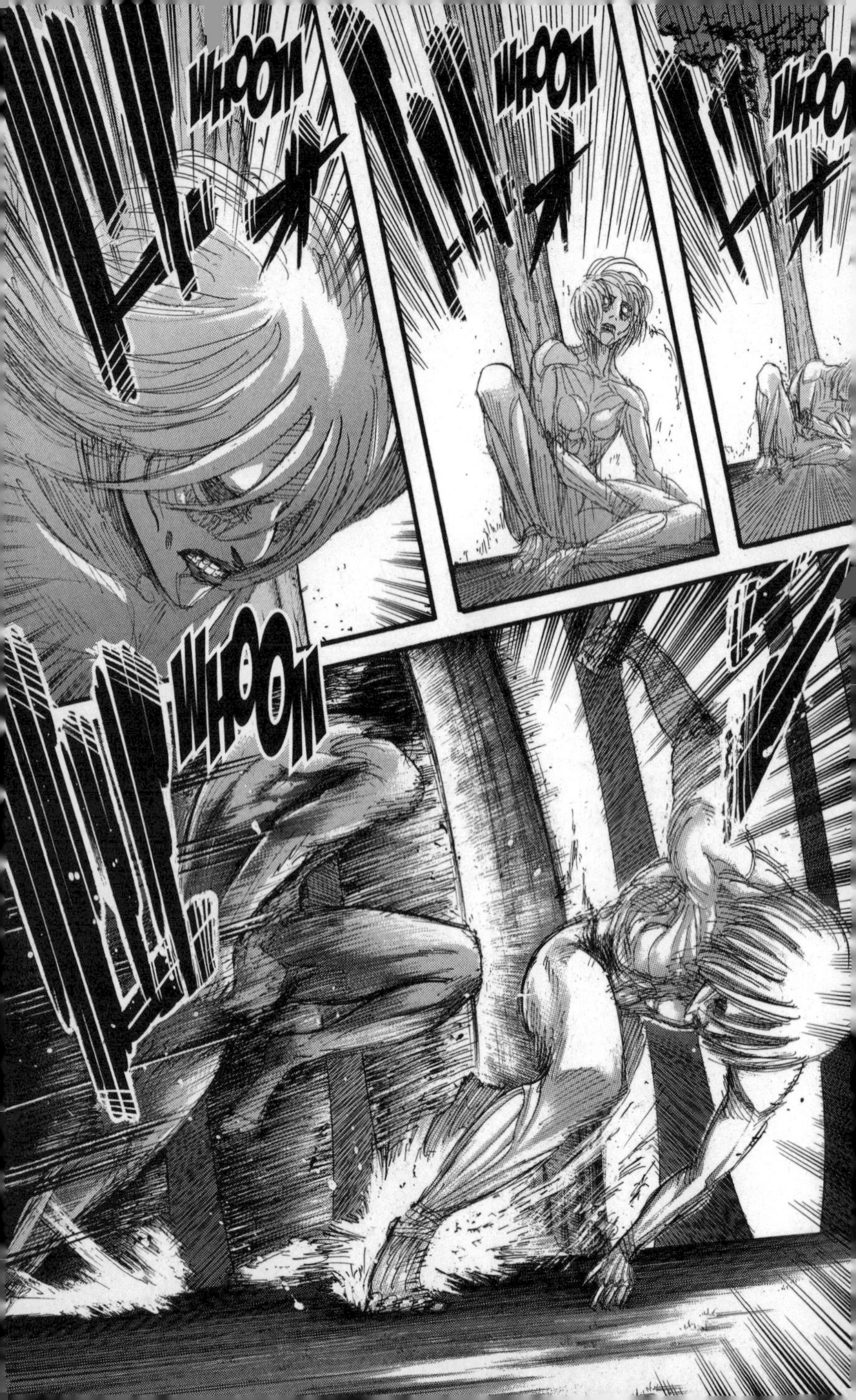
WHOO
WHOOM
WHOOM
WHOOM

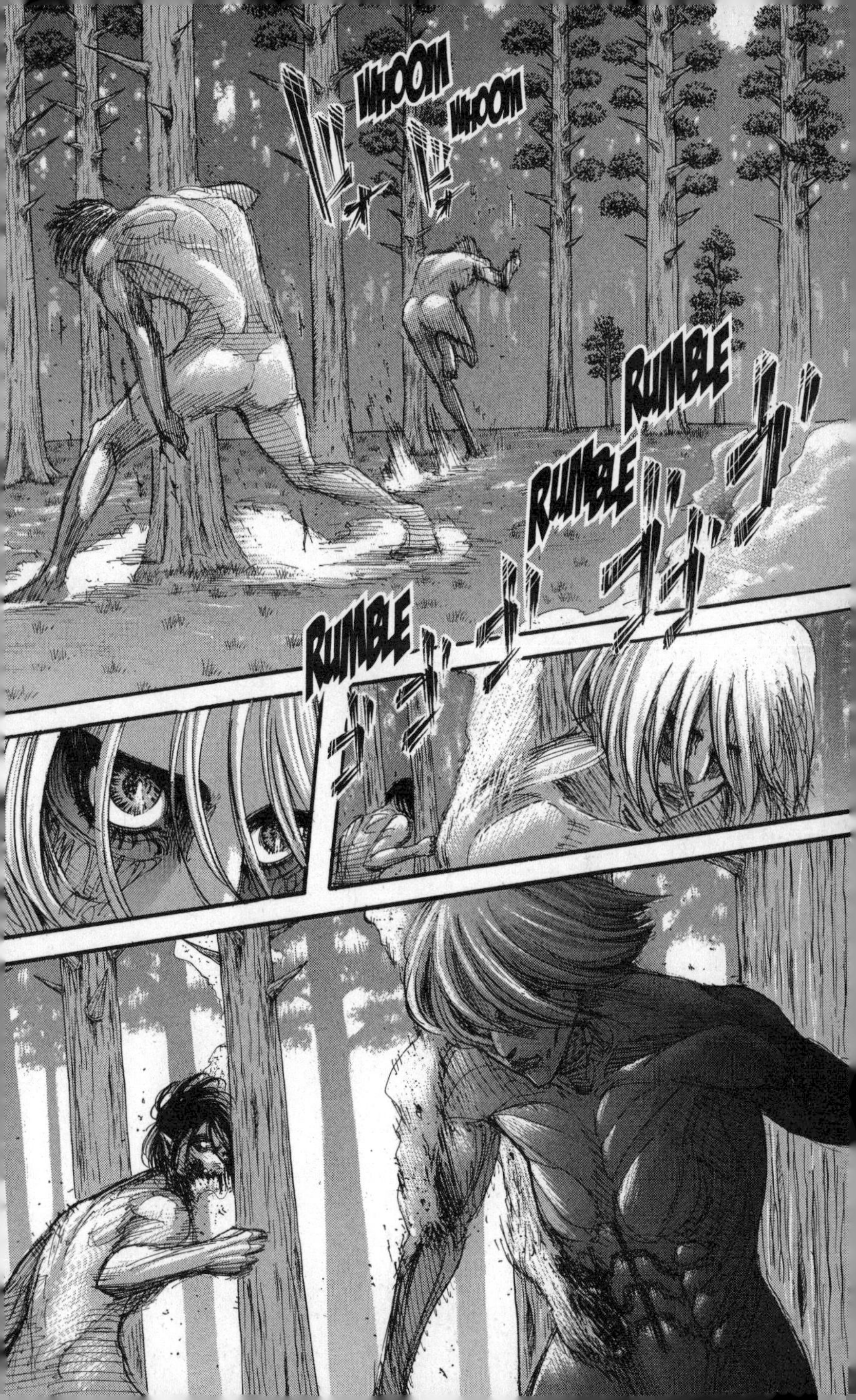
WHOOM
WHOOM
RUMBLE
RUMBLE
RUMBLE

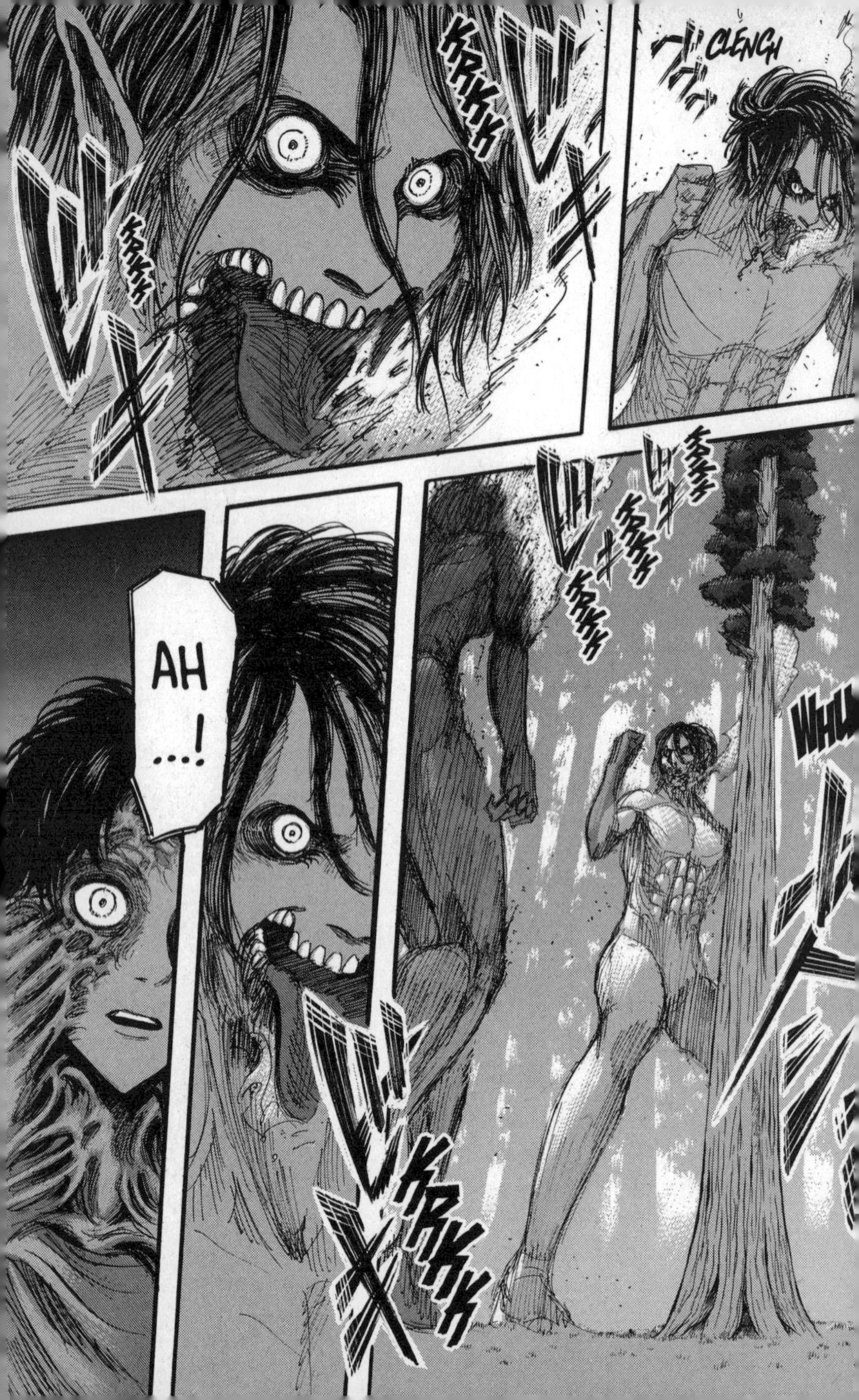
CLENCH
KRKKK
WHU
KRKKK
AH ...!

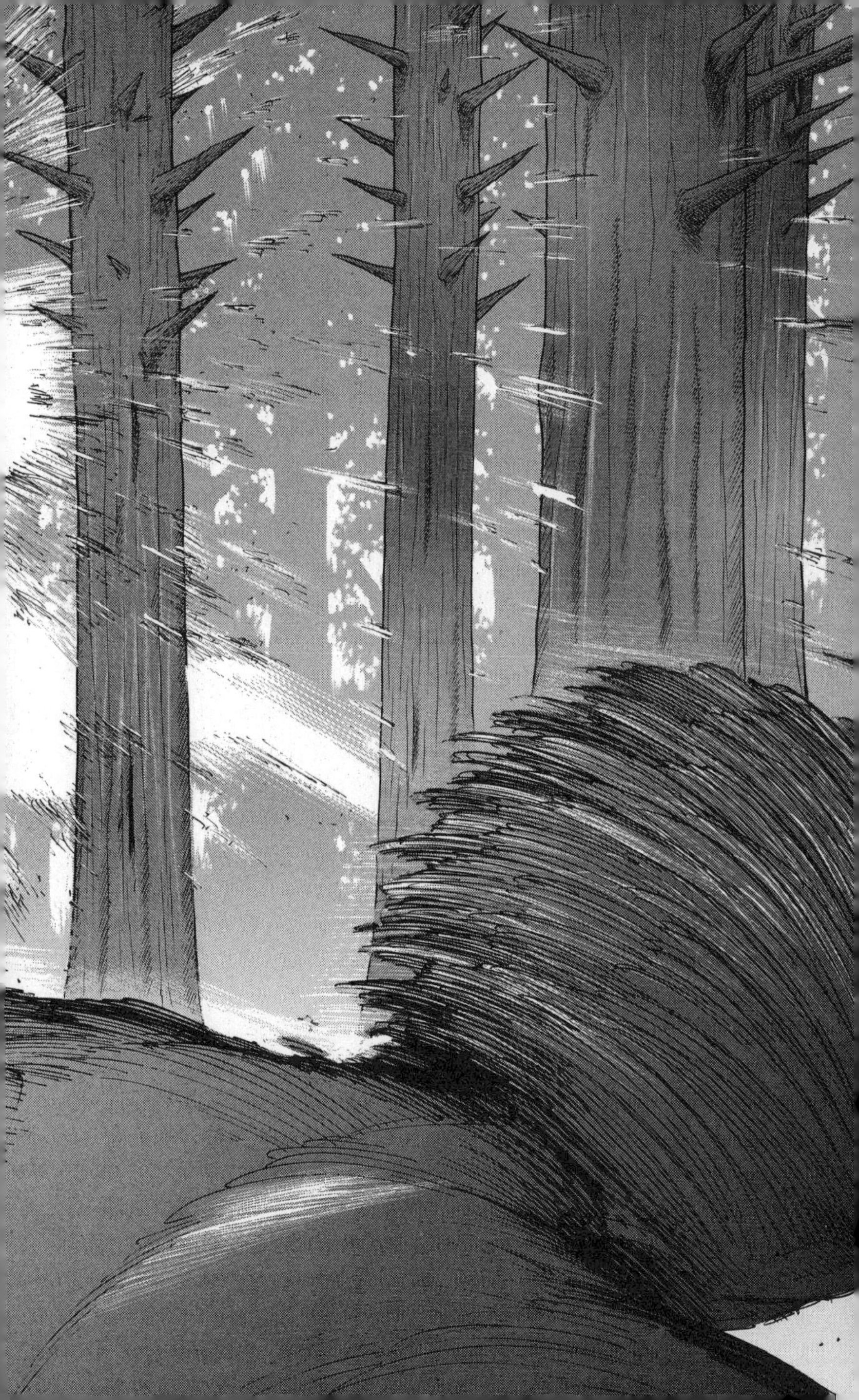

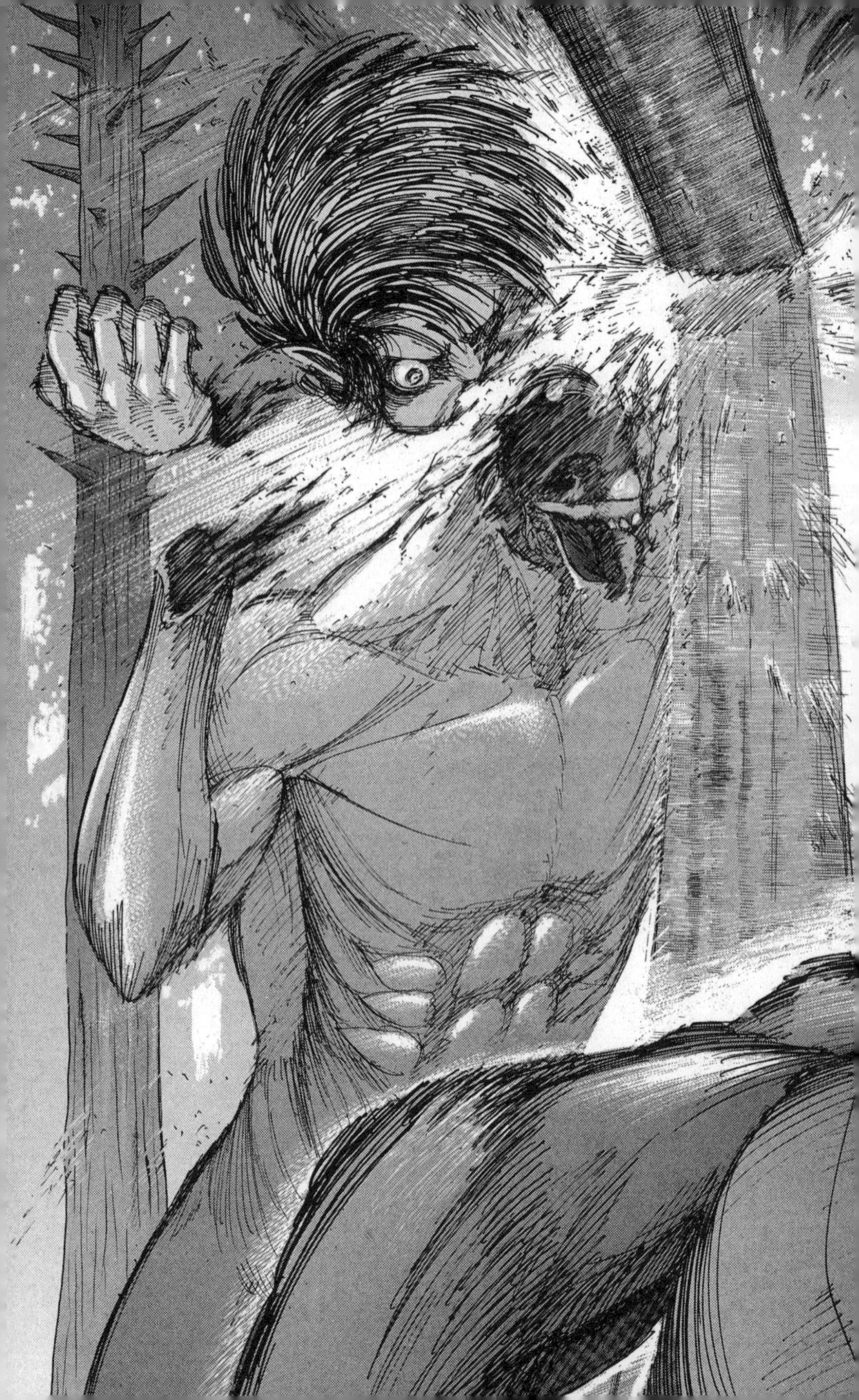

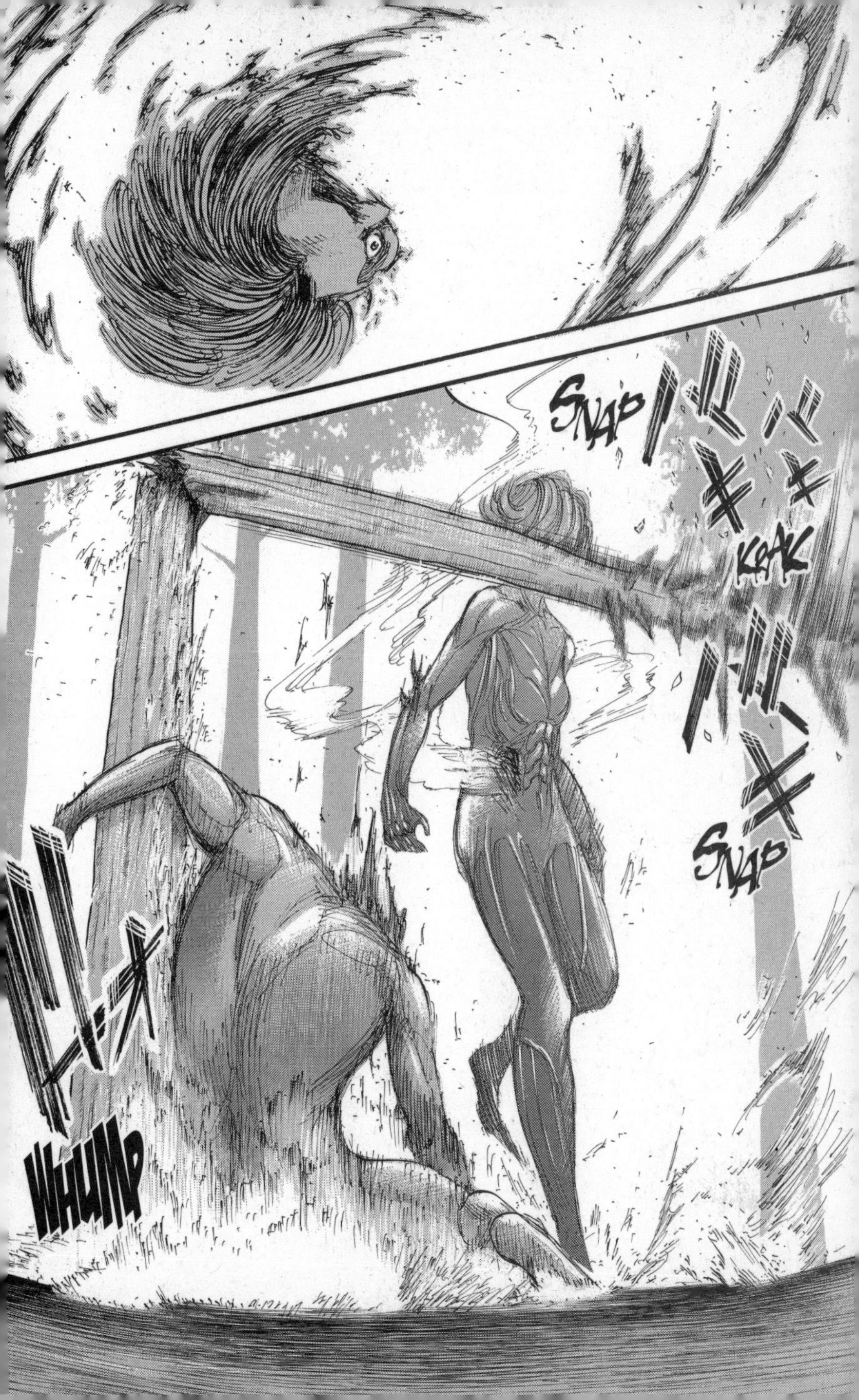
SNAP
KRAK
SNAP
WHUMP

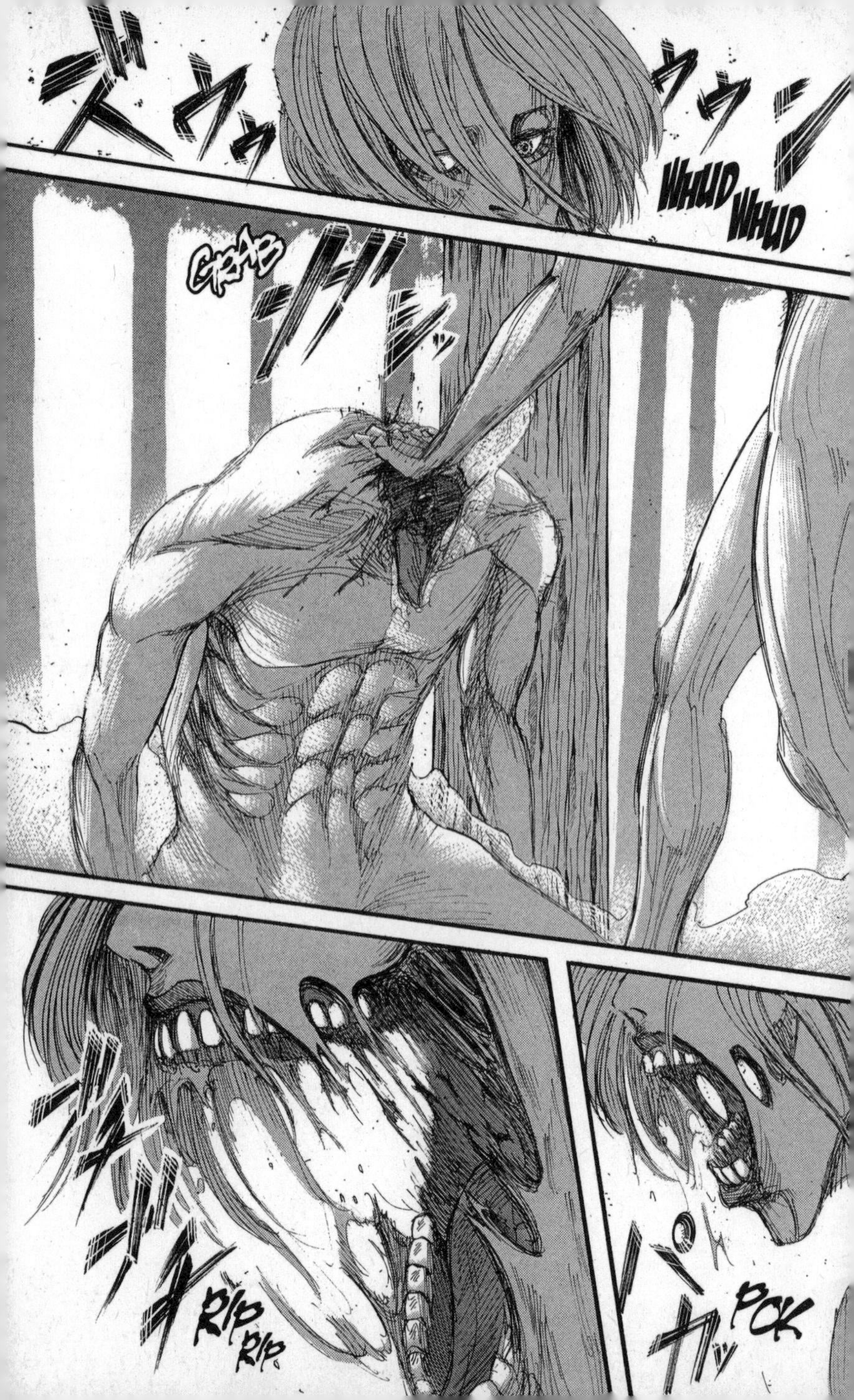
WHUD WHUD
GRAB
POK
RIP RIP

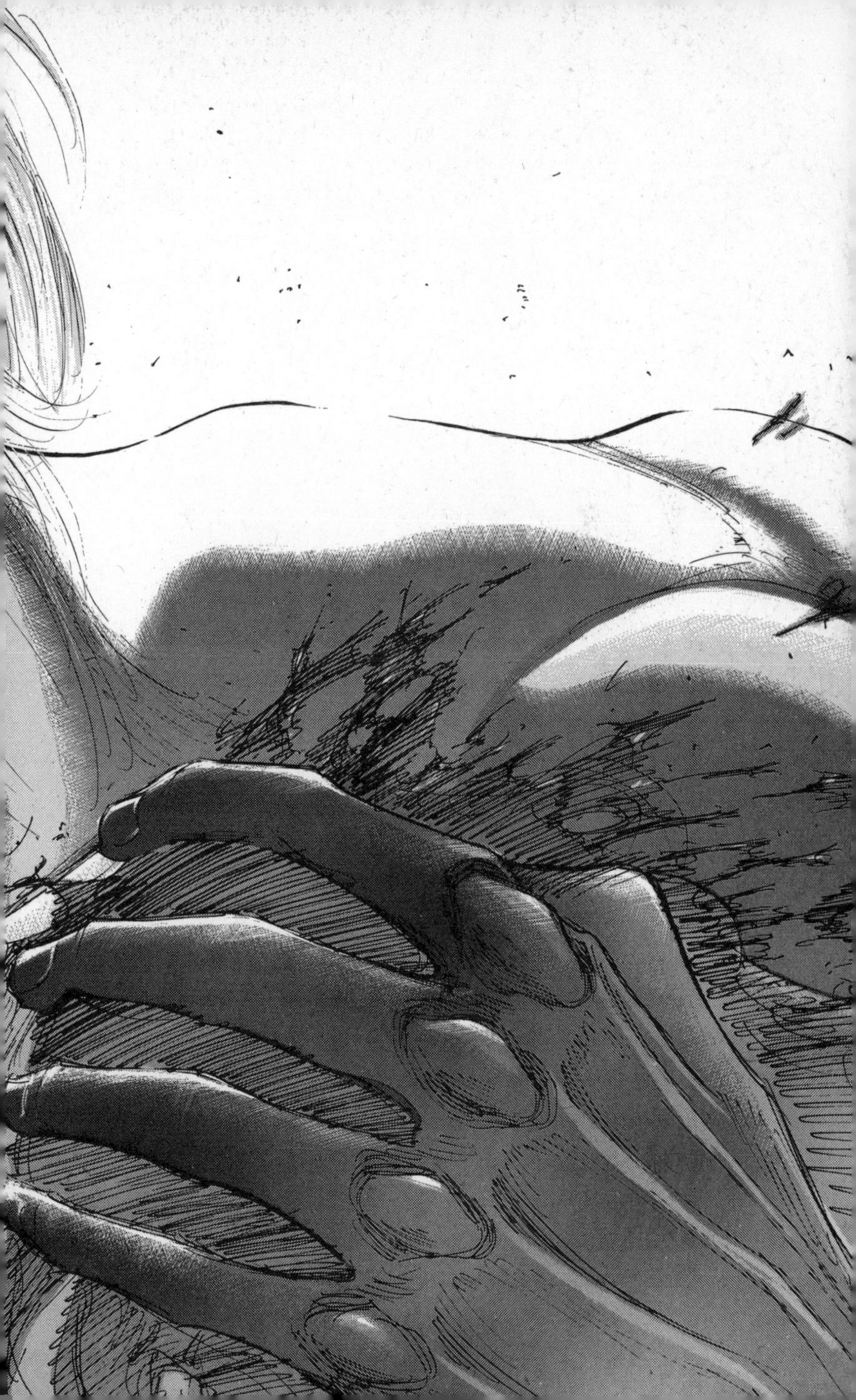

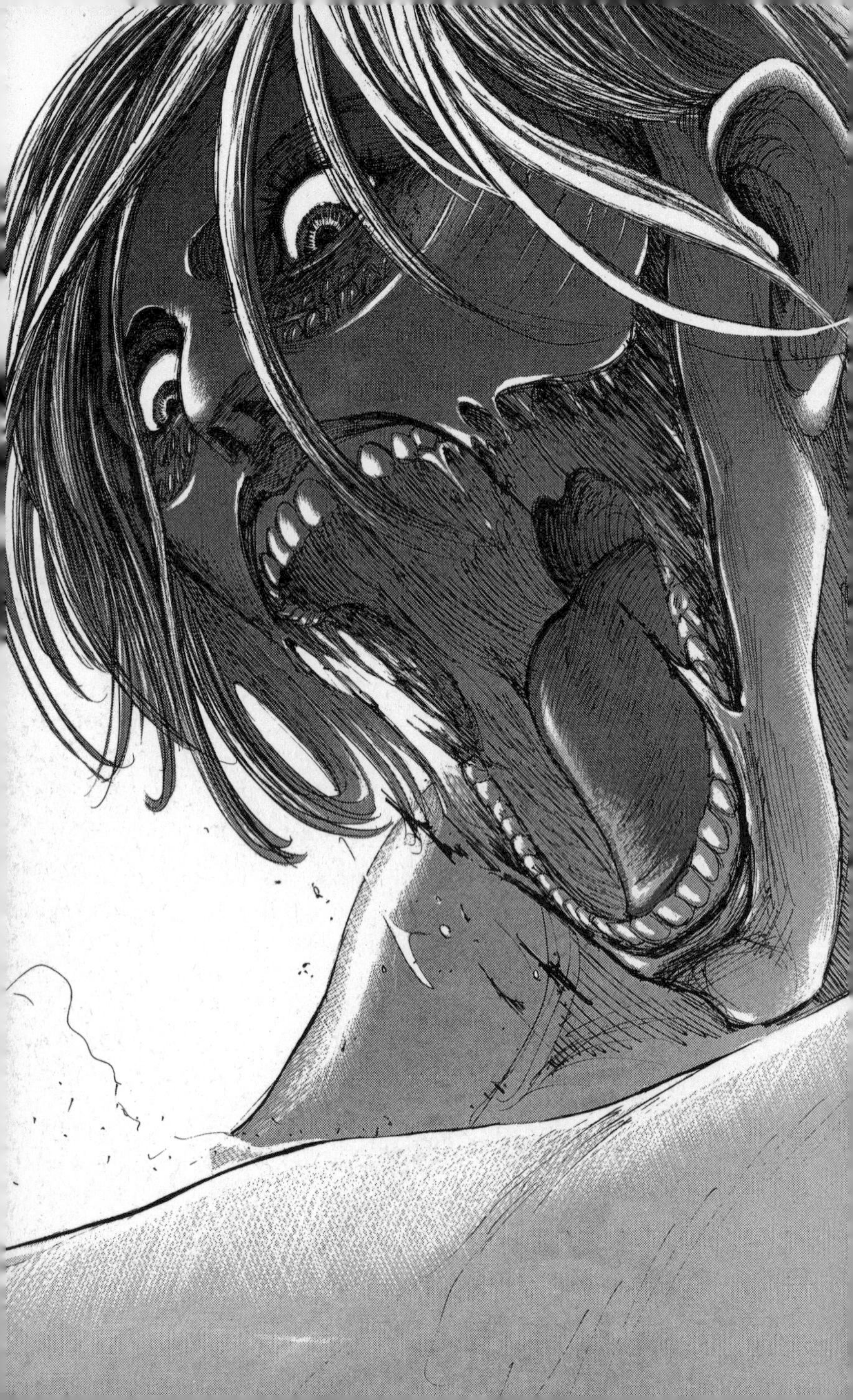

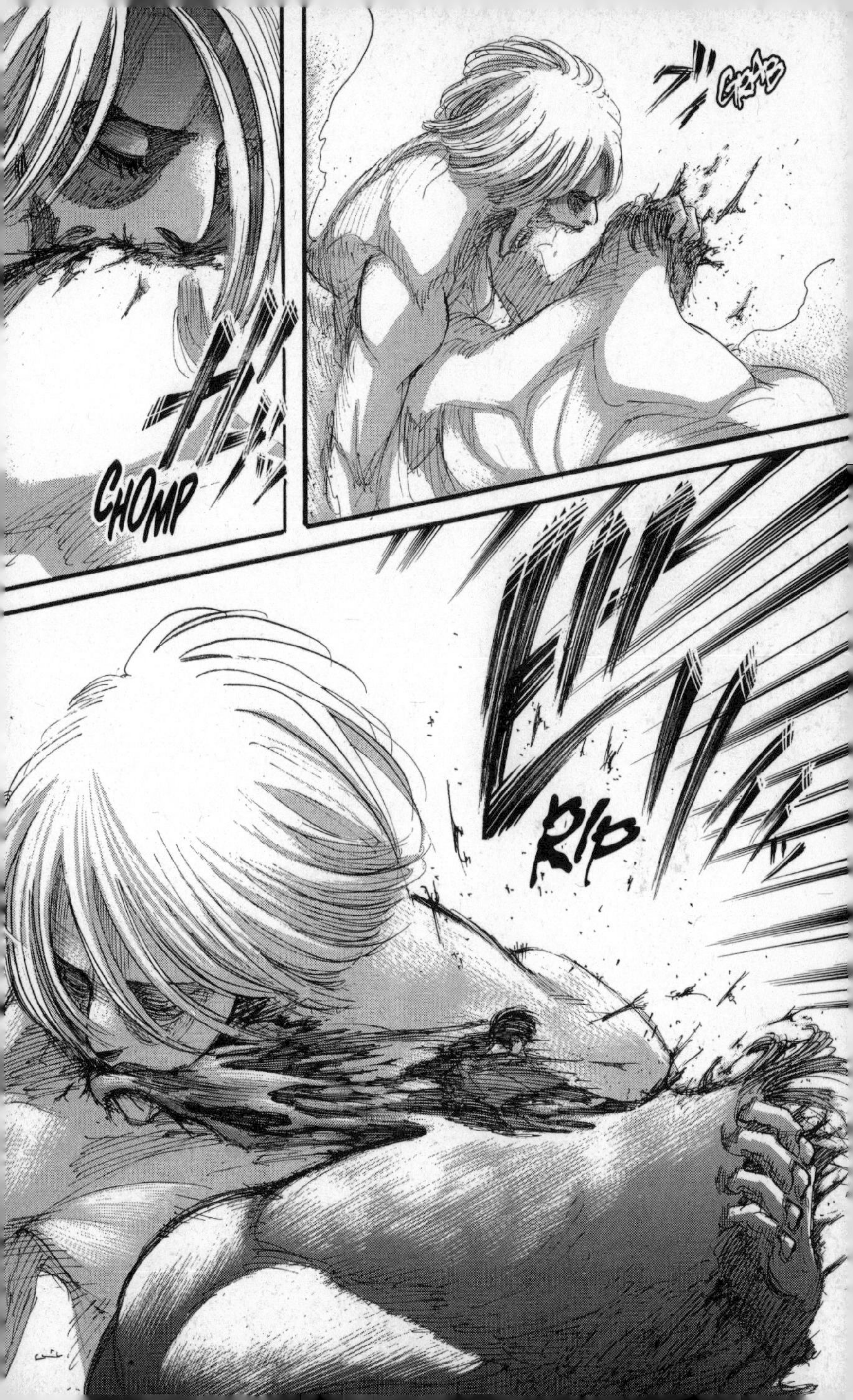
GRAB
CHOMP
RIP

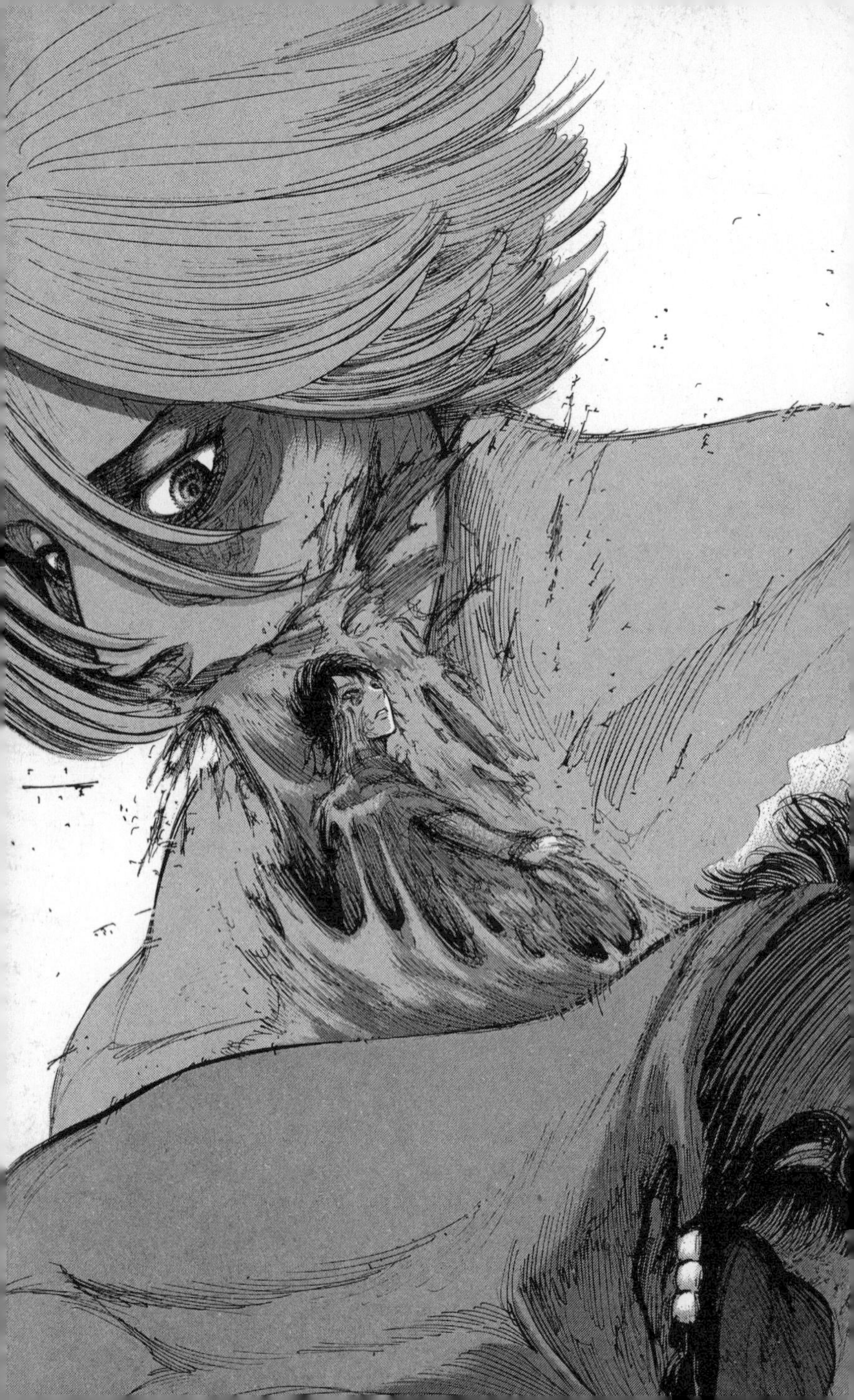

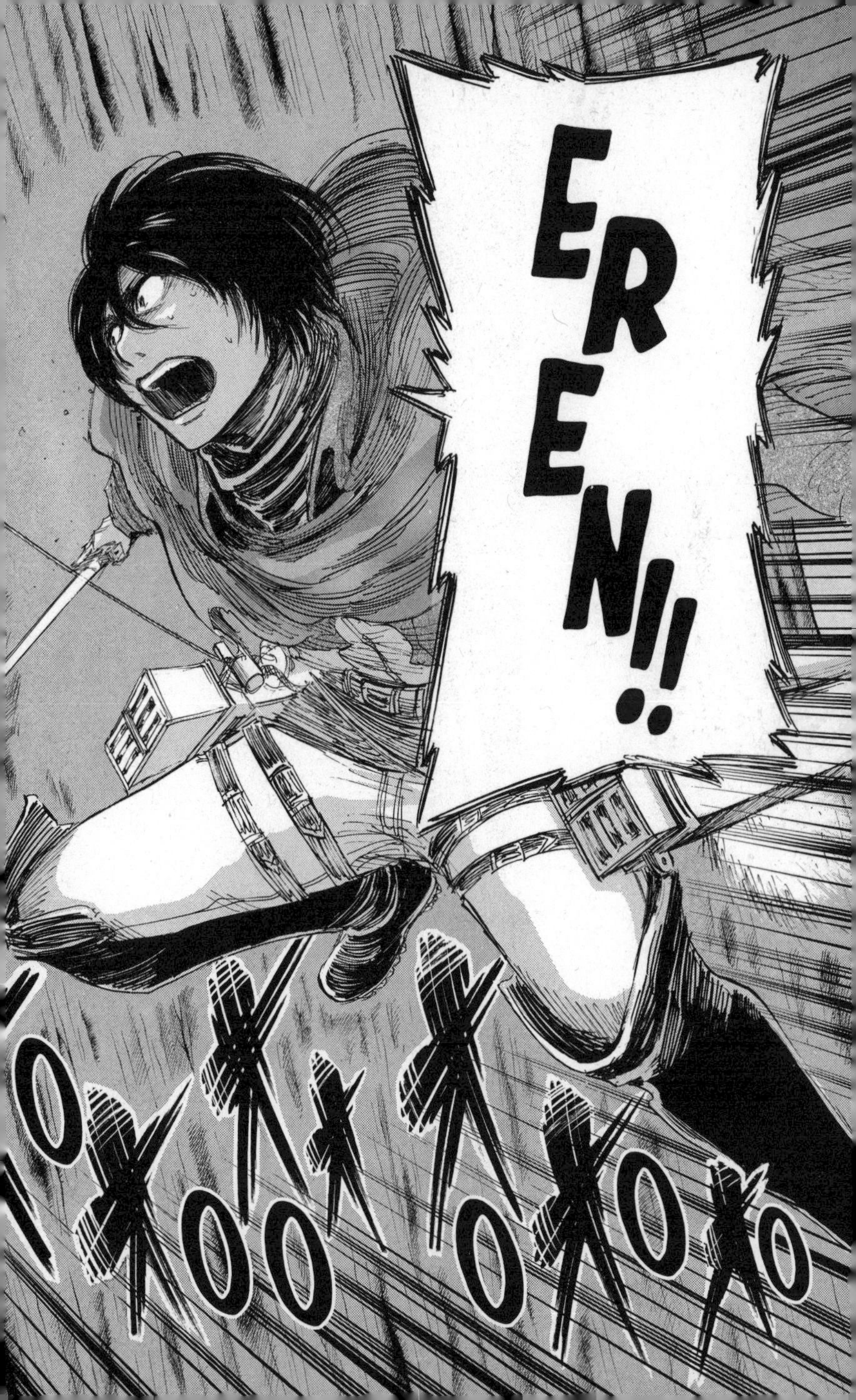
EREN!!

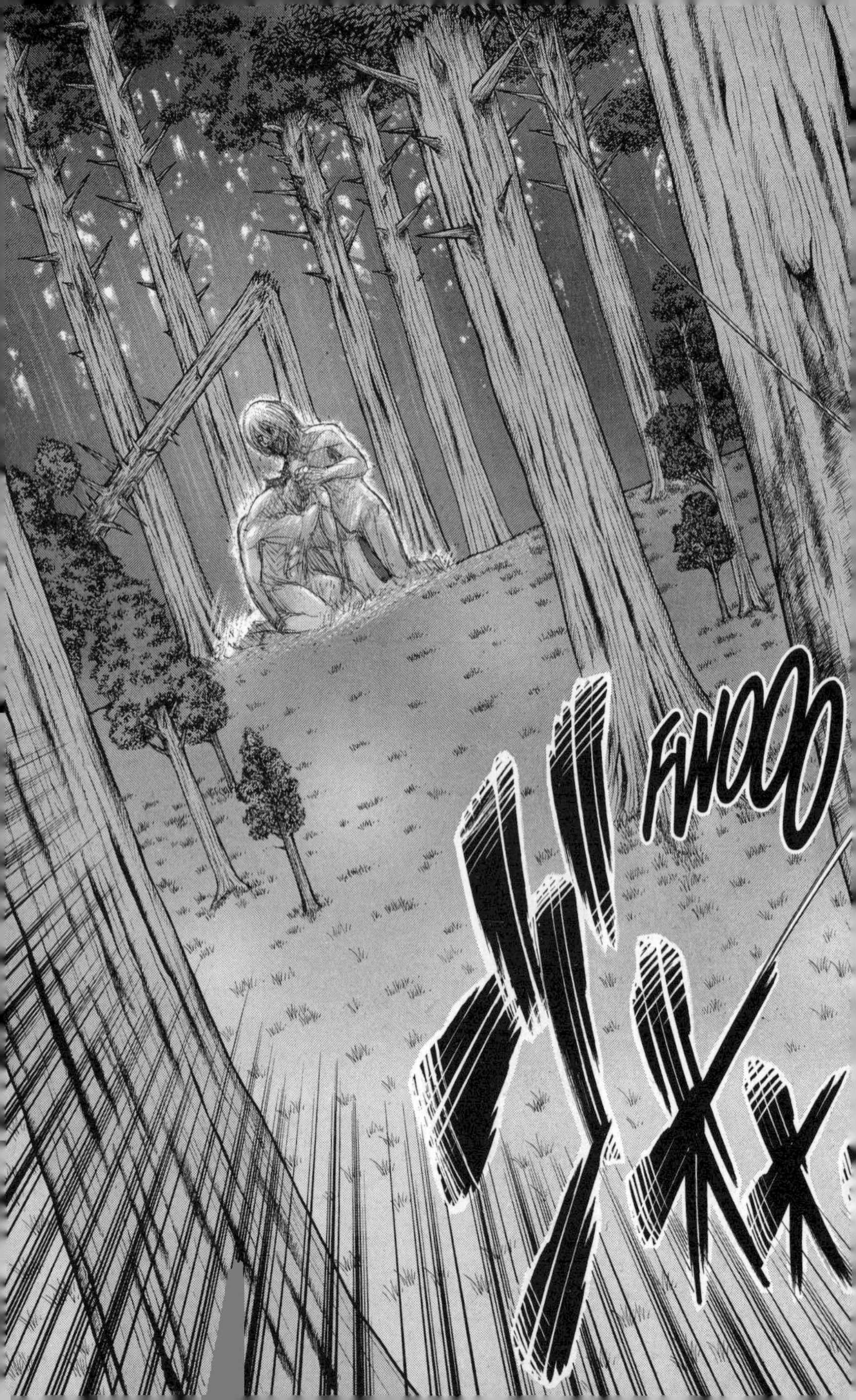
FWOOO

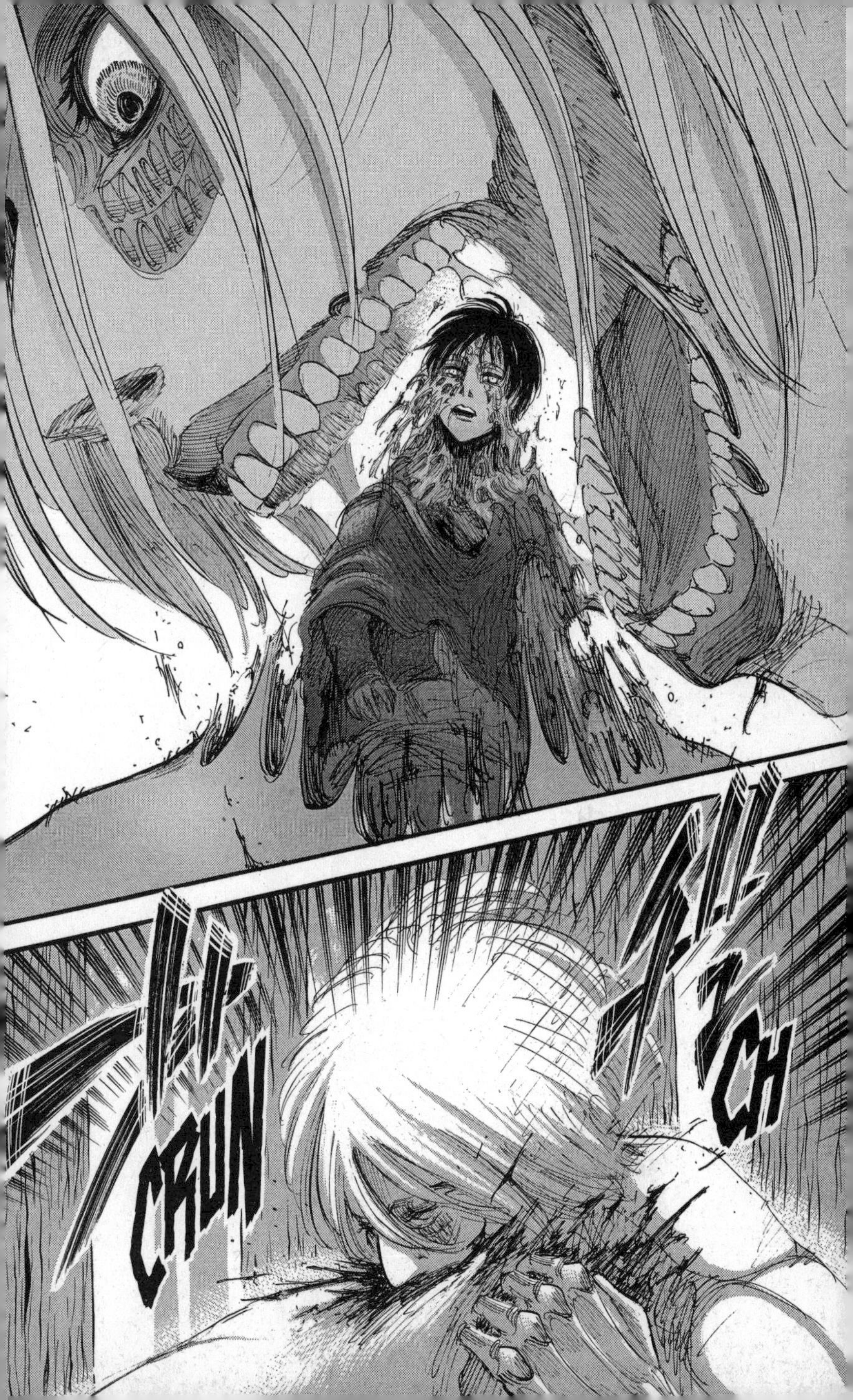
CRUN
CH

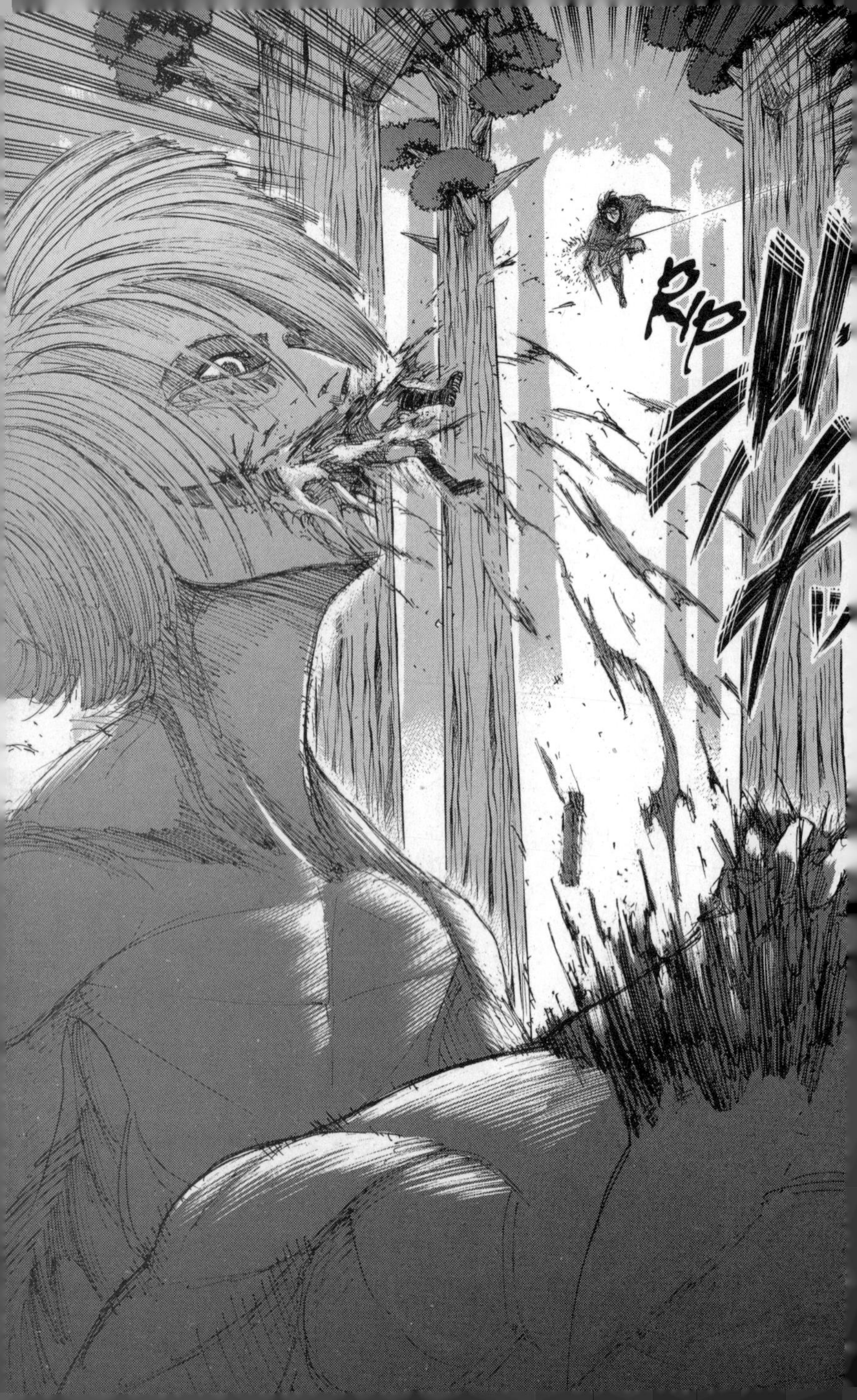
RIP

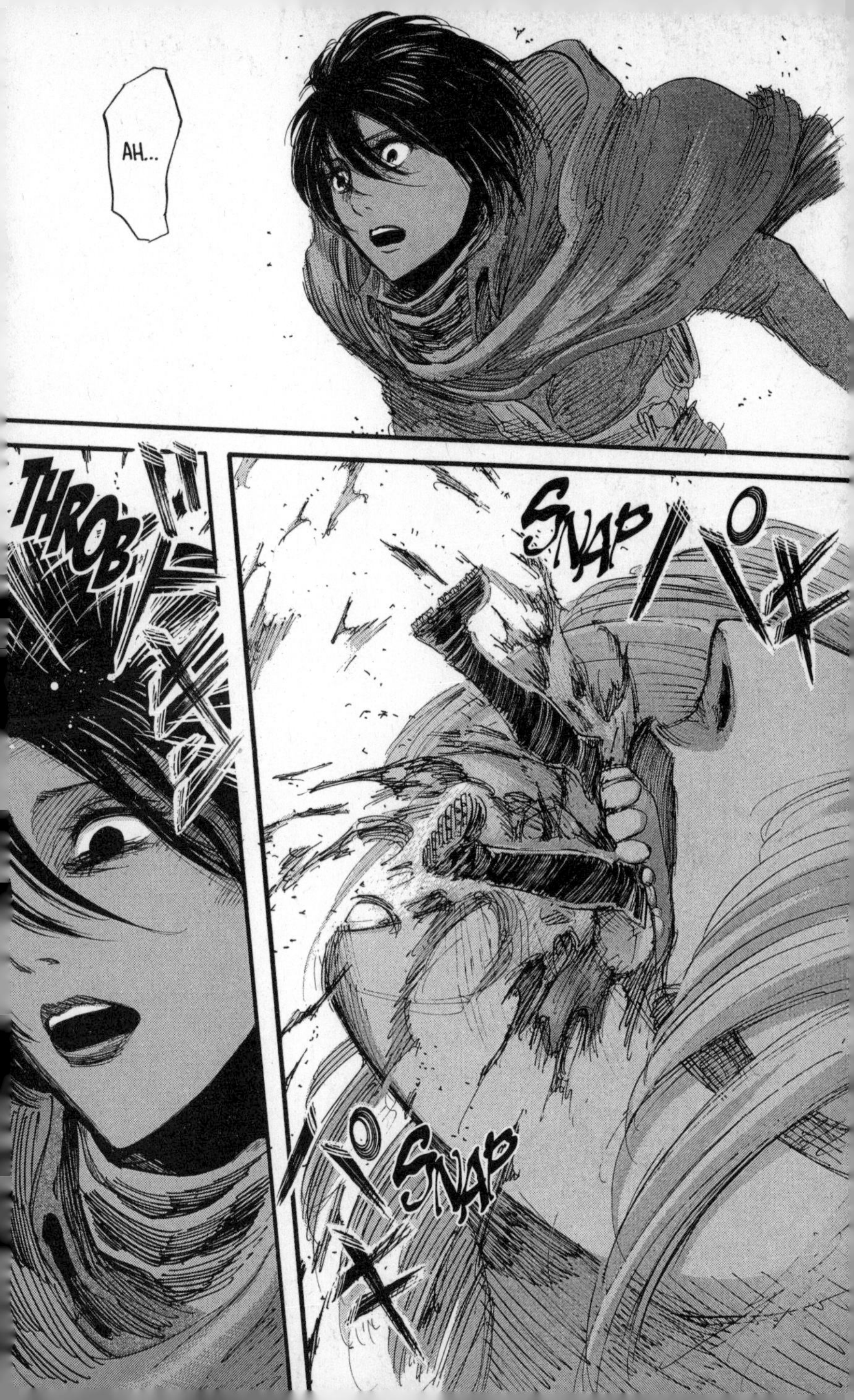
AH...
SNAP
SNAP
THROB!!

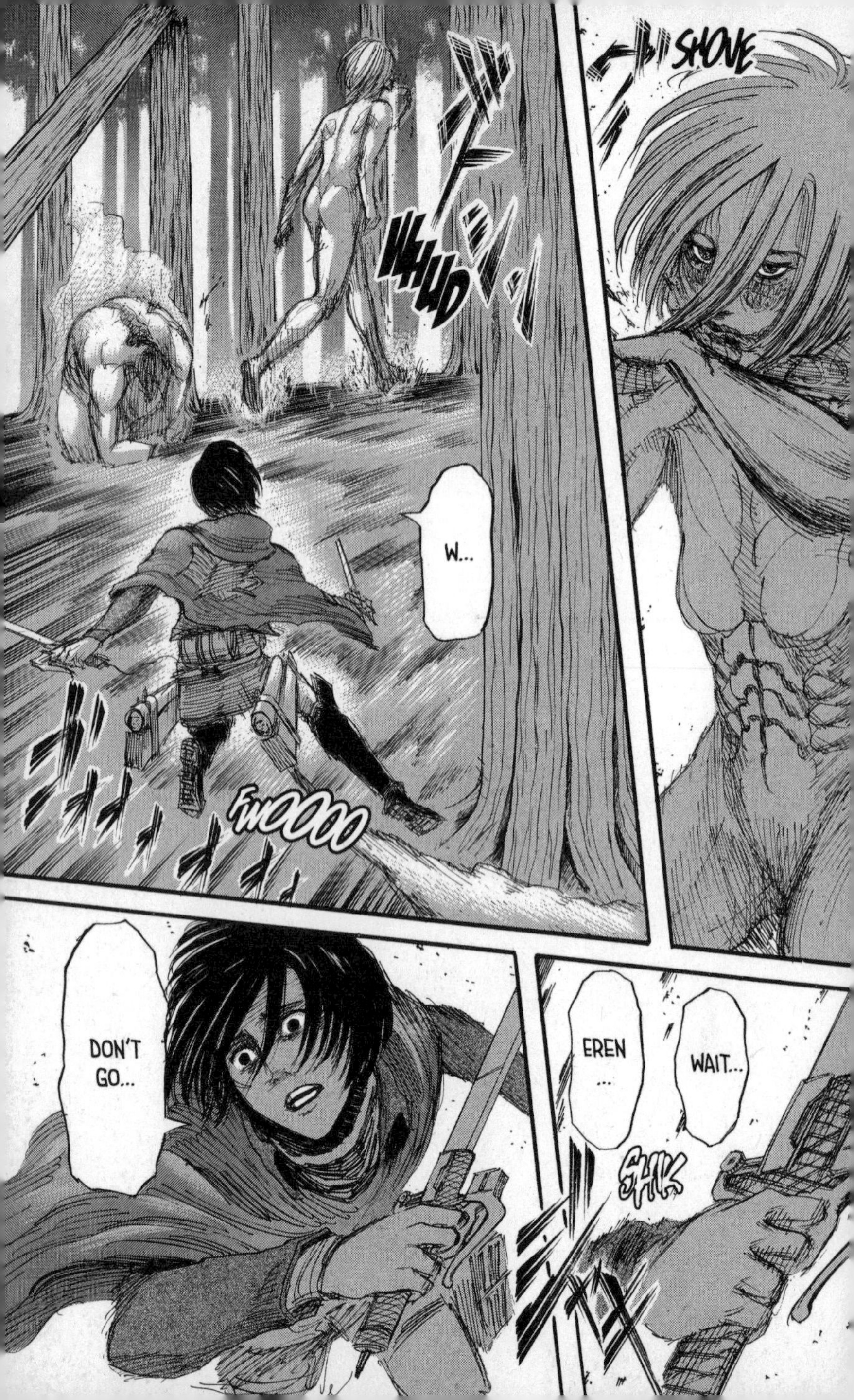
SHOVE
WHUD
W...
FWOOOO
WAIT...
EREN ...
SHIK
DON'T GO...

ATTACK on TITAN

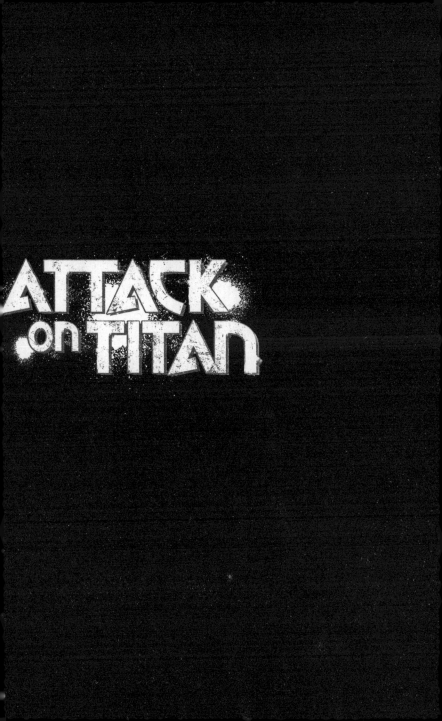

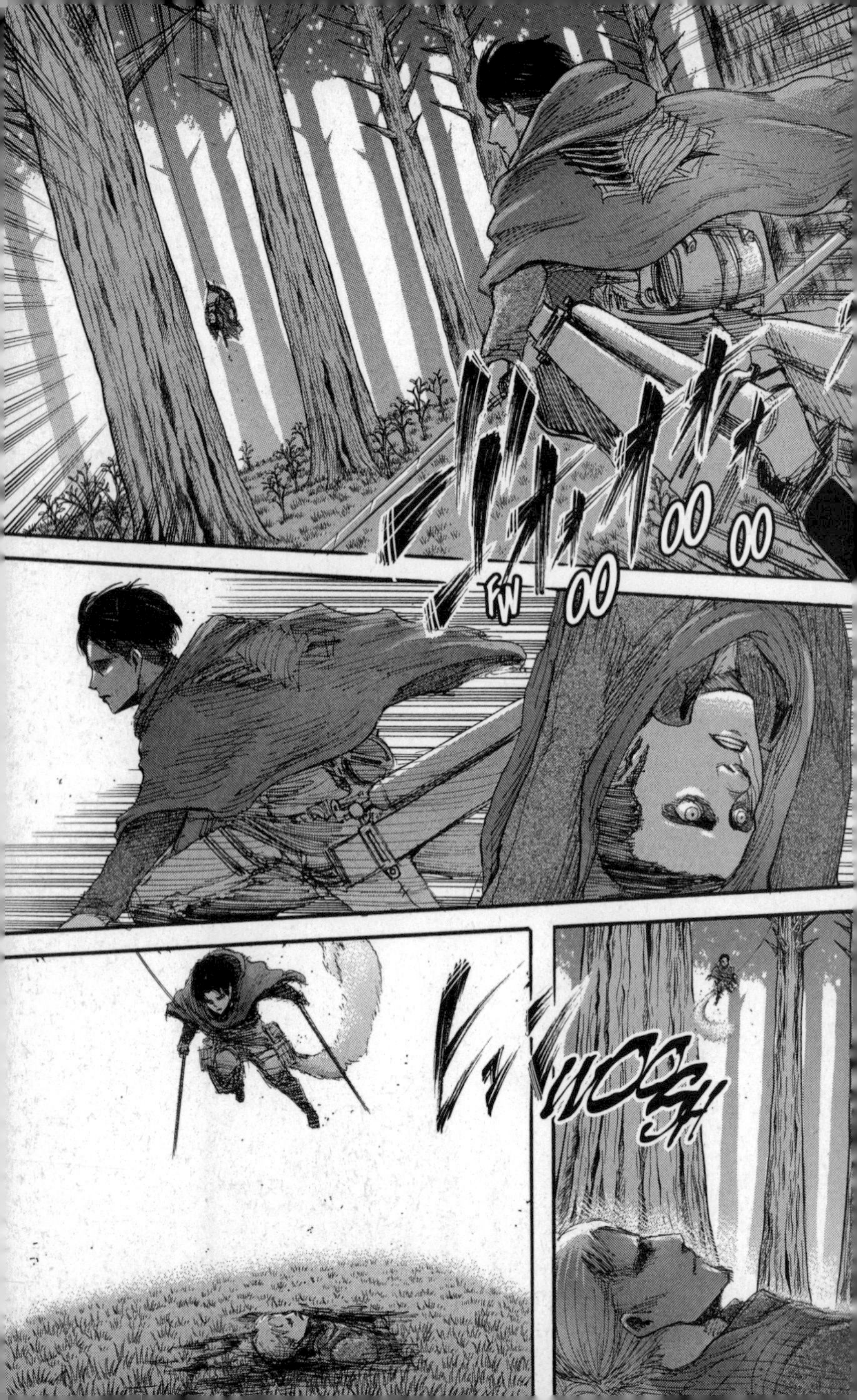
FWOO OO OO
VWOOSH

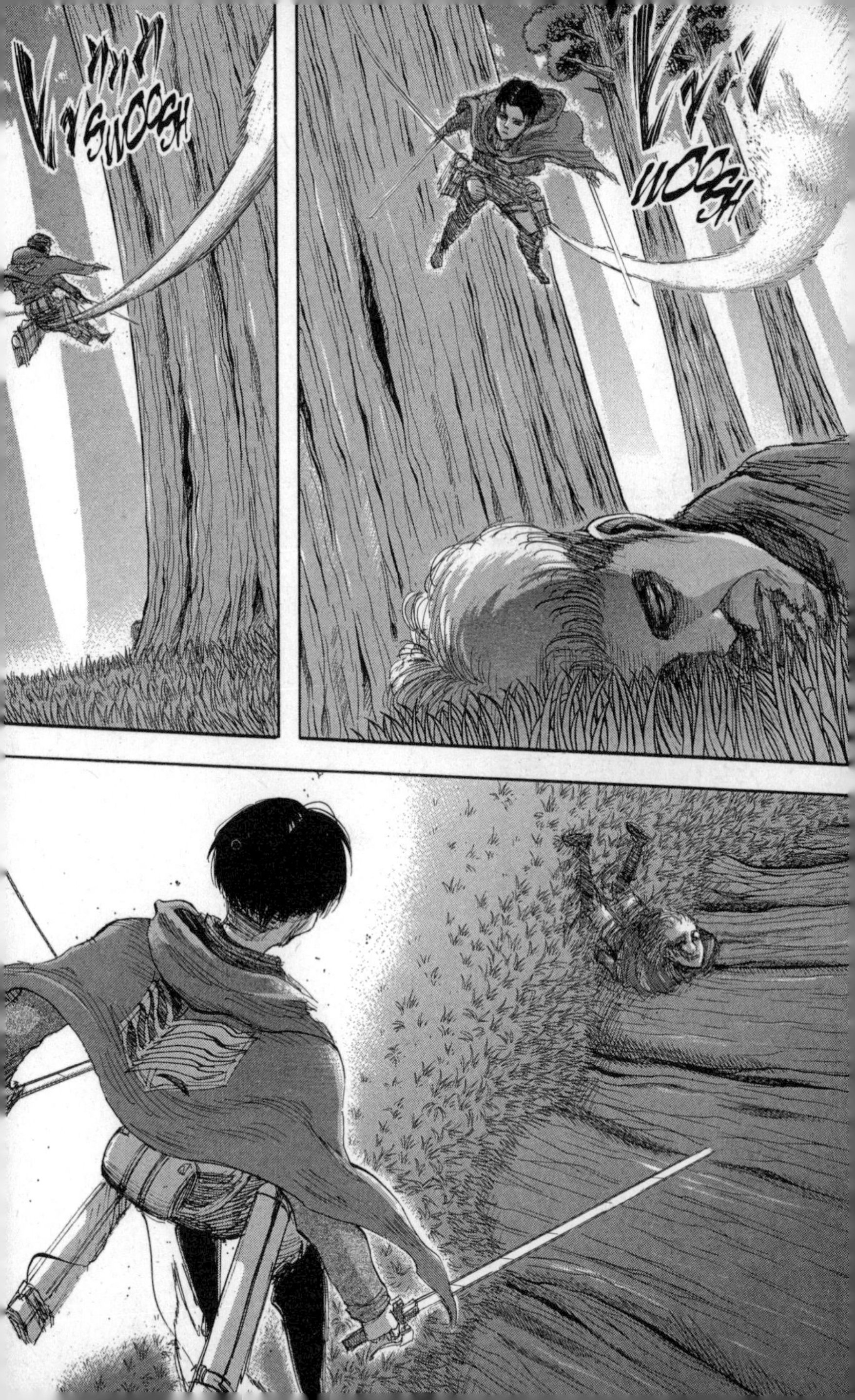
WOOSH
SWOOSH

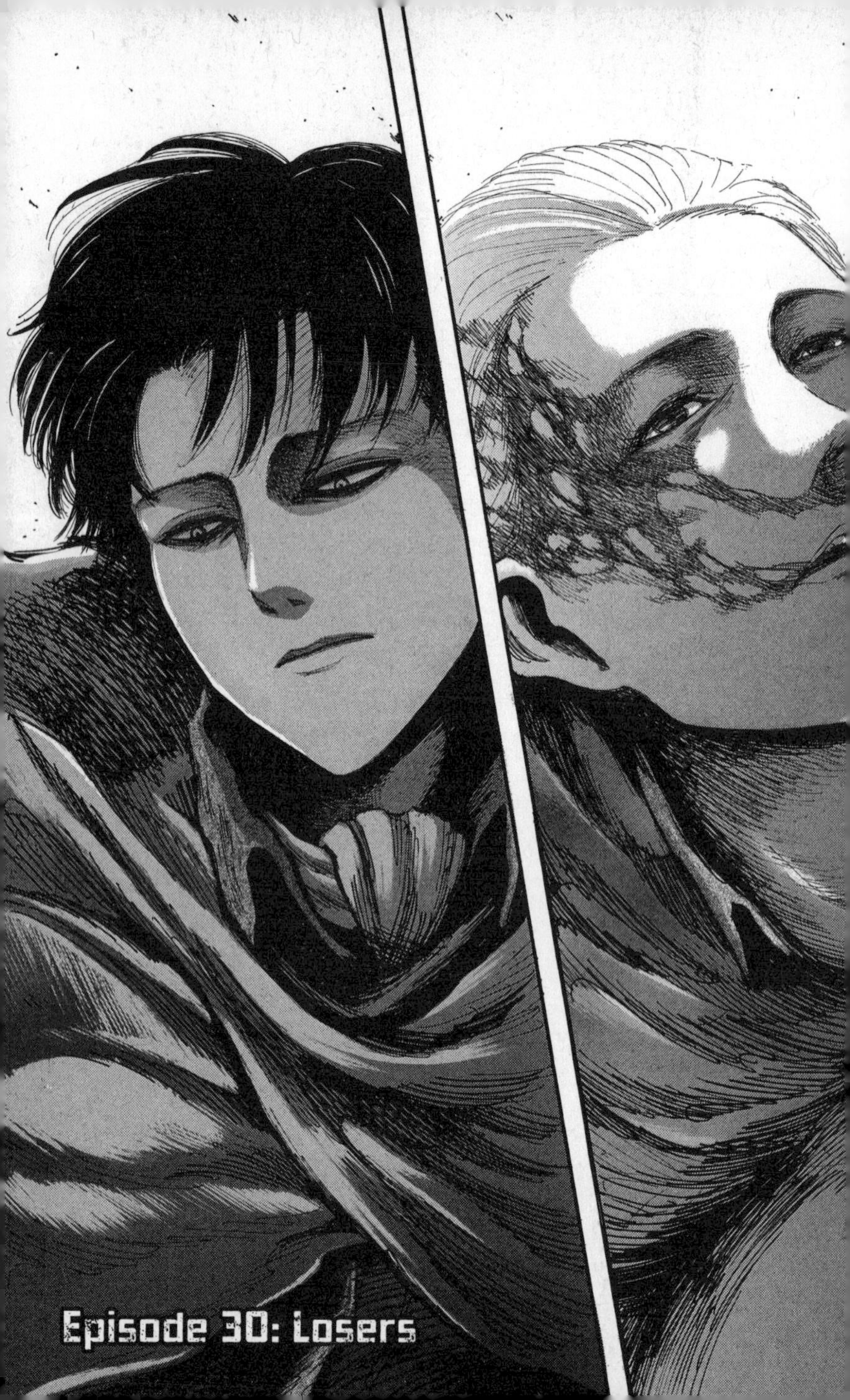
Episode 30: Losers

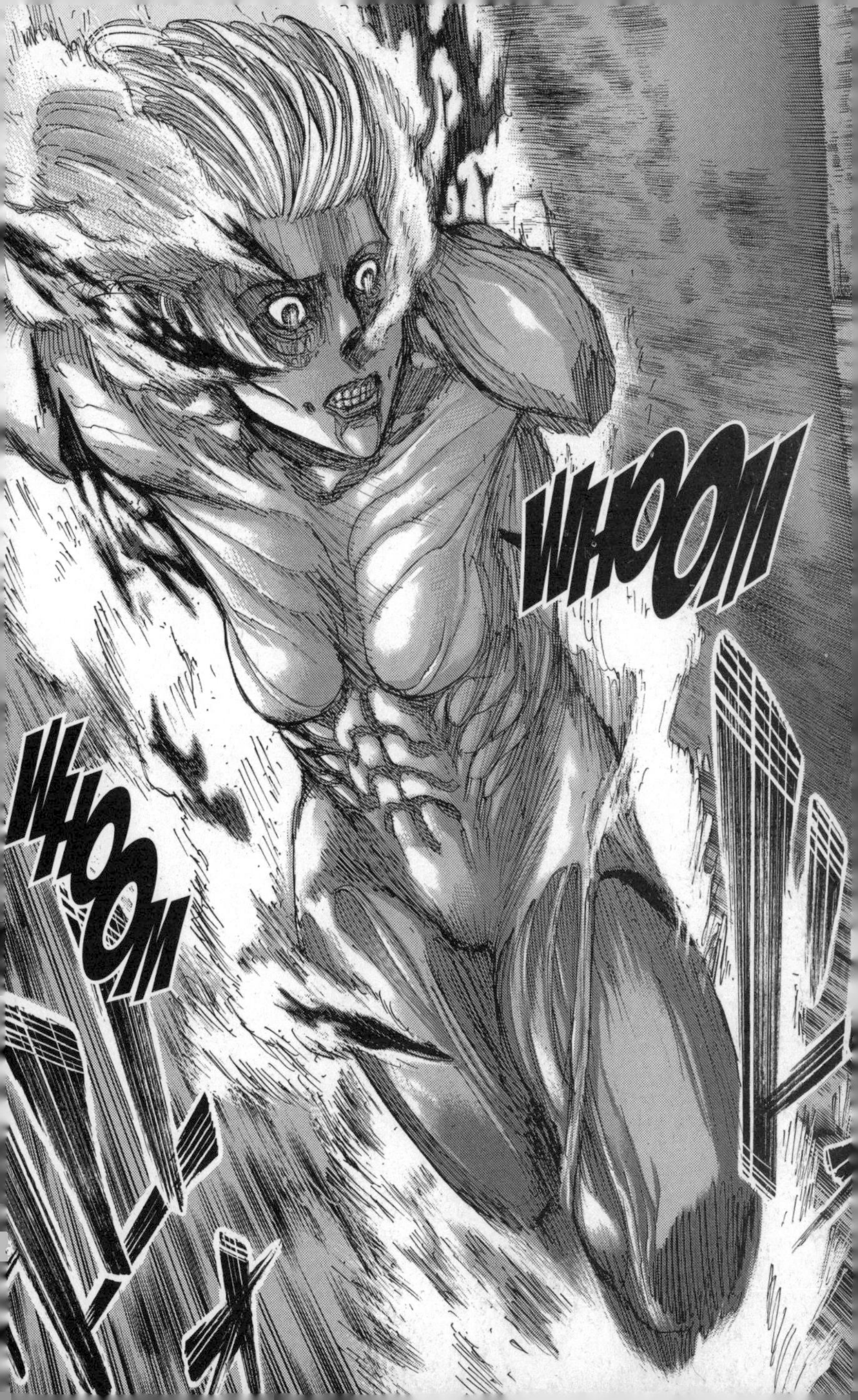
WHOOM
WHOOM

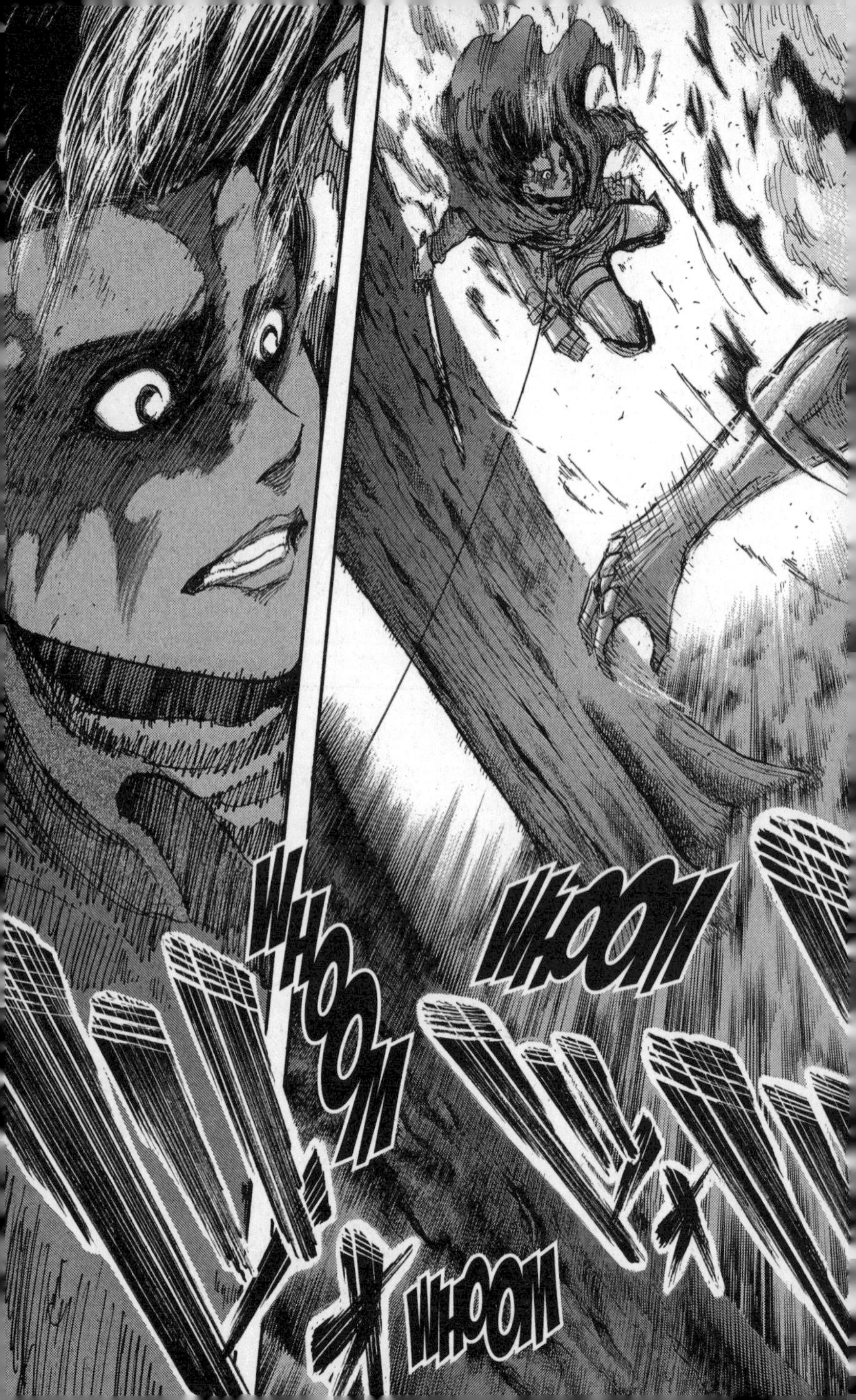
WHOOM
WHOOM
WHOOM

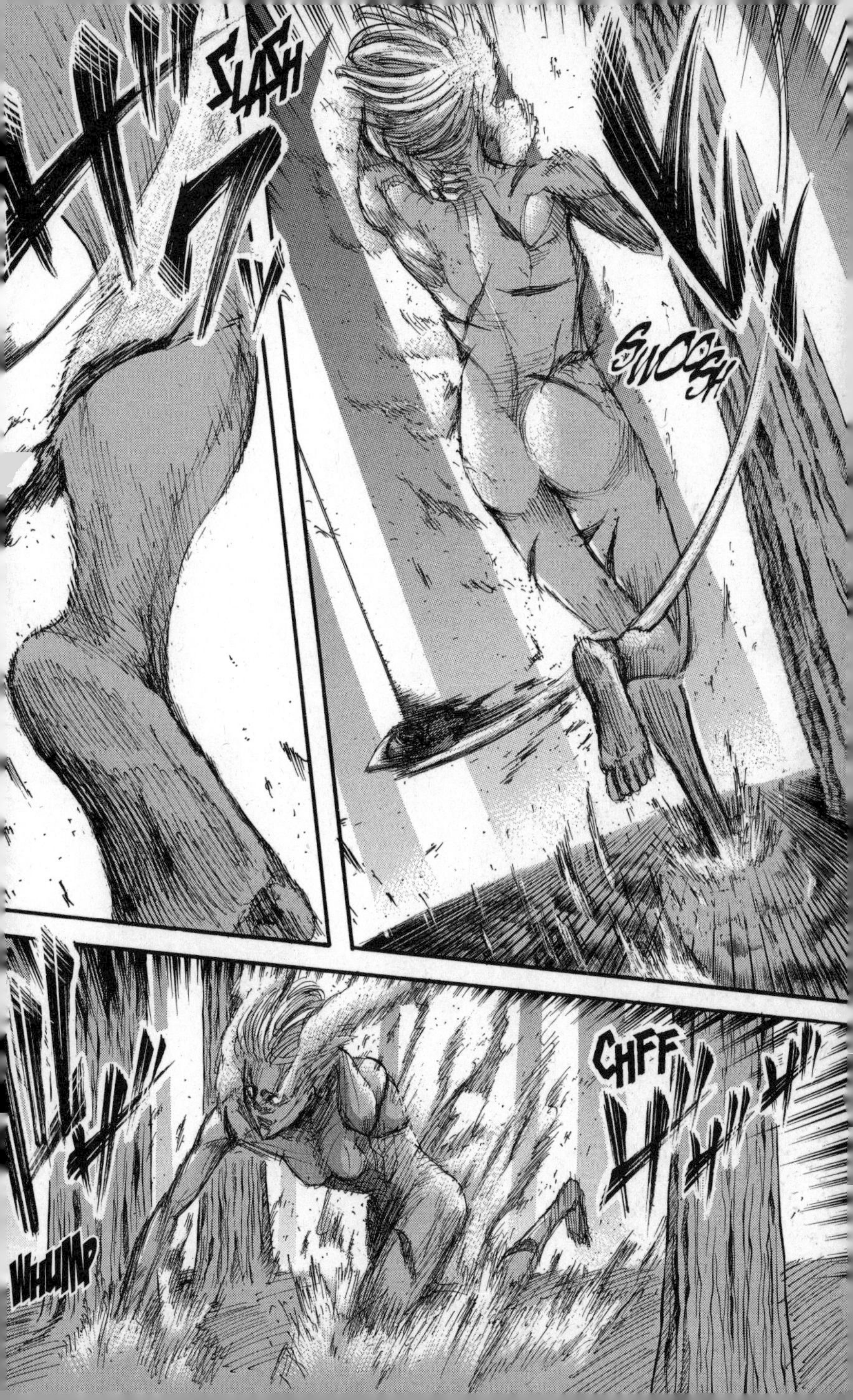
SWOOSH
SLASH
CHFF
WHUMP

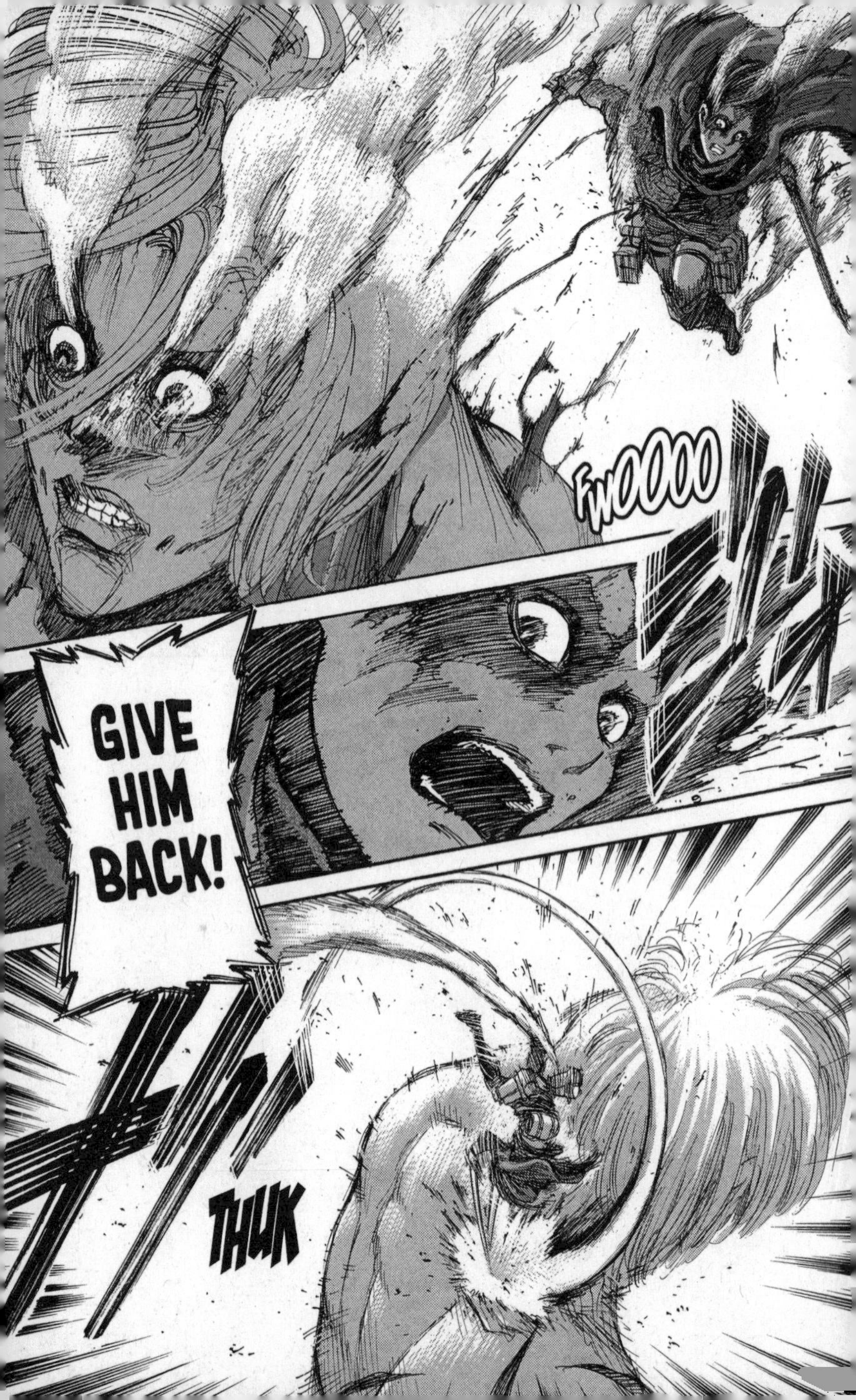
FWOOOO
GIVE HIM BACK!
THUK

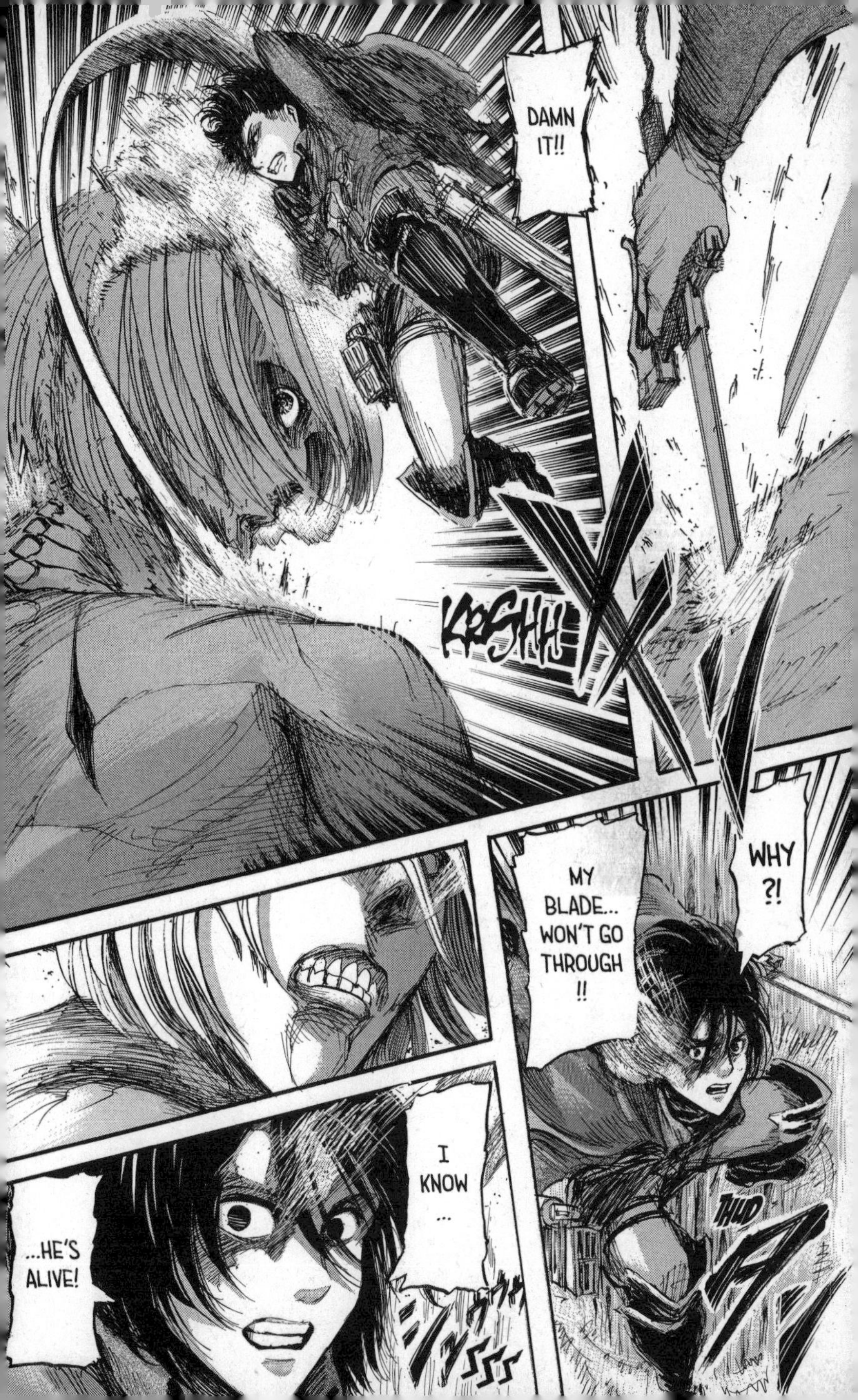
DAMN IT!!
KRSHH!
WHY ?!
MY BLADE... WON'T GO THROUGH !!
THUD
I KNOW ...
...HE'S ALIVE!
SSS

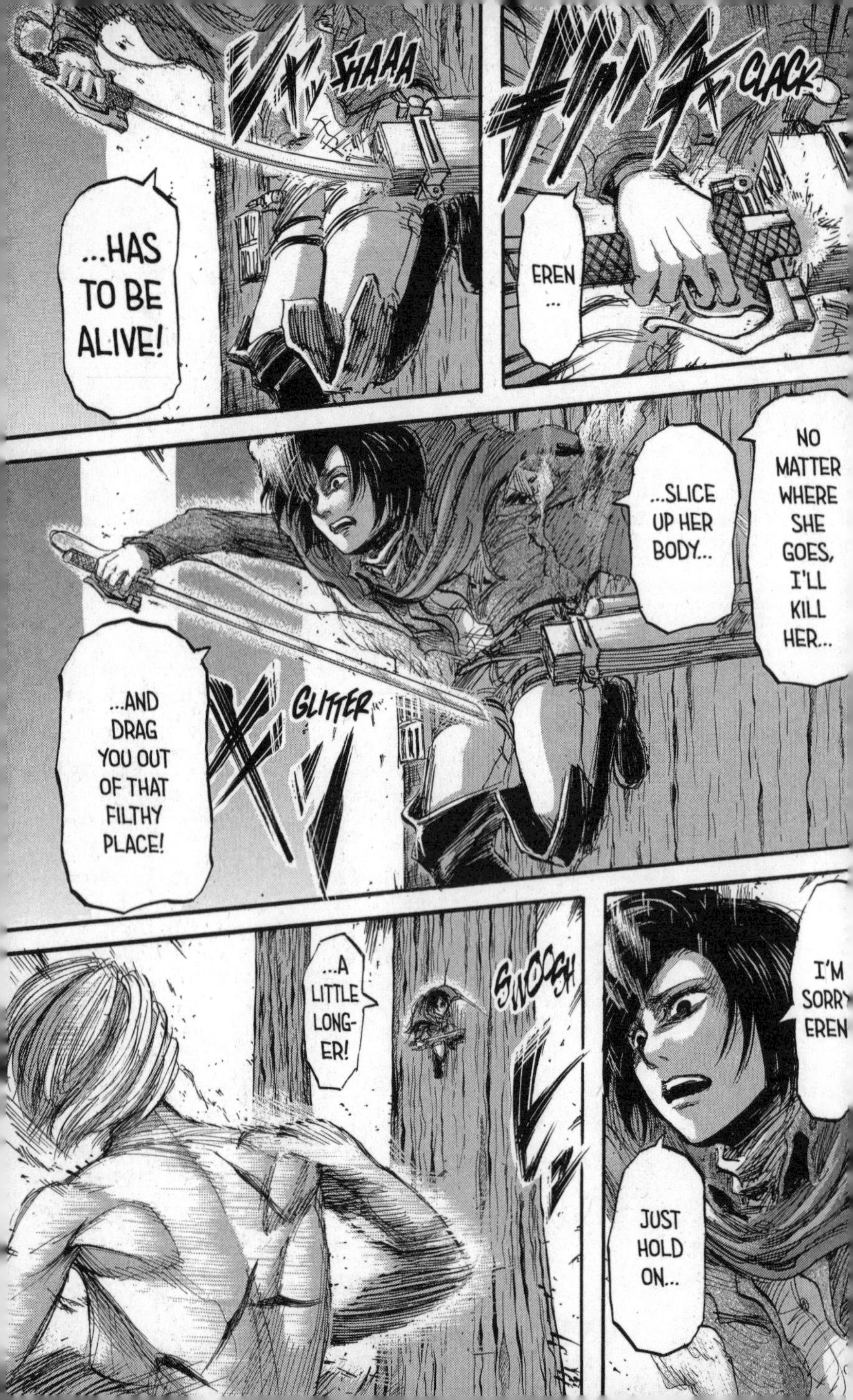
CLACK
EREN ...
SHAAA
...HAS TO BE ALIVE!
NO MATTER WHERE SHE GOES, I'LL KILL HER...
...SLICE UP HER BODY...
GLITTER
...AND DRAG YOU OUT OF THAT FILTHY PLACE!
I'M SORRY EREN
JUST HOLD ON...
SWOOSH
...A LITTLE LONG-
ER!

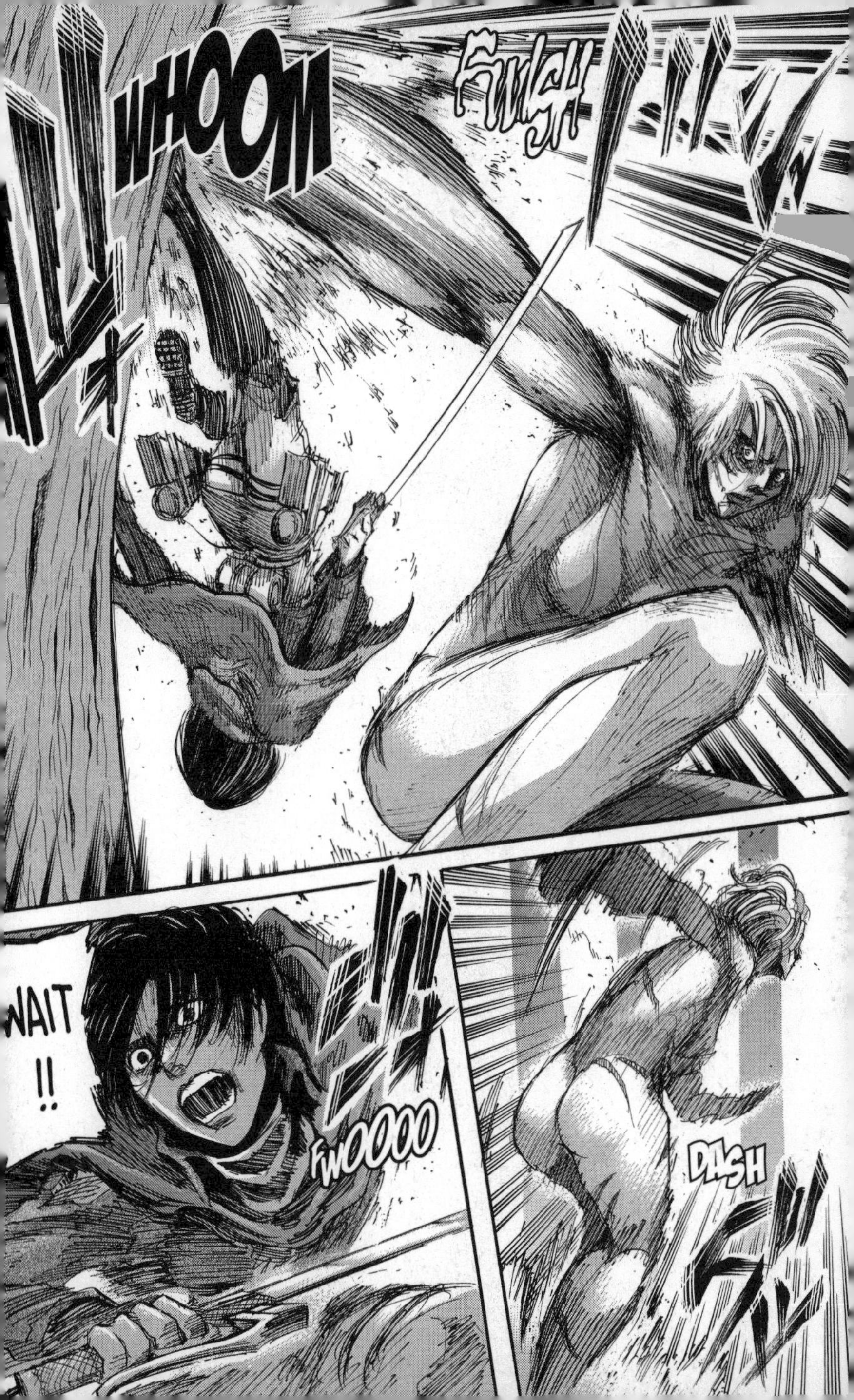
FWISH
WHOOM
DASH
FWOOOO
WAIT !!

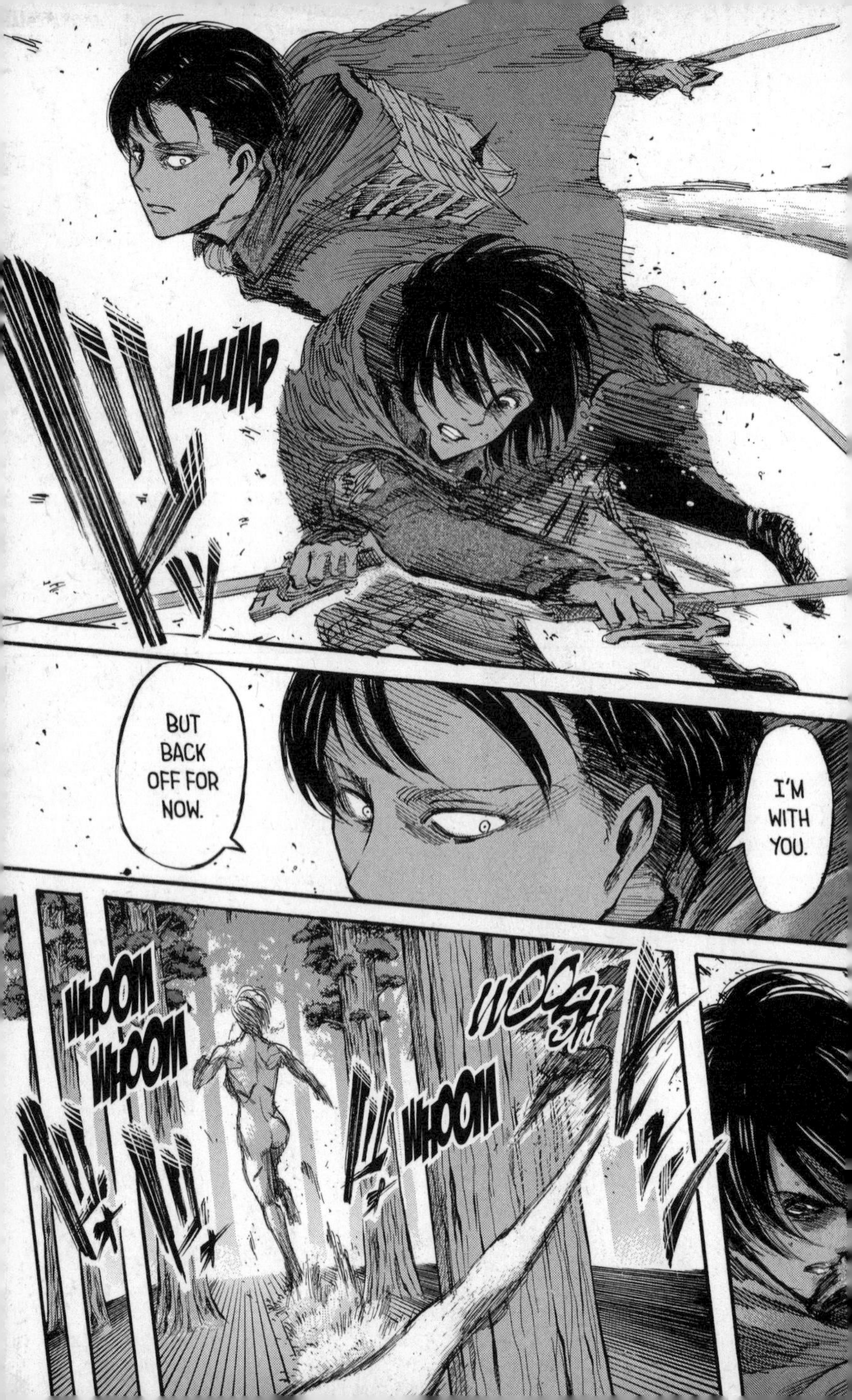
WHUMP
I'M WITH YOU.
BUT BACK OFF FOR NOW.
WOOSH
WHOOM
WHOOM WHOOM

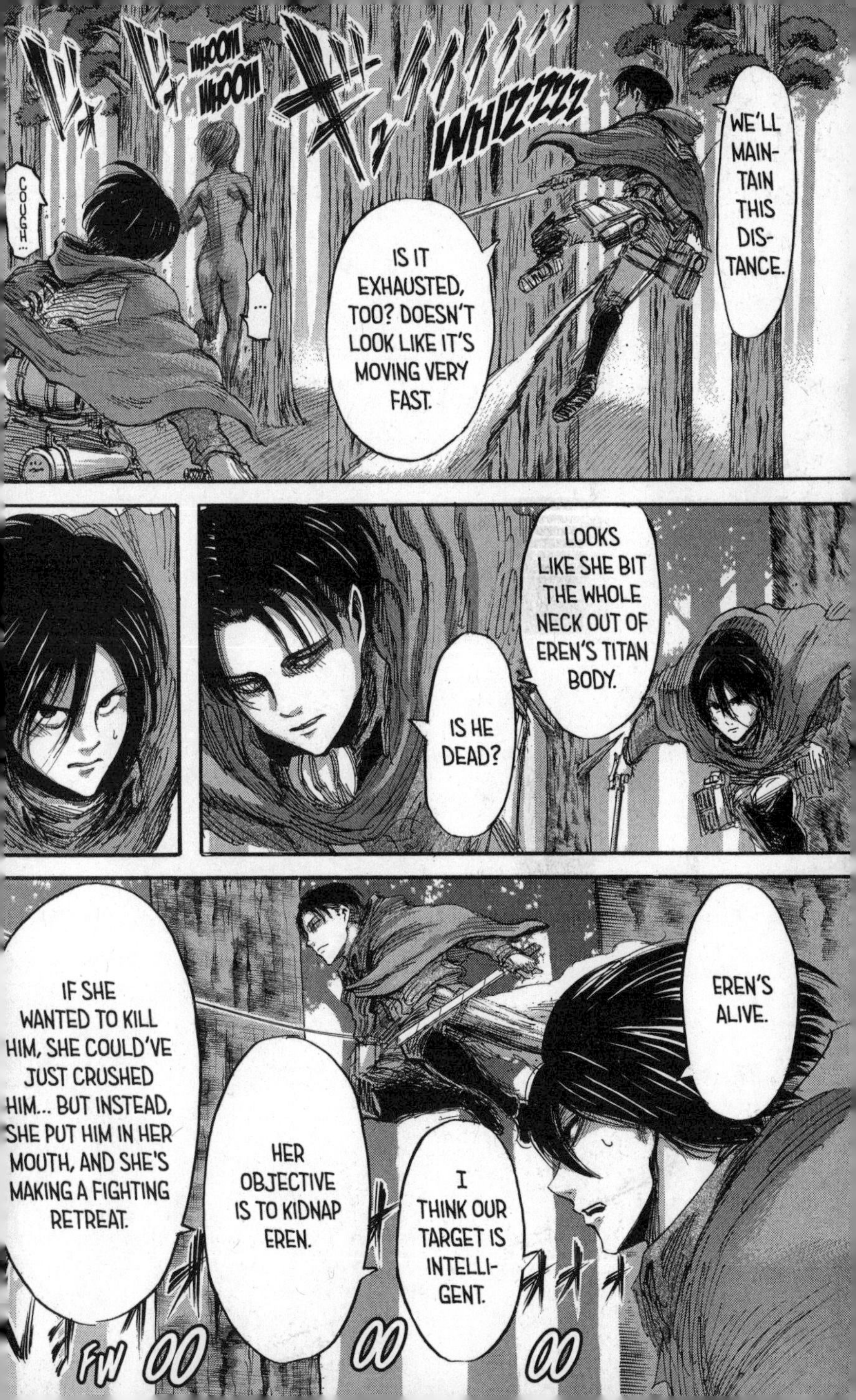
WE'LL MAIN-TAIN THIS DIS-TANCE.
WHIZZZZ
WHOOM WHOOM
IS IT EXHAUSTED, TOO? DOESN'T LOOK LIKE IT'S MOVING VERY FAST.
...
COUGH...
LOOKS LIKE SHE BIT THE WHOLE NECK OUT OF EREN'S TITAN BODY.
IS HE DEAD?
EREN'S ALIVE.
I THINK OUR TARGET IS INTELLI-GENT.
HER OBJECTIVE IS TO KIDNAP EREN.
IF SHE WANTED TO KILL HIM, SHE COULD'VE JUST CRUSHED HIM... BUT INSTEAD, SHE PUT HIM IN HER MOUTH, AND SHE'S MAKING A FIGHTING RETREAT.
FWOOOOOO

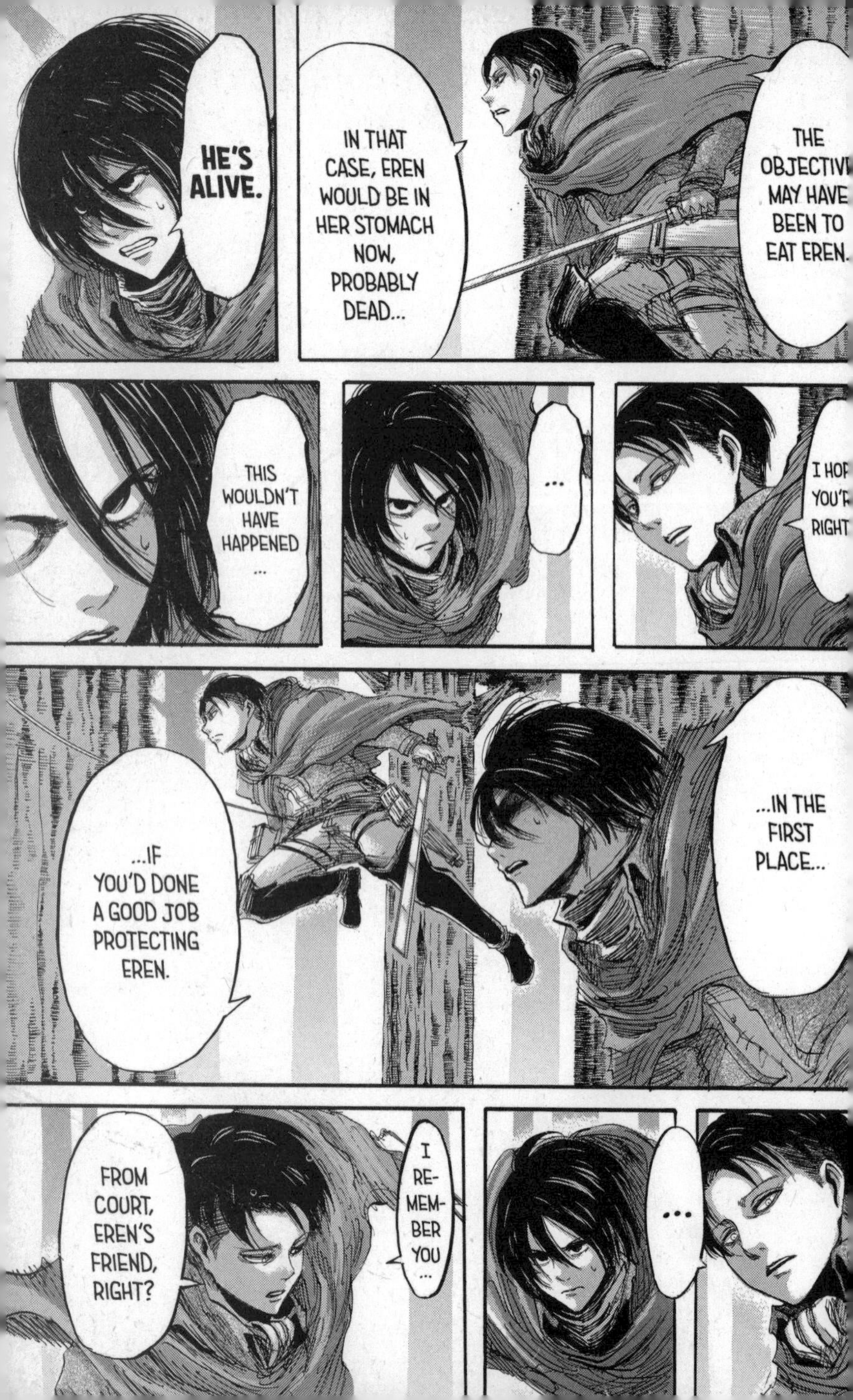
THE OBJECTIV MAY HAVE BEEN TO EAT EREN.
IN THAT CASE, EREN WOULD BE IN HER STOMACH NOW, PROBABLY DEAD...
HE'S ALIVE.
I HOP YOU'R RIGHT
...
THIS WOULDN'T HAVE HAPPENED ...
...IN THE FIRST PLACE...
...IF YOU'D DONE A GOOD JOB PROTECTING EREN.
...
I RE-MEM-BER YOU ...
FROM COURT, EREN'S FRIEND, RIGHT?

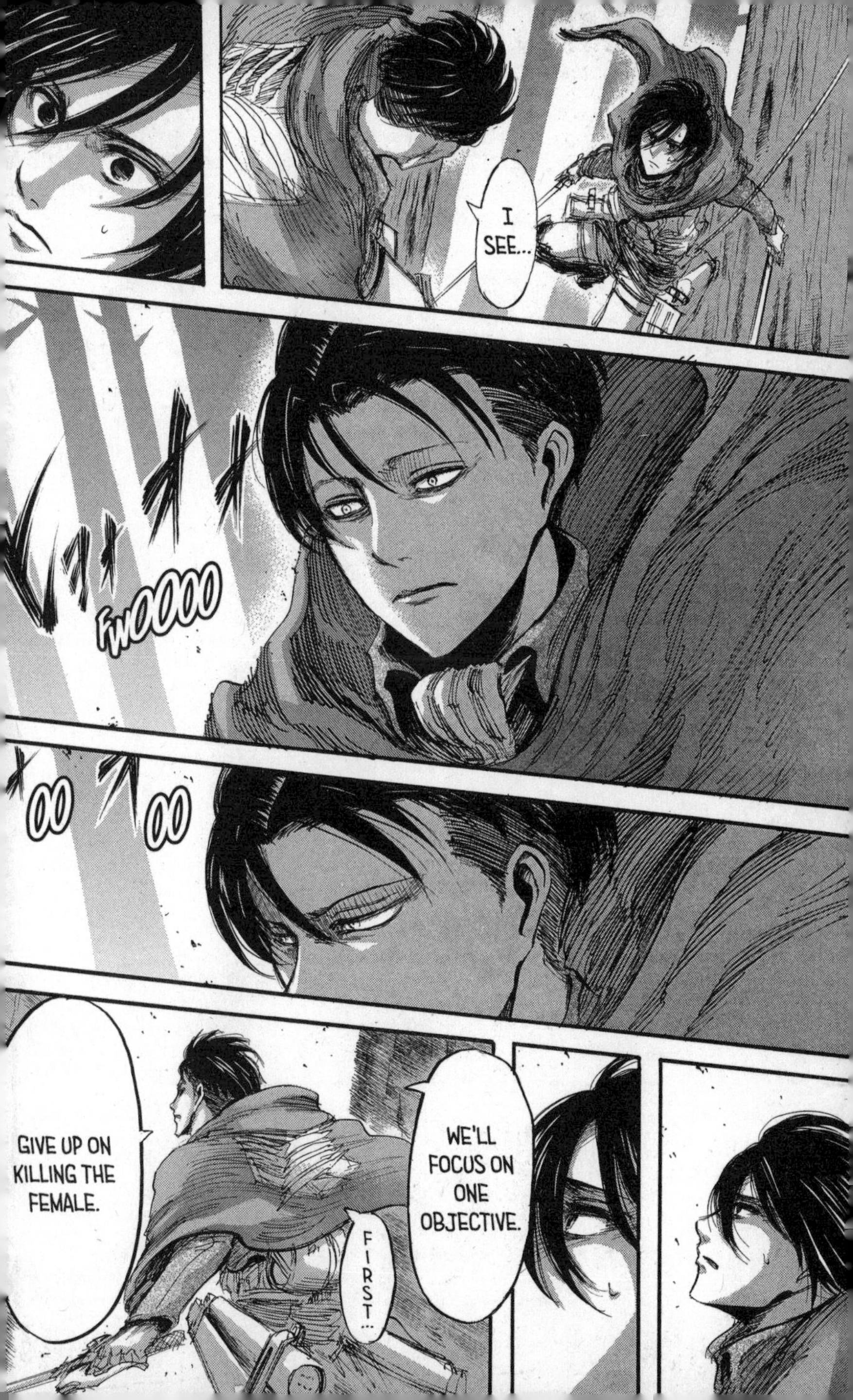
I SEE...
FWOOOO
OO
OO
FIRST...
WE'LL FOCUS ON ONE OBJECTIVE.
GIVE UP ON KILLING THE FEMALE.

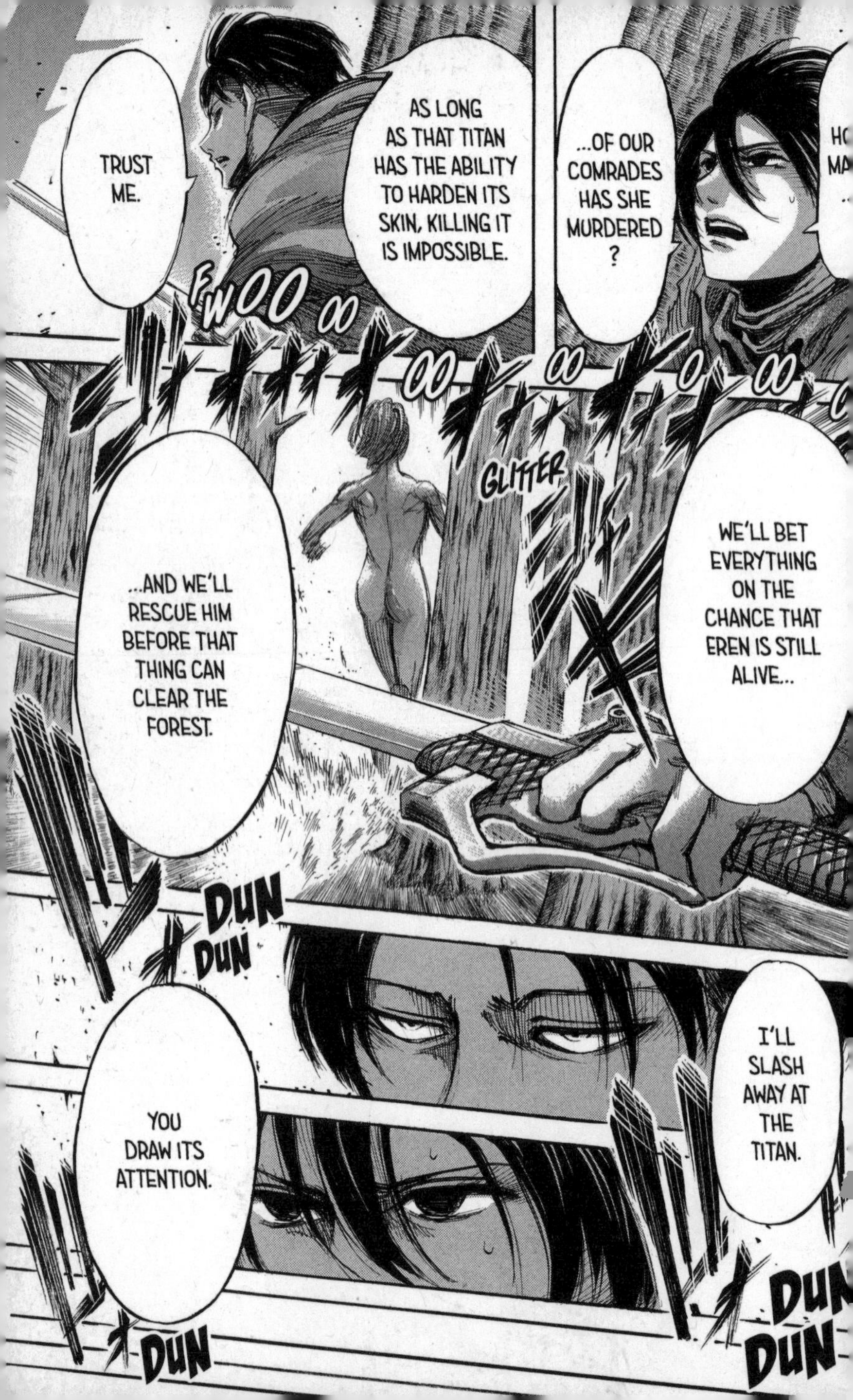
...OF OUR COMRADES HAS SHE MURDERED ?
AS LONG AS THAT TITAN HAS THE ABILITY TO HARDEN ITS SKIN, KILLING IT IS IMPOSSIBLE.
TRUST ME.
FWOOOO OOOO OO OO OO OO
WE'LL BET EVERYTHING ON THE CHANCE THAT EREN IS STILL ALIVE...
GLITTER
...AND WE'LL RESCUE HIM BEFORE THAT THING CAN CLEAR THE FOREST.
DUN DUN
I'LL SLASH AWAY AT THE TITAN.
YOU DRAW ITS ATTENTION.
DUN DUN
DUN

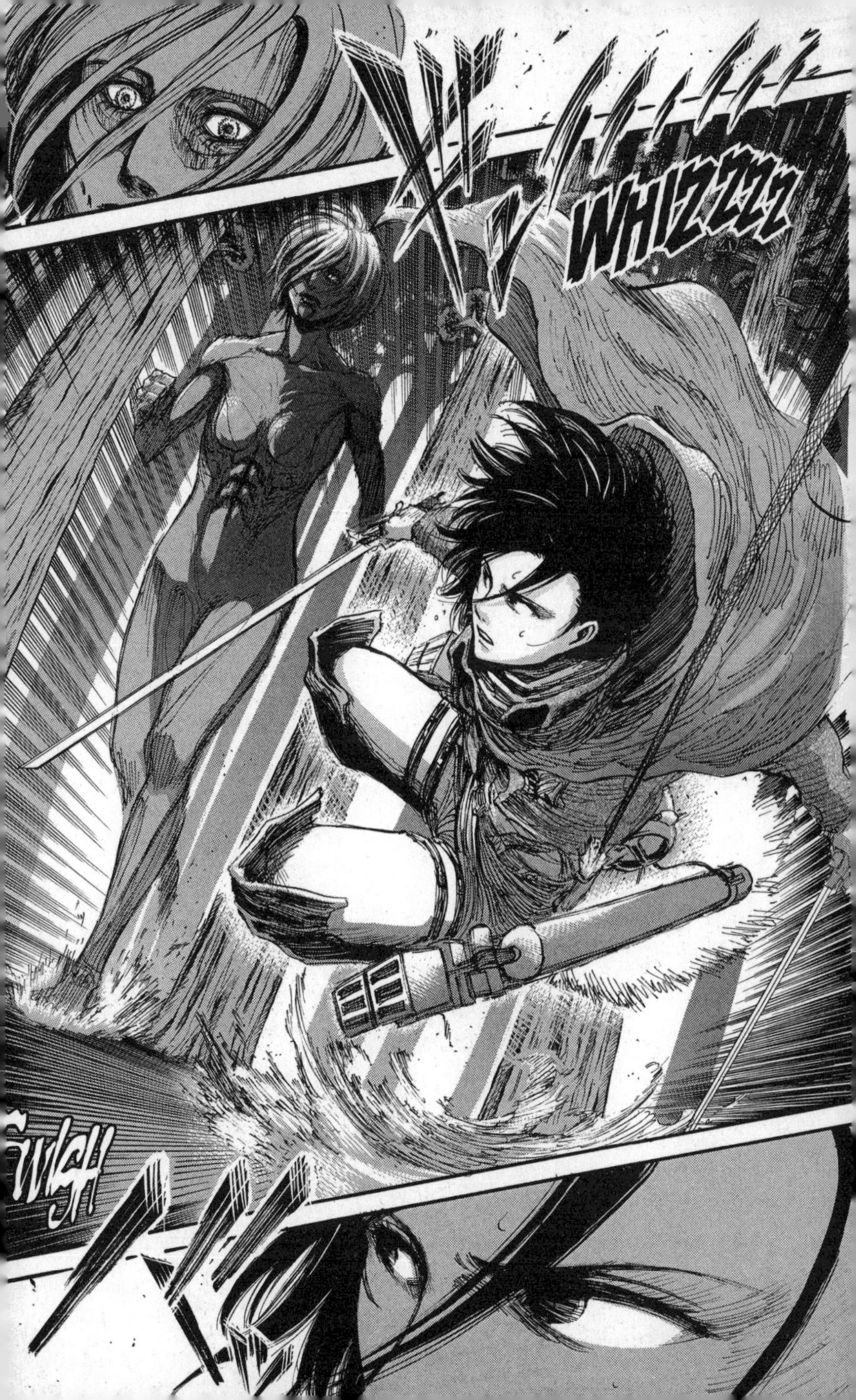
WHIZZZZ
FWISH

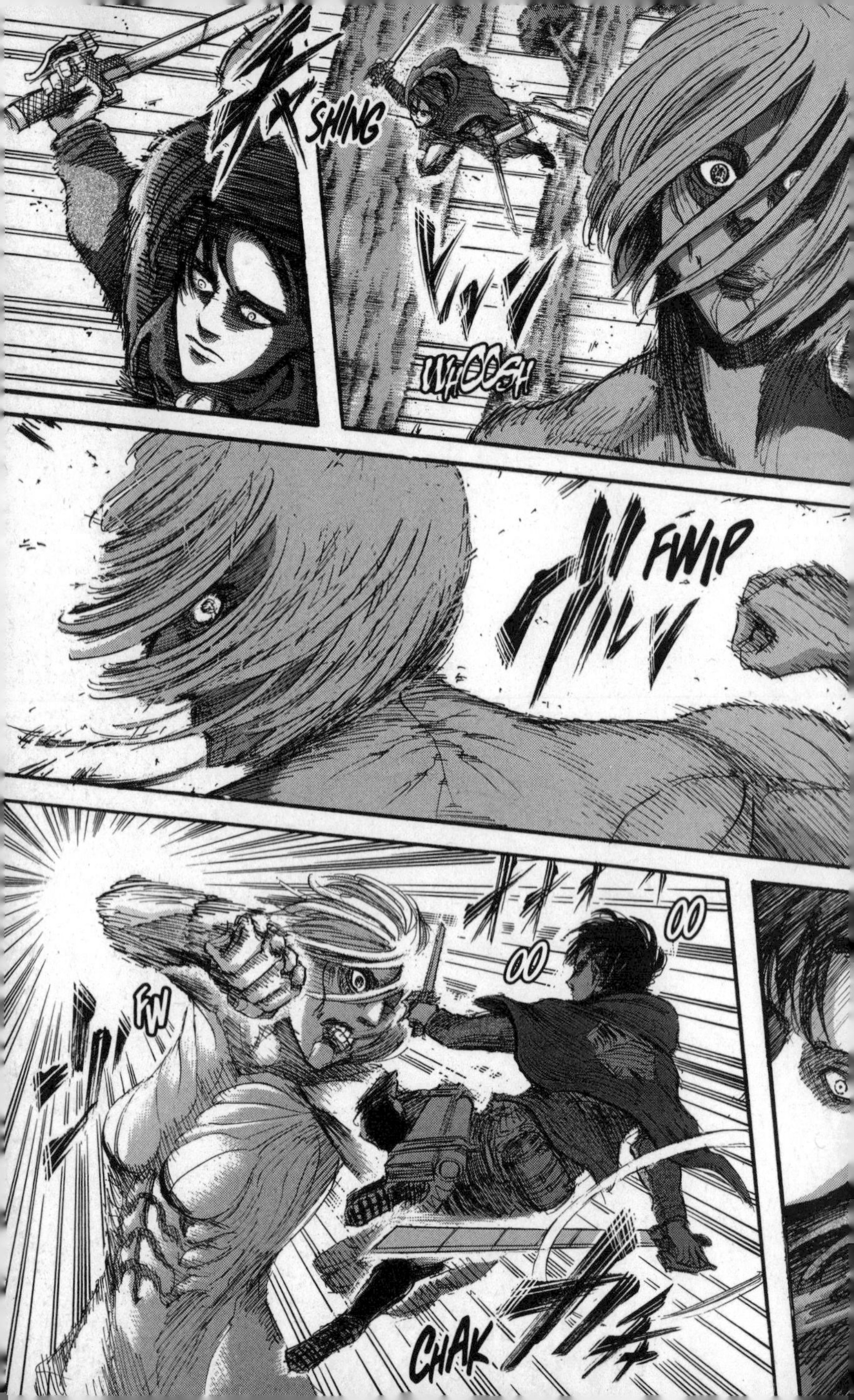
WHOOSH
SHING
FWIP
OO
OO
FW
CHAK

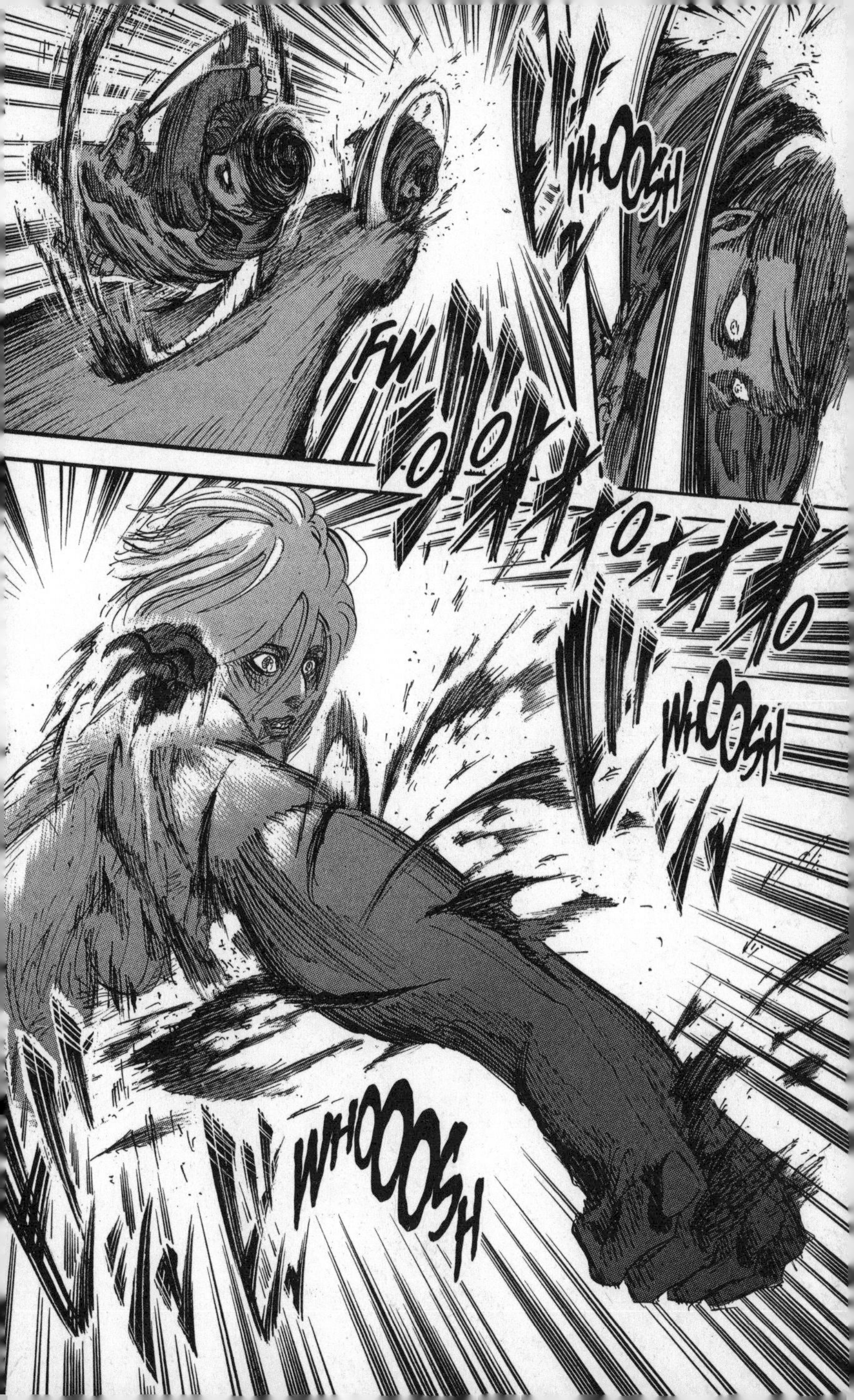
WHOOSH
FWOOOO
WHOOSH
WHOOOOSH

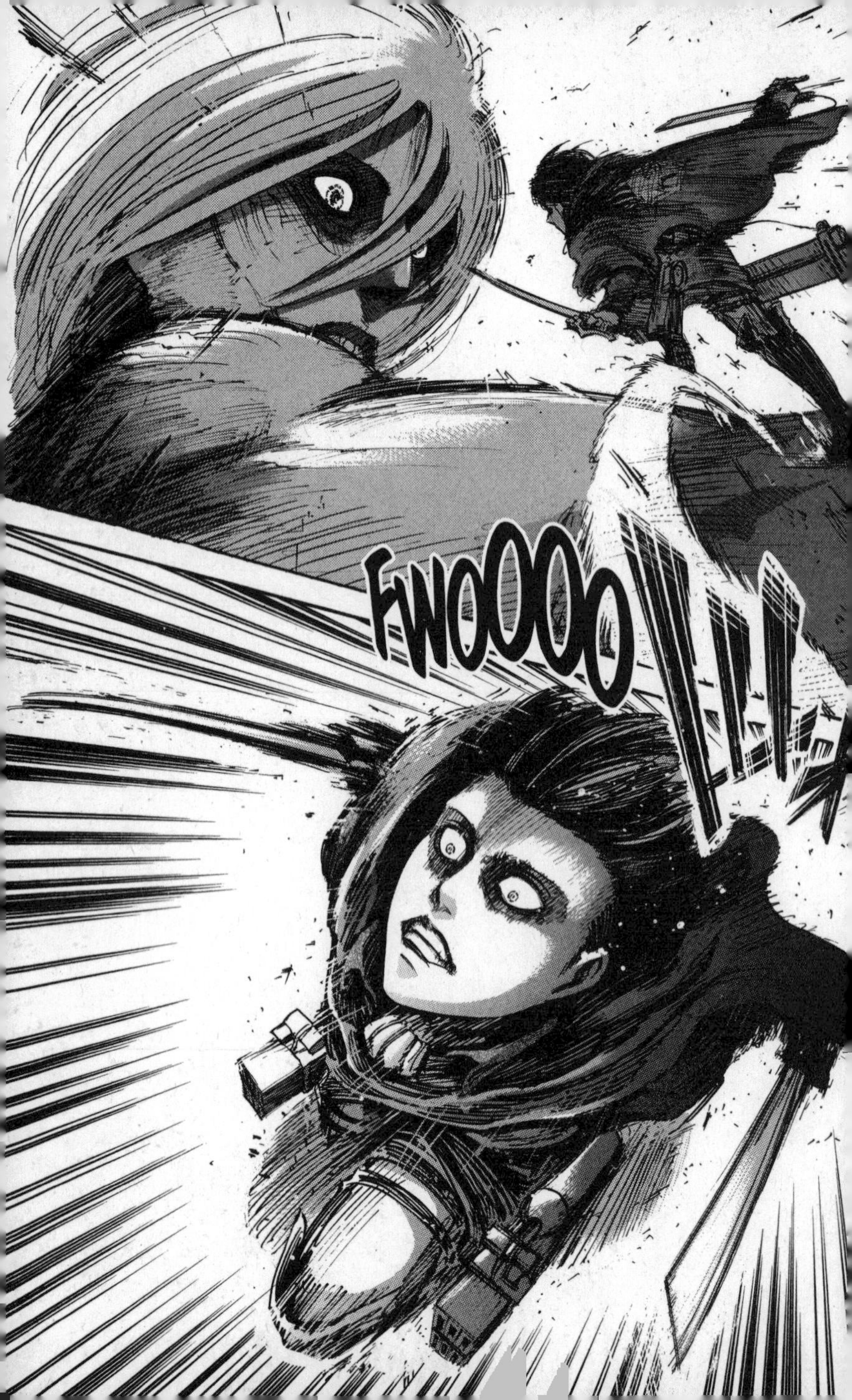
FWOOOO

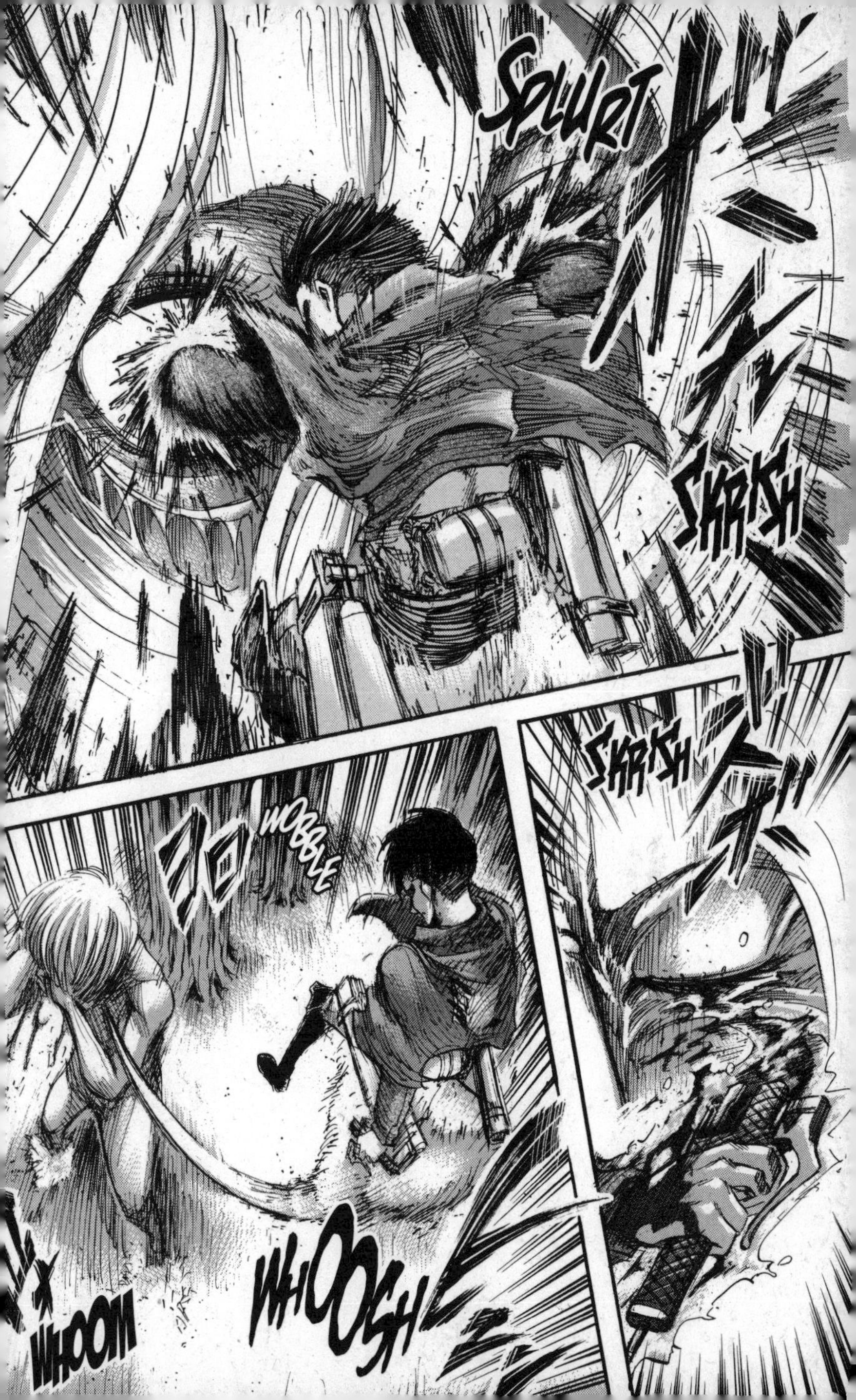
SPLURT
SKRISH
SKRISH
WOBBLE
WHOOSH
WHOOM

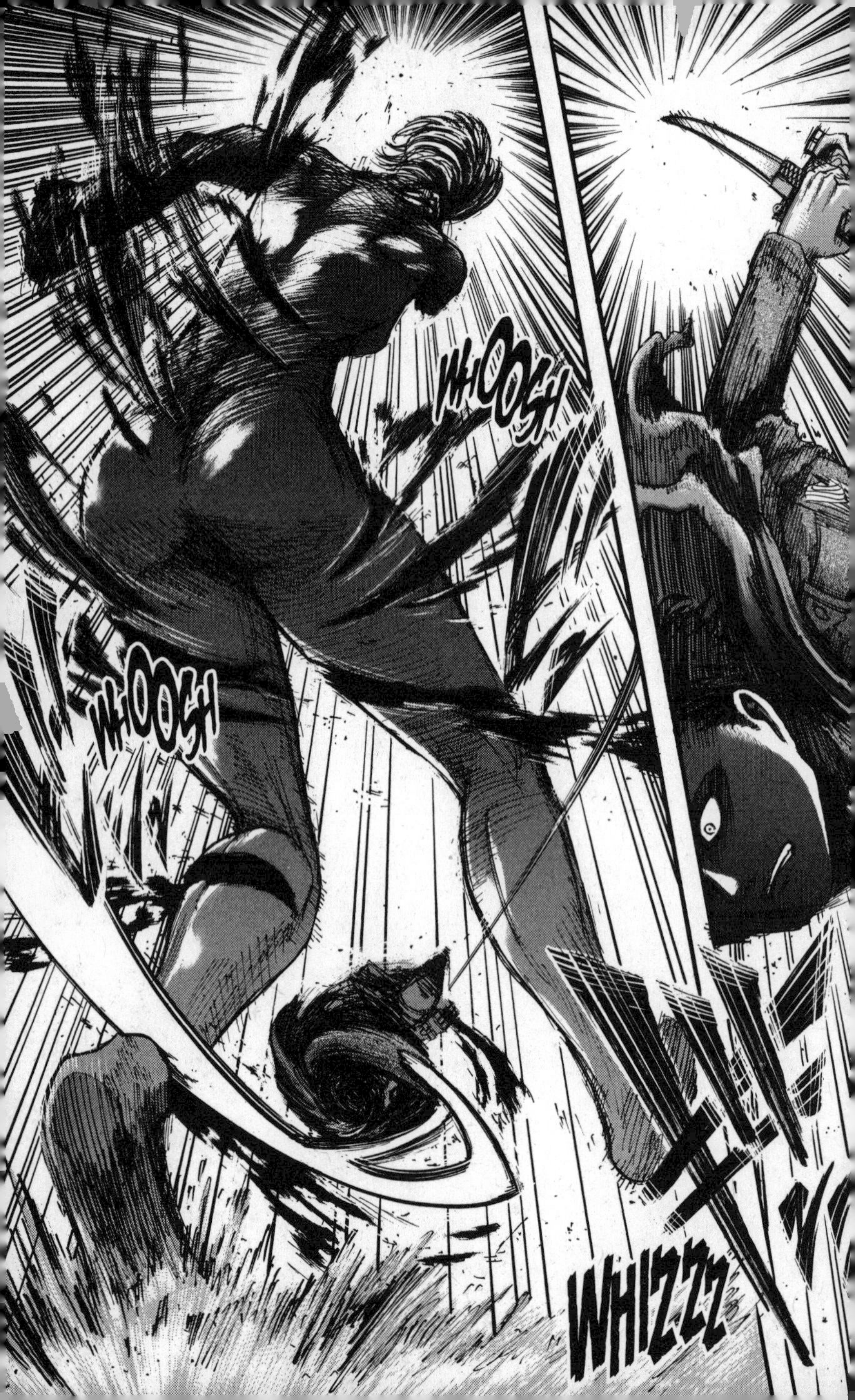
WHOOSH
WHOOSH
WHIZZZ

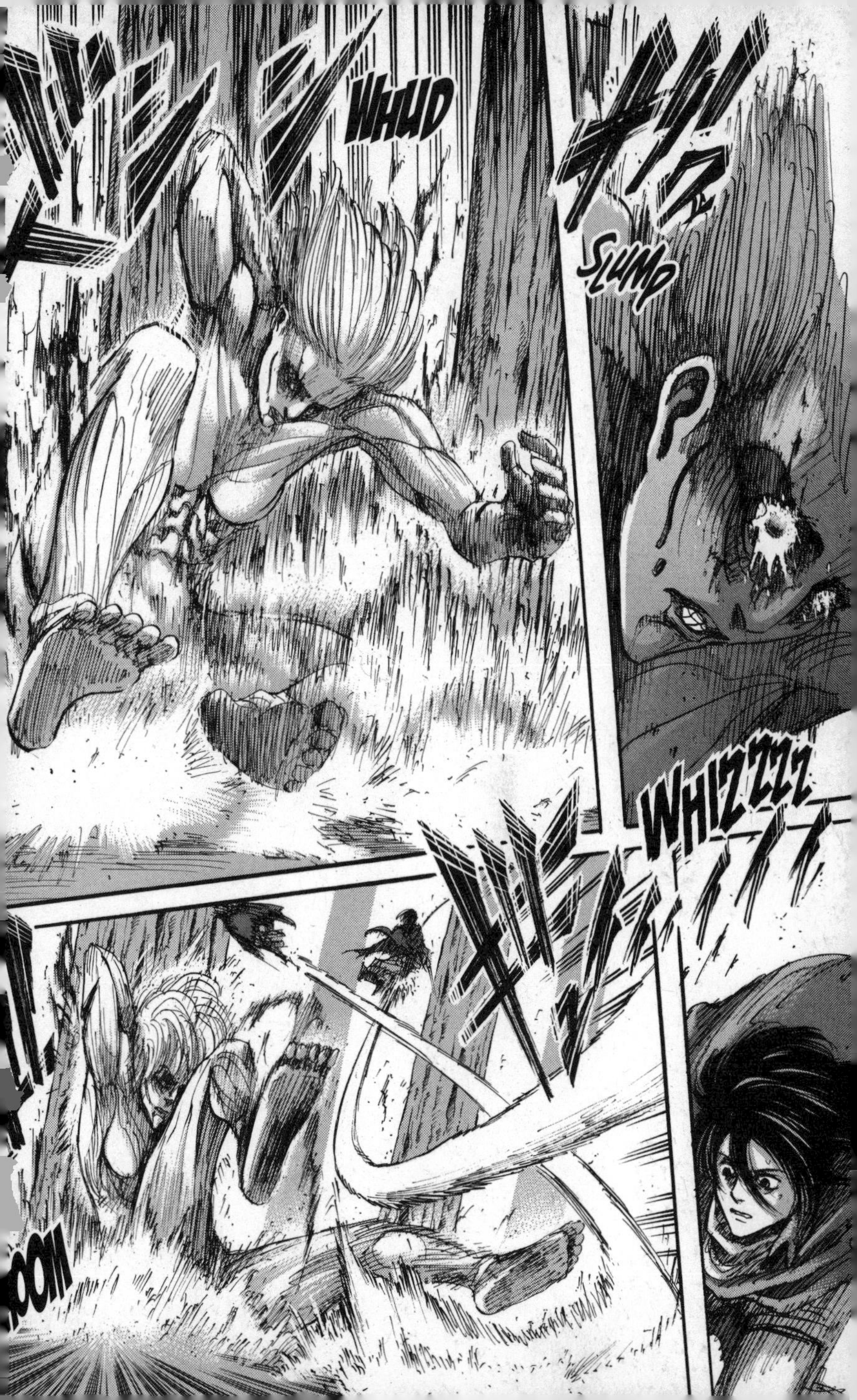
SLUMP
WHUD
WHIZZZZ
OOM

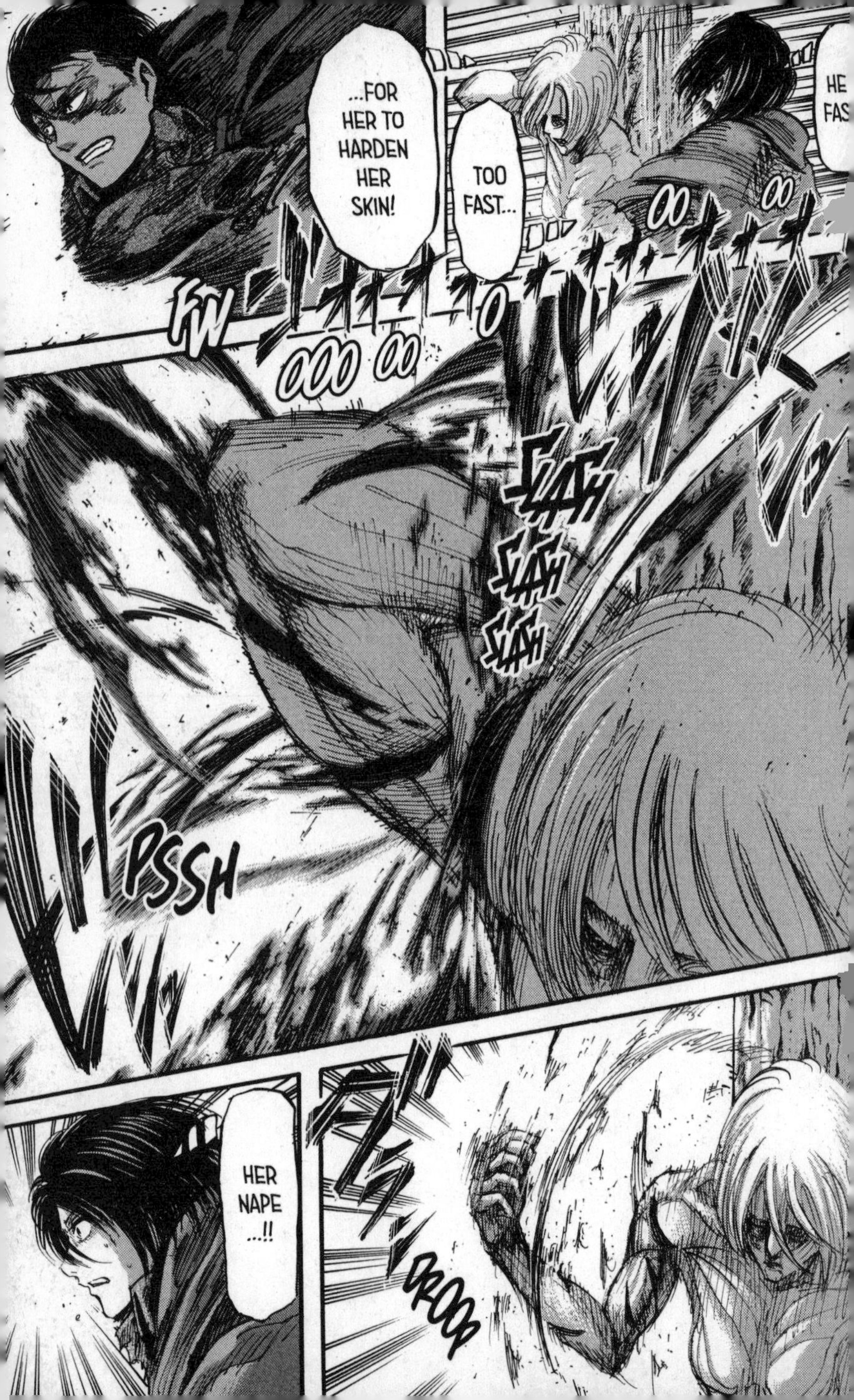
HE FAS
TOO FAST...
...FOR HER TO HARDEN HER SKIN!
FW
OOO OO
OO
OO
SLASH
SLASH
SLASH
PSSH
DROOP
HER NAPE ...!!

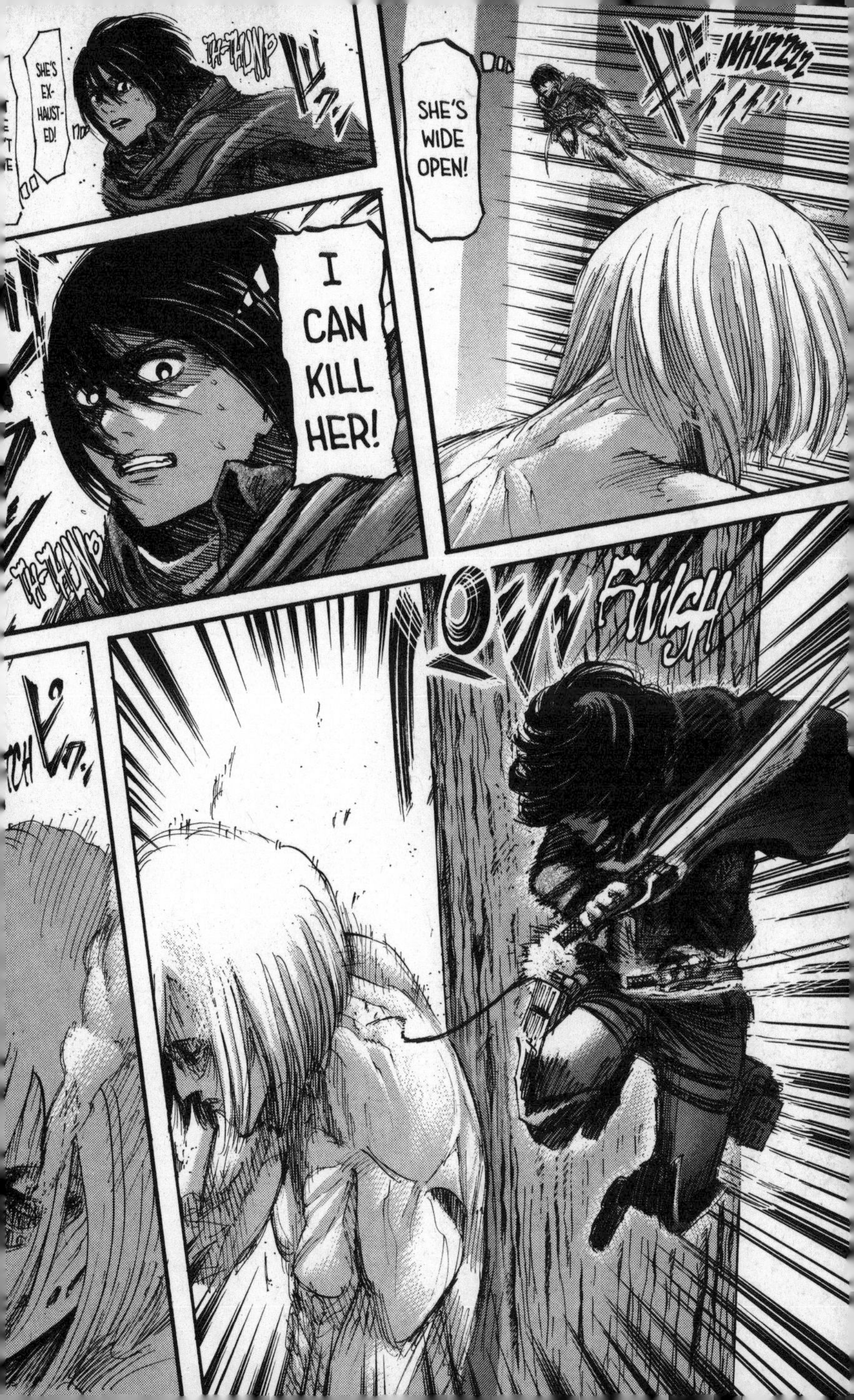
WHIZZZZ
SHE'S WIDE OPEN!
THA-THUNK
SHE'S EX-HAUST-ED!
I CAN KILL HER!
THA-THUNK
FWUSH

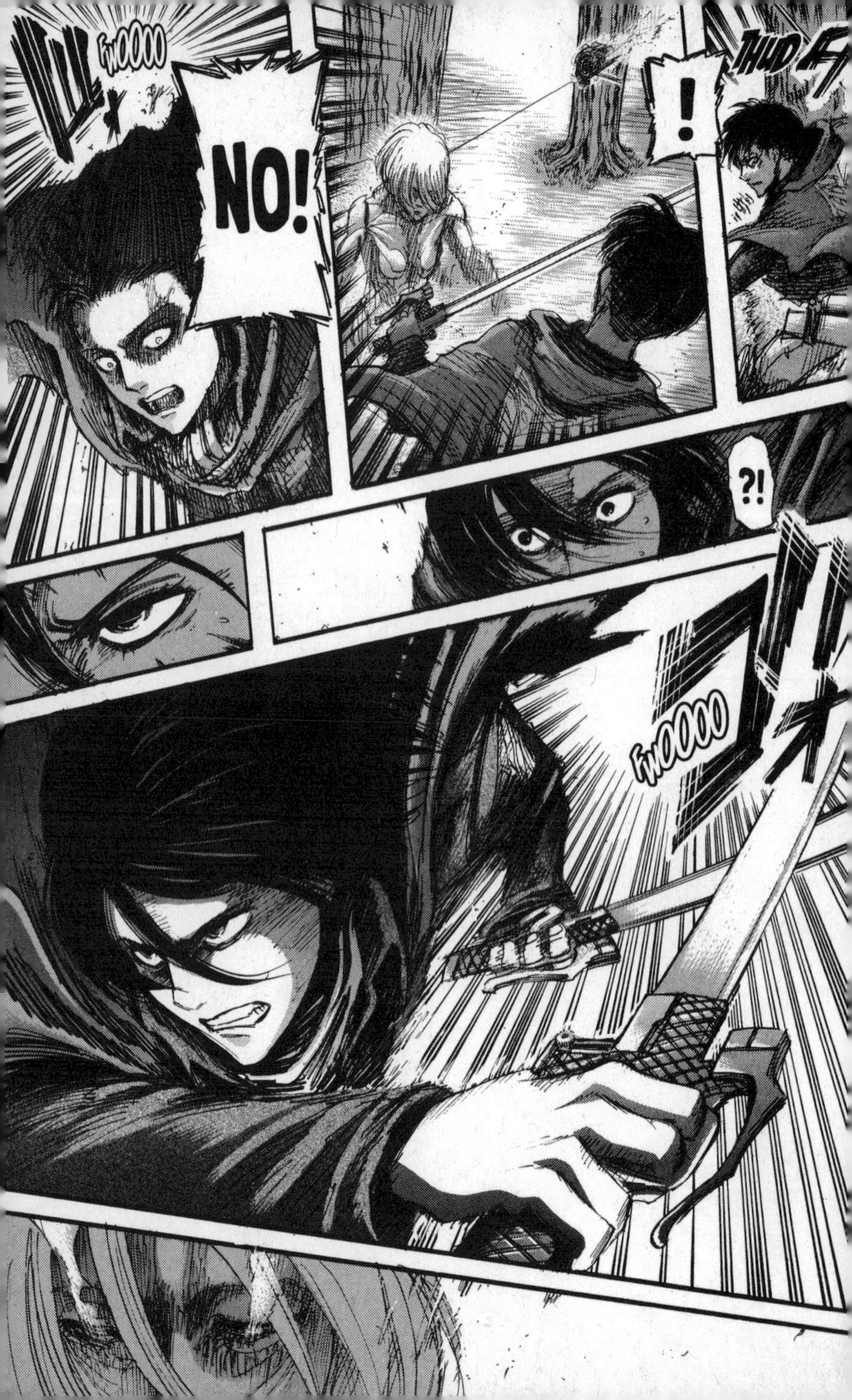
THUD
!
FWOOOO
NO!
?!
FWOOOO

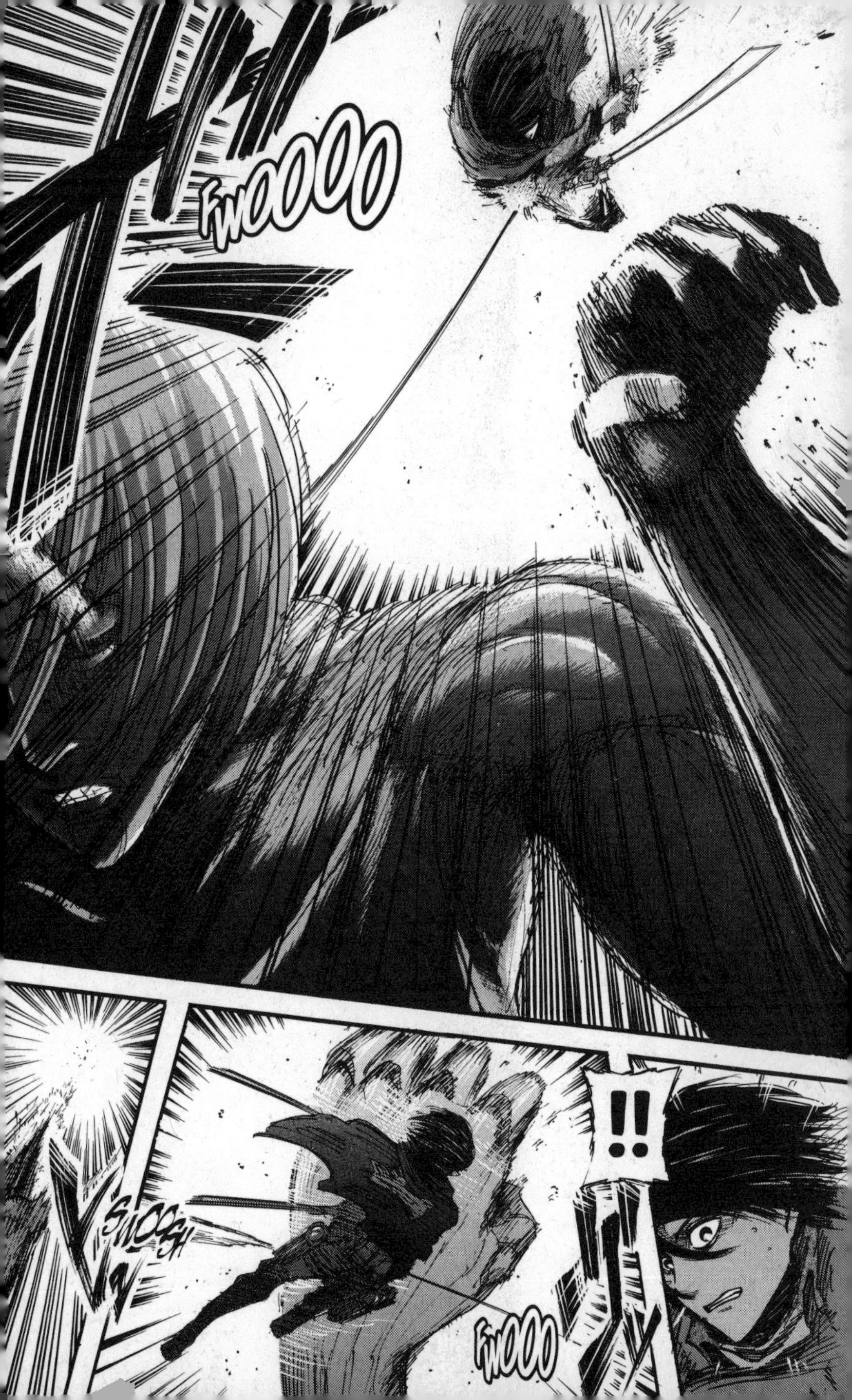
FWOOOO
!!
FWOOO
SWOOSH

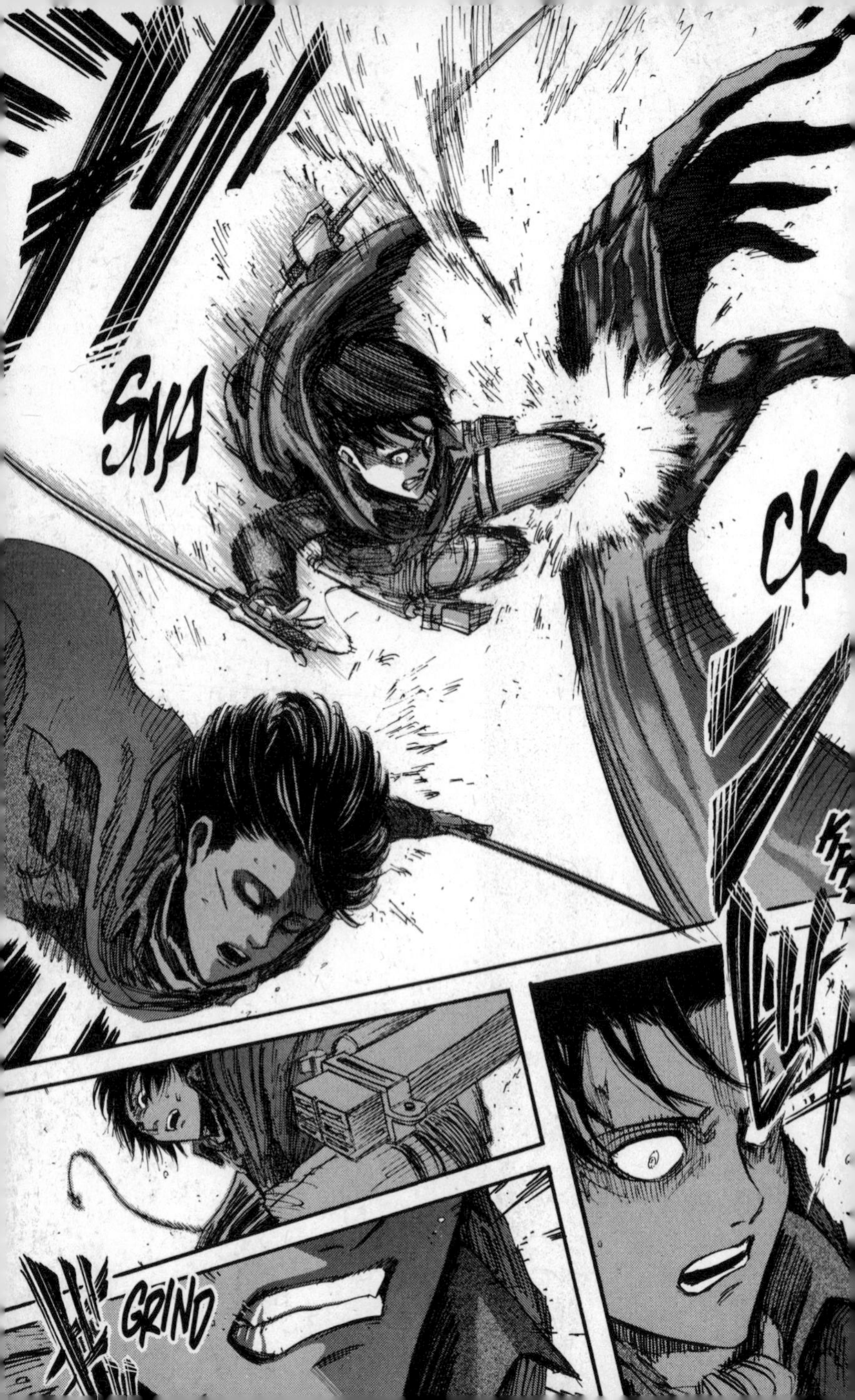
SNA
CK
GRIND

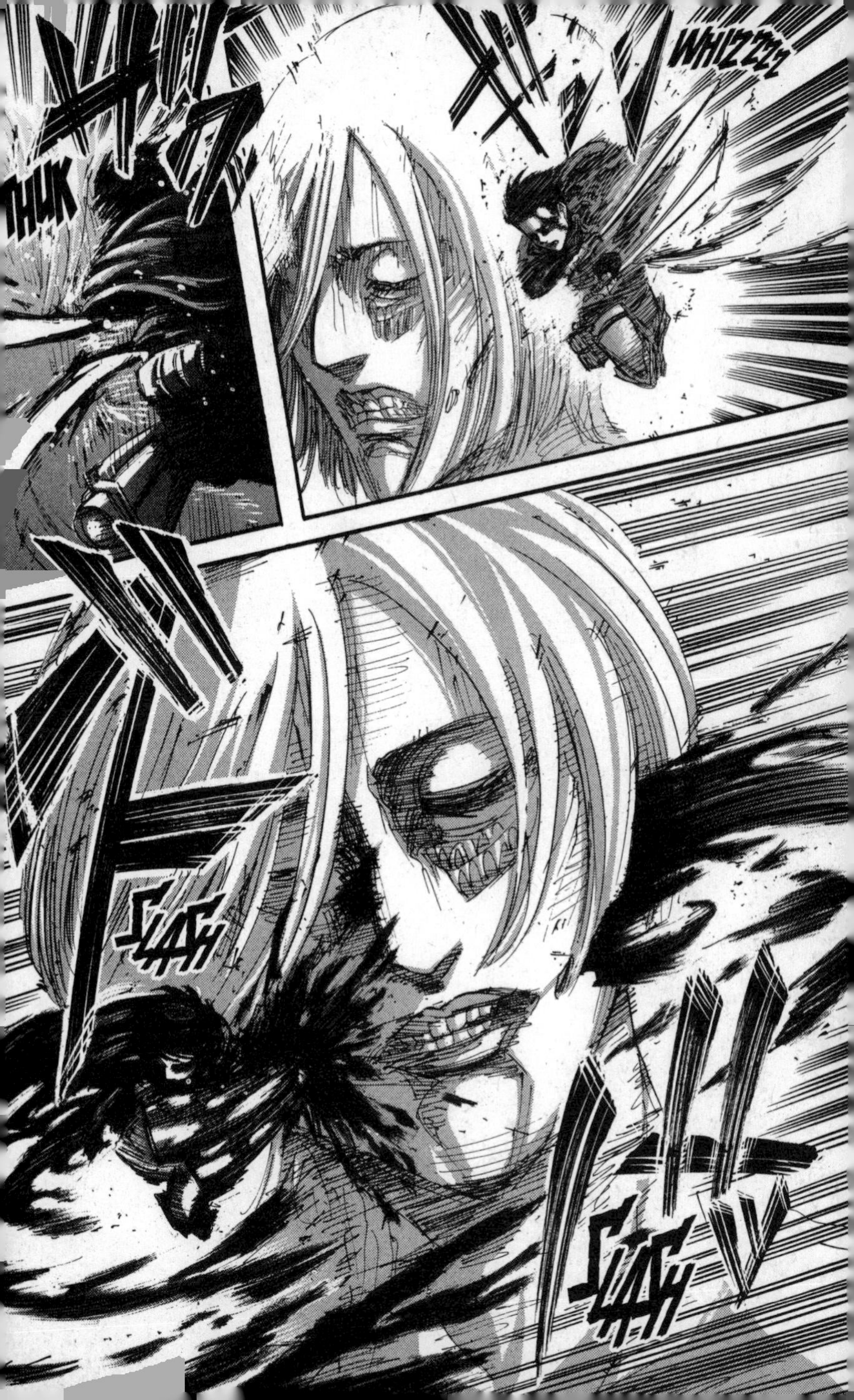
WHIZZZZ
THUK
SLASH
SLASH

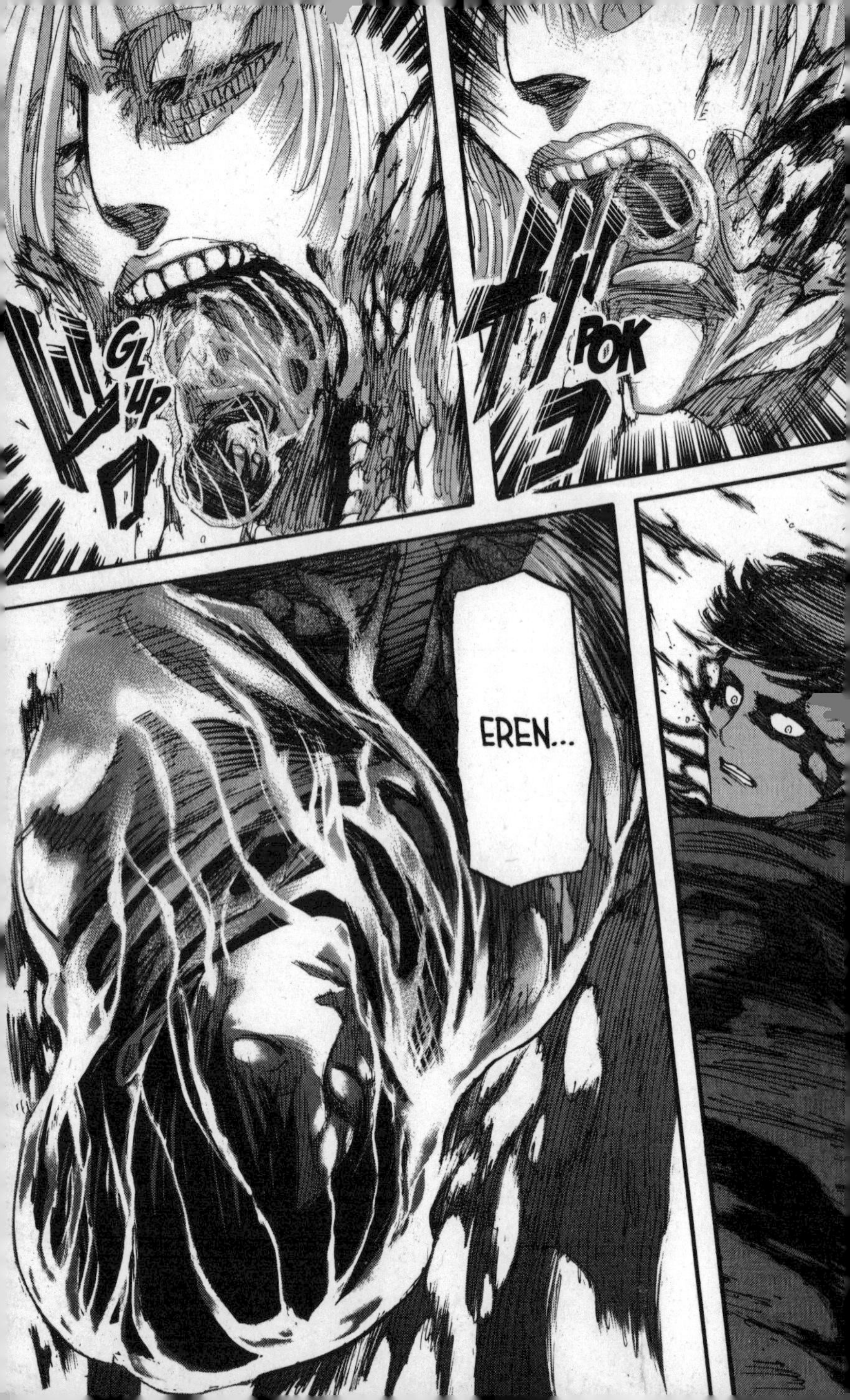
POK
GLUP
EREN...

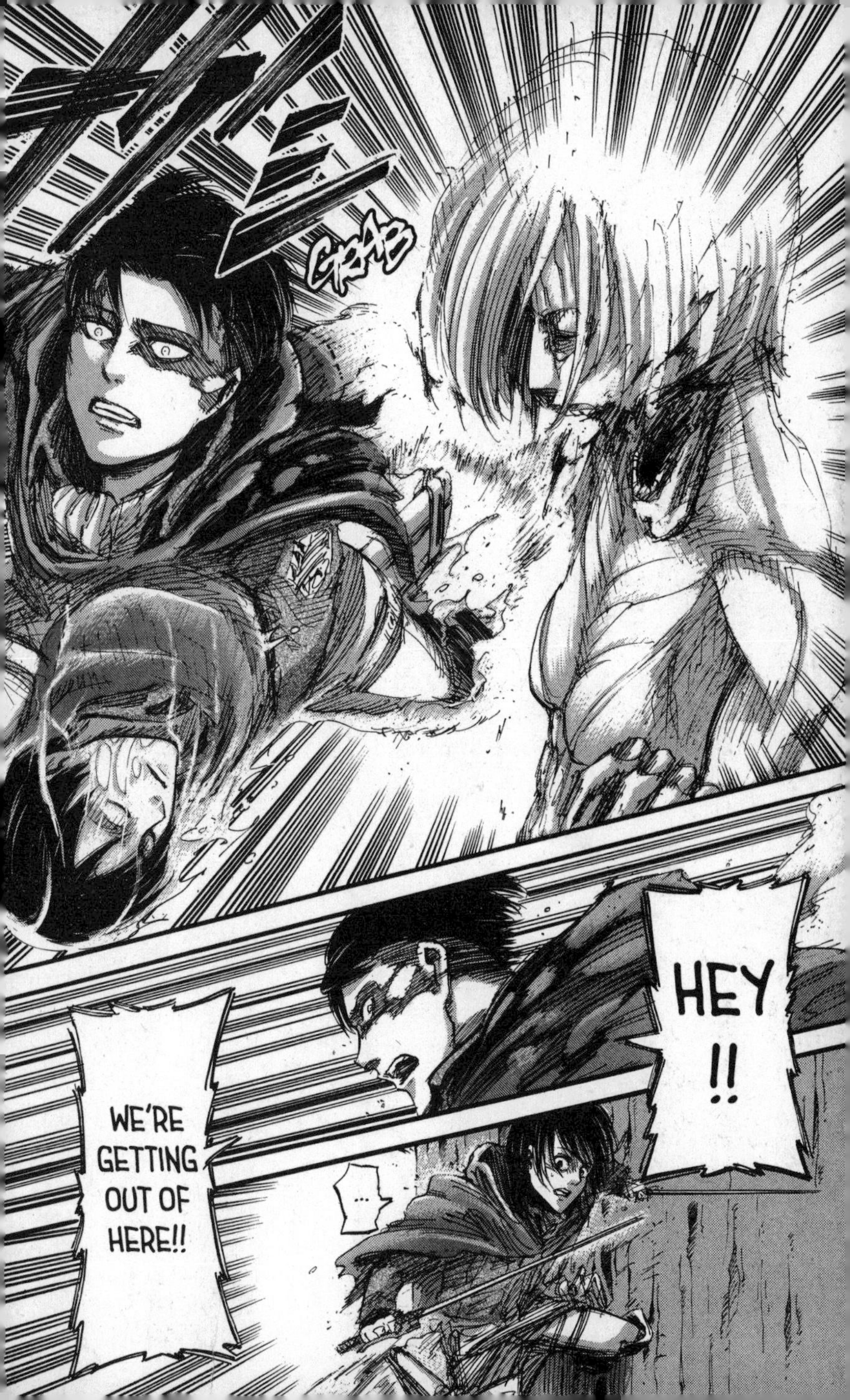
GRAB
HEY!!
WE'RE GETTING OUT OF HERE!!
...

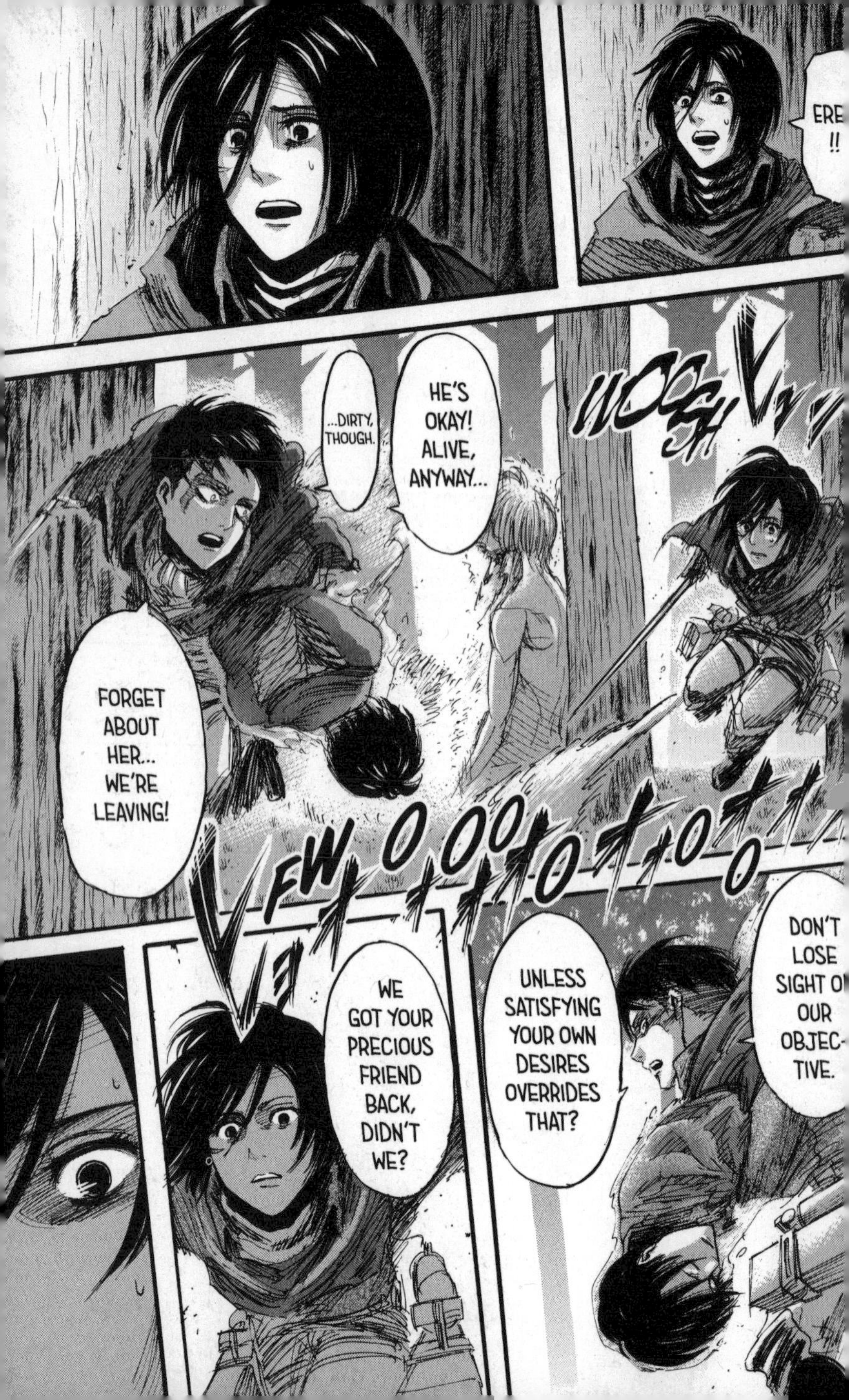
ERE !!
WOOSH
HE'S OKAY! ALIVE, ANYWAY...
...DIRTY, THOUGH.
FORGET ABOUT HER... WE'RE LEAVING!
DON'T LOSE SIGHT O OUR OBJEC-TIVE.
UNLESS SATISFYING YOUR OWN DESIRES OVERRIDES THAT?
WE GOT YOUR PRECIOUS FRIEND BACK, DIDN'T WE?

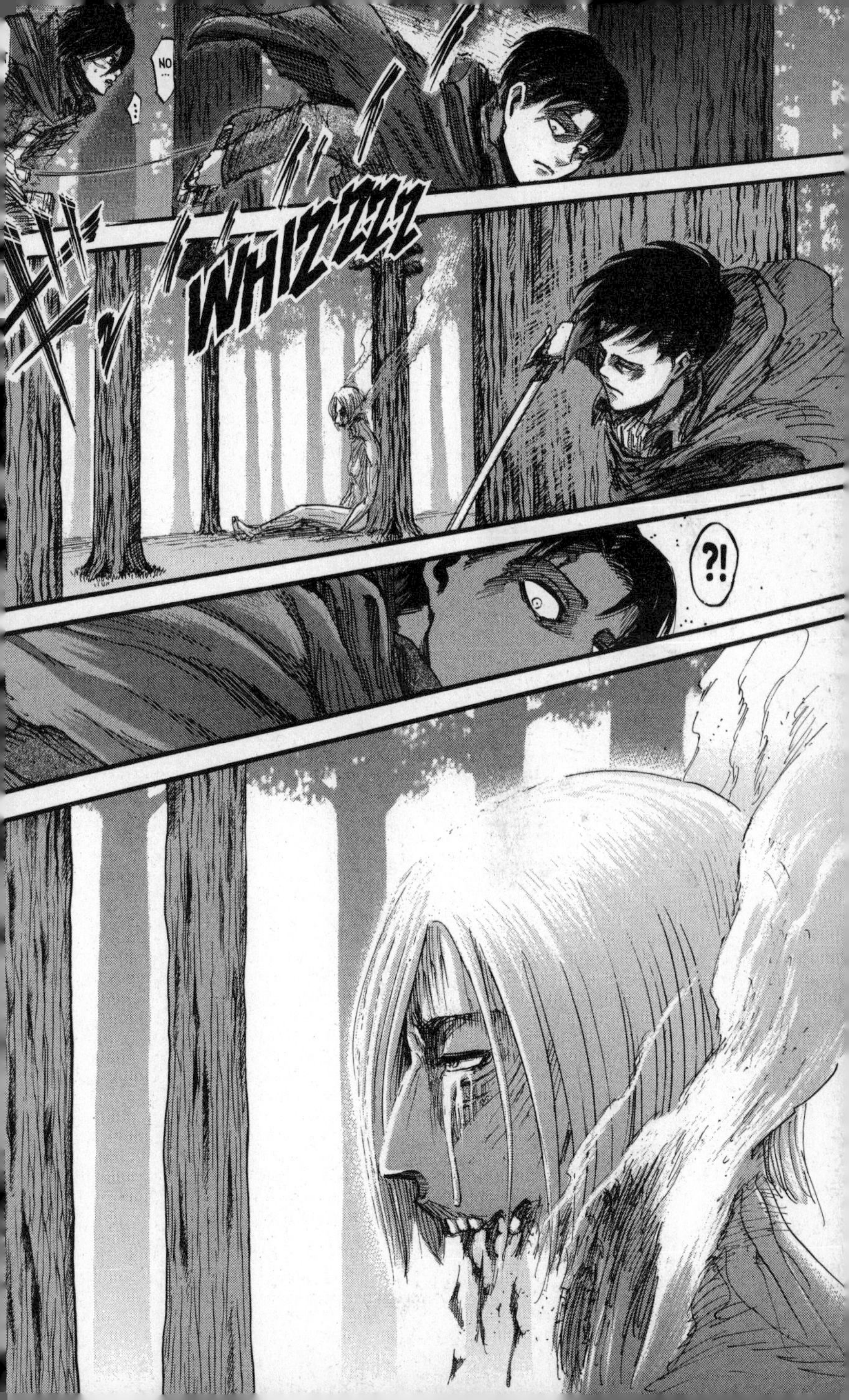
NO ...
...
WHIZZZZ
?!

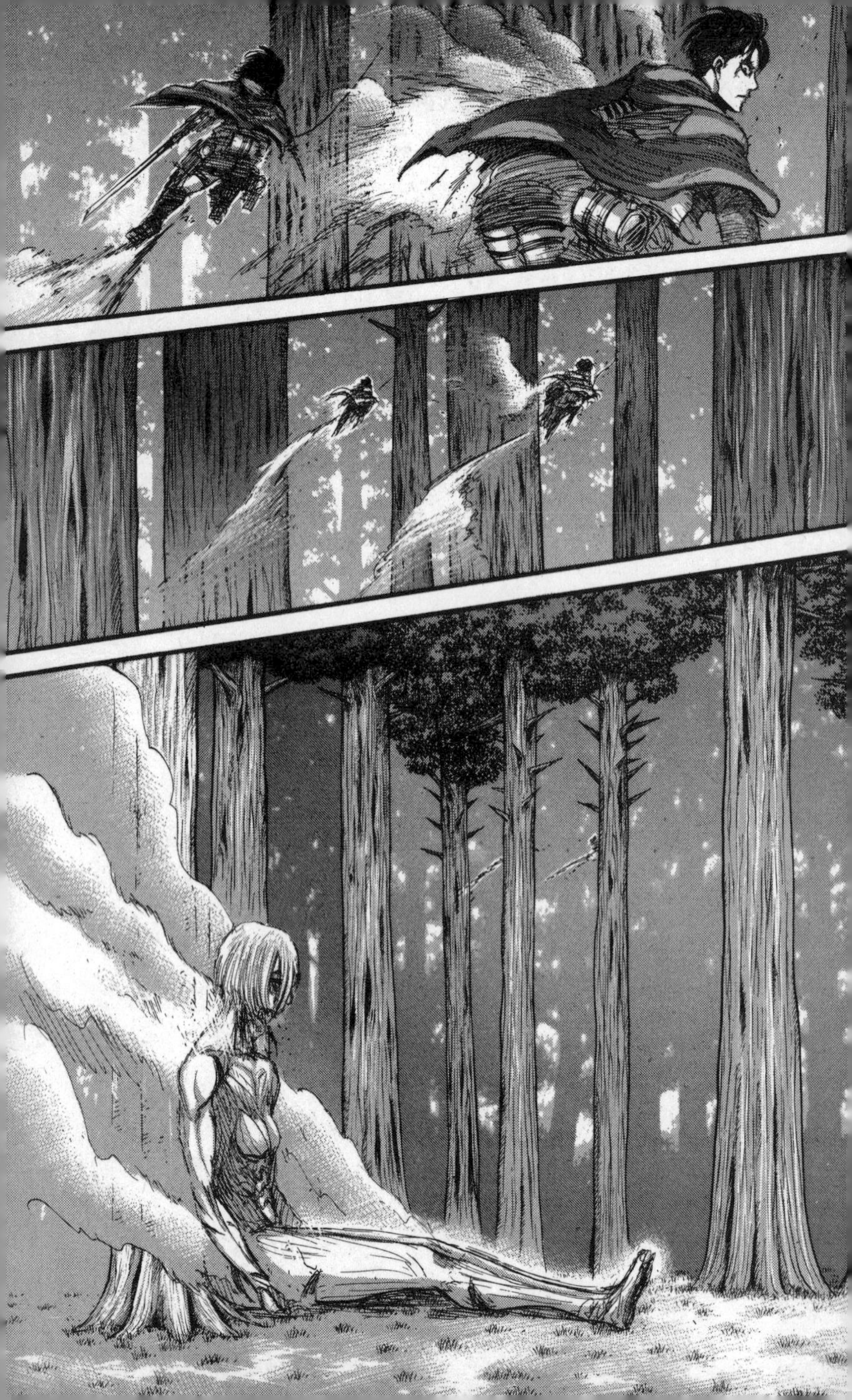

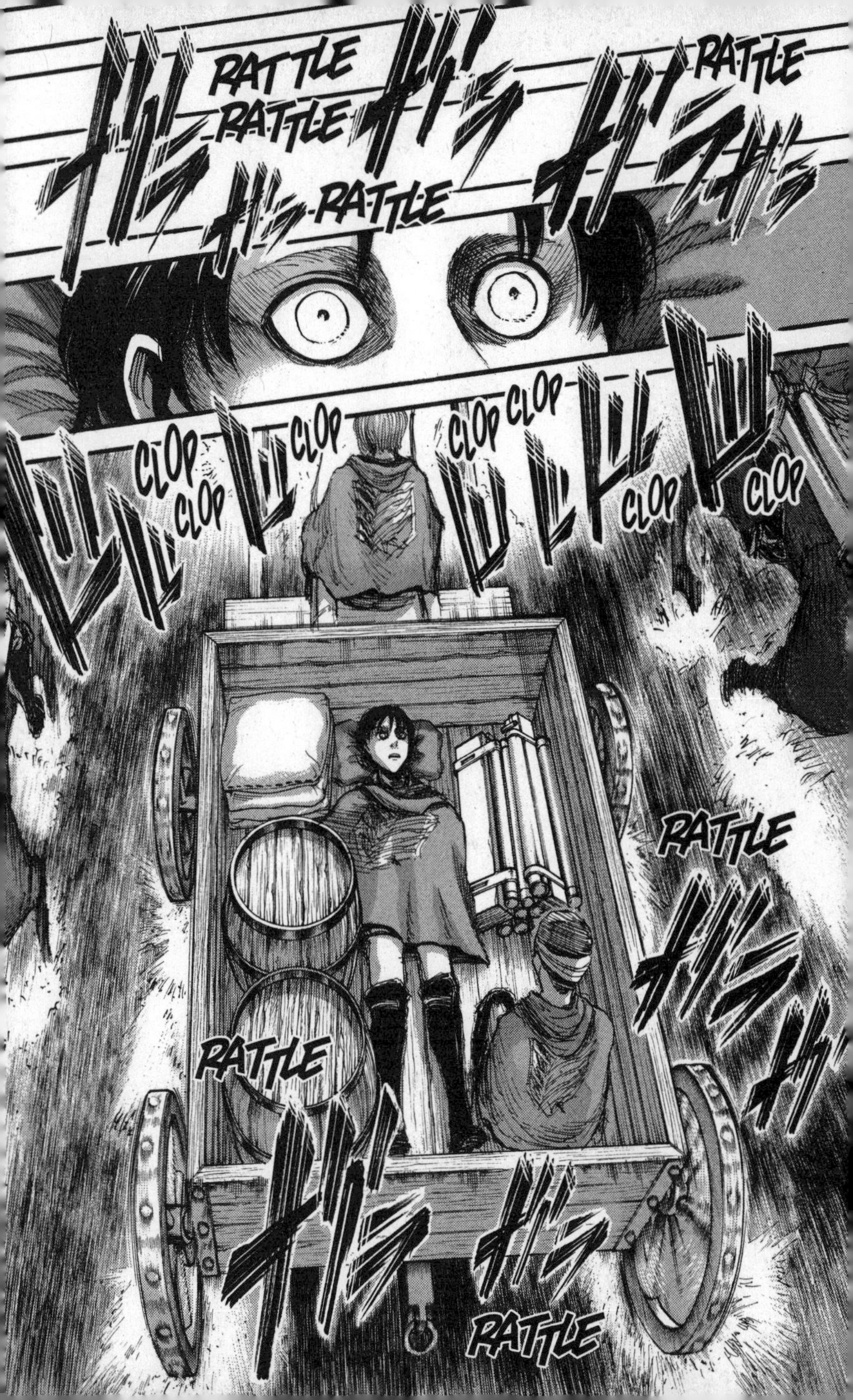
RATTLE
RATTLE
RATTLE
RATTLE
CLOP
CLOP
CLOP CLOP
CLOP
CLOP
CLOP
CLOP
RATTLE
RATTLE
RATTLE

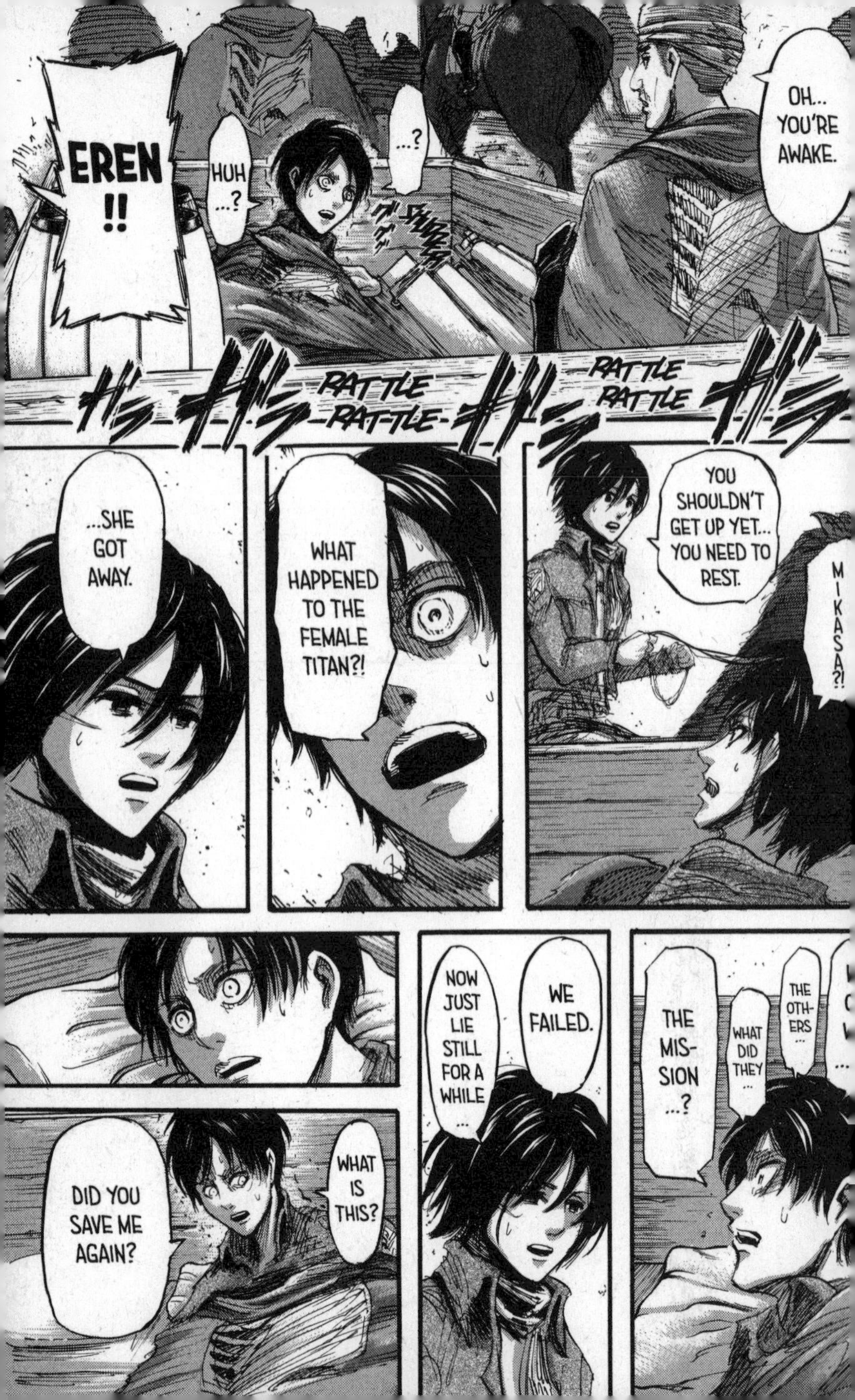
OH... YOU'RE AWAKE.
...?
HUH ...?
EREN !!
RATTLE RATTLE
RATTLE RATTLE
MIKASA?!
YOU SHOULDN'T GET UP YET... YOU NEED TO REST.
WHAT HAPPENED TO THE FEMALE TITAN?!
...SHE GOT AWAY.
THE OTHERS ...
WHAT DID THEY ...
THE MISSION ...?
WE FAILED.
NOW JUST LIE STILL FOR A WHILE ...
WHAT IS THIS?
DID YOU SAVE ME AGAIN?

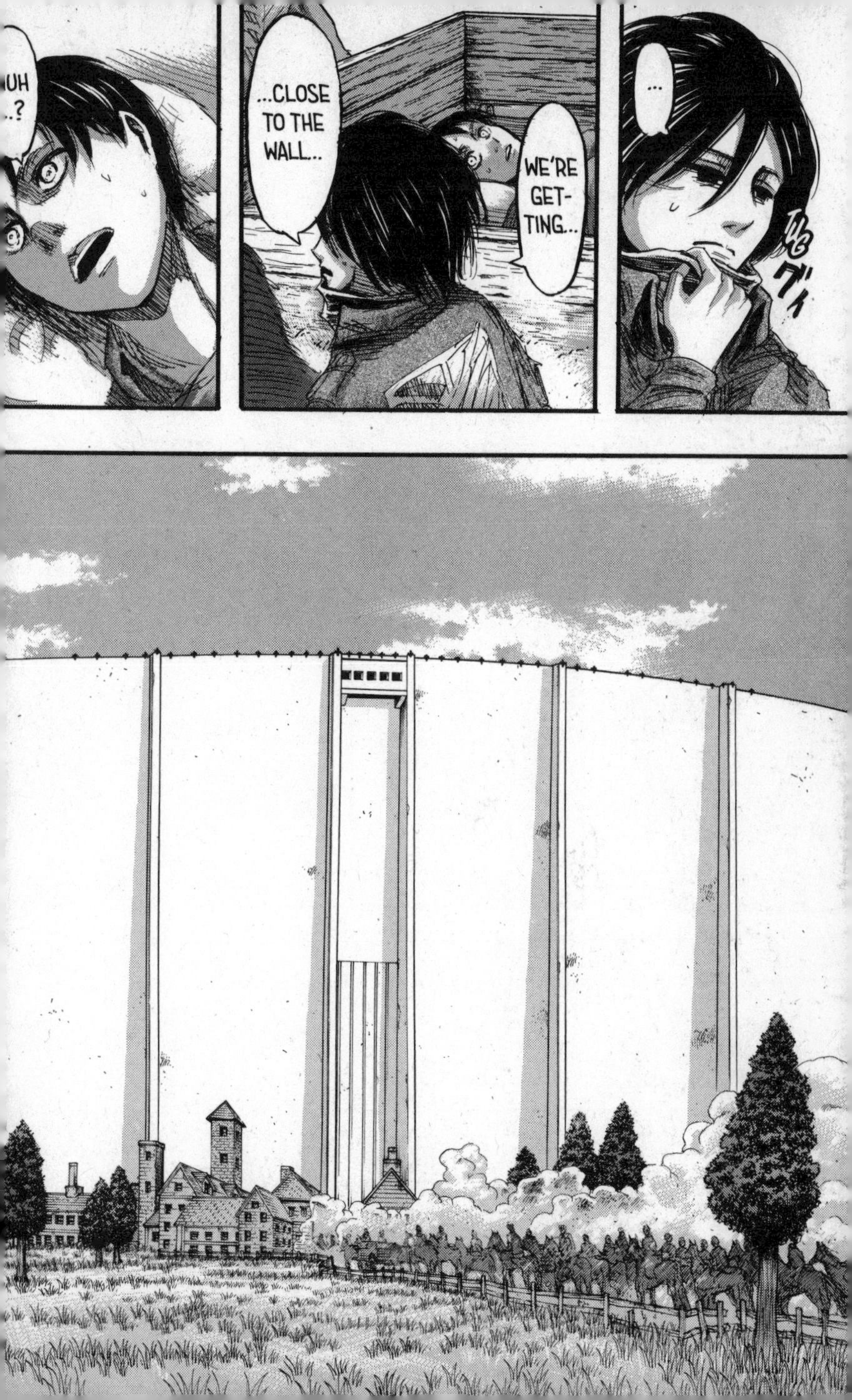
...
TUG
WE'RE GET-TING...
...CLOSE TO THE WALL...
UH ..?

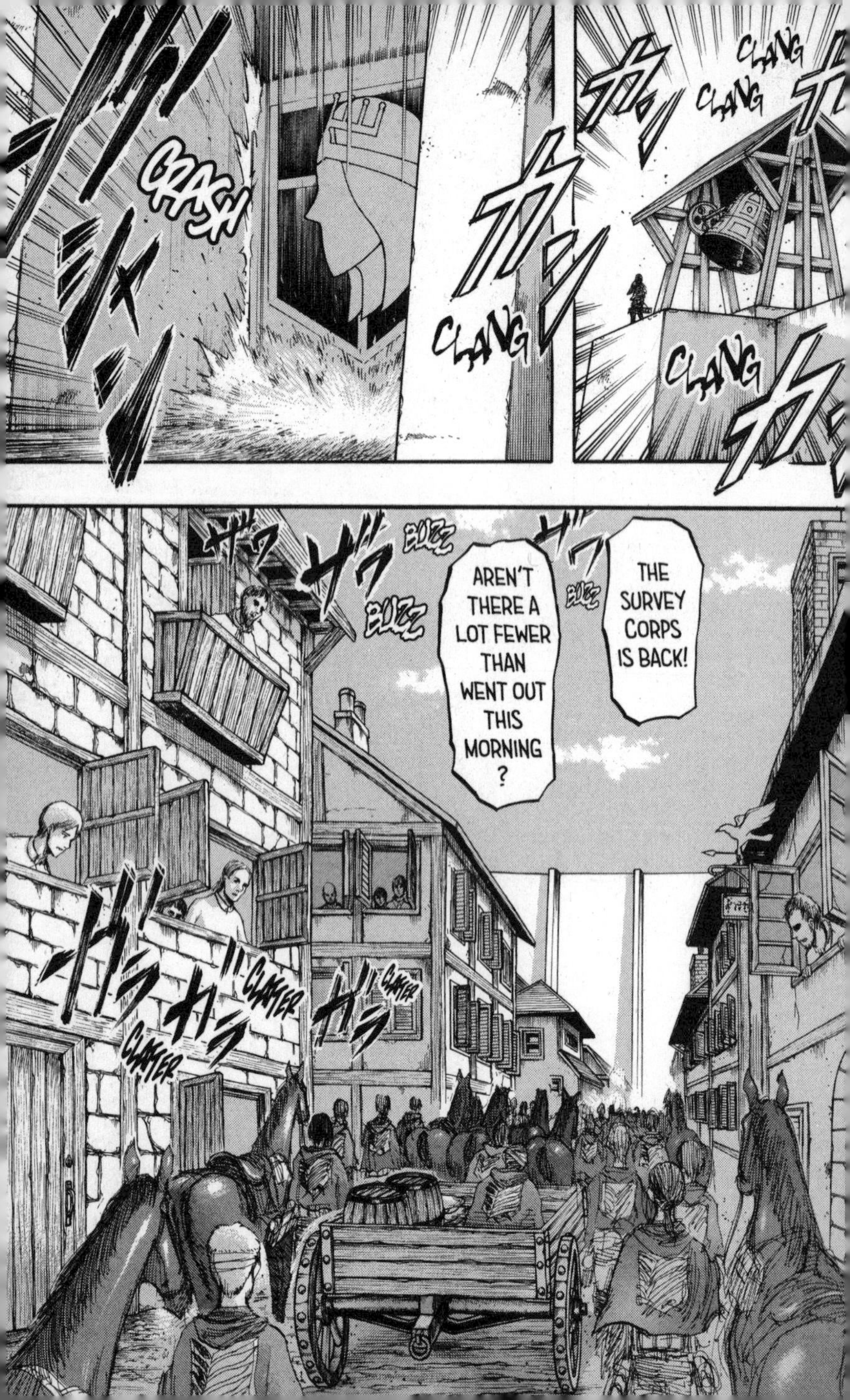
CLANG
CLANG
CLANG
CLANG
CRASH
BUZZ
THE SURVEY CORPS IS BACK!
AREN'T THERE A LOT FEWER THAN WENT OUT THIS MORNING?
BUZZ
BUZZ
CLATTER
CLATTER
CLATTER

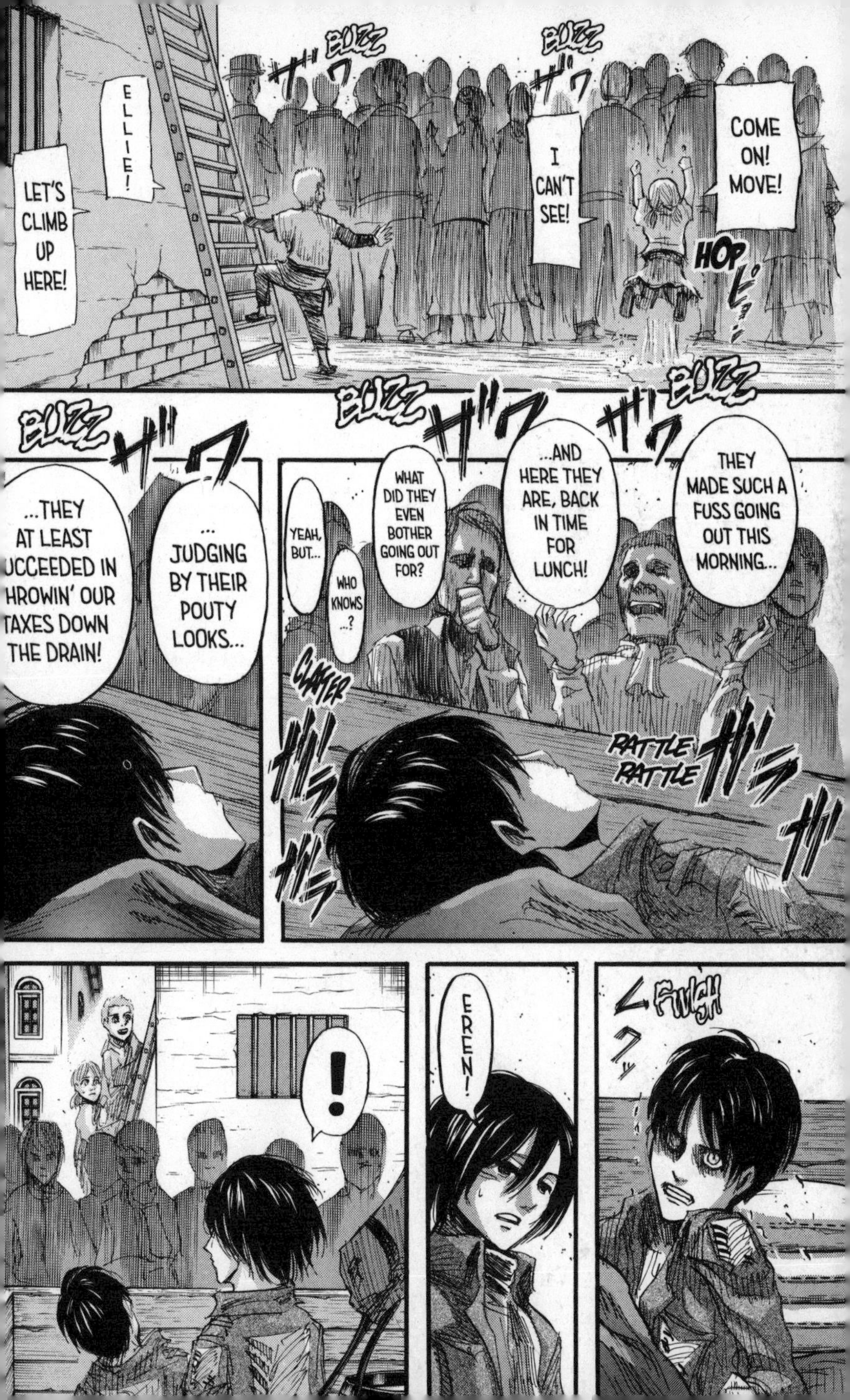
BUZZ
COME ON! MOVE!
HOP
BUZZ
I CAN'T SEE!
ELLIE!
LET'S CLIMB UP HERE!
BUZZ
THEY MADE SUCH A FUSS GOING OUT THIS MORNING...
BUZZ
...AND HERE THEY ARE, BACK IN TIME FOR LUNCH!
WHAT DID THEY EVEN BOTHER GOING OUT FOR?
WHO KNOWS...?
YEAH, BUT...
RATTLE RATTLE
CLATTER
BUZZ
... JUDGING BY THEIR POUTY LOOKS...
...THEY AT LEAST UCCEEDED IN HROWIN' OUR TAXES DOWN THE DRAIN!
FWISH
EREN!
!

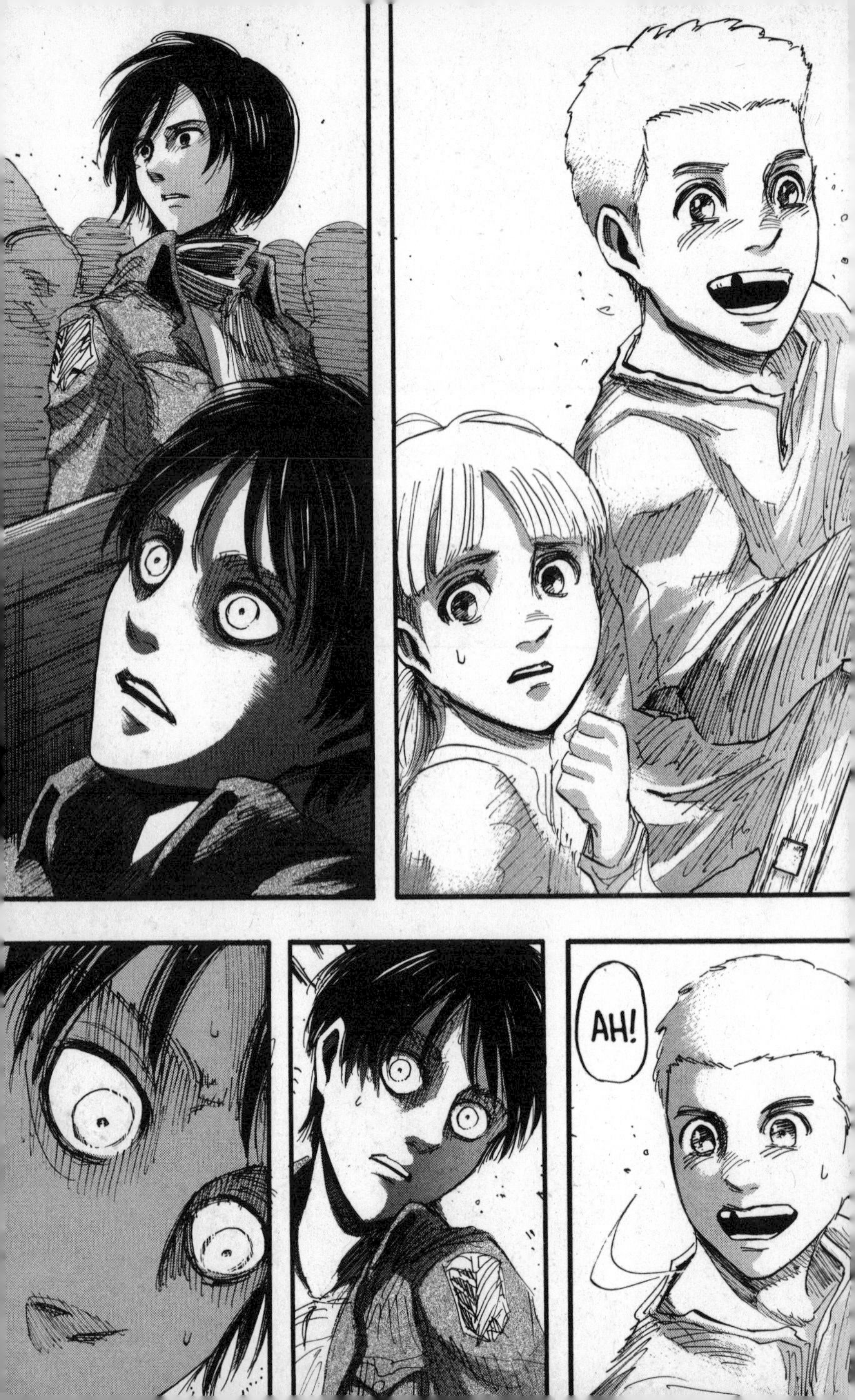
AH!

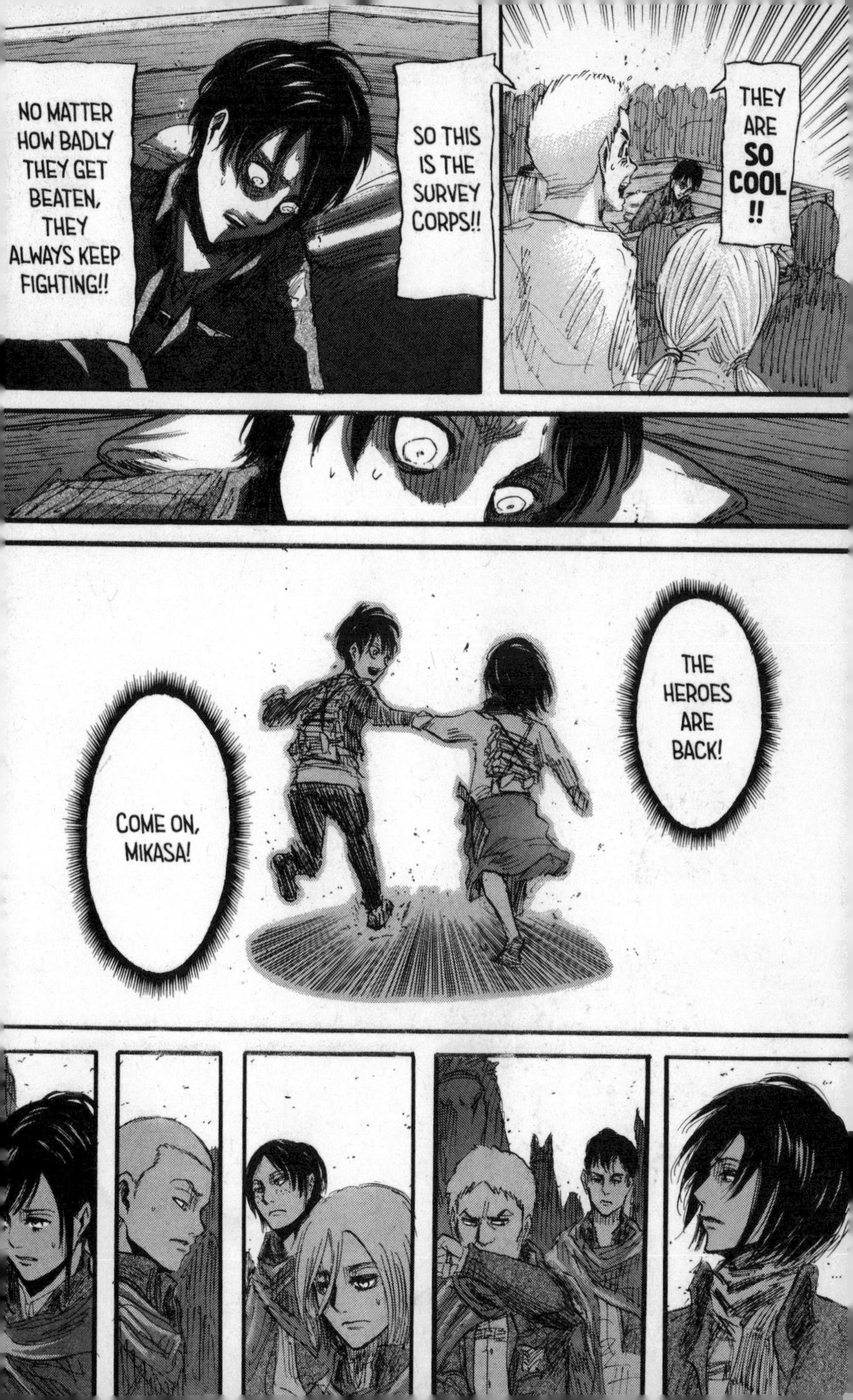
THEY ARE SO COOL!!
SO THIS IS THE SURVEY CORPS!!
NO MATTER HOW BADLY THEY GET BEATEN, THEY ALWAYS KEEP FIGHTING!!
THE HEROES ARE BACK!
COME ON, MIKASA!

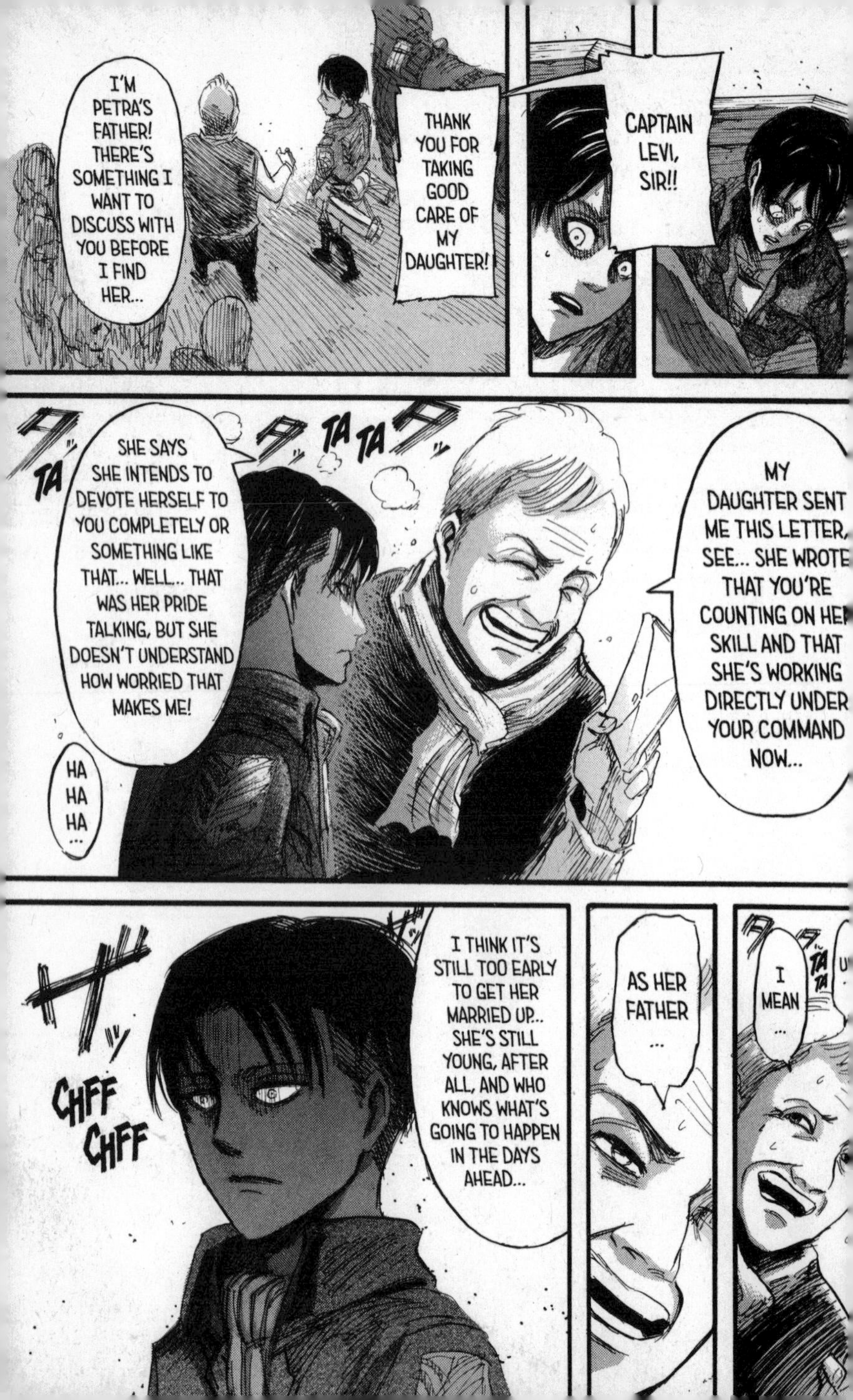
CAPTAIN LEVI, SIR!!
THANK YOU FOR TAKING GOOD CARE OF MY DAUGHTER!
I'M PETRA'S FATHER! THERE'S SOMETHING I WANT TO DISCUSS WITH YOU BEFORE I FIND HER...
TA
TA
TA
TA
MY DAUGHTER SENT ME THIS LETTER, SEE... SHE WROTE THAT YOU'RE COUNTING ON HER SKILL AND THAT SHE'S WORKING DIRECTLY UNDER YOUR COMMAND NOW...
SHE SAYS SHE INTENDS TO DEVOTE HERSELF TO YOU COMPLETELY OR SOMETHING LIKE THAT... WELL... THAT WAS HER PRIDE TALKING, BUT SHE DOESN'T UNDERSTAND HOW WORRIED THAT MAKES ME!
HA HA HA...
TA
TA
I MEAN...
AS HER FATHER...
I THINK IT'S STILL TOO EARLY TO GET HER MARRIED UP... SHE'S STILL YOUNG, AFTER ALL, AND WHO KNOWS WHAT'S GOING TO HAPPEN IN THE DAYS AHEAD...
CHFF
CHFF

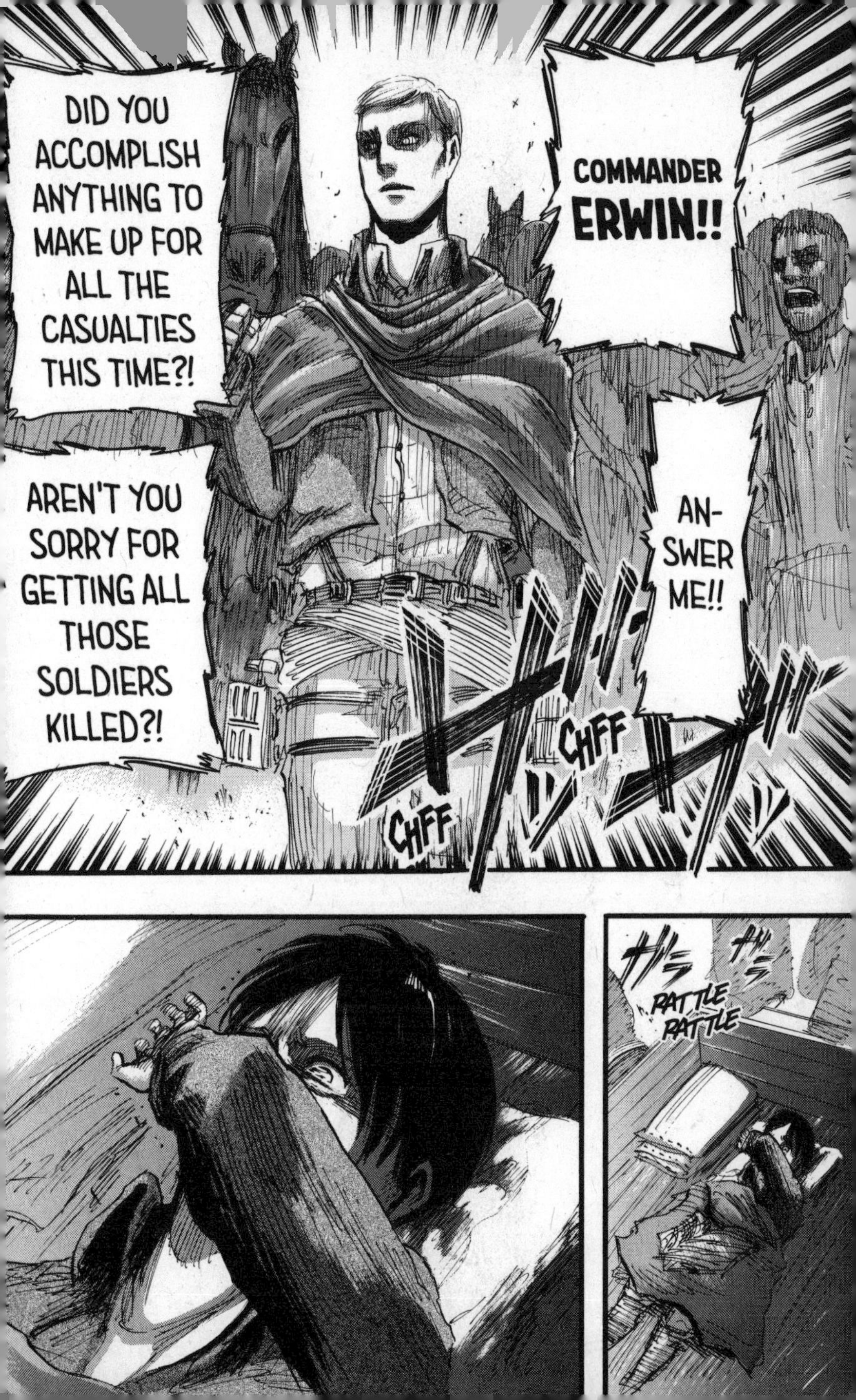
COMMANDER ERWIN!!
DID YOU ACCOMPLISH ANYTHING TO MAKE UP FOR ALL THE CASUALTIES THIS TIME?!
AN-SWER ME!!
AREN'T YOU SORRY FOR GETTING ALL THOSE SOLDIERS KILLED?!
CHFF
CHFF
RATTLE RATTLE

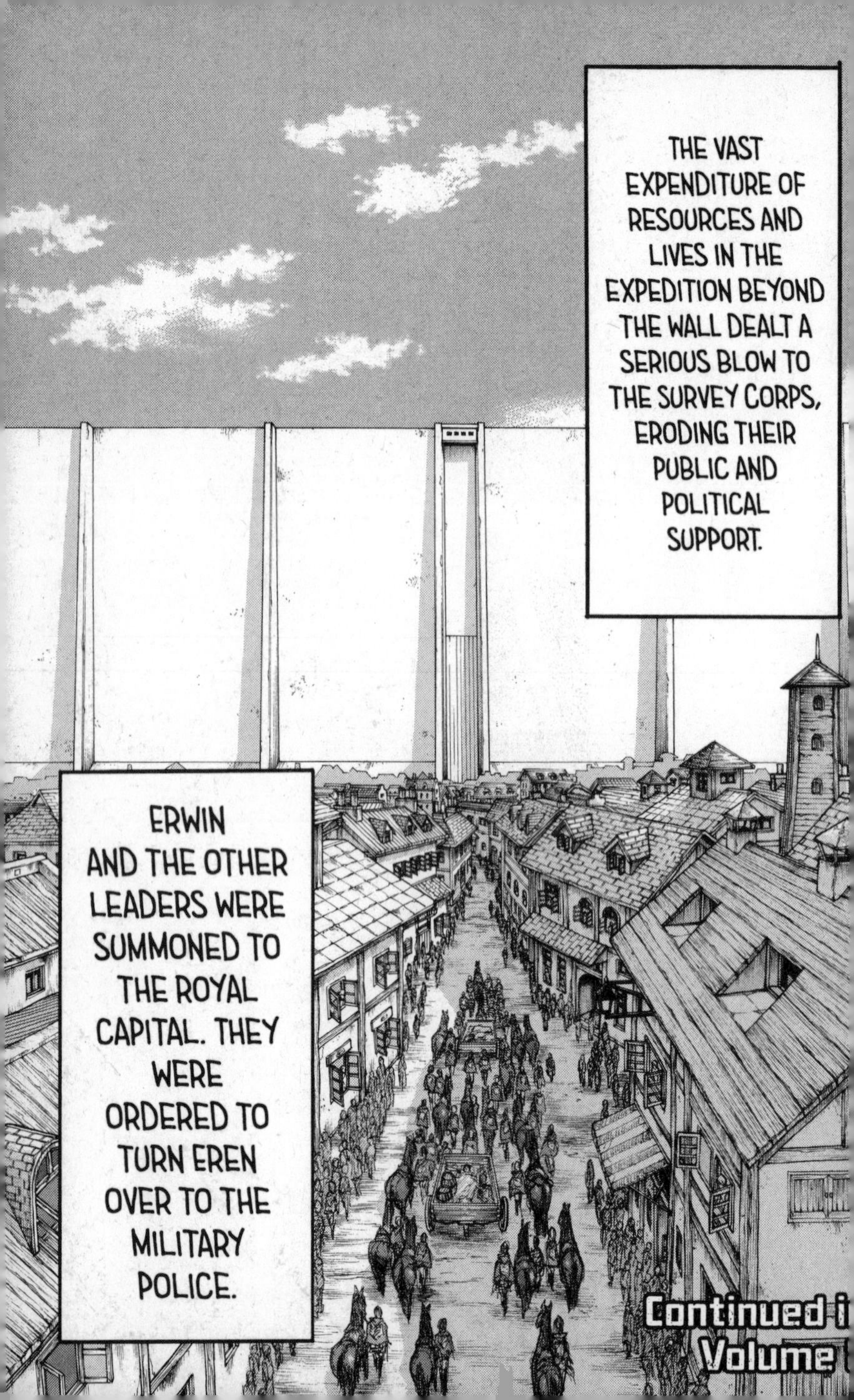
THE VAST EXPENDITURE OF RESOURCES AND LIVES IN THE EXPEDITION BEYOND THE WALL DEALT A SERIOUS BLOW TO THE SURVEY CORPS, ERODING THEIR PUBLIC AND POLITICAL SUPPORT.
ERWIN AND THE OTHER LEADERS WERE SUMMONED TO THE ROYAL CAPITAL. THEY WERE ORDERED TO TURN EREN OVER TO THE MILITARY POLICE.
Continued i
Volume

ATTACK on TITAN

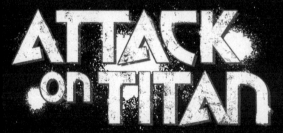

***Rejected Cover Proposal**

The mood just didn't go with the worldview.

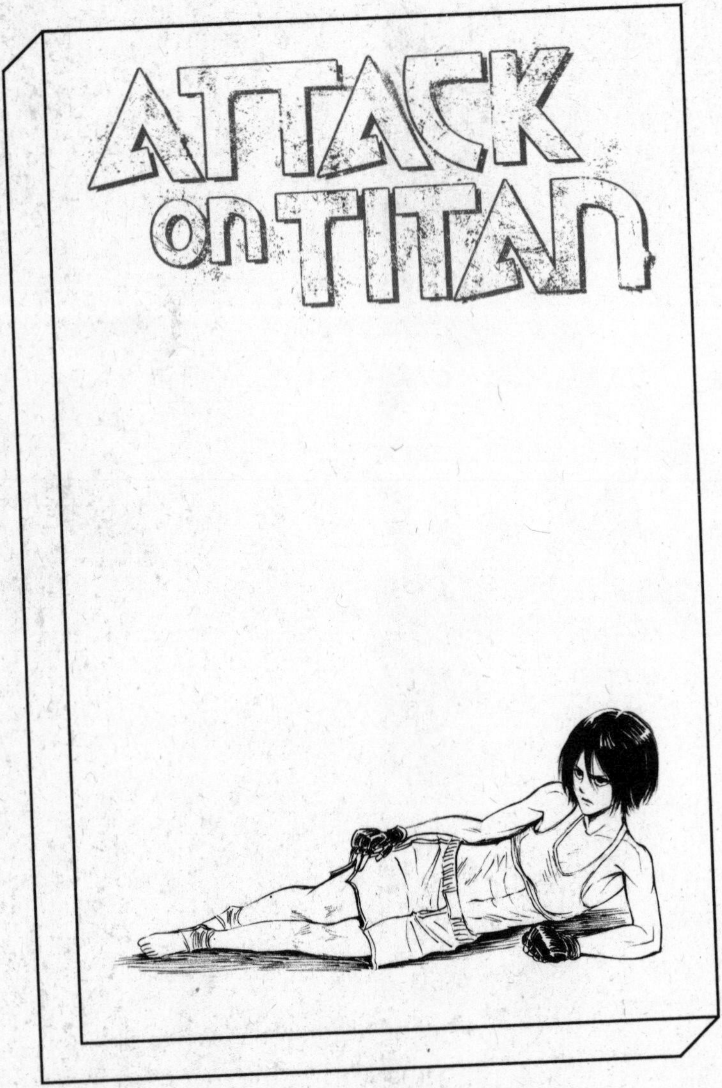
ATTACK on TITAN

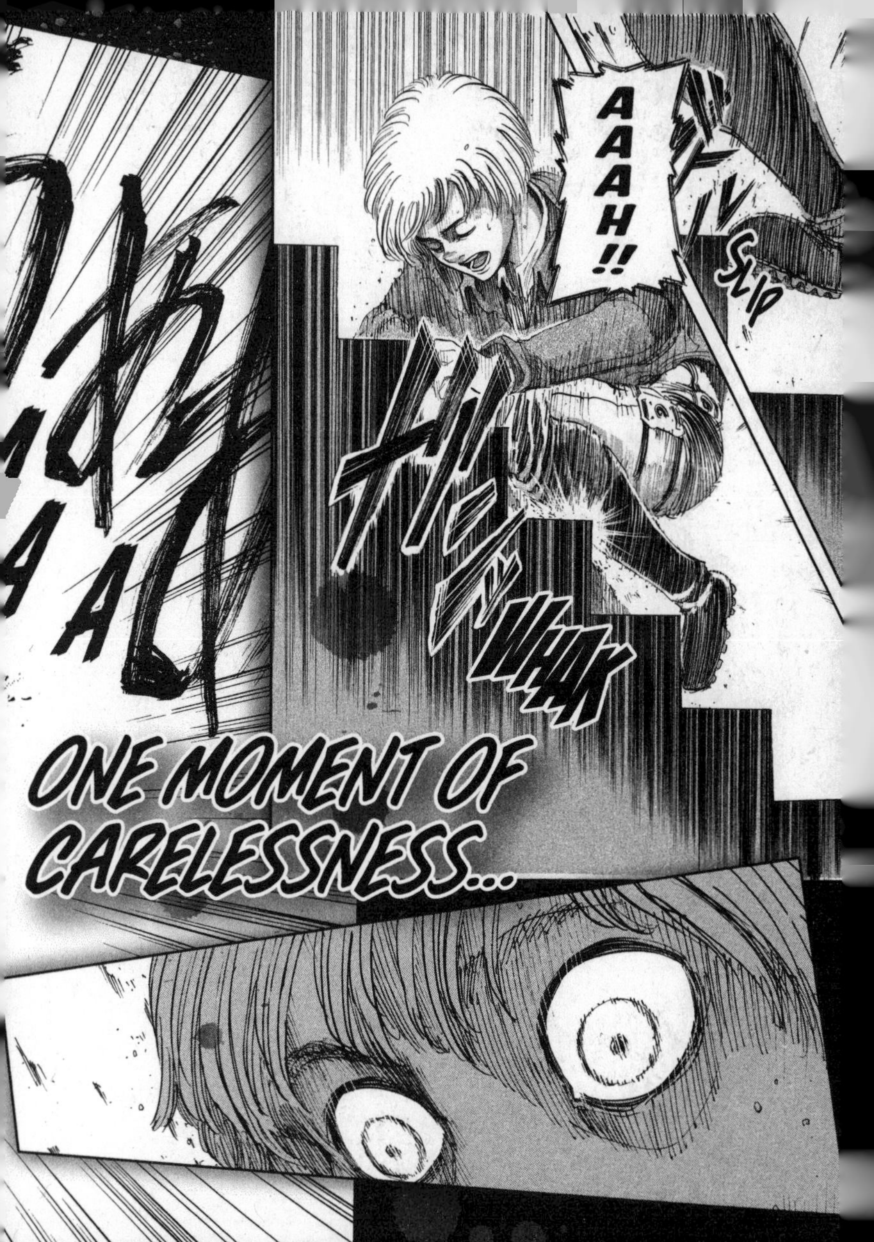
AAAAH!!
SLIP
WHAK
ONE MOMENT OF CARELESSNESS...

COMING SOON!

[REALLY!]

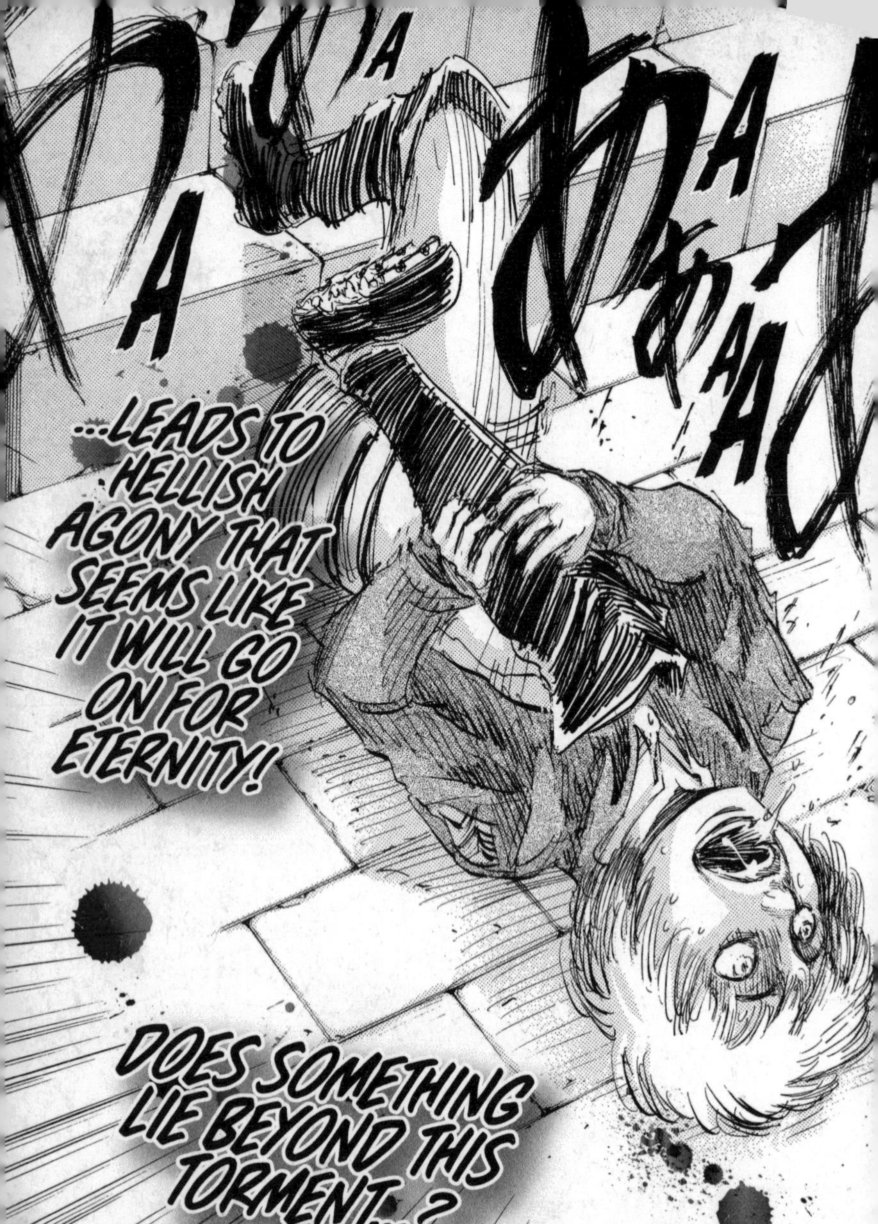
...LEADS TO HELLISH AGONY THAT SEEMS LIKE IT WILL GO ON FOR ETERNITY!
DOES SOMETHING LIE BEYOND THIS TORMENT...?

* Not a real preview.

VOLUME 8

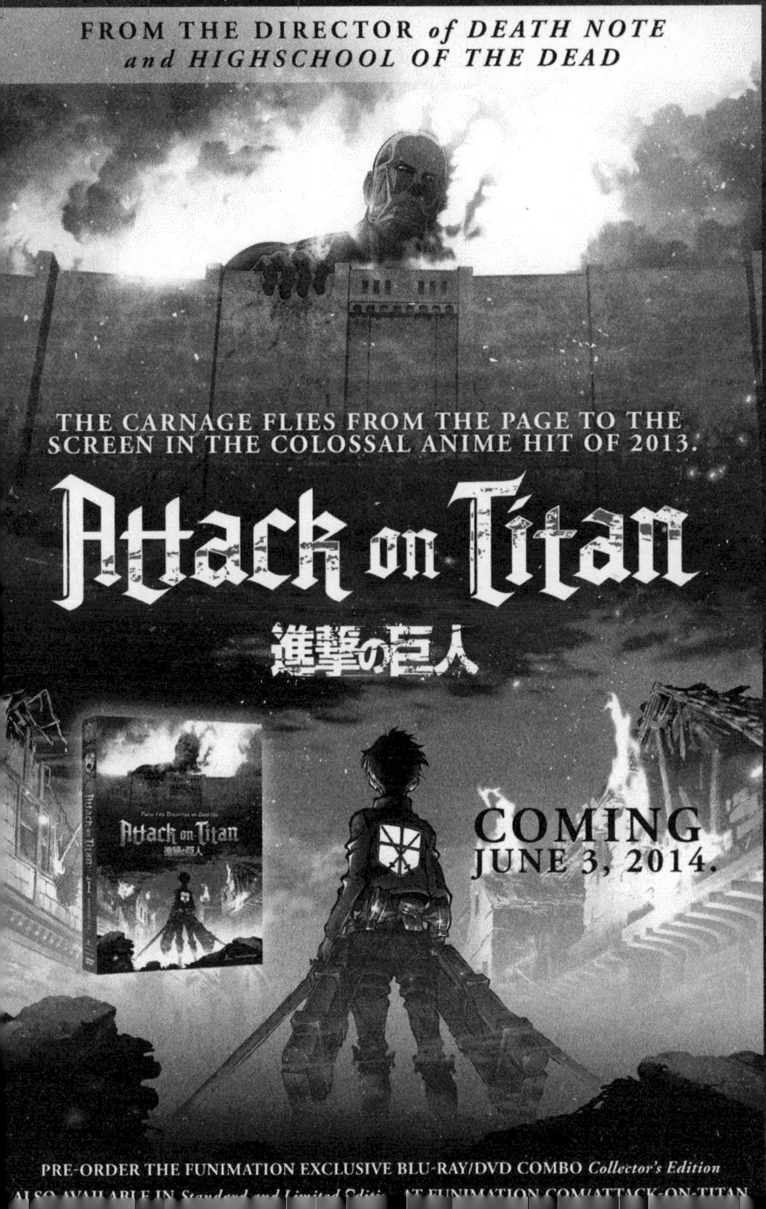
FROM THE DIRECTOR of DEATH NOTE
and HIGHSCHOOL OF THE DEAD
THE CARNAGE FLIES FROM THE PAGE TO THE SCREEN IN THE COLOSSAL ANIME HIT OF 2013.
Attack on Titan
進撃の巨人
Attack on Titan
進撃の巨人
COMING
JUNE 3, 2014.
PRE-ORDER THE FUNIMATION EXCLUSIVE BLU-RAY/DVD COMBO Collector's Edition